THE
Computer
BOOK

THE
Computer
BOOK

LONDON, NEW YORK,
MUNICH, MELBOURNE, DELHI

SENIOR EDITOR Neil Lockley
EDITOR Richard Gilbert
SENIOR ART EDITOR Alison Shackleton
PRODUCTION CONTROLLER Sarah Sherlock
DTP DESIGNER Adam Shepherd

MANAGING EDITOR Adèle Hayward
MANAGING ART EDITOR Karen Self
CATEGORY PUBLISHER Stephanie Jackson
ART DIRECTOR Peter Luff

Produced for Dorling Kindersley Limited by
crosstees.eyes, The Lazy J Ranch,
Vancouver Island, Canada
EDITORIAL MANAGER Ian Whitelaw
EDITORIAL CONSULTANT Rob Beattie
SENIOR DESIGNER Andrew Easton

Cover design by WHSmith

First published in Great Britain in 2001.
This edition published in 2004
for WHSmith by Dorling Kindersley,
80 Strand, London WC2R 0RL

A Penguin Company

2 4 6 8 10 9 7 5 3 1

A CIP catalogue record for this book is available from the British Library.

ISBN 1 4053 0527 4

Printed and bound in Slovakia by TBB

See our complete catalogue at
www.dk.com

ABOUT THIS BOOK

The Computer Book is an easy-to-follow guide to understanding your PC and using it to create documents and spreadsheets, explore the internet, send email, and operate a scanner and printer.

T HIS BOOK WILL HELP YOU TO GET the most out of your computer, whether you are a complete novice or an experienced user approaching Windows for the first time or looking at programs you have never investigated. In eight sections, *The Computer Book* takes you through using Microsoft® Windows® XP Home Edition, Word, Excel, and the internet, as well as making the most of your printer, scanner, and computer.

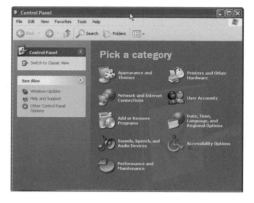

Each section is divided into chapters that deal with specific topics, and within each chapter you will find subsections that cover self-contained procedures. Each of these procedures builds on the knowledge that you will have accumulated by working through the previous chapters.

The chapters and subsections use a step-by-step approach, and almost every step is

accompanied by an illustration showing how your screen should look at that stage. The book contains several other features that make it easier to absorb the quantity of information that is provided. Cross-references are shown within the text as left- or right-hand page icons: and . The page number within the icon and the reference are shown at the foot of the page.

As well as the step-by-step sections, there are boxes that explain the meaning of unfamiliar terms and abbreviations, and give additional information to take your knowledge beyond that provided on the rest of the page. Finally, at the back, you will find a glossary explaining new terms, and a comprehensive index.

For further information on computer software and digital technology, see the wide range of titles available in the *DK Essential Computers* series.

CONTENTS

USING WINDOWS

MANAGING YOUR FILES

USING WORD

DESIGNING DOCUMENTS

USING WINDOWS

BEGINNING TO USE A COMPUTER for the first time is inevitably difficult. There is no other gadget that you can compare with a computer, nor one that can have provided you with any experience to draw on. This section will help to introduce you to the computer. We start by advising you on how to use the keyboard and the mouse, and then show you what the different elements of the opening screen mean when you turn on your computer. The two basic elements of windows and their menus are covered, which naturally lead into how to start using a few of the programs that are provided with Windows XP Home Edition. Using these programs, you will learn how to create and save files, and we also tell you how to organize them. Installing software is considered, and finally, for your relaxation, we show you how to play games on your PC.

KEYBOARD & MOUSE

Your computer's central processing unit, or CPU, allows you to create and manipulate text, images, and numerical data, but without a keyboard and a mouse it is practically useless.

INPUTTING AND MANIPULATING

In order for a computer to fulfil its purpose, it needs information, and the main method of inputting the necessary data is by means of the keyboard, which enables you to key in text and figures. The purpose of the mouse is to help you access the programs on your computer, to use the menus and options that each program offers, and to edit and move words, images, numbers, and graphics within programs. Your keyboard and mouse are your most useful tools.

TYPEWRITER PLUS
● The layout of the alphabet keys on a computer keyboard ⌐ is essentially the same as that on a standard typewriter, with the addition of function keys that tell the computer program to carry out specific commands. An "extended" keyboard also has extra keys at the right-hand side, commonly referred to as calculator, or number pad, keys.

THE MOUSE

A mouse is basically a pointing device that is attached to your PC via a cable and moves the cursor across the screen. The most common type has two buttons on the top, and clicking these allows the user to open documents, drag and drop items on the computer desktop or between applications, and access program menus. In addition, some mice have a wheel situated between the buttons, and this can be used to scroll up and down through documents and web pages on the internet.

MOUSE BASICS

As you move the mouse across a flat surface (a mouse mat is best), the speed and direction of the movement are transmitted to the computer by rollers connected to sensors. Clicking or rolling the mouse wheel also sends instructions to the PC. In this way, the movement of a cursor on the computer screen is controlled by the mouse.

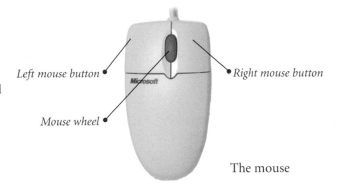

Left mouse button

Right mouse button

Mouse wheel

The mouse

LEFT CLICK

● The click of the left mouse button is probably the most common task performed with a mouse.
● Clicking once or twice with this button on an application's icon, for instance, will open that application. Clicking and holding down the left mouse button on an item, such as a folder, will allow you to drag that item to a another folder on your computer. When you let go of the left mouse button, the item is released. This use of the mouse is called "drag and drop."

RIGHT CLICK

● Clicking on the right mouse button, particularly on a file, usually launches a pop-up menu, which offers extra options or functions related to that file. Right-clicking on the Windows XP desktop, for instance, allows you to arrange icons, create new folders and icons, and alter the properties of your PC.

MOUSE WHEEL

● The mouse wheel is extremely useful when working on the internet, as it allows you to scroll up and down individual pages using the wheel or, by clicking on the wheel, to change the cursor into a directional tool that will cause the page to move up or down on your screen.

will talk -- via NASA downlink -- with teachers participating in the NASA Explorer Schools program.
+ Read More

07.29.03 - Station: 1000 Days in Space
For 1000 consecutive days, seven crews conducted science and assembly tasks aboard Station. The orbiting complex boasts a laboratory with living quarters, galley, and weightless "weight room" along side seven research facilities.
+ Read More

07.28.03 - International Earth Observation Summit
On Thursday, July 31, 2003, senior administration officials and representatives from more than 30 nations will meet in Washington.
+ Read More

07.25.03 - Return To Flight Task Group Members Named
NASA today released the names of the Stafford-Covey Return to Flight Task Group (SCTG).
+ Read More
+ View biographies

07.25.03 - Next ISS Crew Named
Michael Foale and Alexander Kaleri are set to be the eighth crew to live aboard the International Space Station.
+ Read More

+ View Archives

After clicking on the mouse wheel, the cursor can be used to scroll down through the web page

TUNING YOUR MOUSE

The way your mouse behaves on screen can be adjusted to suit the way you work. For example, the speed that you have to double-click in order to open a file can be changed, and so can the speed at which the pointer travels across the screen when you move the mouse. Follow the steps below, and experiment with the settings.

MOUSE PROPERTIES

● First click on the **Start** menu in the bottom left-hand corner of your screen.
● Find **Control Panel** in the main menu and click on it. When the **Control Panel** window opens, double-click on the **Mouse** icon. The **Mouse Properties** dialog box opens.
● The **Buttons** tab enables you to change the mouse from right-handed to left-handed, and to change the double-click speed.
● Clicking on the **Pointer Options** tab allows you to change the pointer speed.

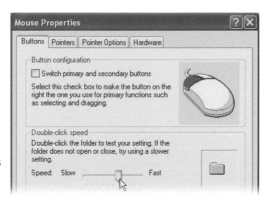

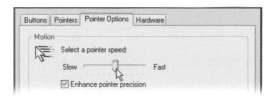

ADJUSTING KEYBOARD SETTINGS

Various aspects of the way the keyboard operates can also be controlled from within the **Control Panel.** Instead of double-clicking on the **Mouse** icon, choose **Keyboard** instead. The **Keyboard Properties** dialog box opens. Under the **Speed** tab you can alter the time you need to hold down a key before it starts to repeat that letter on screen, and you can set the rate at which repeat letters then appear on the screen.

THE KEYBOARD

DISCOVERING THE KEYBOARD LAYOUT

● One of the biggest challenges with your first PC is simply finding the right keys on the keyboard. So before going any further we will briefly look at the layout. In addition to the alphabet, number, and punctuation keys, the PC keyboard also has special keys that provide shortcuts to actions within the various programs. These are described below.

THE KEYBOARD LAYOUT

❶ Tab Key
This key moves the insertion point (the position in which typed letters appear) to an indented position on the page.

❷ Caps Lock
When this key has been pressed, all typed letters will be capital, or upper-case, letters.

❸ Shift Key
To type upper case letters and special symbols, hold down the shift key and press the letter key.

❹ Control Key
In combination with letter keys, the control key allows you to carry out various tasks, such as copying and pasting in Word.

❺ Windows Key
Press and release this to bring up the Windows Start menu.

❻ Alt Key
Like the Control key, this key can be used in combination with letter keys to carry out various tasks.

❼ Space Bar
Pressing the space bar introduces a letter space when keying in text.

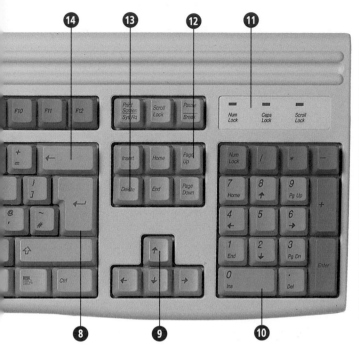

KEYBOARD LEGEND

Control Keys

Alphabet Keys

Punctuation Keys

Number Keys

"Calculator" Keys

Function Keys

Special Control Keys

THE KEYBOARD LAYOUT

8 Return/Enter
Introduces a paragraph end when working with text, and enters a command when an option is highlighted in a program dialog box.

9 Cursor Keys
These keys move the cursor or insertion point up and down, left and right.

10 Calculator Keys
When the Number Lock key

has been pressed, these can be used to key in numbers, and they also work as the number pad for the Windows calculator

11 Indicator Lights
Lights on this panel show when the Number Lock, Caps Lock, or Scroll Lock are active.

12 Page Up/Page Down
Pressing these keys takes you to the page before, or the page after, the current of the document.

13 Delete Forwards
Deletes the character to the right of the insertion point.

14 Delete
This key deletes a character to the left of the insertion point, and will also delete any highlighted element.

WELCOME TO XP

Windows XP has been developed with the home PC user in mind, and with this latest offering, Microsoft is aiming to make the PC an even better environment in which to work.

WHAT IS WINDOWS XP?

Windows XP is an operating system – the backbone of your day-to-day computing environment. Windows XP has simplified the PC experience by removing some irritations of earlier versions of Windows and introducing improvements of its own.

RECOGNIZE ME?

In the early 1990s, Microsoft released its first version of Windows, known as Windows 3.x (the "x" stood for the different version numbers). This was a great advance on the old operating system, known as MS-DOS. In 1995, Windows 95 was released, which was a smaller step forward than 3.x. Three years later, Windows 98 appeared, with some small improvements, and it was quickly followed by Windows Me, which added more minor tweaks. Windows XP is a major revamp, with a radical new look, many more features, and improved stability.

Technically Speaking...

Windows is a Graphical User Interface (GUI), which means that instead of typing commands into your computer, as MS-DOS required, you use a mouse to point and click to issue instructions to the machine.

FEATURES OF WINDOWS XP FOR EXPERIENCED USERS

● MEDIA PLAYER

Media Player can access digital media on the internet, from movies and music to radio stations. You can also download and play MP3 files. A database called Media Library allows you to organize your music and videos into one source. You can copy CDs to your hard disk and, if you have a re-writable CD drive, create compilation CDs of your own from the songs in the Media Library.

● MOVIE MAKER

Movie Maker captures video from a camcorder, VCR, or webcam and enables you to edit the footage before saving it as a movie. As it imports the video, it automatically breaks it up into short clips that are easy to manage and manipulate. You can also add your own background music and narration. Movie Maker is best suited for producing short, highly compressed movies for e-mailing to friends. You will probably need additional hardware, such as a video capture card to transfer the original video onto your PC. The latest version of Movie Maker includes many more special effects, a one-click instant movie-maker, and the ability to copy movies straight onto CD.

● HOME NETWORKING

Connecting PCs used to be complicated, but with the Windows XP Network Setup Wizard creating a home network to share disk drives and folders, as well as printers, internet connections, and other devices, is much simpler. You can also connect digital music players, digital camcorders, and wireless devices over a network. For example, a clock radio and a thermostat can communicate over the network to turn on the heating before the alarm goes off in the morning.

● WINDOWS UPDATE

Windows Update runs periodically, checking the Microsoft website for the latest program patches, updates, and fixes. It allows you to download these and install them so that your copy of Windows XP stays up to date. If you are installing Windows XP on a new computer, a companion program called Dynamic Update will run during setup, offering to download the latest updates to be added during installation.

● PERSONAL FIREWALL

Windows XP includes a personal firewall that helps prevent your PC from being accessed by unauthorized users while you are connected to the internet. Although such attacks occur rarely, this is an important new feature.

● SYSTEM RESTORE

This feature enables the computer's system to be returned easily to its previous settings. System Restore regularly takes a "snapshot" of your system settings and does so each time you install a new program or driver. If a problem occurs, you can wind the system back to the point at which it last worked properly. This feature is significantly improved in Windows XP.

THE WINDOWS XP DESKTOP

When you first start your computer, the Windows XP desktop appears. It is from this location that every action that you carry out on your computer begins. From here, you can launch programs, search for documents, surf the internet, and play games. The desktop is also a place where you can keep all your letters, documents, photographs, and much more. The desktop is also highly customizable.

FEATURES KEY

❶ My Documents
The My Documents folder is a place to store and organize any files you need.

❷ My Computer
The My Computer window displays all the folders, documents, and programs on your computer.

❸ My Network Places
This tool links your computer to any others that are on the same network.

❹ Recycle Bin
The Recycle Bin ⬜ is where you place items that you want to delete.

❺ Internet Explorer
If your computer is set up correctly, then double-clicking this icon ⬜ will connect you to the internet.

❻ Start Button
The Start button provides shortcuts to the document folders, files, and programs stored on the computer.

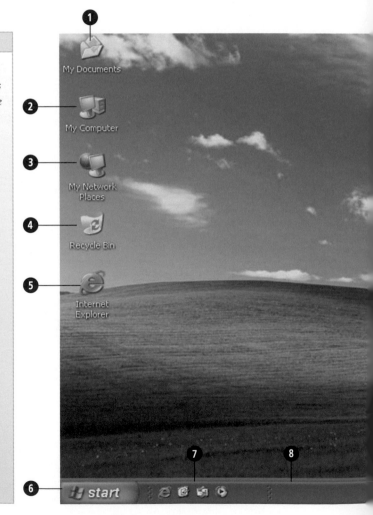

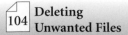

STARTUP PROBLEMS?

When you turn on your PC, it should go through a procedure known as booting up. If this fails to happen, or if the computer fails to start up as it should, carry out these checks. First make sure that the power cable is plugged in and that the power is turned on. Second, check there isn't a floppy disk in the floppy disk drive. Third, check all interconnecting cabling from the PC.

FEATURES KEY

7 The Quick Launch Toolbar
Icons of frequently-used applications can be added here to provide easy access.

8 Taskbar
The Taskbar gives quick access to programs and documents that are open on your desktop.

9 Show/Hide Icons
Clicking on this arrow alternately displays and hides the icons in the System Tray to the right of the arrow (see below).

10 System Tray
The System Tray contains the icons of special utilities, allowing you quick access to these programs by double clicking on them.

11 The Desktop
The Windows XP desktop is where you work. Programs open here, and you can store files for as long as you need.

9 10

05:12

EXPLORING XP

Now that we have seen the Windows XP desktop, it's time to explore your surroundings further and discover what the taskbar does, as well as the different menus and help screens.

USING THE TASKBAR

The taskbar is a panel initially located at the foot of the screen. It contains the **Start** button, from where programs can be launched, the Quick Launch bar, the System tray, and the buttons for all your open files, programs, and windows.

NAVIGATING BETWEEN WINDOWS

● As you use, experiment, and play with Windows XP, you will find that you can easily have many different applications and windows open at the same time, and that, from time to time, your screen may resemble the example on the right.

All the documents and windows that are active have a corresponding button on the taskbar

• Clicking on a program button on the taskbar brings the program to the foreground where it is ready to use. Here, we have clicked on the **3D Pinball for Windows** button to open its window.

*Note that **3D Pinball for Windows** is now in the foreground and active*

Clicking on a button makes the application active

USING THE MOUSE BUTTONS

Generally speaking, the left mouse button is used to activate applications or menu options by clicking once. It is also used for scrolling through windows and menus 🖰, and for dragging and dropping 🖰. If you right-click with the mouse on an object, for instance, the **My Computer** icon on the desktop, a menu of options appears (right). This allows you, among other options, to open, browse, create a shortcut to, rename, and view the properties of that object.

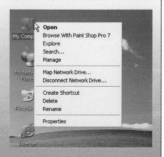

SHOWING THE DESKTOP

- To minimize all windows when you start to lose track of where they all are, right-click on a blank area of the taskbar and then click on **Show the Desktop** in the menu that appears.

Right click in a blank space •

RESTORING A WINDOW

- All the applications have been minimized and the desktop is clear. However, any one of the windows can still be accessed through the taskbar by left-clicking on its taskbar button.

Single-click on the application •
that you wish to open

MINIMIZING AND MAXIMIZING INDIVIDUAL WINDOWS

❶ Minimize
Clicking on this button minimizes the window. The window is still available by left-clicking on its button on the taskbar.

❷ Maximize
*The **Maximize** button expands the window to fill the whole screen. Once maximized, the button then changes its name to **Restore Down**.*

❸ Restore
*Clicking on the **Restore Down** button returns the window to its previous dimensions and location onscreen.*

❹ Close
*To shut down an application or to close a window, such as Windows Explorer, click the **Close** button. If you need to save an open file before closing, Windows will prompt you.*

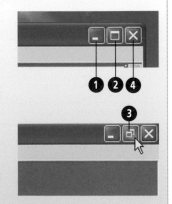

USING THE START MENU

The Windows **Start** button is the main starting point for finding and accessing files and documents, installing and using programs, and changing and customizing the settings on your computer to suit your own requirements. It is also the location from where you can access the **Help** options, and, paradoxically, is the place where can you restart your computer or shut it down at the end of a session.

OPENING THE START MENU

● Place the cursor over the **Start** button and click the left mouse button once.

● The Start menu pops up. Any one of the options can be clicked on to select it. Throughout Windows XP, any option that has a right-pointing arrowhead next to it (such as **All Programs**) will display a submenu of further options when you click on it.

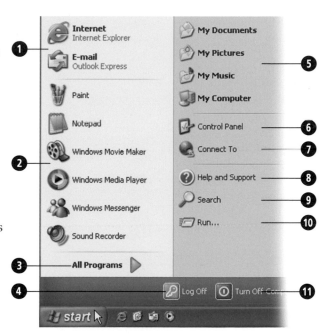

START MENU KEY

❶ Shortcuts to web browser and email

❷ Recently used programs

❸ All Programs Menu
see p.24

❹ Log Off Option
To log off as a user

❺ Frequently used folder shortcuts, *see* p.29

❻ Control Panel
see p.26

❼ Connect Menu

❽ Windows Help and Support

❾ Search Menu
see p.27

❿ Run Command
see p.25

⓫ Turn Off Computer Option
see p.29

THE ALL PROGRAMS MENU

The **All Programs** menu lists the software, sometimes called "applications," that you use to perform tasks on your computer.

This menu also provides access to further submenus where related applications are grouped together, for example **Games**.

FAVORITE PROGRAMS

● The list above the **All Programs** menu contains the programs you use most frequently or those that you have used most recently. Double-click on any of them to start the program.

● When you initially move the cursor over the **All Programs** arrow in the **Start** menu, you'll see some of the programs that are included with Windows XP, such as Internet Explorer and Windows Media Player.

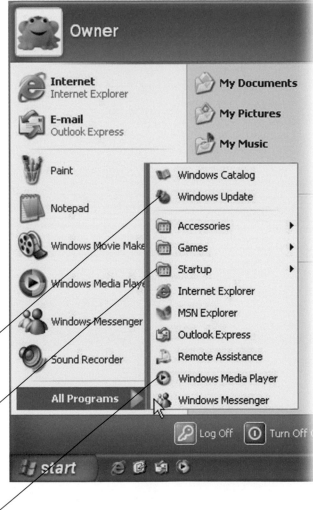

You can update your version of Windows XP with the latest patches, upgrades, and fixes by clicking on **Windows Update** ●

The **Startup** *submenu contains utility programs that Windows loads automatically when the computer is turned on* ●

Clicking on this option immediately launches **Windows Media Player** ●

ACCESSORIES

● The **Accessories** menu contains applications that are installed along with Windows XP. They include a calculator, text-editing tools, and an address book.

● In addition, this menu also contains its own submenus.

The Run Command

An alternative method of launching a program is to click on **Run** in the **Start** menu and type the name of the file that is needed to run the program. This option is generally used by more experienced users of Microsoft Windows.

GAMES

● The **Games** menu contains a selection of simple applications for passing time.

● Not only are there a number of games that can be played on your own, but there are also five that can be played over the internet. With Windows XP, you can now play games from your home or office against someone sitting on the other side of the world.

THE CONTROL PANEL MENU

The **Control Panel** menu contains options that include customizing and fine-tuning the working of your computer, connecting to another computer, handling printers, and selecting the elements that appear in the **Start** menu and in the taskbar.

CONTROL PANEL

- The **Control Panel** menu allows you to access many of Windows XP's important settings. You can change everything from your computer screen's color scheme to your internet connection from here.
- The **Control Panel** also has facilities to add and remove hardware and programs, alter the settings for your peripherals and network. It also includes **Accessibility Options**.

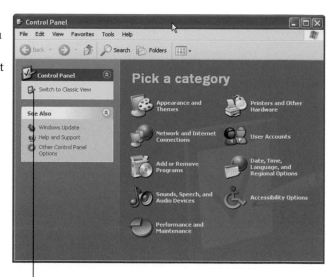

*If you are familiar with an earlier version of Windows, clicking here will display the **Control Panel** in the classic style*

THE CLASSIC VIEW

- In the classic view, the **Control Panel** is no longer divided into categories, but more options can be seen at a glance.

*In this view, the **Control Panel** options are displayed in alphabetical order*

USING THE SEARCH MENU

The **Search** menu provides the means for finding any files, folders, documents, or photographs that are stored on your computer. If you have an internet connection, you can also use it to find information stored on a website .

1 SEARCHING FOR PICTURES

● Click once on the **Start** button and select **Search** by clicking on it. The **Search Companion** appears.

● The **Search Companion** offers several search options. Click on the **Pictures, music, or video** option at the top of the left-hand column.
● The search criteria dialog box appears, allowing you to focus your search still further. To locate all images stored on your computer's hard disk, check the box next to **Pictures and Photos** by clicking on it, and leave the **All or part of the file name** text box empty.
● Click on **Search**, and all the pictures and photos on your computer will be listed in the search results that appear in the right-hand panel.

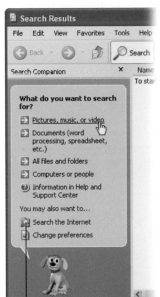

● *There is also the option to **Search the Internet**, but you will need your computer to be connected to the internet to use this option*

2 SEARCHING FOR DOCUMENTS

● You can also search for a specific document. Click the **Start** button and choose **Search**.

● Click the **Documents** (**word processing, spreadsheet, etc.**) option.

● In the criteria dialog box, click in the **All or part of the document name** panel and enter as much of the name as you know. We are looking for a missing letter that was created in the last week, so check the **Within the last week** radio button and click on **Search** to see the results.

3 SEARCHING THE INTERNET

● To search the internet, choose the **Search the Internet** option in the **Search Companion**.

● In the screen that appears, type in your search word or words and click the **Search** button. If you are connected to the internet, your connection opens and the results, which are links to websites, are displayed below the **Search** button.

● Clicking on any of these links will display that particular web page in the right-hand window.

THE MY DOCUMENTS OPTION

The **My Documents**
option in the **Start** menu
opens files that you have
been working on recently.
Click on the **Start** menu,
then on **My Documents**,
and then double-click on
the file or folder that you
want to open.

RESTARTING AND SHUTTING DOWN

Turning off a computer is different from
switching off the television. There are
internal settings that a computer has to

maintain, and these have to be recorded
before shutdown. However, with Windows
XP, shutting down is now much faster.

1 LAUNCHING TURN OFF COMPUTER
● Click on the **Start** button
and click on the **Turn Off
Computer** button.

2 SELECTING THE RIGHT OPTION
● **Stand By** puts your
computer into a low power-
consumption mode.
● **Turn Off** switches the
computer off completely.
● **Restart** is the equivalent
of turning the computer off
and starting it again.

WINDOWS XP PROGRAMS

When you start Windows XP, and take a look around for the first time, you will notice that there are various programs available for use. Let's take a look at a few of them.

NOTEPAD

Notepad is a basic text editor, used mainly for creating, viewing, and editing documents that only contain text, and do not contain any images.

Notepad has some very useful features. Text can be cut, copied, and pasted; and there is also an option to add the date and time if you want to include those details.

1 LAUNCHING NOTEPAD

● The first step in using any program or tool on a computer is to open, or launch, it. There may be shortcuts available, but to begin with, using the **Start** button is the simplest method.

● Click on the **Start** button, move to **All Programs, Accessories**, and then finally to **Notepad**.

WHAT IS A PROGRAM?

A program allows you to perform a specific task or function on your computer. Programs can also be called applications, which is a slightly broader term. Programs and applications are also called software. Windows XP is a piece of software that creates a "platform" for other applications.

2 THE NEW DOCUMENT

- A new, blank document screen opens with a blue title bar at the top and a menu bar below it.
- A cursor flashes at the top left of the window and shows where text will appear when you begin typing.

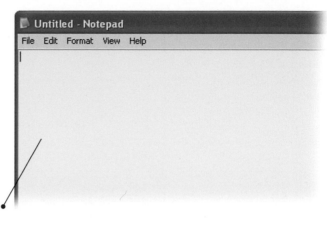

The Notepad main window

- When you begin typing, the cursor disappears.

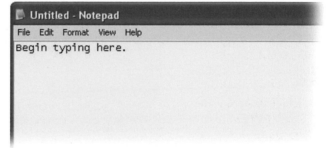

3 SAVING THE DOCUMENT

- Once you have created your first document, you can save it. This allows it to be opened again at any time.
- When you save a file for the first time, Windows asks you to give it a name and select a location where it is to be saved on your hard drive.
- Click on **File** in the Menu bar, and from the drop-down menu click on **Save**.

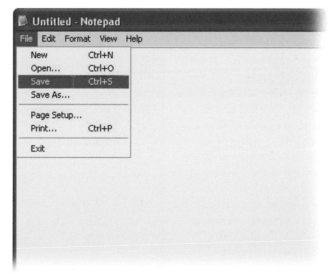

- The **Save As** dialog box opens. By default, Windows directs the file to the **My Documents** folder, which is a useful location for your files when you first start .
- In the **File name** text box, type in a descriptive name for the document.
- Click on the **Save** button. The **Save As** box closes and your document is saved.

4 OPENING AN EXISTING FILE

- At some time, you are likely to need to open a file that you have saved to edit it or print it out. There are two main ways of opening a file.
- The first method is carried out from inside Notepad. Open Notepad as before, then click on **File** in the Menu bar, and click on **Open**.
- The **Open** dialog box opens. Notepad makes the assumption, by default, that any documents created previously have been saved to the **My Documents** folder.
- Click on the file that you wish to open (in this case, we are opening the **Monday Shopping List**).

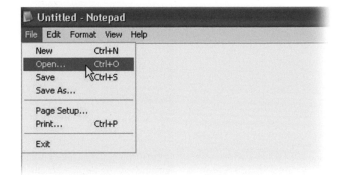

● Now move the cursor down to the **Open** button at the bottom right-hand corner and click on it.

● The file will open onscreen and you can make changes and then resave it.

*Click on the **Open** button* ●

● The second method of opening an existing file is more direct than the first.

● Select the folder that contains the file you want to open. In this case, it is the **My Documents** folder. Double-click on the folder icon to open its window.

● In the **My Documents** window, double-click on the file that you wish to open. The file automatically opens in the program that was used to create it – in this case, Notepad.

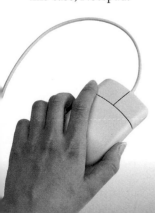

PAINT

Paint is a piece of graphics software that is used to create and work with images. An image you have created can then be pasted into another document, and you can even edit photographs that have been scanned in. Paint also has its own text tool.

LAUNCHING PAINT

● You can launch Paint in the same way that Notepad was launched . Click on the **Start** button, move up to **All Programs**, select **Accessories**, and then click on **Paint**.

● A window opens that contains painting tools, a color palette, and the main Paint window.

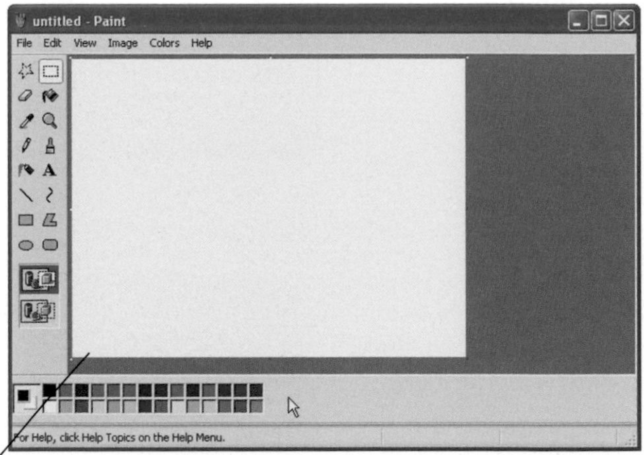

The main Paint window ●

DRAWING WITH PAINT

● Using the **Pencil** tool , we have drawn an outline of a tree, and with the **Fill With Color** tool we have started to color the image.

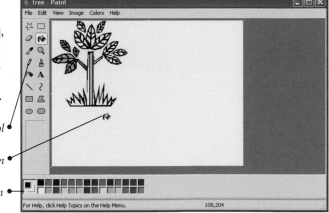

*The **Pencil** tool* ●

Fill With Color tool icon ●

*The **Color palette** from which you can select a color by clicking on it* ●

30 **Launching Notepad**

35 **Paint Tools**

THE FINISHED DRAWING

● Using just two tools from the range that Paint provides, and selecting green and brown from the color palette, we have created a simple picture of a tree.

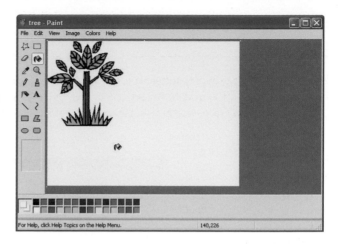

THE PAINT TOOLS PALETTE

● There are many tools available in Paint, from a simple line tool to an airbrush. With time and patience, these tools can soon be mastered.

Find Out More...

We have only been able to give an overview of Paint here. The **Help** drop-down menu within the program contains numerous hints and tips for greater creativity.

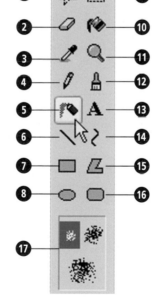

PAINT TOOLS

❶ Free-Form Select
❷ Eraser/Color Eraser
❸ Pick Color
❹ Pencil
❺ Airbrush
❻ Line
❼ Rectangle
❽ Ellipse
❾ Select
❿ Fill With Color
⓫ Magnifier
⓬ Brush
⓭ Text
⓮ Curve
⓯ Polygon
⓰ Rounded Rectangle
⓱ Airbrush Nozzles

Note: The Airbrush Nozzles Palette only becomes visible once the Airbrush tool has been selected.

MOVIE MAKER

Movie Maker warrants a book in its own right. With this program you can import video from a camcorder, VCR, or webcam, and then edit the footage to create your own movie, complete with special visual effects and background music.

QUICK AND FUN

● Movie Maker is very easy to use. Once you have captured your video, Movie Maker slices it up into scenes and places them in the middle window.

● Scenes can be dragged onto the filmstrip at the bottom of the screen in any order, and wipes, fades, and other special effects can be placed between scenes.

● Scenes that are too long can be cut until they are the correct length.

● Movie Maker includes a special "AutoMovie" feature that will create a complete movie for you with just a few mouse clicks.

● Finished movies can be sent as emails, posted to a website, or recorded back onto a digital video camera. If you have a CD writer, you can also save movies to a blank CD-ROM.

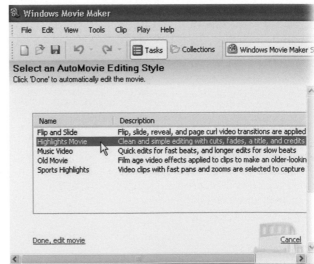

WORDPAD

Wordpad takes text editing further than Notepad. With Wordpad, you are able to design and produce colorful documents, and insert photographs or graphics that you may have created (see p.38) or downloaded from the internet. You will see that Wordpad has a far more extensive range of tools than Notepad.

1 ENTERING AND SELECTING TEXT

● Wordpad, like Notepad and Paint, is opened from the **Start** menu, moving to **Programs**, choosing **Accessories**, and then **Wordpad**.

● When you start typing into the document that opens, a font size of 10 points is used automatically. However, the font size can be reduced or enlarged.

● Hold down the mouse button when the cursor is at the end of the line, then drag the cursor over the text to highlight the line.

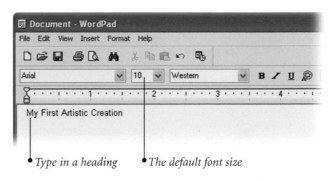

● *Type in a heading*   ● *The default font size*

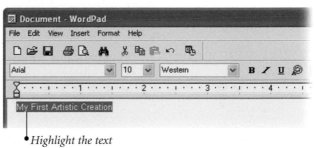

● *Highlight the text*

2 SELECTING THE FONT SIZE

● Click on the down arrow to the right of the **Font Size** box, and in the drop-down menu click on a larger font size. Here, a font size of **22** points is being selected.

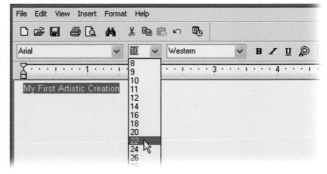

● The text changes to the selected size.
● Click the cursor at the end of the line of text to deselect it, and press [Enter ←] twice.

The cursor is now here ●———————|

3 INSERTING AN OBJECT

● Click on **Insert** in the Menu bar and click on **Object** in the drop-down menu that appears.

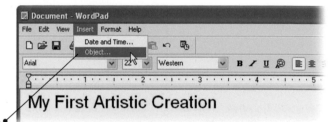

Click on Object ●

4 BROWSING FOR AN IMAGE

● The **Insert Object** dialog box opens. As the image to be inserted is in a file, click on the **Create from File** radio button.

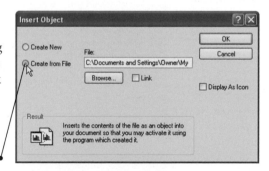

Click on Create from File ●

● The contents of the dialog box change to show a text field where the names of folders and files can be displayed.
● Click on the **Browse** button to navigate to the location of the graphic.

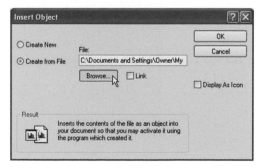

5 OPENING MY PICTURES

● The **Browse** dialog box opens. The image of the tree, which was created using Paint , is stored in the **My Pictures** folder.
● Double-click on that folder to open it.

6 SELECTING THE IMAGE

● Other than the sample pictures that are supplied with Windows XP, the tree is the only image contained in the **My Pictures** folder.
● Click on the image and then on the **Open** button.

7 INSERTING THE SELECTION

● The filename is shown in the text field, and you can now click on **OK**.

8 THE INSERTED GRAPHIC

● The picture is inserted into the document below the heading.
● The techniques shown here can be used for a variety of different purposes in different documents – from letter-heads to greeting cards.

35 **The Finished Drawing**

INSTALLING SOFTWARE

Having Windows XP installed on your computer means that you have a great many new and exciting programs to explore and enjoy. However, the time will come when you will want to develop and expand your computing and gaming horizons. This means that you will want to start installing software.

WHERE CAN YOU OBTAIN SOFTWARE?

There are many ways to source software, and thousands of applications are available – from the latest games to a program to help redesign your backyard. Where you look for software depends on what you want. Large graphics-creation programs are available from computer stores and an immense range of mail-order websites. Computer utilities are available as downloads or from CDs free with computer magazines.

Websites are a useful source of software.

WHAT DIFFERENT FORMS OF SOFTWARE ARE AVAILABLE?

The bulk of the software you will install is the commercially available form that you install on one computer and make one backup copy 🗋. Another form of software is shareware, which you can try before paying a fee to use it. After a trial period, you are then asked to pay a registration fee, which is less than you would pay for commercial software, and which funds the author to support the software, update it, and develop new programs. In some cases, you may receive updates and manuals.

A NOTE OF CAUTION

Installing software is far from being a completely safe operation. New programs can sometimes want to work in parts of your computer where other programs are working, leading to conflicts. Programs can occasionally try to install themselves in the system tray at the right-hand end of the taskbar, which should be reserved for programs that need to be running all the time, such as antivirus software. The most important precaution you can take is to monitor each installation closely. Read what each window says, and if it's unclear or unwanted, just click on the "No" option.

| 45 | **The Problem of Software Piracy** |

INSTALLING FROM A CD

For this example, a piece of software is going to be installed from a CD-ROM that was supplied with a popular home computing magazine. These discs can contain fully functional programs or trial versions with a limited life.

1 AUTORUN FEATURE

● Most CDs that are free with magazines have an autorun feature that automatically opens the CD-ROM when it is placed in the drive.
● A screen appears that usually lists the software available and advertisements for other products.

2 CHOOSING YOUR SOFTWARE

● Choose the program that you want to install. In this case, we are going to install the latest version of WinZip, which is a file-archive and compression utility.
● After clicking on the **Install Software** command, the setup begins.

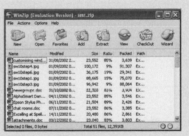

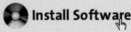 **Install Software**

WHAT IS FILE COMPRESSION?

WinZip – as we have mentioned – is a file compression and archiving utility. File compression is a method of making files smaller in size, and therefore saving disk space, without losing quality or data, which is vital for files you want to archive. WinZip is probably the most common program used for this function. A trial version of WinZip can be downloaded from the internet from its own website: **http://www.winzip.com**.

● The **WinZip Setup** window appears.
● Click on **Setup** to continue the installation.

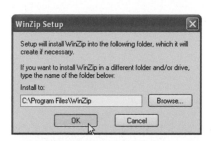

3 CHOOSING A LOCATION

● Programs usually install themselves in a location that they select, and to which you can agree by clicking on **OK**.

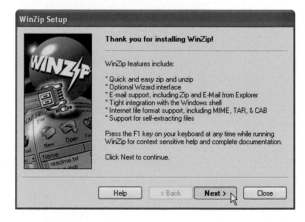

● A screen appears, providing information on the software you are about to install.
● After reading the information, click on **Next** to continue.

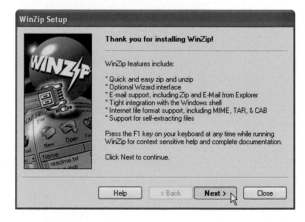

4 LICENSE AGREEMENT

● The License Agreement is where the lawyers briefly take over from the programmers. Some applications present you with the whole agreement. WinZip's option is simpler where you can simply click on **Yes** to agree.

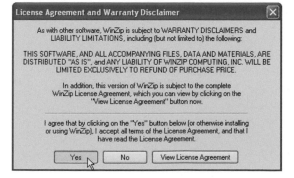

5 CONTINUING INSTALLING

● You are offered the opportunity to print or view useful information about the installation and the use of WinZip.

● Click **Next** to continue with the installation.

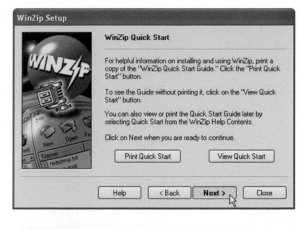

● WinZip has almost completed its installation. It now needs to know which type of WinZip you wish to start with. In this example, we have chosen to start with WinZip Classic. Read the text in the dialog box carefully and make your own choice.

We have chosen to start with WinZip Classic ●

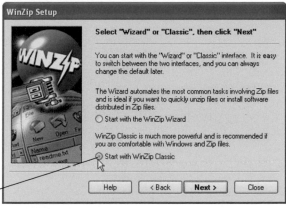

● When you are given the choice, click in the radio button next to **Start with WinZip Classic**. Don't be deterred by the fact that this is recommended for people already familiar with Zip files – you will not be performing any tasks within the program yet.

● Click on **Next**.

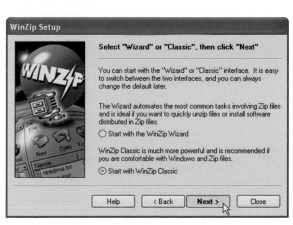

● Click in the radio button next to **Express setup (recommended)**.
● Click on **Next**.

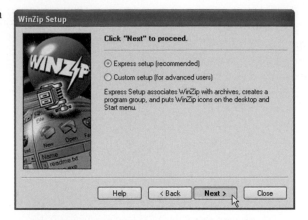

● This dialog box gives experienced users the opportunity to fine tune some of WinZip's settings. Just leave everything as it is and click on **Next** to continue.

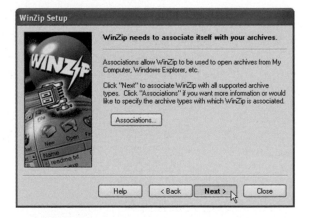

● Once the installation process is complete, click on the **Finish** button.

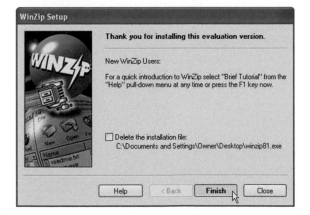

6 CLOSING WINZIP

- You can now close the the program by clicking on the **Close** button.
- In future, WinZip will automatically expand compressed files when you download them to your computer.

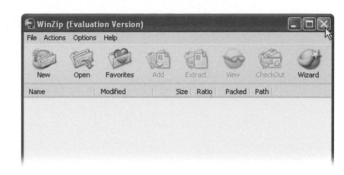

- As well as installing the software on your computer, other changes have been made. A shortcut to WinZip has automatically been placed on the desktop.

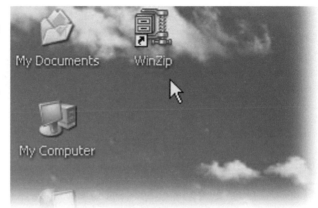

THE PROBLEM OF SOFTWARE PIRACY

- The ease with which computer software can be copied from computer to computer makes it very tempting to copy programs for friends. However, when you buy a program, you are buying a license to install the program only on one computer and to make a backup copy for archiving purposes only. Any use of computer software beyond those activities is illegal.

- In the US, the Copyright Act gives the copyright owner the exclusive rights to reproduce the work and distribute copies. Buying software does not include the purchase of those legal rights of reproduction and distribution as well.

- In addition to being illegal, software piracy is very risky. The computer from which the software is copied may contain a virus that is also copied. The version may not be fully functional, and it will not have manuals or technical support. Neither is there access to patches, upgrades, or innovations. Piracy also deprives the software manufacturers of their legitimate earnings.

FUN AND GAMES

As you do your day's work, or complete that letter to the bank manager, Windows XP can offer some light relief, whether for playing or recording CDs, or listening to internet radio.

THE MULTIMEDIA EXPERIENCE

One of the biggest advances in Windows XP over previous versions of Windows is the collection of facilities contained in Windows XP for managing digital media files. Here we look at Windows Media Player for Windows XP, which encompasses all the latest audio/visual technologies in one package, including playing and recording music CDs. We look at customizing Media Player and using the visualizer. We also examine the Explorer Media button and playing XP's games.

LAUNCHING MEDIA PLAYER

● You can use Media Player to play video/animation files, CDs, and CD-ROMs.

● Media Player can be accessed from the **Start** menu, from **All Programs**, or from the Quick Launch section of the taskbar.

● Note that when Media Player is open but nothing is yet playing, several of the options and buttons are inaccessible.

•*Windows Media Player Quick Launch icon*

THE MEDIA PLAYER WINDOW

To enjoy Windows Media Player, you will need a sound card, a modem, and speakers attached to your computer. All modern computers include all these items as standard, but if you have an older PC, you may have to purchase one of these.

MEDIA PLAYER TOOLS

❶ Drop-down Menus
❷ Web browser-style navigation buttons
❸ Hide/Show Playlist
❹ Main Visual Window
❺ Change color scheme of Media Player screen

❻ Switch to skin mode
❼ Audio/Video Controls
❽ Skin Chooser
❾ Find multimedia subscriptions on the web
❿ Burn a CD or copy to a portable music player

⓫ Radio Tuner
⓬ Media Library
⓭ Copy music from a CD to your hard disk
⓮ Guide to multimedia on the internet
⓯ Now Playing

PLAYING A MUSIC CD

When you insert an audio CD into the CD-ROM drive on your computer, Media Player automatically detects it and starts playing immediately. If you click on **Now Playing** while an audio CD is playing, some visual changes occur onscreen.

MEDIA PLAYER TOOLS

❶ Now Playing Button
Click here to watch currently playing media, such as the details of an audio CD.
❷ Main Visual Window
The main visual window

contains album art retrieved from the internet. It can also display a "visualization" of moving colored patterns.
❸ Track Details Window
The right-hand window has the

track listing of artist, album, and track information including track times, if known.
❹ Audio/Visual Controls
All of the audio/visual controls are now displayed.

WHAT ELSE CAN MEDIA PLAYER DO?

THE MUSIC MACHINE
Not only can Media Player play your CDs, it can also store the songs on your computer in Windows Media Format. This makes the files very small and means they take up very little hard disk space. In addition, if you are connected to the internet, Media Player will automatically find and retrieve the name of the artist, the title of the album, and track listings for every song that you have recorded on your PC. Once you have built up a collection of music, Media Player allows you to create your own personal playlists that can be any length you choose, and if you have a recordable CD drive, you can make customized CD compilations. Media Player can also play and store MP3 and WAV files.

MEDIA GUIDE
With Media Guide, it is possible to download music, videos, and movie trailers via the website: **windowsmedia.com**.

RADIO
Now you can listen to the immense variety of radio stations available from around the world with Media Player. You can choose between AM, FM, or internet-only radio.

CUSTOMIZING MEDIA PLAYER

Even the experience of playing a music CD can be heightened by personalizing the way that Windows Media Player looks onscreen. You can change the size of the player, dress it up in an elaborate or a fun skin to change its appearance, and even select a visualization effect to suit the music or your mood.

CHANGING THE APPEARANCE
● You can alter the way that Media Player looks by changing its skin. The player has to be displayed in full mode to do this.
● Click on the **Skin Chooser** button.

● The main Skin Chooser window opens. On the right-hand side of the window, there is an image of the skin that you are using at the moment; in this case, it is the default Media Player skin. In the left-hand window, there is a list of the optional skins that are supplied with Media Player.

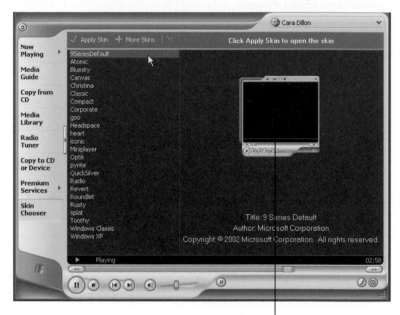

The preview window ●

● Clicking on each of the skin names displays a preview of the design in the right-hand window.
● Click through each of the names in turn until you find a skin that you like.

*A chic, retro Media Player skin called **Radio*** ●

MORE SKINS

● If you don't like any of the optional skins that come with Media Player, **windowsmedia.com** has an immense selection of alternatives that you can browse through.

● Begin by clicking on the **More Skins** button at the top of the main Skin Chooser window.

● Your internet connection opens the **windowsmedia. com** website at the first skins page. Here you can browse through page after page of weird and wonderful skins. You can even find out how to design a Media Player skin yourself.

VISUALIZATIONS

Visualizations in Media Player provide a relaxing series of light shows that respond to and accompany the rhythms of the music as it plays. There are many visualizations to choose from, and they are grouped according to specific themes.

MEDIA PLAYER VISUALIZATIONS

● When a CD is playing, the visualization starts, whether the player is in full or compact mode. Some skins do not have the facility to accommodate visualization, particularly in compact mode.

By clicking on the left and right arrows, you can scroll through the many visualization effects in Windows Media Player ●

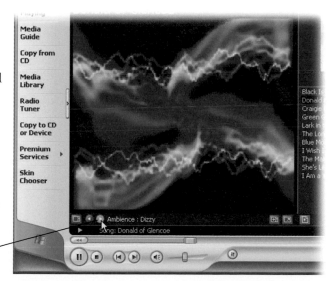

EXPLORER RADIO BAR

As well as internet-only radio stations, many national and local stations broadcast live over the internet. These will run in the background while you browse the web. Internet Explorer's Radio Guide provides links to hundreds of radio stations.

1 LOCATING THE MEDIA BUTTON

● In the Internet Explorer window, find the **Media** button icon on the Internet Explorer toolbar and click on it once.

2 LOCATING THE GUIDE

● Find the **Media Options** panel at the bottom of the left pane, click on it once, and choose **Radio Guide** from the drop-down menu that appears.

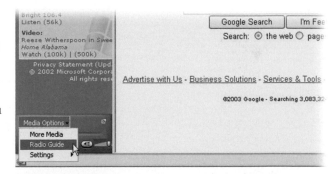

3 LOCATING THE STATIONS

● A list of radio stations is now displayed in the right-hand window. You can display more stations by selecting a category on the right, such as **Country**.

There are many radio stations available to suit all tastes

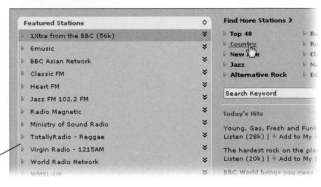

WINDOWS XP GAMES

Windows XP is designed to make playing games easier and faster, so after figuring out your finances or writing a letter to your aunt, take it easy and have some fun, either playing a game solo or online against opponents anywhere in the world.

1 PLAY ON THE INTERNET

● To launch a game on the internet, begin by clicking on the **Start** button, then move to **All Programs,** and then to **Games.**

● From the collection that is available in the **Games** submenu, we'll choose to play a game of **Internet Checkers.**

2 CONNECT TO THE INTERNET

● The first time that you play across the internet, the **Zone.com** dialog box opens onscreen.

● You can click in the **Show this every time** check box to deselect it if you don't want to see this box each time you start to play online.

● When you're ready, click on the **Play** button.

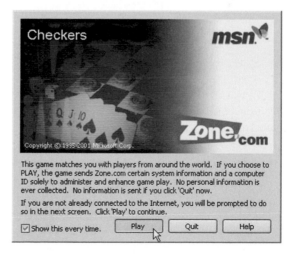

3 CONNECT TO GAMES SERVER

● A message tells you that an attempt is being made to connect you to the games server, which is at **Zone.com**.

Connecting to the Internet game server...

4 STARTING THE GAME

● Now you are launched straight into the fray, pitting your wits against an opponent who could be thousands of miles away.

If you decide after a while that you just cannot win, you could always tactfully resign ●

*If you have the **Chat** button turned on, you can talk to your opponent by selecting a remark from the **Select a message to send** drop-down menu* ●

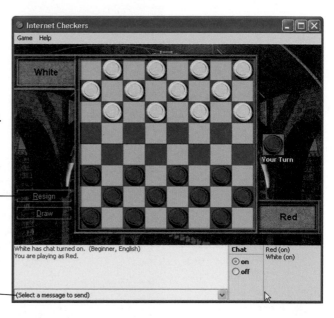

5 EXCHANGING MESSAGES

● Don't worry if you are playing someone whose language you do not understand, as the message that you send from your computer will be translated at their end into their language and vice versa.

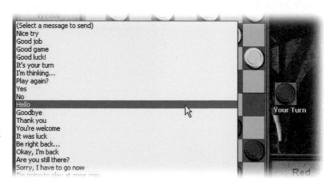

6 PLAYING ANOTHER GAME

- If you lose your game dismally, as we did here, either of the players can suggest another game, or the program offers you an opportunity to play another game against a new opponent.

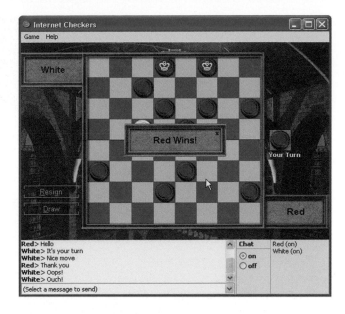

3D PINBALL SPACE CADET

- If you prefer a more fast-paced and immediate style of gaming, **3D Pinball Space Cadet** is worth trying – it's an exciting electronic version of a classic arcade pinball machine.
- The menu bar contains options to customize the game, and you can even listen to music or sound effects while you play.

GAMING ZONE

Microsoft's Gaming Zone, at **http://zone.msn.com**, has a **Game Index** link that lists all the games currently being played; one visit showed 110 games. Click on a game to see a list of games rooms and the total numbers playing.

MANAGING YOUR FILES

Whether you are a complete beginner or are already using Windows XP at a basic level, the ability to manage the documents on your computer efficiently is essential. This section explains in simple terms how to view the files on your computer, navigate through the many levels of folders on your hard disk, set up a personal filing system, and maintain the good organization of your documents in the future.

By working your way through the section from the beginning and following the tasks in sequence, you will achieve a thorough understanding of the principles involved in managing your files. At the same time, the tasks that you complete will prepare your computer for the next time you come to save new documents. Afterwards, you can return to the individual tasks and use them as a quick-reference guide.

VIEWING YOUR FILES

Managing files is easy once you are familiar with how they appear on your computer. There are many different ways to view files, and you can adopt a preference that suits you.

LOOKING INSIDE MY COMPUTER

All of the programs and files on your computer are stored on the hard disk: **Local Disk (C:)**. This is located in **My** Computer – the main "entrance" into your PC. Here you will also find access to the floppy disk and CD-ROM/DVD drives.

OPENING MY COMPUTER

● Position your cursor over the **My Computer** icon in the top left corner of the Windows desktop.
● Double-click the left mouse button and the **My Computer** window opens. Note that the taskbar now displays a button for the open window .

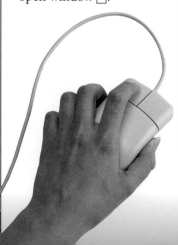

Clicking on this taskbar button will return you to the window at any time

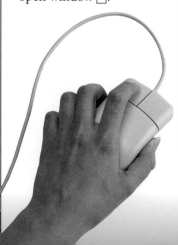

20 Using the Taskbar

The floppy disk drive

Your computer's hard disk, where the programs and files on your computer are stored

A removable disk – for example a Zip disk

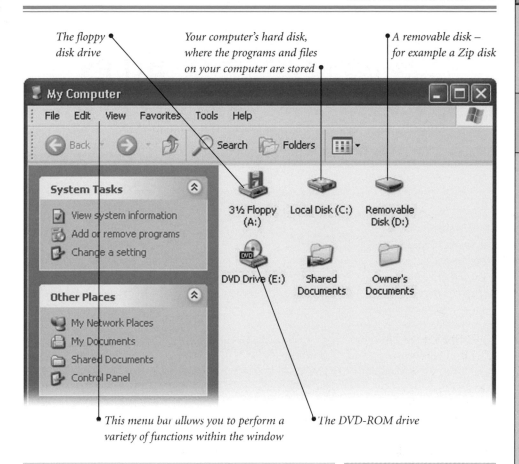

This menu bar allows you to perform a variety of functions within the window

The DVD-ROM drive

MINIMIZING, MAXIMIZING, AND CLOSING A WINDOW

The three buttons in the top right of an open window control how it appears onscreen. Clicking on the minimize button (–) makes the window disappear, but you will see a button remain on the taskbar. The maximize button (□) makes the window fill the

screen. You can click on it again to restore the window to its original size. The (X) button closes the window.

RESIZING A WINDOW

You can make a window larger or smaller by clicking in the bottom right corner and dragging the window to a new size.

VIEWING FILES IN WINDOWS

The default setting for Windows XP is to display the contents of open windows as large icons, showing nothing more than the name of the file and an icon to indicate its file type 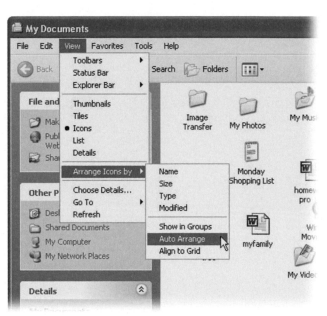. However, there are many ways to organize and view items within windows by changing the appearance of files, and by arranging them in a particular order.

1 SELECTING AUTO ARRANGE

● A window's contents displayed as large icons can often appear disordered, but you can arrange a window's contents by using **Auto Arrange**.

● Folders created in the **My Documents** folder may display their contents in this disorganized way, so open this window by double-clicking on its icon.

● With a "messy" folder open, select **Arrange Icons by** from the **View** menu and choose **Auto Arrange** from the submenu.

2 THE CONTENTS REARRANGED

● The menu closes and the icons rearrange themselves neatly within the window. With the **Auto Arrange** feature left on, the icons always automatically align themselves with one another when you resize a window or add new folders.

File Name Extensions and File Icons

3 ARRANGING IN OTHER WAYS

● As well as arranging icons automatically, it is also possible to arrange the icons by **Name**, **Size**, **Type**, or date **Modified** – just as you can by sorting files in **Details** mode ⌐.

● Experiment by using the same procedure as **Auto Arrange**, but select one of the other options under **Arrange Icons by** option in the **View** menu.

● In this example the items are arranged by their size.

Menu options...

Wherever relevant, the steps in this section show you how to select options from the menus found at the top of open windows. Often, many of these functions are also available by clicking on the right mouse button within a window, or by using a keyboard shortcut. By experimenting, you will become more familiar with your computer and develop methods of performing these tasks with which you feel most comfortable.

LINING UP THE CONTENTS OF A WINDOW

Under the **Arrange Icons by** menu you will also see **Align to Grid**. This is similar to the other ways of arranging the icons, but does not place them in any order. It simply aligns them in columns and rows by moving them slightly from their current positions.

4 VIEWING AS A FILM STRIP

● Next, we are going to look at how Windows XP can display photographs.
● With the **My Documents** folder still open 🗂, double-click on the **My Pictures** folder icon.

● Inside the **My Pictures** folder you will find a folder of sample photographs that are included with Windows XP. Double-click on the **Sample Pictures** folder icon to open it.

● The **Sample Pictures** window opens. Click on the **View** menu and choose **Filmstrip** by clicking on it.
● Windows XP now displays the pictures in the folder in a line along the bottom of the screen. Click on any of these to see an enlarged version displayed in the middle of the screen.

5 VIEWING AS A LIST

● Display the **View** menu again, but this time select **List** from the options.

● The contents retain their small icons, but now appear as a list arranged vertically in the window.

6 VIEWING DETAILS

● Now select **Details** from the **View** menu.

● When you select this option, certain information appears alongside the icons such as **Type** and **Total Size**.

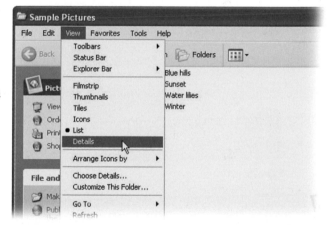

● Later, when you start to view windows containing individual files and folders in this way, you will also see their modification date.

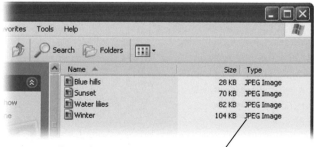

Further information appears in the list ●

ORGANIZING A WINDOW'S CONTENTS

When you view the contents of a window in **Details** 🗋 mode, you will see that a series of small boxes appears along the top of the open window containing headings for each category of information shown. By clicking on these headings you can reorganize the contents of the window into different lists according to different criteria.

1 ORGANIZING FILES BY NAME

● To explore the different ways of organizing your files in **Details** mode, double-click on **My Computer** in the **Other Places** task panel.

● When the My Computer window opens, double-click on **Local Disk (C:)**.

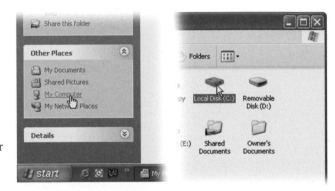

● When the **Local Disk (C:)** window opens, you will see that the items are automatically sorted into alphabetical order by name. Folders are always shown at the start of the list, with files listed at the end.

● Click on **View** in the toolbar and select **Details**.

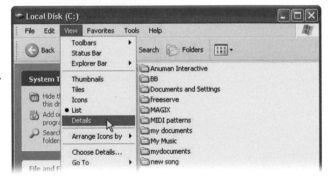

● This view provides additional information about the items in the list. Clicking on the **Name** heading box presents the items in reverse alphabetical order and places files before folders.

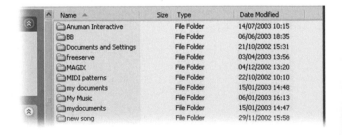

🗋 **Viewing**
63 | **Details**

2 ORGANIZING FILES BY SIZE

● You can view items listed by size by clicking on the **Size** heading box at the top.

● The files are listed from smallest to largest, and folders are again grouped at the top of the list.

● Click again on the **Size** heading box if you want to view the files listed in reverse size order.

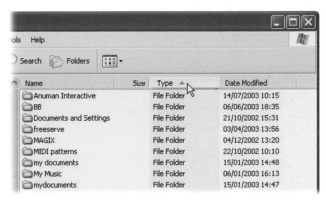

3 ORGANIZING FILES BY TYPE

● Click on the **Type** heading box.

● The items in the window are grouped according to their different types, which are listed alphabetically.

● As before, you can click again on the heading box to view the groups in reverse alphabetical order.

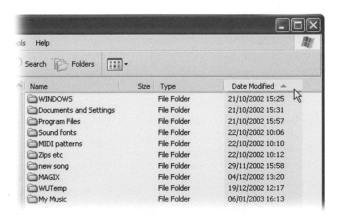

4 ORGANIZING FILES BY DATE

● Click on the **Date Modified** heading box.

● The files and folders are now reordered so that the oldest items are shown at the top of the list.

● If you want to view the newest files, click again on the heading box. The date order of the list is reversed.

VIEWING FILES IN WINDOWS EXPLORER

The last few pages have shown you the basic methods for viewing files within open windows. However, Windows XP has an additional tool, Windows Explorer, which provides you with another means of viewing and managing your files.

It allows you to do all the same things that you would do by using Windows conventionally, but also shows you exactly where a file is saved by guiding you visually through the hierarchy of folders on your computer's hard disk.

1 LAUNCHING EXPLORER

● To launch Windows Explorer, click once on the **Start** button in the bottom left corner of the taskbar ⬚. ● Choose **All Programs** from the pop-up menu, then **Accessories**, and then select **Windows Explorer** from the submenu that appears at the side.

● Either release the mouse button, or left-click, and Windows Explorer opens.
● By default, the window displays the contents of the **My Documents** folder.

● To make the window fill the screen, click on the **Maximize** button 🔲.

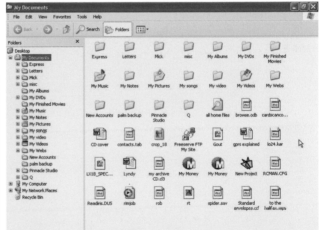

RESIZING THE WINDOW PANELS

If the folders displayed in the left-hand panel are obscured, place the cursor over the gray vertical bar that divides the two parts of the window. The cursor changes to a double-headed arrow. Hold down the mouse button and drag the bar to the right. When the left-hand panel is sufficiently large to reveal the list of folders, release the mouse button.

59 **Minimizing, Maximizing, and Closing a Window**

2 NAVIGATING WITH EXPLORER

● When you first launch Windows Explorer, a diagram is displayed in the left-hand panel listing items that branch from the **Desktop** – the top level of your computer.

● You will see that the folder **My Documents** is automatically highlighted in the list because this is where the majority of the folders and files that you are most likely to want to access are stored.

● The folders that this folder contains are listed below its name. As each folder is highlighted, its contents will appear automatically in the panel to the right. Note that individual files are not shown in the list to the left, but they do appear along with the folders in the main panel.

● By moving up the column of folders and then to the left, you see that **My Pictures** is stored in **My Documents,** which, in turn, can be found on the **Desktop.**

● Many options appear as buttons in a menu bar

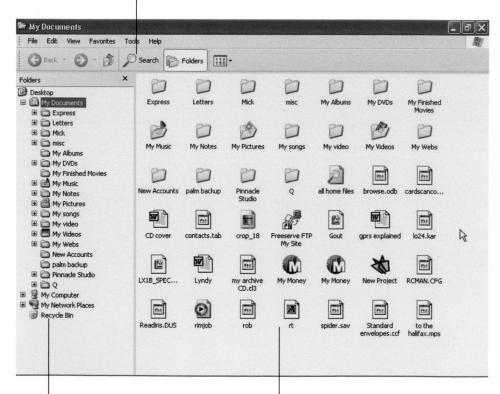

● The left-hand panel displays a diagram showing the hierarchy of all the drives and folders on your computer

● When a folder or drive in the left-hand diagram is highlighted, the files and folders it contains appear in the panel to the right

WHY USE WINDOWS EXPLORER?

It is purely personal preference whether you want to use Windows Explorer to manage your files. With Explorer, you can perform all the operations – copying , renaming , and deleting  – that you might carry out across open windows. The main advantage of using Windows Explorer is the ability to navigate your way through the entire contents of your computer within a single open window. This avoids constantly opening and closing different windows, or having a number of windows open at the same time.

FOLDERS WITHIN FOLDERS

In the diagram, you will see that many folders have a small square next to them containing either a plus symbol (+) or a minus symbol (–). This is a quick way of seeing whether a folder contains other folders that aren't currently displayed. A plus sign (+) next to a folder means that it contains other folders (known as subfolders), but they are not presently displayed in the diagram. A minus symbol (–) next to a folder shows that it is open and other folders it contains are listed in the diagram. If there is no symbol next to a folder, there are no other folders inside it. This does not necessarily mean that the folder is empty, as it could still contain individual files.

3 REVEALING THE SUBFOLDERS

● Position the cursor over one of the squares in the diagram that contains a plus symbol (+) and left-click once.

● A new list of folders appears underneath, branching from the folder you selected, and the plus symbol (+) changes to a minus symbol (–).

| 95 | **Copying Files to Other Locations** | 102 | **Renaming Files and Folders** | 104 | **Deleting Unwanted Files** |

4 REVEAL FOLDER CONTENTS

● To see all the files that the folder contains, click once on the folder that you just clicked next to.

● The folder becomes highlighted and its contents are now displayed in the main right-hand panel.

The contents of the folder are displayed in this panel

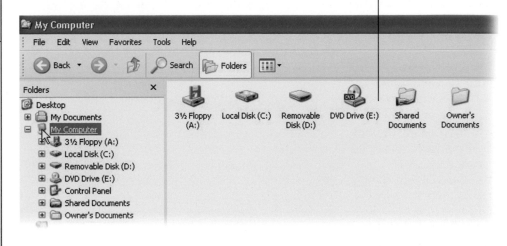

5 HIDING THE SUBFOLDERS

● Place the cursor over the square that now contains a minus symbol (–) and left-click once.

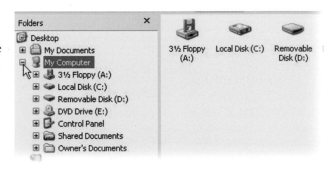

● The folders that stem from your selected folder disappear, and the symbol in the square becomes a plus sign (+) again.

FILE NAME EXTENSIONS AND FILE ICONS

Whenever you save a file, three letters are added to the name, which indicate its file type. This is known as a file name extension, but it isn't always visible. In addition, the file is also given a graphic symbol called an icon – which is always visible – so you can instantly recognize the file type, or the program used to create it.

VIEWING THE FILE EXTENSIONS

● Open a window that contains some of your files and select **Folder Options** from the **Tools** menu. Under the **View** tab, click in the square next to **Hide extensions for known file types** to remove the check mark. When you click on **OK**, the extensions appear after the file names.

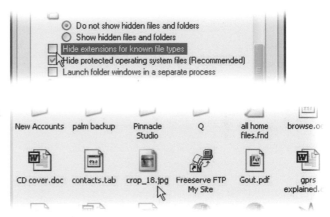

FILE NAME EXTENSIONS

Here are some common extensions that you may see following file names:

- **.doc** Word/WordPad document
- **.xls** Excel spreadsheet
- **.txt** Text document
- **.psp** Paint Shop Pro image file
- **.tif** Tagged Image File Format
- **.pdf** Portable Document Format
- **.png** Portable Network Graphic file

COMMON FILE ICONS

Files are given a unique icon depending on the program they were created in. These icons provide you with a simple way of distinguishing text files from graphics files, and so on.

A document created in NotePad

A graphics file created in Paint

A document created in Microsoft Word

A spreadsheet created in Microsoft Excel

An image file created in Paint Shop Pro

A pdf created in Adobe Acrobat

OPENING AND SAVING

These two operations are among the first that you will carry out on your computer. However simple they may seem, saving your files correctly is a crucial part of good file management.

OPENING FILES FROM A WINDOW

A common way of opening documents is first to open the program used to create it, and then select **Open** from the **File** menu. However, a simpler way to open a file is to locate it on your computer (using the navigation techniques described in the previous chapter) and open it directly from the folder window containing the file.

1 SELECTING A FILE TO OPEN

- Open the window of the folder containing the file that you wish to open.
- Click once on the file icon to highlight it.

2 OPENING THE FILE

- Click on **File** in the Menu bar at the top of the window and select **Open** from the drop-down menu.
- The program that was used to create the file launches automatically, and the file you selected opens onscreen.

OPENING A RECENT FILE

Windows XP contains a feature that allows most programs to add files to a list of up to 15 files in the **Start** menu. These are the files that you have been working on most recently. This feature provides a quick and easy way of opening a recent file.

1 OPENING FROM THE START MENU

- Click once on the **Start** button in the bottom left corner of the taskbar ⬚.
- Choose **My Recent Documents** from the pop-up menu. You will see that your most recent files are listed in the submenu that appears.
- Highlight a file and release the mouse button.
- As before, the program launches and your chosen file opens.

The most recent files that you have been working on appear in this list

---

OPENING FILES THE QUICK WAY

Once you gain confidence in handling files within their windows, the easiest, and by far the quickest, way to open them is by simply double-clicking on the file icon. Within an open window, double-click on the file icon (there is no need to highlight it first by selecting it). The program launches and the file opens to be worked on.

SAVING A FILE TO MY DOCUMENTS

Although saving is a very simple process, it is not without its pitfalls. If you don't have logical locations on your computer to save your files, you can soon create filing havoc on your computer's hard disk. The next few steps show the default location of your files when you save them, and how you can modify that location.

1 CREATING A NEW DOCUMENT

● Before you can familiarize yourself with saving files, you first need to create a new document with which to experiment. If the document from the previous task is open, then close it and create a new file.

● In the example shown below, we are using a new document created in WordPad, which is a simple word processing program that comes with Windows XP. It can be found in the **Start** menu under **All Programs** and then under **Accessories**.

37 | **Wordpad**

2 SELECTING SAVE AS

● With the new WordPad document open, click on **File** in the Menu bar and select **Save As** from the drop-down menu.

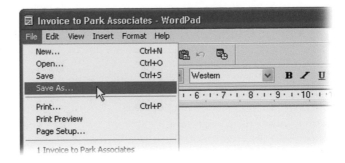

3 SELECTING THE LOCATION

● The **Save As** dialog box opens. At the top there is a text box with the words **Save in** written alongside. This is where you select the location in which to save your document.

● The current location shown in the box is **My Documents**. Your computer automatically selects this location when you open a program and select **Save** or **Save As** for the first time.

● Any other folders that are also contained in this location are displayed in the window. Although you can choose to save the document loose in **My Documents**, try placing it into one of the existing folders by double-clicking on the folder's icon. If there are no folders, you can create a new one in which the document can be saved 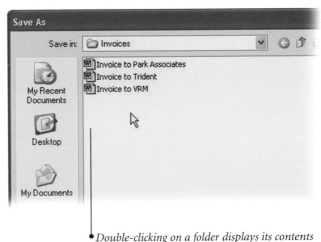.

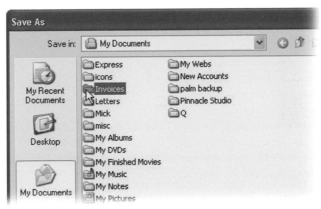

●Double-clicking on a folder displays its contents in the window, and selects it as the new location

83 **Creating New Folders as You Save**

4 NAMING THE DOCUMENT

- Click in the **File name** text box at the start of the default name (**Document**). The cursor changes to a blinking insertion bar.
- Hold down the mouse button and drag the insertion bar over the name to highlight it.
- Type in the new name.

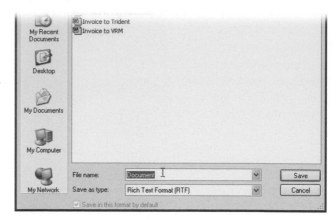

5 SAVING THE DOCUMENT

- Click on the **Save** button and your document is saved, with the name that you have given it, in the location you have chosen.
- Close the program and check that the file has been saved to the correct location by opening the folder window containing your document.

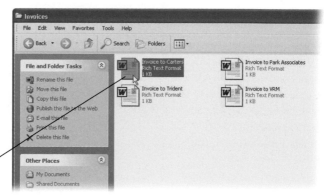

The file has been saved in your chosen location

I Can't See the My Documents Folder on the Desktop...

If for any reason the **My Documents** folder doesn't appear on your desktop, then it can be found within **My Computer** . Double-click on the **My Computer** icon on the desktop to view its contents. The main drives of your computer, as well as the principal folders, appear in the list. Double-click on the **Owner's Documents** folder – this is the same as the **My Documents** folder.

CHANGING THE FILE TYPE

When you save a file for the first time, the program that you are running saves the document as a specific file type 🗋, usually a basic format recognized only by that particular program. However, it is possible to change the file type of the document you are saving so that it can be recognized by other software packages or a different computer operating system (such as the Apple Macintosh system, for example).

1 OPEN THE SAVE AS DIALOG BOX

● Save a file through the **Save As** dialog box as usual 🗋, choosing its location and giving the document a name. Before you save, click on the arrow next to the **Save as type** box to see a list of file type options.

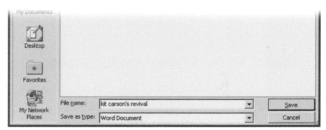

2 SELECTING THE FILE TYPE

● In this example we are going to save a Word document as an RTF (**Rich Text Format**) file.
● Highlight this option in the list and click on **Save**.

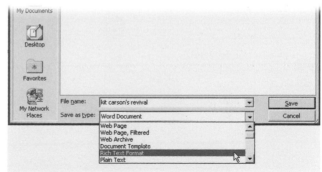

SELECTING A FILE TYPE FOR TEXT DOCUMENTS

The most common format for transferring text documents is **Plain Text**. Although this file format is widely used and recognized, be aware that it will remove the formatting (indents, text styling, etc) from your document, and strip it down to simple unformatted text. Because of this, it makes more sense to save your text documents in a standard format, then make a copy (saved as **Plain Text**) to use for file transfer.

YOUR FILING SYSTEM

The key to good file management is not only understanding where files on your computer are stored – you also need to develop your own system for saving files in organized folders.

BETTER FILE MANAGEMENT

You can, if you want, save your documents loose within the **My Documents** folder. However, as you create more files, the folder will soon become very full and disorganized, and you will begin to lose track of what each file contains. This can be time-consuming and frustrating when you want to return to documents. The next few pages take you through all the steps involved in setting up a filing system.

KEEPING IT ORGANIZED

You will be surprised by just how many files you create as you begin to use your computer's potential. In addition to simple word processing and spreadsheets, you may also want to create graphics and pictures by using image-based software. If you are connected to the internet, you will want to save emails, as well as files that you download, for future reference. Not only will you be doing all these things as a home user, you may also be creating documents that are work-related. If you have two or three family members using the PC for their own purposes, you will soon begin to understand why good file management is essential.

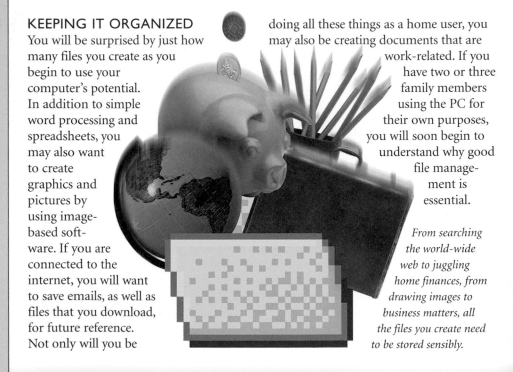

From searching the world-wide web to juggling home finances, from drawing images to business matters, all the files you create need to be stored sensibly.

DESIGNING YOUR NEW FILING SYSTEM

It is essential to start using a logical system for saving your files as soon as possible. It is easy to overlook this in your haste to "play" with your new PC, but it will be a long and arduous task to return and organize all those files later. Before creating a filing system on the computer, begin by planning it on paper.

1 WHO WILL BE USING YOUR PC?

● First, make a list of all the people who will be using your computer. In the case of a home PC, this is most likely to be the members of your household.

● These people become first-level entries in your new filing system.

● Even if you are the only person using your computer, still put your name at the top of the list.

2 WHAT WILL THEY BE USING IT FOR?

● Each person that uses your PC will do so for a variety of reasons.

● Against each user's name, list the categories of the different types of work that they are likely to undertake. These might include work, personal projects, home finances, college, etc. You may have to repeat some of the categories, for example, most of the users will have their own personal projects.

● These categories become second-level entries in the system.

3 LIST SPECIFIC PROJECTS

● Next to each category, make a third-level list of more specific projects or jobs relevant to the particular category.

● The entries in this third level will eventually become folders to contain all the text documents, graphics, emails, and other files that are associated with a particular job or project.

● This level will constantly expand, but begin by listing as many specific projects as possible that are already on your computer.

YOUR FINAL DESIGN

Using connecting lines between the levels of folders, this illustration shows how Windows Explorer might represent your new filing system. Later, we will be creating all the folders shown in the diagram on your computer. These folders will form the basis of your filing system.

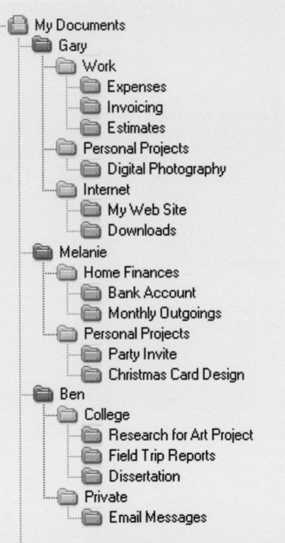

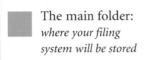

The main folder:
where your filing system will be stored

Level one folders:
for each user

Level two folders:
for project categories

Level three folders:
to contain documents

Just the beginning...

Remember that this is just the starting point for your new filing system. Over time, you will need to modify your use of folders, indeed you will certainly have to create many more levels of subfolders to store individual projects. Where you choose to save your files is not set in stone, and you can easily modify your system later by moving files and folders to new locations 🗋.

All documents associated with a particular project or job should be stored within individual third-level folders

🗋 **Moving Files Between Locations** 93

CREATING NEW FOLDERS

A folder on your computer should be used to store files that are associated with one another. This means that all your documents are kept in logical groups and are easy to find. In order to create your filing system, you will need to make a number of new folders on your PC, in which you can place your files. You can create as many folders and subfolders as you wish, and you should develop the habit of creating a new folder for each new job or project that you undertake.

1 OPENING MY DOCUMENTS

● We are going to use the existing folder, **My Documents**, as the location for housing your new filing system.

● Double-click on the **My Documents** icon on the desktop.

● The **My Documents** window opens. There are some standard folders that will already exist in this location, including **My Pictures** and **My Webs.**

● If you are not using your computer for the first time, there are also likely to be some other existing files, and possibly folders, saved in the **My Documents** folder as well. These will have to be organized into your new filing system, but for now we are going to put them all out of the way into one folder so that you can return and sort through them later.

*Your **My Documents** folder is likely to contain a number of disorganized files and folders*

2 CREATING A NEW FOLDER

● Within the window of the **My Documents** folder, click on **Make a new folder** in the list of **File and Folder Tasks** in the left-hand panel.

● A new folder appears in the **My Documents** window.

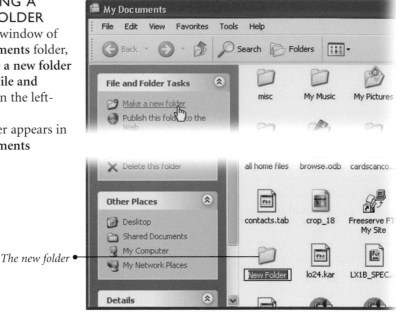

The new folder ●

3 NAMING THE NEW FOLDER

● With the new folder highlighted, type in a new name, **Files to sort**. Press the [Enter ←] key and deselect the folder by clicking once in any blank area of the window.

● You have now created a new folder that is ready to be used to store all those disorganized files.

● To keep the window neat while you create your new filing system, we are going to place the files and folders, currently saved in **My Documents**, into the new folder.

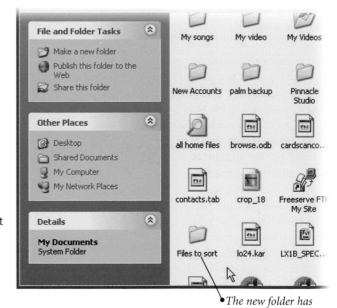

●*The new folder has been renamed*

4 PUT AWAY YOUR EXISTING FILES

● Click on an existing file and keep the mouse button held down. The file becomes highlighted.

● Move the file into the new folder by dragging the icon over the folder and releasing the mouse button. The file is now placed in the folder.

● Repeat this process for each of the files and folders in the window. If there are a number of items to move, refer to the section dealing with making multiple selections ⌐. You can leave the standard folders – such as **Pictures, Music,** and **Webs** – where they are.

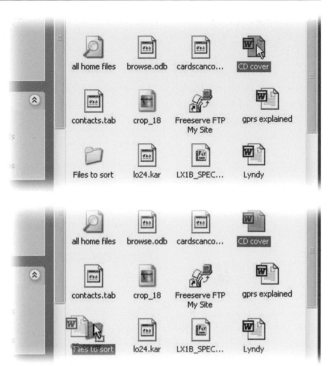

CREATING NEW FOLDERS AS YOU SAVE

Another way to make new folders is to create them at the same time as saving a document. You will find this a useful feature once your new filing system is in place because you can create folders for new projects as you save documents, rather than preparing them in advance. When you select **Save As,** to save a document for the first time ⌐, select a location for your file as normal,

but do not click on **Save** immediately. Instead, click once on the **Create New Folder** button – a new

Create New Folder button •

folder appears in the list. The folder's name is automatically highlighted so that you have the opportunity to give it a more specific name. Once you have typed in the folder's new name, double-click on it to select the folder, then name the new document by typing it into the **File Name** box. When you click on the **Save** button, the document is saved into your new folder.

| 90 | **Selecting Your Files** | | 74 | **Saving a File to My Documents** |

CREATING YOUR NEW FILING SYSTEM

We are now going to continue creating new folders within **My Documents** to set up the filing system you designed on page 79. The following steps also show you how to create folders within folders, which are known as subfolders.

1 CREATING YOUR MAIN FOLDERS

● Beside the folders you have chosen to leave, there should now only be one folder currently in view in the **My Documents** window, named **Files to sort**, which contains all the other files and folders that were already saved in this location. Make sure that it is not selected by clicking on any blank area in the window.

● Click on the **Make a new folder** command in the **File and Folder Tasks** panel.

● Give the new folder the name of one of your computer users from the top level of your design, in this case – **Gary**.

● Continue to create new folders for each of the users, naming each of the folders as you create them.

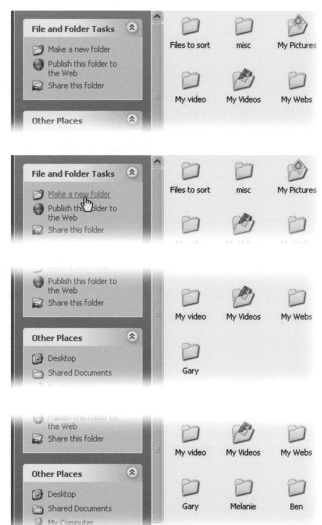

2 CREATE A USER'S SUBFOLDERS

● We are now going to place a series of folders within the user's main folder, corresponding to the second level in the design.

● Select a user's folder by double-clicking on its icon in the window. A new window opens to reveal the contents of that particular folder which, of course, is currently empty. Any folders that you now create are saved directly into that user's folder.

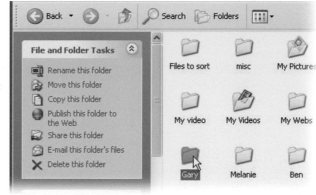

● Create a folder in the new window in the usual way and give it a category name, in this case – **Work**.

● Make new folders for each of the categories listed underneath this particular user in the second level of your design.

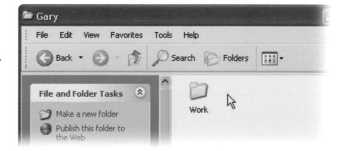

3 FURTHER SUBFOLDERS

● Before repeating the above process for each of the other users, first complete the filing system for your currently selected user. In the same way as shown in step 2, you need to create further subfolders within the category folders you have just made. These will correspond to the third level in your design.

● Double-click on a category folder to view its contents.

● In the new window, create new folders for each of the third-level entries under the currently selected category.

4 MOVING TO THE NEXT CATEGORY

● To create third-level folders in the remaining second-level categories, you will need to return to view the contents of your current user in level one.

● Keep clicking on the **Back** button in the menu bar until you return to the window that displays the folders for each second-level category.

● Double-click on the next category to open its window.

- Create the third-level folders for this category.
- Repeat step four for each second-level category.

5 MOVING TO THE NEXT USER

- Having completed the filing system for one user, you need to repeat the process for each of the others. Remember that the window will currently display the contents of a second-level subfolder for your first user.

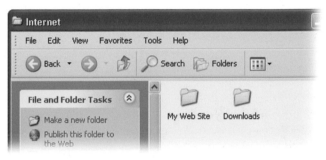

- Return to your first level of folders by clicking on the **Back** button.
- Repeat steps 2 to 5 for each of the people listed in the design of your filing system.

See your filing system in all its glory...

Remember that once you have completed your filing system, you can check its complete structure by viewing it through Windows Explorer ⌐.

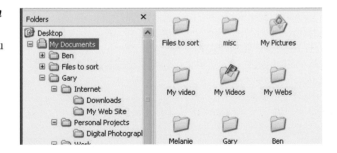

CREATING A SHORTCUT TO A FOLDER

If there is a particular folder, or folders, in your filing system that you need to access regularly, then it may be worth creating a shortcut on the desktop. A shortcut made from a folder acts as a direct link taking you directly to an open window for that particular folder, instead of having to "drill down" through many levels of folders to reach it. With this in mind, a shortcut can become a valuable time-saving device if your chosen folder is buried within many levels of subfolders.

1 CHOOSING THE FOLDER

● Open the window that contains the folder for which you wish to create a shortcut.
● Click once on your chosen folder so that it is highlighted.

2 CREATING THE SHORTCUT

● Click on **File** in the menu bar at the top of the open window. In the drop-down menu, click once on **Send To**, then click on **Desktop (create shortcut)** in the submenu.

Selecting this option creates a shortcut in the same location

3 YOUR SHORTCUT IS CREATED

● Close the window and the shortcut that you created appears on the desktop. Shortcuts are distinguished by a small arrow in the bottom left-hand corner of the icon.

● *This arrow indicates that the folder is a shortcut*

4 OPENING FROM A SHORTCUT

● To open the folder linked to the shortcut, simply double-click on the shortcut's folder icon.

● The window for that specific folder opens immediately.

SHORTCUTS FOR FILES AND PROGRAMS

You can create shortcuts for individual files and programs in the same way as folders. Be careful about this though. You may have just created a thoroughly efficient filing system on your computer, but creating too many shortcuts can very quickly make an unusable mess of your desktop!

MOVING AND COPYING

An important part of organizing your files is the ability to move and copy your documents between different locations within your filing system.

SELECTING YOUR FILES

Moving and copying both use simple "drag and drop" techniques that involve picking up a file, or folder, from one open window and placing it into another. For this to happen, you need first to select the files that you want to move. You can select individual files, or several at a time. To become familiar with the different methods of selecting, we are going to organize all the files that you stored under **Files to sort** earlier in the book ⬆. If you don't have some old files to organize, the following steps are equally as relevant for selecting and moving files in the future.

1 SELECTING A SINGLE FILE

● Open the window to display the contents of the **Files to sort** folder.
● Within this window you should see a variety of files and folders, as shown here.
● To select a file, click once on its icon in the window. The file becomes highlighted to show that it is now selected.

2 SELECTING GROUPS OF FILES

● You can continue to select further files that are positioned next to your currently selected file.

● With the file still selected, place the cursor over the next file to be selected.

● Hold down the `⇧ Shift` key and now, when you click on your second file, both are highlighted.

● Holding down the `⇧ Shift` key can also be used to select files in a block by clicking on two files that occupy the opposite corners of a grid.

3 SELECTING UNGROUPED FILES

● You can select several files from the window, cvcn if they are not positioned next to one another.

● Click on any empty area of the window to deselect any highlighted files.

● Select your first file, as described in step 1.

● Hold down the `Ctrl` key and click on a second file anywhere in the window, and both files then become highlighted.

● Keep the `Ctrl` key held down to select further files.

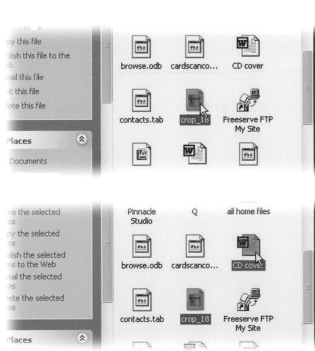

4 SELECTING ALL FILES

● To select all the items in an open window, click on **Edit** in the menu bar. Choose **Select All** from the drop-down menu.

● When you release the mouse button, the menu closes and the entire contents of the window are highlighted.

5 DESELECTING FILES

● To deselect a single file from this group of selected files, hold down the Ctrl key.
● Click on the file that you would like to deselect. The file is now no longer highlighted.
● Keep the Ctrl key held down to deselect further files.

INVERTING A SELECTION

You can reverse which files are selected and deselected by choosing **Invert Selection** from the **Edit** menu within the window. When you select this option every file that is currently highlighted will become deselected and the files that are deselected become highlighted.

MOVING FILES BETWEEN LOCATIONS

We are now going to use the selection methods described in the previous task to move your existing files into your new filing system. When you move a file, it means that the place where that file is saved on your computer changes from one location to another. This is different from copying 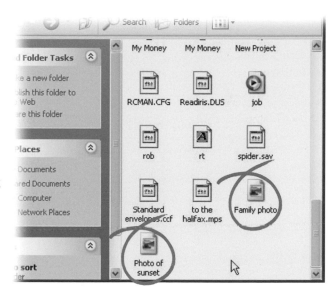, where the file that you copy and move can result in copies being stored in any number of locations.

1 CHOOSING THE FILES TO MOVE

● Open the window of the **Files to sort** folder to display its contents.
● Decide which file(s) you are going to move first, for example, all files that are connected by belonging to one of the users.
● In this case, we are going to move all the photographic files that belong to Gary into the relevant folder in the filing system.

2 CHOOSING THE NEW LOCATION

● Select the files that are to be moved.
● Click on the **Move the selected items** command in the **File and Folder Tasks** panel in the left-hand side of the window.

● The **Move Items** window opens onscreen.

● Before moving a file, you need to decide where to move it to. The files that we have chosen belong in the new folder called **Digital Photography**, found within Gary's folders.

● Navigate to this folder using the techniques shown on pages 66–70 , and click on the folder to select it.

● Click on the **Move** button.

3 VIEWING THE MOVED FILES

● The files will move from one location to the other.

● You can check this by opening the window for the new location. The files will be visible in the window.

Continue sorting...
Check your computer for files that may have been accidentally saved to other locations on your hard drive and move these into your filing system as well.

BEWARE OF WHAT YOU MOVE

Although moving your own files around your computer is a simple task, don't be tempted to start "organizing" other aspects of your computer's hard drive. To make everything work properly, the operating system "knows" where important system files are stored, and uses these to launch the programs that you run on your computer. If you inadvertently move files that the computer requires, you can expect a time-consuming, and possibly expensive, process to fix it. This is why it is safest to restrict all your file management to the **My Documents** folder.

COPYING FILES TO OTHER LOCATIONS

The process of copying files is similar to moving them – however, the original file remains in place and a duplicate file appears in a new location. Probably the main reason for copying files to different locations on your computer is to create backups in case anything goes wrong with your original file. Remember though, copying is not like making a shortcut – when you make a copy, both files become independent of one another, whereas a shortcut is a link to the original. This means that changes made to the original file are not reflected in the copy until you overwrite it with a new copy. For more information on backups, see page 114.

1 CHOOSING THE FILE TO COPY

● Let's assume that you already have a file saved on your computer that needs to be located in two different folders within your new filing system. During your reorganization, the file will have been moved into one of the relevant folders.
● Open the window containing the file you wish to copy and select it.

2 COPYING THE FILE

● Select the **Copy this file** command from the **File and Folder Tasks** panel.

Creating a Shortcut to a Folder

- The **Copy Items** window opens.
- Navigate to the folder into which you would like to place the duplicate file, and click on the folder once to select it.
- Click on the **Copy** button.

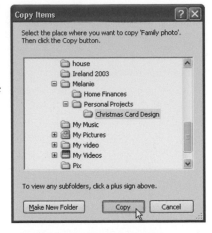

- A copy of the file is placed in the new location, leaving the original file in place.

USING DRAG AND DROP

Another way to move or copy files and folders between locations is by "dragging and dropping" them between two or more open windows. In order to do this you must first change the default Windows XP settings so that different folder contents open in independent windows, rather than opening in the same one.

1 CHANGING THE SETTINGS

- With the **My Documents** window open, select **Folder Options** from the **Tools** menu. The **Folder Options** window opens.

● Within the **Browse folders** section, click once in the radio button next to **Open each folder in its own window,** so that a bullet appears in it.
● Click on the **OK** button.

● Now, when you double click on folder icons their contents are displayed in separate windows.
● As before, select the files that you wish to move and, while keeping the left mouse button pressed down, drag the files from one window to the other.
● To copy files between locations – rather than moving them – hold down the Ctrl key as you release the mouse button.

AN ALTERNATIVE WAY OF MOVING AND COPYING

Instead of using the Ctrl key to ensure that you are copying rather than moving, you can also make the choice from a menu. Drag a file into a second location using the technique described, regardless of whether you would like to make a copy or not. As you drag the file from one window to

another, hold down the right-hand mouse button rather than the left. When you release the mouse button, a pop-up menu appears from which you can select either **Copy Here** or **Move Here.** It is purely personal preference, but you may want to adopt this technique until you are confident about using

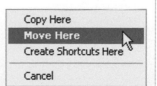

keyboard commands to perform certain tasks. Note also that you can create a shortcut within your chosen location by using this method.

COPYING FILES TO A FLOPPY DISK

So far we have only made copies of files to different locations on the same hard disk. This is fine for making temporary back-ups, or if you need to use the same file for several projects, but what happens if your whole computer should develop some kind of fault that prevents you from accessing your files? Having copies on a floppy disk will mean that you still have access to those files. Or you may want to take a file to work so that you can continue working on it. Perhaps you want to give someone else a copy of one of your files. These are all good reasons why you may want to copy files to an external device – commonly a floppy disk.

1 INSERTING A DISK

● Insert a formatted floppy disk into the computer's disk drive with the metal edge facing forward and the circular metal disc on the underside. Push the disk in firmly and you will hear it snap into position in the drive.

Storage Capacity…
There are two types of 3½" floppy disk – Double Density, which can store 720KB, and High Density, which can store 1440KB (1.44MB). High Density disks display an HD symbol.

2 SELECTING THE FILES

● Open the window of the folder containing the files that you wish to copy to the floppy disk. Remember, you can change the view of the window to **Details** so that you can check the size of the files and make sure that they will fit on the disk ◻.
● Select the files ◻.

These files are particularly small and will easily fit onto a floppy disk

| 63 | **Viewing** **Details** |

| 90 | **Selecting** **Your Files** |

3 COPYING THE FILES

● With the files high-lighted, click on **File** in the menu bar and select **Send To** from the drop-down menu. You will see that the floppy disk drive appears in the submenu as: 3¹/₂ **Floppy (A:)**. Click once on this option.

● Copies of the files that you selected are placed on the floppy disk.

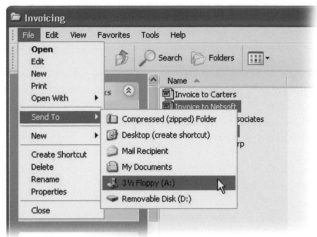

FORMATTING A FLOPPY DISK

When you buy new floppy disks, they are usually preformatted so that you can start to use them immediately. If you insert an unformat-ted disk into your floppy disk drive, your computer will not be able to recognize the disk and will display an alert message. To format a disk, select the drive 3¹/₂ **Floppy (A:)** from within the **My Computer** window, and click on **Format** in the **File** menu. Select the relevant options in the **Format** window to format the disk.

VIEWING THE CONTENTS OF A FLOPPY DISK

The above steps assume that you are using a new disk with maximum storage capacity. If you want to use a disk that already has files stored on it, you can view the contents of the disk in a window, just like any other drive or folder on your computer. With the floppy disk inserted, double-click on **My Computer** on the desktop. In the window there will be an icon for the floppy disk drive, 3¹/₂ **Floppy (A:)**. Double-click on the icon, and a window appears display-ing the contents of the floppy disk currently in the drive. From this window, you can edit or delete the contents of the disk as normal, for example, to create more storage space on the disk.

FINDING YOUR MISPLACED FILES

No matter how well-managed your filing system might be, over time you are bound to misplace some files, or forget what they are called. Because the filing system you have created is housed in one location (the **My Documents** folder), it is a relatively easy procedure for the computer to search for your misplaced files. To do this, you have to enter a few details about the file, and tell the computer where to look.

1 OPENING SEARCH COMPANION

● Click once on the **Start** button at the left-hand end of the taskbar.
● Select **Search** from the right-hand menu.
● The **Search Results** dialog box appears.

2 ENTERING THE SEARCH DETAILS

● Within the panel on the left there are several options to help you find particular files.
● Choose the **All files and folders** option by clicking on it.
● Click inside the text box next to **All or part of the file name**. Type in a few details about what the file is called. Be as specific as possible – if you know the file name, then enter the complete name into the box. If you can't remember the name exactly, then

enter as much as you can. In this example, a missing invoice is being searched for on the hard drive, and we are fairly sure the word "invoice" is in the filename.
● The next box down, labeled **A word or phrase in**

the file, allows you to enter specific words that you know are contained within the file. For example, we know the invoice we are looking for was addressed to **Park Associates**, so this is entered into the box.

3 FINDING THE FILE

● To tell the computer specifically where to look for your file, click on the arrow next to the **Look in** text box and select the folder in which you think the file is stored. If the filing system has been used as described so far, the file should be in the **My Documents** folder.

● Click on the **Search** button to begin the search.

4 VIEWING THE RESULTS

● Any files that match your search criteria are displayed in the window.

● If you want to open the file immediately, you can easily do so by double-clicking on the file icon.

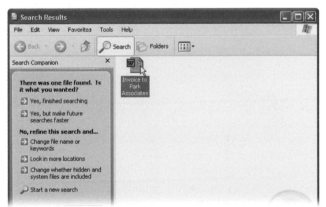

MAXIMIZING YOUR SEARCH SUCCESS

The more information with which you can provide the computer, the more likely it is that the files you are looking for will be found. To help, you can click on the arrow buttons to right of **When was it modified?**, **What size is it?**, and **More advanced options** to enter information about when the file was last modified, its size, and location.

MODIFYING YOUR FILES

Now that all your files are efficiently organized, it is time to examine the different ways in which you can modify them to ensure your filing system is kept in good working order.

RENAMING FILES AND FOLDERS

Over time, as you expand your filing system to include new folders and, certainly, many more files, it will become necessary to rename certain items. Follow the steps below to change the names of both folders and files.

1 SELECTING THE FILE

● In an open folder window, click once on the file that you wish to rename so that it becomes highlighted (you can only rename one file at a time). Here, we are renaming the file that we copied from one location to another on page 95, so that they clearly become different files.

File Names

Windows XP allows you to use up to 255 characters when naming your documents. On one hand this is obviously a benefit, because you can provide a full and precise description of your document. On the other hand, however, Windows will only make the beginning of very long file names visible when you view your documents in certain modes ⌐. This can become confusing if you have many files with a similar beginning, so try to differentiate file names as much as possible using just 20 to 30 characters.

60 | **Viewing Files in Windows**

2 RENAMING THE FILE

● Click on the **Rename this file** command in the **File and Folder Tasks** panel.

● A box appears around the current file name. If you want to change the name completely, press the ⌜Delete⌝ key and type in the new name. If you want to modify the name, for example, by adding to it, place the cursor at the point in the name that you want to alter and left-click.

● Rename the file and press the ⌜Enter ↵⌝ key.

● Your file is now displayed with its new name.

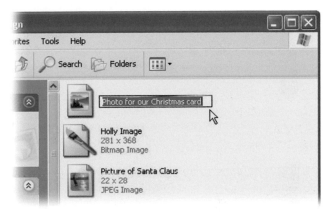

RENAME FILES WITH CAUTION!

Just as you should exercise caution when moving files ⌐, the same applies to renaming files. Changing the name of a file or folder that has not been created by you can give you and your computer a big headache when you try to perform certain functions or run applications. Limit any renaming you do to your own filing system.

DELETING UNWANTED FILES

Deleting files from your computer is just like throwing something away – you put it in the wastebasket. Be ruthless when it comes to removing files from your computer, and only keep what you are sure you need. It won't take long for you to accumulate hoards of worthless files, including those that you believe you might *possibly* need later! In practice, you will not return to them, eventually forget what they are, and use up valuable storage space on your computer in the process.

1 SELECTING THE FILE

● In this example we are going to delete the files that are deemed not important enough to keep in the filing system. These are the files that were left in the folder called **Files to sort**. By deleting the folder you are also throwing away all the files that it contains – this saves you having to delete each file one by one.

● In the open window, click once on the folder to be deleted. If necessary, you can also use the selecting techniques to delete many files in one process.

2 DELETING THE FILE

● Click on the **Delete this folder** command in the **File and Folder Tasks** panel.

● A box appears onscreen asking you to confirm the deletion. Click on the **Yes** button to confirm.

● The folder disappears from the window.
● You can also delete files either by right-clicking on them and choosing **Delete** from the pop-up menu (below right) or by dragging them to the Recycle Bin.

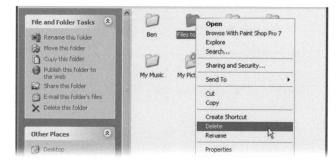

HAVING REGULAR CLEANUPS

An important part of maintaining your filing system is to have a regular review of the files stored there. If there are files that have been forgotten about, then consider whether you really need them, and if you start seeing several updated versions of the same file appearing in your folders, then you can be even more ruthless.

MANAGING THE RECYCLE BIN

Rather than deleting files immediately, the computer really moves them into the **Recycle Bin** positioned on the desktop. From this location you can restore files, so there's no problem if you suddenly realize you have made a mistake by performing the deletion. Files are only deleted permanently when you empty the **Recycle Bin**.

1 VIEWING THE BIN'S CONTENTS

● Position the cursor over the **Recycle Bin** icon on the desktop, and double-click. Note that the icon for the bin shows that there are files contained inside it. The **Recycle Bin** window opens and displays the files you have thrown away since the bin was last emptied.

2 RESTORING YOUR DELETED FILES

● All is not lost if you place a file in the **Recycle Bin** that you later decide you need – as long as you haven't yet emptied the bin.
● Highlight the folder that you deleted in the previous task. By selecting the folder, the entire contents of that folder are also selected.
● Click on the **Restore this item** command in the **Recycle Bin Tasks** window.
● The folder disappears from the window. It has been restored to the location from which you deleted it.

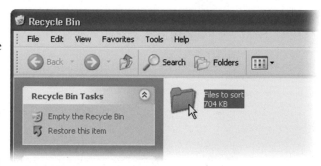

3 THROWING AWAY DELETED FILES

● For this task, delete the **Files to sort** folder again so that we can now dispose of it permanently.

● In the **Recycle Bin** window, click on the **Empty the Recycle Bin** command in the **Recycle Bin Tasks** window, or select **Empty Recycle Bin** from the **File** drop-down menu.

● A box appears onscreen asking you to confirm the deletion. You cannot be selective about the files that you permanently remove – clicking on the **Yes** button deletes all the files displayed in the window.

● The contents of the window vanish, and the icon for the **Recycle Bin** shows that it is now empty.

● *No documents are shown in the bin, indicating that the **Recycle Bin** is empty*

Too nervous to bin those files?

If you really can't bear to dispose of certain files then store them on some form of external device, such as a floppy disk. At least you won't be using up your hard disk space – and the files will be available, just in case!

EMPTYING THE RECYCLE BIN

You should empty the **Recycle Bin** frequently so that you do not clog up your computer's hard disk with unwanted files. However, before doing so, remember that this is your last chance to save any files from permanent deletion from your computer. Once you have emptied the **Recycle Bin**, the lost files cannot be restored.

VIEWING FILE PROPERTIES

Identical features, known as "properties," are assigned to every new file that you create on your computer, and they make the file function in certain ways. By changing a file's properties you can control the operations that can be carried out on it.

These changes include locking a file so that no modifications can be made to it (**Read-only**), hiding the file to make it invisible to others (**Hidden**), and "tagging" a file so that it is selected and backed-up automatically by your computer (**Archive**).

1 SELECTING THE FILE

● Select any file in an open folder window so that it becomes highlighted.

2 OPEN THE FILE PROPERTIES BOX

● Click on **File** in the menu bar and select **Properties** from the drop-down menu.

● The **Properties** of the file appear in a dialog box.

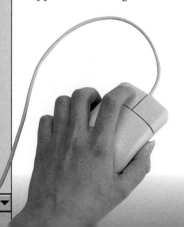

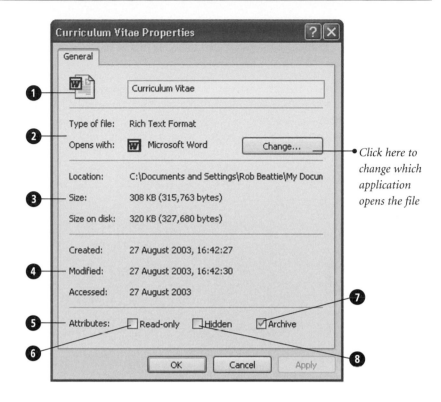

Click here to change which application opens the file

THE FILE PROPERTIES BOX

1 *The top part of the box displays the name of the file, along with an icon ⬜ to indicate which program it was created in.*

2 *Here you can see what type of file it is and which program is assigned to open it (in this case, the file is a Word document called* **Curriculum Vitae***). You can modify which program opens*

the file by clicking on the **Change…** *button.*

3 *The location where the file is saved and its size (in this case, shown in kilobytes and bytes) is specified in this part of the box.*

4 *This area tells you when the file was created and when it was last modified and last accessed.*

5 *The attributes in this part of the box can be modified by clicking in the check boxes.*

6 *Click on the* **Read-only** *option to lock your files. You will be able to open the document, but not modify or delete it.*

7 *When the* **Archive** *box is checked, this particular file will be included in an automated backup.*

8 *Selecting the* **Hidden** *option makes files invisible on your computer ⬜.*

CREATING HIDDEN FILES

A hidden file remains where it is on your computer, but becomes invisible. In other words, you cannot see an icon for the file within a folder window, or its file name in an **Open** menu. This is a basic form of security because another user will not immediately be aware that the file exists. Beware though – for anyone who knows how to make it accessible, it is a relatively simple process to display the file.

1 SELECTING THE HIDDEN OPTION
● Before you perform this operation, make a note of the file name because you won't be able to see it while the file is hidden.
● Open the **Properties** box for the file that you want to hide.
● Click in the check box next to **Hidden** so that a check mark appears.
● Click on **OK** and close the **Properties** box.

Location:	C:\Documents and Settings\Rob Beattie\My Docun
Size:	707 bytes (707 bytes)
Size on disk:	16.0 KB (16,384 bytes)
Created:	27 August 2003, 16:54:24
Modified:	27 August 2003, 16:54:26
Accessed:	27 August 2003
Attributes:	☐ Read-only ☑ Hidden ☑ Archive

OK   Cancel   Apply

2 HIDING THE FILE
● Your file only becomes hidden once you have changed the **View** options for the folder window that it appears in.
● Open the window to display the contents of the folder where your hidden file is located.

*The file is grayed-out to indicate that the **Hidden** property is applied, but it is still visible in the window*

● The file to which you applied the **Hidden** property may still be visible in the folder window. If it is, click on **Tools** in the menu bar, followed by **Folder Options** from the drop-down menu.

● When the **Folder Options** dialog box opens, click on the **View** tab.

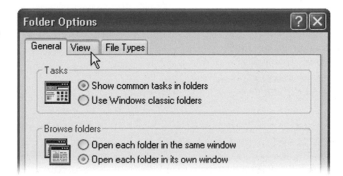

● Click on the radio button next to **Do not show hidden files and folders** so that a bullet appears in the button.
● Click on the **OK** button. Now, when you view the contents of the window, your hidden file will be invisible.

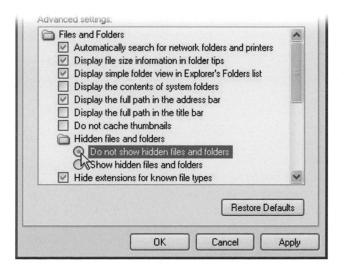

3 HIDING THE STATUS BAR

● Although the file is now hidden, if the **Status Bar** is visible it will show that the file exists in the location.

*The **Status Bar** shows there is one hidden file in the location* ●

● To hide the **Status Bar** click on **View** and select **Status Bar** from the drop-down menu.

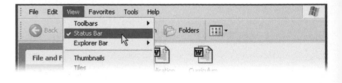

● When the menu closes the **Status Bar** disappears and there is no indication that your hidden file is saved within this location.

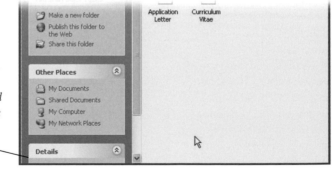

*The **Status Bar**, and the information that it contained, are no longer visible* ●

4 OPENING A HIDDEN FILE

● Launch the program in which you want to open your hidden file.
● Select **Open** from the **File** drop-down menu.

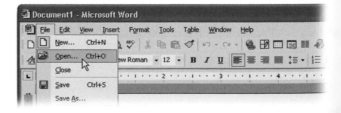

● When the **Open** dialog
box appears, select the
location of your file in the
Look in box, and then type
the name of your file into
the **File name** text box.
● Click on the **Open**
button, and your hidden
document now appears
onscreen.

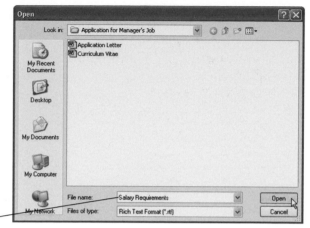

Enter the name of the file here ●

5 VIEWING HIDDEN FILES

● To make hidden files
visible again, reopen the
Folder Options box via
the **Tools** menu, and click
once in the radio button
next to **Show hidden
files and folders** so that a
bullet appears.
● Click on the **OK** button
to close the **Folder Options**
box. Any hidden files now
reappear in the window.
Be aware, however, that
anyone else can also follow
this procedure.

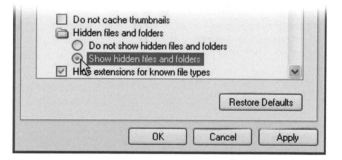

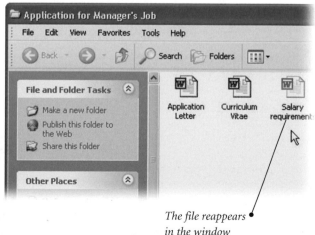

The file reappears ●
in the window

BACKING UP YOUR FILES

Now that your filing system is in place and you are managing your files effectively, it is time to consider safeguarding your work against accidental loss.

WHY BACK UP YOUR FILES?

Think for a moment about all the work that is stored on your computer. It represents a huge commitment of not only your money, but more importantly, your time. If your computer should fail, or is stolen, it will be virtually impossible for you to recreate the documents that were stored on your hard drive. For this reason, creating back ups on a regular basis is crucial. This simply involves copying files from one location to another that is separate from the computer itself.

PERMANENT ARCHIVES

The principle reason for backing up your files is to insure that you have access to them should anything happen to your computer or to the original files. However, the situation may also arise when it becomes very difficult or even impossible to store any more files on your computer. You may have used up your hard disk space, or the volume of files and folders on your hard drive becomes too unwieldy to manage. The only option left may be to remove files from your computer and store them on an external device. Good practice is to remove documents from your filing system as you finish with them. This

means that there is always maximum storage capacity on your computer, and the backing up process takes minutes rather than hours.

Backing Up to CD

See the final section of this book for detailed information on how to back up your valuable data using a recordable CD drive and Windows XP.

CREATING A COMPRESSED ARCHIVE

Unless you are regularly transferring large files to and from your computer, you may not have any device available to you apart from a floppy disk drive. If this is the case, you will need to maximize the amount of space available so that you can fit as many files as possible. File compression enables you to store many times the normal amount of files on a floppy disk by compacting them into a single "archive."

USING WINZIP

Probably the most commonly used file compression software for Windows is WinZip. If you wish, you can download a free evaluation version of this software from the internet and use it for a limited time before you have to purchase the full copy.

Visit **www.winzip.com** to download the program and follow the onscreen instructions to install it onto your computer. You will be asked a few questions in order to set up WinZip. When you are given the option, choose to run WinZip Classic – this is the simplest means of creating a basic archive file for the purpose of backing up.

WinZip has many more features than those shown below and, to appreciate its potential fully, you should treat the following steps as an introduction only. File compression is also very useful for transferring files between computers, especially if you are sending attachments by email. You can experiment with the program to see what best suits your archiving needs.

1 CREATING A NEW ARCHIVE

● Once the Winzip setup is complete, the WinZip window opens.
● Before you start, insert a floppy disk into your computer [].
● Click on the **New** button at the top of the window to create a new archive.

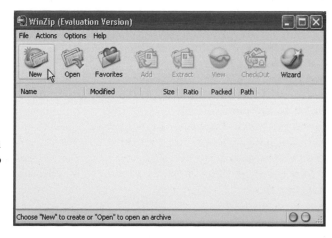

2 CHOOSING THE LOCATION

● The **New Archive** dialog box opens.

● In the **Save in** box, choose a location in which the archive is to be saved. In this case you can select the floppy disk directly by highlighting **3¹/₂ Floppy (A:)**.

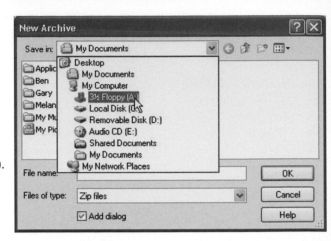

3 NAMING THE ARCHIVE

● It makes sense to create separate archive files that correspond with the names of the folders you use in your filing system.

● Decide which files you are going to archive first, and give the archive the same name as the folder where they currently reside.

● Click on the **OK** button.

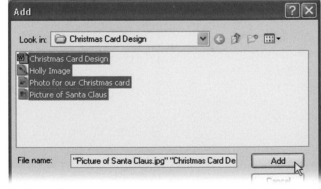

4 SELECTING THE FILES

● The **Add** dialog box opens. Select the location where the files are currently saved, and highlight them in the main window.

● Once the files are selected, click on the **Add** button.

5 THE ARCHIVE IS CREATED

● The WinZip window displays the contents of your archive file, which has now been saved onto your floppy disk.

● Close the window.

● It is now safe for you to delete the original files from your computer.

6 OPENING FROM AN ARCHIVE

● You can open the archive file by double-clicking on its icon. Then, whenever you want to open one of your archived files, simply double-click on it in the WinZip window.

● To restore files to your computer, click on the **Extract** button at the top of the window. You can then select the individual files you want to restore from the archive to your PC.

Label your disks... File management doesn't stop there! Remember to label your floppy disks clearly to keep track of where your files are saved.

COMPARING FILE SIZES

You can see how much space you have saved by comparing the file properties of the original folder with those of the archive file. The original files created a 545KB folder, whereas the archive is 156KB.

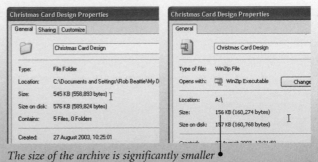

The size of the archive is significantly smaller ●

USING WORD

W ORD'S ESSENTIAL FEATURES are presented in separate chapters within this section. The tasks that are covered include launching this word-processing program on your PC, understanding the Word window and the toolbars, keying in text, and changing its appearance. This section also shows you how to save your documents and organize them in folders, print them, improve them using Word's tools, templates, and wizards, and how to carry out a mail merge.

MICROSOFT WORD

Microsoft Word has been around for well over a decade and, with each new release, adds to its reputation as the world's leading word-processing program.

WHAT CAN WORD DO?

The features contained in Word make it one of the most flexible word-processing programs available. Word can be used to write anything from shopping lists to large publications that contain, in addition to the main text, illustrations and graphics, charts, tables and graphs, captions, headers and footers, cross references, footnotes, indexes, and glossaries – all of which are easily managed by Word. Word can check spelling and grammar, check text readability, search and replace text, import data, sort data, perform calculations, and provide templates for many types of documents from memos to web pages. The comprehensive and versatile design, formatting, and layout options in Word make it ideal for desktop publishing on almost any scale. In short, there's very little that Word cannot do.

WHAT IS A WORD DOCUMENT?

In its simplest form, a Word document is a sequence of characters that exists in a computer's memory. Using Word, a document can be edited, added to, and given a variety of layouts. Once the document has been created, there are a large number of actions that can be carried out, such as saving, printing, or sending the document as an email.

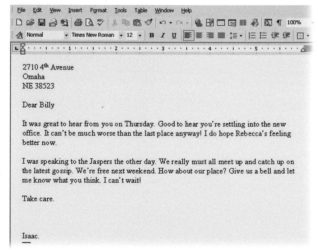

LAUNCHING WORD

Word launches just like any other program running in Windows. With the Windows desktop onscreen, you can launch Word as the only program running, or you can run Word alongside other software to exchange data with other applications.

1 LAUNCHING BY THE START MENU

- Place the mouse cursor over the **Start** button on the taskbar and click with the left mouse button.
- Move the cursor up to the **All Programs** panel, and a submenu of programs appears to the right.
- Move the cursor across and up the menu to **Microsoft Word** and left-click again. (If **Microsoft Word** is missing from the **Programs** menu, it may be under **Microsoft Office**.)
- The Microsoft Word window opens ⬁.

2 LAUNCHING BY A SHORTCUT

- You may already have a Word icon onscreen, which is a shortcut to launching Word. If so, double-click on the icon.
- The Microsoft Word window opens ⬁.

THE WORD WINDOW

At first, Word's document window may look like a space shuttle computer display. However, you'll soon discover that similar commands and actions are neatly grouped together. This "like-with-like" layout helps you quickly understand where you should be looking on the window for what you want. Click and play while you read this.

THE WORD WINDOW

❶ Title bar
❷ Menu bar
Contains the main menus.
❸ Standard toolbar
Buttons for frequent actions.
❹ Formatting toolbar
Main layout options.
❺ Tab selector
Clicking selects type of tab.
❻ Left-indent buttons
Used to set left indents.
❼ Ruler
Displays margins and tabs.
❽ Right-indent button
Used to set right indent.
❾ Insertion point
Shows where typing appears.
❿ Text area
Area for document text.
⓫ Split box
Creates two text panes.
⓬ Scroll-up arrow
Moves up the document.
⓭ Scroll-bar box
Moves text up or down.
⓮ Vertical scroll bar
Used to move through text.

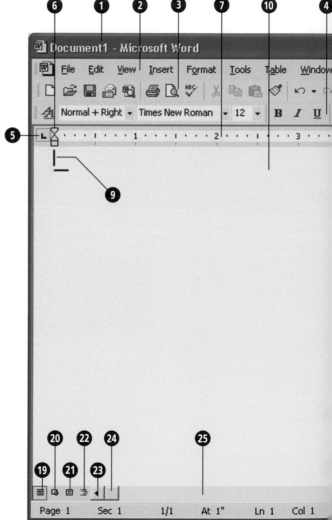

126 Insertion Point

144 Indenting the Address

THE WORD TASK PANE

28 Task Pane arrow
Scrolls through the various task pane commands.
29 Open tasks
Opens recent documents.

30 "New from" task
Base new document on existing.
31 Templates
Load ready-made documents from your PC or the internet.

To hide the Task Pane and increase the usable screen area, click on **View** in the toolbar and uncheck the box next to **Task Pane**.

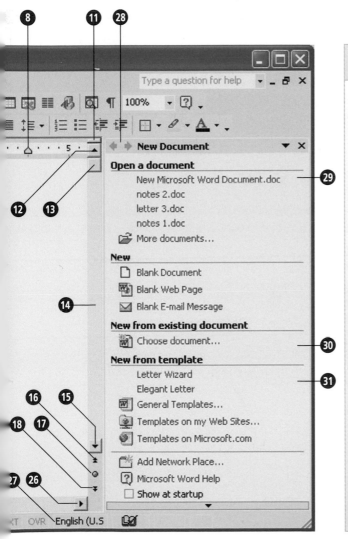

THE WORD WINDOW

15 Scroll-down arrow
Moves down the document.
16 Page-up button
Shows previous page of text.
17 Select browse object
Opens browse options menu.
18 Page-down button
Displays next page of text.
19 Normal view
Default document view.
20 Web layout view
Web-browser page view.
21 Page layout view
Printed-page view of text.
22 Outline view
Shows document's structure.
23 Left-scroll arrow
Shows the text to the left.
24 Scroll-bar box
Moves text horizontally.
25 Horizontal scroll bar
To view wide documents.
26 Right-scroll arrow
Shows the text to the right.
27 Language
Spelling, thesaurus, and proofing settings.

THE WORD TOOLBARS

Word provides a range of toolbars where numerous commands and actions are available. The principal toolbars are the Standard toolbar and the Formatting toolbar, which contain the most frequently used features of Word. There are also more than 20 other toolbars available for display. Click on **Tools** in the Menu bar, move the cursor down to **Customize**, and click the mouse button. The **Customize** dialog box opens. Click the **Toolbars** tab to view the variety of toolbars available.

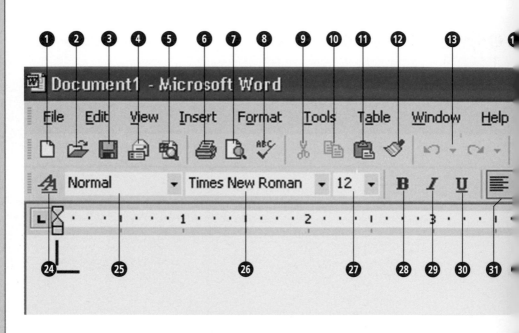

THE STANDARD TOOLBAR

1. New document
2. Open folder or file
3. Save
4. Email
5. Search
6. Print
7. Print preview
8. Spelling and grammar
9. Cut text
10. Copy text
11. Paste text
12. Format painter
13. Undo/redo action(s)
14. Insert hyperlink
15. Tables and borders
16. Insert table
17. Insert Excel worksheet
18. Columns
19. Drawing toolbar
20. Document map
21. Show/hide formatting marks
22. Zoom view of text
23. Microsoft Word help

163 Printing Quickly	**160** Print Preview	**129** Formatting Marks

CUSTOMIZING A TOOLBAR

To add a **Close** button to a toolbar, click on the **Commands** tab of the **Customize** box (see left). Place the cursor over the **Close** icon, hold down the mouse button, drag the icon to the toolbar, and release the mouse button.

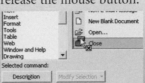

ScreenTips

It isn't necessary to memorize all these buttons. Roll the cursor over a button, wait for a second, and a ScreenTip appears telling you the function of the button.

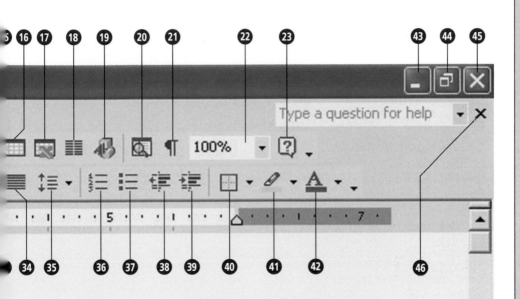

THE FORMATTING TOOLBAR

- ㉔ Styles and formatting
- ㉕ Style selector
- ㉖ Font selector
- ㉗ Font size selector
- ㉘ Bold
- ㉙ Italic
- ㉚ Underline
- ㉛ Left-aligned text

- ㉜ Centered text
- ㉝ Right-aligned text
- ㉞ Justified text
- ㉟ Line spacing
- ㊱ Numbered list
- ㊲ Bulleted list
- ㊳ Decrease indent
- ㊴ Increase indent

- ㊵ Outside border
- ㊶ Highlight color
- ㊷ Font color
- ㊸ Minimize Word
- ㊹ Restore Word
- ㊺ Close Word
- ㊻ Close document

150	Font and Font Size
150	Quick Ways to Format Fonts
149	Quick Ways to Align Text

YOUR FIRST LETTER

Microsoft Word makes the process of writing a letter and printing it out easier than ever. This chapter takes you through the few simple steps involved in creating your first letter.

TYPING THE LETTER

The first image on your screen when you start Microsoft Word is a blank area with a blinking cursor, surrounded by buttons and symbols that may mean nothing to you. Don't worry about them for now. To begin with, the only thing you need to concentrate on is to start writing your letter on that blank screen.

1 BEGINNING TYPING

● Type the first line of your address. As you type, the insertion point moves with your text. Don't worry about mistakes – they are easily corrected ⌐.

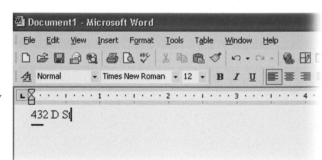

2 STARTING A NEW LINE

● Press the [Enter ↵] button.
● The insertion point has now moved to the beginning of a new line.

Insertion point ●

INSERTION POINT

This is a blinking upright line that precedes your text as you type. If you are ever unsure about where your typing will appear on the page, check where the insertion point is.

3 COMPLETING THE ADDRESS

- Finish typing your address, pressing [Enter ←] at the end of each line.
- At the end of the last address line, press [Enter ←] twice to leave a line space.

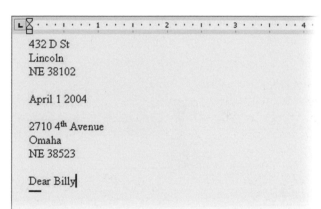

```
432 D St
Lincoln
NE 38102
```

4 STARTING THE LETTER

- Now type the date, leave another line space, then type the recipient's address.
- Leave two line spaces (by pressing [Enter ←] three times) and type your greeting.

```
432 D St
Lincoln
NE 38102

April 1 2004

2710 4th Avenue
Omaha
NE 38523

Dear Billy
```

5 CREATING PARAGRAPHS

- Leave another line and start your first paragraph. When typing paragraphs in Word, just keep typing until the end of the paragraph, and only then press [Enter ←]. At the end of each line, Word "wraps" your text round to start a new line.
- To start a new paragraph, press [Enter ←] to end the first paragraph, and press [Enter ←] again to leave a line space. You are ready to start the new paragraph.

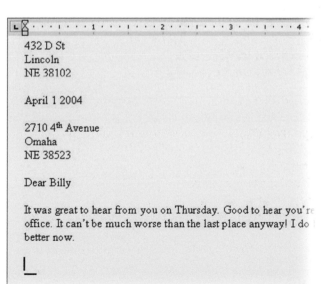

```
432 D St
Lincoln
NE 38102

April 1 2004

2710 4th Avenue
Omaha
NE 38523

Dear Billy

It was great to hear from you on Thursday. Good to hear you'r
office. It can't be much worse than the last place anyway! I do
better now.
```

6 FINISHING THE LETTER

- If your letter is longer than can fit on the screen, Word moves the text up as you type. If you need to go back to it, simply hold down the ⬆ arrow key. The insertion point moves up the text to the top of your letter.
- Type a farewell after the last paragraph. Press Enter⏎ a few times to leave room for your signature. Then type your name.
- You have now typed your first letter using Word.

Dear Billy

It was great to hear from you on Thursday. Good to hear you're office. It can't be much worse than the last place anyway! I do better now.

I was speaking to the Jaspers the other day. We really must all the latest gossip. How about our place? We're free next weeke me know what you think.

Take care

Isaac.

Page 1   Sec 1   1/1   At 5.4"   Ln 24   Col 7   REC TRK

start   Document1 - Microsof...

CORRECTING ERRORS AS YOU TYPE

1 REMOVING THE ERROR

- You have misspelled a word as you are typing.
- To remove the misspelled word, first press the Backspace (← Bksp) key. This removes text one letter at a time to the left of the insertion point.
- Keep tapping ← Bksp until the word is gone.

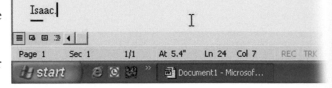

It was great to hear from you on Thursday. Good to hear you're office. It can't be much worse than the last place anyway! I do better now.

I was speaking to the Jaspers the other day. We really must all the latest gossip. How aubot

It was great to hear from you on Thursday. Good to hear you're office. It can't be much worse than the last place anyway! I do better now.

I was speaking to the Jaspers the other day. We really must all the latest gossip. How

2 REPLACING THE ERROR

● Now type the word again. Remember to leave a space before it – ⬚←Bksp⬚ also removes spaces and line spaces if they are immediately to the left of the insertion point.

● You have corrected the error and you can carry on typing your letter.

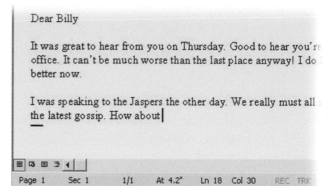

Dear Billy

It was great to hear from you on Thursday. Good to hear you're office. It can't be much worse than the last place anyway! I do better now.

I was speaking to the Jaspers the other day. We really must all the latest gossip. How about|

Page 1   Sec 1   1/1   At 4.2"   Ln 18   Col 30   REC TRK

FORMATTING MARKS

Word uses invisible markers (called formatting marks) within your text to mark the spaces between words, and where you have decided to leave line spaces. Formatting marks do not appear on paper when you print out. Initially you don't see them on your screen, which makes the text on the screen appear exactly how it will print out. However, you may want to see the formatting marks so that you can see double spaces and control where you want the line spaces to be placed. To see the formatting marks, click on the button with the paragraph mark at the top right-hand end of your toolbar. You are now able to see the formatting marks. Click the button again when you want to turn off the formatting marks. Alternatively, click on **Tools** in the toolbar, select **Options**, click on the **Views** tab in the **Options** dialog box, and select which **Formatting Marks** you wish to see.

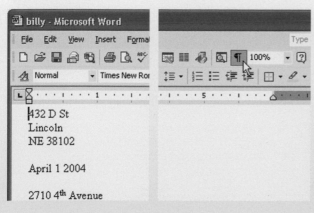

CORRECTING ERRORS FROM EARLIER IN THE TEXT

It is inevitable that errors are going to be made as you type, such as misspellings and duplicate words. If Word alerts you to a typing error higher up in your letter, you can easily move the insertion point back to the error and correct it.

1 MOVING TO THE ERROR

● The misspelled word is higher in the text than the insertion point. You may be familiar with using the mouse to relocate the insertion point, but you may be less familiar with using the arrow keys.

● Move the insertion point up to the line containing the error by using the ⬆ arrow key.

● Use the ⬅ and ➡ arrow keys until you've placed the insertion point at the end of the misspelled word.

It was great to hear from you on Thursday. Good to hear you'r office. It can't be much worse than the last place anyway! I do better now.

I was spaeking to the Jaspers the other day. We really must all the latest gossip. How about our place? We're free next weeke me know what you think.

It was great to hear from you on Thursday. Good to hear you'r office. It can't be much worse than the last place anyway! I do better now.

I was spaeking to the Jaspers the other day. We really must all the latest gossip. How about our place? We're free next weeke me know what you think.

2 CORRECTING THE ERROR

● Remove the misspelled part of the word and type in the correct spelling.

● You have now corrected the error. Use the ⬇ arrow key to return the insertion point to where you left off. You can now continue with your typing.

It was great to hear from you on Thursday. Good to hear you' office. It can't be much worse than the last place anyway! I do better now.

I was speaking to the Jaspers the other day. We really must all the latest gossip. How about our place? We're free next weeke me know what you think.

ADDING WORDS IN THE MIDDLE OF THE TEXT

Word makes it easy for you to change your text at any time while writing your letter. If you decide to add something further, or suddenly realize that an important point has been left out, you can type it in by first using the insertion point.

1 POSITIONING THE INSERTION POINT

● Move the insertion point to the place in the text where you want to add words. Use the arrow keys on your keyboard again for further practice. Remember, you can only move to where text has already been typed.

Insertion point ●

> 2710 4ᵗʰ Avenue
> Omaha
> NE 38523
>
> Dear Billy
>
> It was great to hear from you on Thursday. Good to hear you'r℮ office. It can't be much worse than the last place anyway! I do better now.
>
> I was speaking to the Jaspers the other day. We really must all the latest gossip.│ How about our place? We're free next weeke₁ me know what you think.
>
> Take care
>
> Isaac.

2 ADDING THE WORDS

● Start typing the new text. If the insertion point is in the middle of a paragraph, you'll notice that Word automatically moves text along to accommodate what you are adding.
● Use the arrow keys to return to the place where you left off typing.

> Dear Billy
>
> It was great to hear from you on Thursday. Good to hear you'r℮ office. It can't be much worse than the last place anyway! I do better now.
>
> I was speaking to the Jaspers the other day. We really must all the latest gossip. I can't wait!│ How about our place? We're free bell and let me know what you think.
>
> Take care

MANIPULATING PARAGRAPHS

Paragraphs organize your text, help with the sense of your document, and make your document more readable. With Word, it's easy to create a new paragraph when another is needed, and to combine them when two paragraphs aren't required.

1 SPLITTING A PARAGRAPH

● To split a paragraph into two, move the insertion point to the start of the sentence that will begin the new second paragraph. Then press [Enter ←] twice. You now have two paragraphs.

better now.

I was speaking to the Jaspers the other day. We really must all the latest gossip. I can't wait! How about our place? We're free bell and let me know what you think.

Take care

I was speaking to the Jaspers the other day. We really must all the latest gossip. I can't wait!

How about our place? We're free next weekend. Give us a bell think.

Take care

2 COMBINING PARAGRAPHS

● If you want to join two paragraphs together to make one, place the insertion point at the beginning of the second paragraph. Then press [← Bksp] twice to remove the line spaces. Your two paragraphs now form one larger paragraph.

Dear Billy

It was great to hear from you on Thursday. Good to hear you're settling into the new office. It can't be much worse than the last place anyway! I do hope Rebecca's feeling better now.

I was speaking to the Jaspers the other day. We really must all meet up and catch up on the latest gossip. I can't wait! How about our place? We're free next weekend. Give us a bell and let me know what you think.

Take care

3 PARAGRAPH MARKS

● Pressing the [Enter ↵] key ends a paragraph and inserts a paragraph mark. You can see these marks by turning on the formatting marks ⛫. Deleting the line space between paragraphs is just a matter of deleting the paragraph mark just like any other character.

Dear Billy

It was great to hear from you on Thursday. Good to hear you're settling into the new office. It can't be much worse than the last place anyway! I do hope Rebecca's feeling better now. I was speaking to the Jaspers the other day. We really must all meet up and catch up on the latest gossip. I can't wait! How about our place? We're free next weekend. Give us a bell and let me know what you think.

Take care

USING WORD TO START A NEW PAGE

If you want to begin a new page, before the text has reached the end of the current page, you can use Word to split the page into two. Move the insertion point to the position in your letter where you want the new page to start. Hold down the [Ctrl] key and press [Enter ↵]. Word inserts a "manual" page break. You can delete this page break by placing the insertion point at the top left of the second page and pressing [← Bksp].

It was great to hear from you on Thursday. Good to hear you're settling into the new office. It can't be much worse than the last place anyway! I do hope Rebecca's feeling better now.

I was speaking to the Jaspers the other day. We really must all meet up and catch up on the latest gossip. I can't wait! How about our place? We're free next weekend. Give us a bell and let me know what you think.

It was great to hear from you on Thursday. Good to hear you're settling into the new office. It can't be much worse than the last place anyway! I do hope Rebecca's feeling better now.

-------------------------------- Page Break --------------------------------

I was speaking to the Jaspers the other day. We really must all meet up and catch up on the latest gossip. I can't wait! How about our place? We're free next weekend. Give us a bell and let me know what you think.

129 **Formatting Marks**

SAVING YOUR LETTER

Now that your letter is finished and correct, you should save it as a file on your computer's hard disk so that if you need to find it later, or make changes after you have printed it out, you will be able to bring it back up on the screen.

1 SAVING THE FILE

● Move your mouse pointer over the word **File** in the Menu bar at the top of the screen and left-click to display its menu. Move the mouse pointer down and click on **Save**.

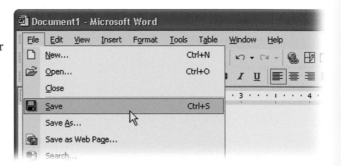

● The **Save As** dialog box pops up in the middle of your screen. In this box you are able to give your letter a file name and decide where you want to save it. Word automatically uses the first line of your text as the file name, but you can change this by typing over it.

2 NAMING AND SAVING

● Choose a file name that identifies the letter for you and type it into the **File name** box.
● Select a folder in the **Save in** box and click on the **Save** button. The dialog box closes and your letter is saved to disk.

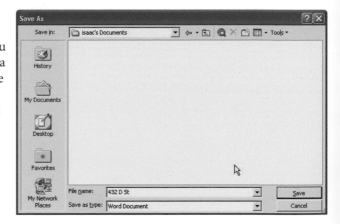

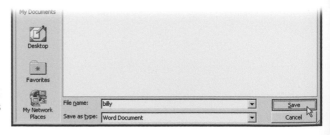

PRINTING YOUR LETTER

1 CHOOSING TO PRINT

● Click on the **File** menu. The **File** menu drops down.
● This time choose **Print** from the **File** menu by clicking once on **Print**.

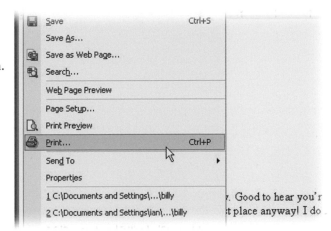

2 PRINTING YOUR LETTER

● The **Print** dialog box pops up. Don't worry about any of the features here at this stage. Just make sure that the printer is plugged into the computer and is switched on.
● Click on the **OK** button at the bottom of the dialog box and your letter begins to print.

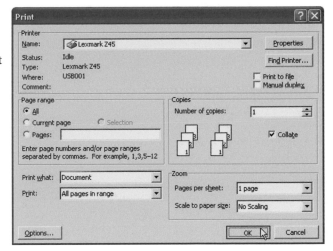

Well done...
You have now typed, corrected, saved, and printed your first letter using Word. These simple steps have shown you the basic process that you use to create a letter with Microsoft Word. Now we go into more detail and explore each step of the process in detail.

WORKING WITH TEXT

This chapter deals with methods of working with text:
moving around text, shifting text from one place to another,
deleting text, and copying text.

MOVING AROUND YOUR TEXT

There are many different ways to move around and see different parts of your letter. Here are some techniques to move through your letter that make use of either the mouse or the different actions that are available through the keyboard.

1 GET TO THE START OF THE LETTER

● The insertion point is midway through or at the end of the letter.

● Hold down the [Ctrl] key and press the [Home] key on your keyboard.

● The screen now shows the top of the letter. The insertion point is at the very beginning of the text.

The insertion point moves to the start of the letter

Dear Billy

It was great to hear from you on Thursday. Good to hear you're office. It can't be much worse than the last place anyway! I do better now.

I was speaking to the Jaspers the other day. We really must all the latest gossip. I can't wait! How about our place? We're free bell and let me know what you think.

432 D St
Lincoln
NE 38102

April 1 2004

2710 4th Avenue
Omaha
NE 38523

Dear Billy

2 GET TO THE END OF THE TEXT

● Hold down the Ctrl key and press the End key on your keyboard.

● The screen now shows the foot of the letter. The insertion point is at the very end of the text.

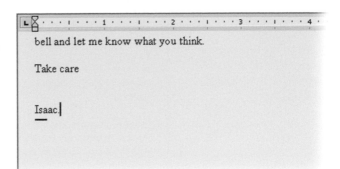

bell and let me know what you think.

Take care

Isaac.

3 SCROLLING THROUGH TEXT

● If you can't see the part of the letter you want, position the mouse cursor over the sliding box in the scroll bar.

Hold down the left mouse button and move the box up and down the bar to scroll through the text.

● Alternatively, use the buttons at the top and bottom of the scroll bar. Click on them to scroll the text up and down.

● Stop when the section of the text appears that you want to work on.

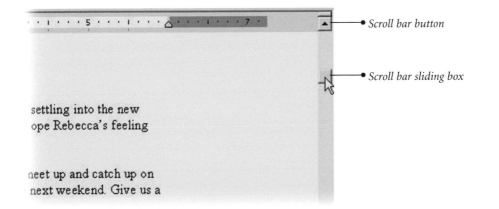

Scroll bar button

Scroll bar sliding box

settling into the new
ope Rebecca's feeling

neet up and catch up on
next weekend. Give us a

MOVING AROUND WITHOUT THE MOUSE

If you want to move quickly around your letter without using the mouse, you can use the PgUp and PgDn keys on your keyboard to move up or down your letter one screen at a time. This method moves the insertion point directly. You can use the arrow keys to place the insertion point in the exact position in the text where you need to make your changes.

4 CLICKING ON TEXT

● Move the mouse pointer to the exact point in the text where you want the insertion point to go.
● Left-click once. The insertion point appears.

Dear Billy

It was great to hear from you on Thursday. Good to hear you're office. It can't be much worse than the last place anyway! I do better now.

I was speaking to the Jaspers the other day. We really must all the latest gossip. I can't wait! How about our place? We're free bell and let me know what you think.

Take care I

SELECTING TEXT

Before Word can carry out any changes that you want to make, you first need to tell Word what parts of the text you want it to work on. This is done by selecting text, which is one of the most frequently used operations when using Word.

1 USING THE KEYBOARD

● Move the insertion point to the start of the text you want to select.
● Hold down the ⇧ Shift key and press the → arrow key. This has the effect of creating a block of selected text one letter at a time.

better now.

I was speaking to the Jaspers the other day. We really must all the latest gossip. I can't wait! How about our place? We're free bell and let me know what you think.

Take care

office. It can't be much worse than the last place anyway! I do better now.

I was speaking to the Jaspers the other day. We really must all the latest gossip. I can't wait! How about our place? We're fre bell and let me know what you think.

Take care

● If the block you want to select extends over more than one line, keep the ⇧ Shift key held down, and press the ↓ key to select whole lines at a time. Then use the ← and → keys to choose the end of the block. Don't release the ⇧ Shift key until you have selected the entire block of text that you want.

It was great to hear from you on Thursday. Good to hear you'r office. It can't be much worse than the last place anyway! I do better now.

I was speaking to the Jaspers the other day. We really must all the latest gossip. I can't wait! How about our place? We're free bell and let me know what you think.

Take care

Isaac.

Vanishing Point

You will notice that when you have selected and highlighted a block of text, there is no longer an insertion point in your Word window. What has happened is that the block of selected text becomes one very large insertion point. It is important to be careful here because if you press any character key on the keyboard while your block is selected, your entire block will vanish and be replaced by whatever you type.

2 USING THE MOUSE

● Move the mouse pointer to the precise point where you want to start your selected block of text.

● Hold down the left mouse button and move the mouse pointer to the position that marks the end of the block that you want.

● Release the mouse button. Your block of text is now selected.

● If you make a mistake, simply click outside the selection and go through the process again.

Dear Billy

It was great to hear from you on Thursday. Good to hear you'r office. It can't be much worse than the last place anyway! I do better now.

I was speaking to the Jaspers the other day. We really must all

NE 38523

Dear Billy

It was great to hear from you on Thursday. Good to hear you'r office. It can't be much worse than the last place anyway! I do better now.

I was speaking to the Jaspers the other day. We really must all

3 SELECTING ALL THE TEXT

● Click on **Edit** on the menu bar. The **Edit** menu drops down.

● Now click on **Select All** in the **Edit** menu.

● The whole of your letter is now selected.

● Alternatively, you can move the mouse cursor to the left of your text where it changes from pointing left to pointing to the right. Hold down the Ctrl key and click on the left mouse button. The whole of your text is now selected.

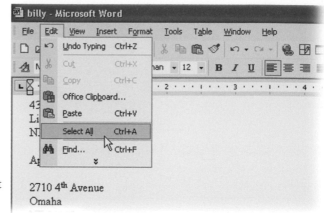

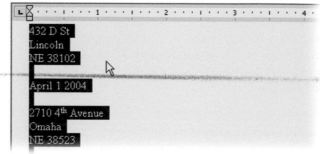

4 SELECTING LINES AT A TIME

Selecting blocks of text by lines can save time. Move the mouse pointer to the left of the first line that you want to select. Hold down the left mouse button and move the mouse pointer to the last line of your chosen block. Release the mouse button and the block is selected.

2710 4th Avenue
Omaha
NE 38523

Dear Billy

It was great to hear from you on Thursday. Good to hear you're
office. It can't be much worse than the last place anyway! I do
better now.

I was speaking to the Jaspers the other day. We really must all
the latest gossip. I can't wait! How about our place? We're free
bell and let me know what you think.

Take care

MOVING TEXT – CUT AND PASTE

You can move whole blocks of text either within your document or between documents when using Word. The easiest way to do this is by "cutting" selected blocks of text from your letter and "pasting" them back into a different place.

1 CUTTING TEXT

● Select a block of text ◻.
● Click on **Edit** on the menu bar. The **Edit** menu drops down.
● Click on **Cut** in the **Edit** menu. Your block of text will disappear, but it is not lost. The rest of the text will move back into place around it.

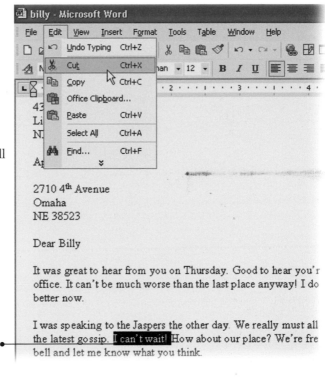

Block of text to be cut ●——

Cutting has removed the text ●——

2 PASTING TEXT

● Position the insertion point where you want the text to reappear.

● Click on **Edit** in the Menu bar, then on **Paste** in the drop down menu.

● The text is pasted back into your letter exactly where you want it.

COPYING TEXT

You may want to copy a block of text to a new location while leaving the original block in its old position. Simply go through the cut and paste procedures detailed on these pages, but when you come to cut the text, select **Copy** instead of **Cut** on the **Edit** menu. The block will stay where it is, but you will be able to paste copies of it whenever you want.

Dear Billy

It was great to hear from you on Thursday. Good to hear you'r office. It can't be much worse than the last place anyway! I do better now.

I was speaking to the Jaspers the other day. We really must all the latest gossip. How about our place? We're free next weeke me know what you think.

Take care.

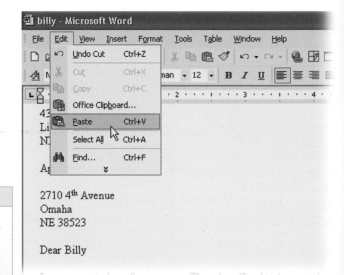

2710 4th Avenue
Omaha
NE 38523

Dear Billy

Dear Billy

It was great to hear from you on Thursday. Good to hear you'r office. It can't be much worse than the last place anyway! I do better now.

I was speaking to the Jaspers the other day. We really must all the latest gossip. How about our place? We're free next weeke me know what you think. I can't wait!

Take care.

MOVING TEXT – DRAG AND DROP

This method is a quicker way of moving text around and uses only the mouse. Once you've told Word what part of the text you want to move, you can then "drag" it to the position where you want to move it, and "drop" it into place.

1 SELECTING THE TEXT

● Select a block of text using one of the methods that you have already learned ⌐.

It was great to hear from you on Thursday. Good to hear you're settling into office. It can't be much worse than the last place anyway! I do hope Rebecca better now.

I was speaking to the Jaspers the other day. We really must all meet up and c the latest gossip. How about our place? We're free next weekend. Give us a me know what you think. I can't wait!

Take care.

2 MOVING THE TEXT

● Place the mouse cursor over the block of selected text. Hold down the left mouse button and move, or "drag," the mouse cursor to the position in your letter where you want the text to appear. Don't release the mouse button until the mouse pointer is in exactly the right place.

● Now release the mouse button and the text appears in the new location.

It was great to hear from you on Thursday. Good to hear you're settling into office. It can't be much worse than the last place anyway! I do hope Rebecc better now.

I was speaking to the Jaspers the other day. We really must all meet up and the latest gossip. How about our place? We're free next weekend. Give us a me know what you think. I can't wait!

Take care.

It was great to hear from you on Thursday. Good to hear you're settling into office. It can't be much worse than the last place anyway! I do hope Rebecc better now.

I was speaking to the Jaspers the other day. We really must all meet up and the latest gossip. We're free next weekend. How about our place? Give us a me know what you think. I can't wait!

Take care.

138 **Selecting Text**

CHANGING THE LAYOUT

In this chapter we deal with how to lay your text out on the page in the way you want it. The most common layout changes that you'll be making are indenting and aligning.

INDENTING THE ADDRESS

1 SELECTING YOUR ADDRESS

● Using either the mouse or the keyboard, select the lines of your address as a block of text ⌐.

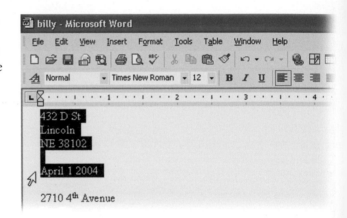

2 CHANGING THE INDENT

● Directly above the text on the screen is a numbered line. This is the ruler.
● Move your mouse pointer to the small symbol called the left indent marker shown at right.
● Click on the box at the base of the left indent marker, and hold down the left mouse button.

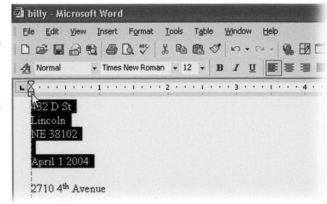

138 Selecting Text

● Drag the left indent marker, by using the box, across the ruler however far you want your address to be indented.

● Now release the mouse button. Your address has moved across the screen.

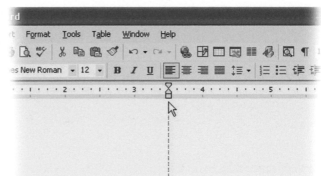

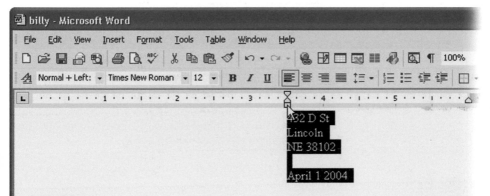

432 D St
Lincoln
NE 38102

April 1 2004

2710 4th Avenue
Omaha
NE 38523

Dear Billy

It was great to hear from you on Thursday. Good to hear you're settling into the new office. It can't be much worse than the last place anyway! I do hope Rebecca's feeling better now.

I was speaking to the Jaspers the other day. We really must all meet up and catch up on the latest gossip. We're free next weekend. How about our place? Give us a bell and let me know what you think. I can't wait!

Take care.

INDENTING PARAGRAPHS

You may want to make each of your paragraphs begin a little further into the page than the main text (a "first line indent"). Or you may want the body of text indented except for the lines beginning each paragraph (a "hanging indent"). These steps take you through how to do each of these procedures.

1 SELECT THE PARAGRAPHS

- Select only the paragraphs of text in your letter and not the addresses, date, greeting, and sign-off.

2710 4th Avenue
Omaha
NE 38523

Dear Billy

It was great to hear from you on Thursday. Good to hear you're
office. It can't be much worse than the last place anyway! I do
better now.

I was speaking to the Jaspers the other day. We really must all
the latest gossip. We're free next weekend. How about our plac
me know what you think. I can't wait!

Take care.

2 FIRST LINE INDENT

- Move your mouse pointer over the left indent marker on the ruler.
- When the pointer is on the top part of the left indent marker, hold down the left mouse button.
- Drag the pointer along the ruler to however far in you want the indent.

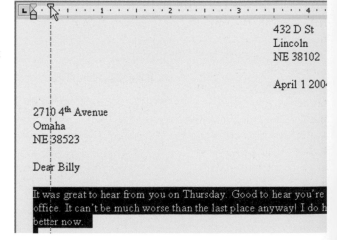

432 D St
Lincoln
NE 38102

April 1 200

2710 4th Avenue
Omaha
NE 38523

Dear Billy

It was great to hear from you on Thursday. Good to hear you're
office. It can't be much worse than the last place anyway! I do h
better now.

● Release the mouse button. The first lines of each of your paragraphs are now indented.

2710 4ᵗʰ Avenue
Omaha
NE 38523

Dear Billy

It was great to hear from you on Thursday. Good to hear yo office. It can't be much worse than the last place anyway! I do better now.

I was speaking to the Jaspers the other day. We really must on the latest gossip. We're free next weekend. How about our p let me know what you think. I can't wait!

Take care.

3 HANGING INDENT

● For a hanging indent, go through Step 1 (opposite) to select the text.
● Now, move the mouse pointer until it is over the left indent marker ⌐.
● Position the pointer over the middle part of the left indent marker, (avoiding the other two parts of the left indent marker may need some practice).
● Hold down the left mouse button and drag the pointer over to the right as far as you want the paragraphs to be indented.
● Release the mouse button. Your paragraphs are now formatted with a hanging indent.

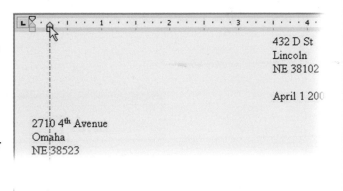

432 D St
Lincoln
NE 38102

April 1 200

2710 4ᵗʰ Avenue
Omaha
NE 38523

2710 4ᵗʰ Avenue
Omaha
NE 38523

Dear Billy

It was great to hear from you on Thursday. Good to hear you're office. It can't be much worse than the last place anyway! I feeling better now.

I was speaking to the Jaspers the other day. We really must all the latest gossip. We're free next weekend. How about our let me know what you think. I can't wait!

Take care.

144 **Indenting the Address**

ALIGNMENT

At the moment all your text except for your address is aligned to the left – the left side is straight while the right is ragged, like text created with a typewriter. Word can make the right side straight as well, like text in a book (this is called "justified text"). Other possibilities include aligning your text to the right, which leaves the left side ragged, or centering the text exactly down the middle of the page.

1 JUSTIFIED TEXT

● Select the text you want to realign.

● Drop down the **Format** menu from the menu bar at the top of the screen.

● Click on **Paragraph** in the Format menu and the **Paragraph** dialog box opens onscreen.

● Click on the drop-down button next to the **Alignment** option. A small menu will drop down.

● Click on the word **Justified** in this menu.

● Click on **OK** and the dialog box closes.

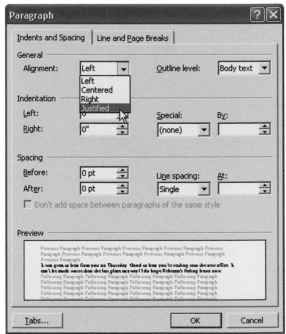

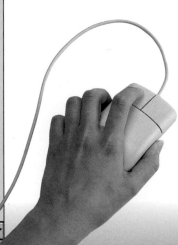

● Your text is now justified with the left- and right-hand sides of all complete lines of text both straight.

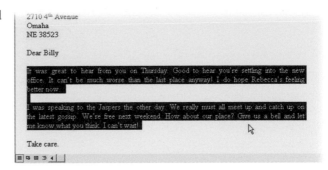

2 RIGHT-ALIGNED TEXT

● Follow Step 1 (opposite) until you get to the **Alignment** drop-down menu in the **Paragraph** dialog box.

● This time click on **Right** and then on **OK**.

● Your text has been aligned to the right.

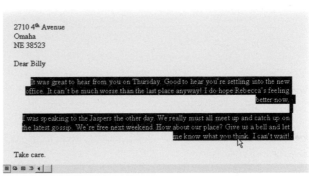

3 CENTERED TEXT

● Follow Step 1 until you get to the **Alignment** drop-down menu in the **Paragraph** dialog box.

● Click on **Center** this time, then on **OK**.

● Your text has been centered on the page.

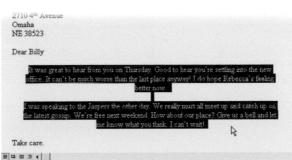

QUICK WAYS TO ALIGN TEXT

You are also able to realign text by using the alignment buttons (shown at left) on the toolbar at the top of the screen. First select the text and then click on the button you need. From left to right, the buttons mean: left-align, center, right-align, and justify.

APPEARANCE

Your letter now looks better than it did before. However, there are many other tweaks and touches that can transform your text to just the way you want it to appear.

FONT AND FONT SIZE

The font is the kind of lettering that Word uses to display your text. You may wish to use different fonts in different kinds of letter: a stern, professional-looking font for business letters, and a lighter, friendlier font for your personal letters. You may also wish either to increase or decrease the size of the font that you use.

1 THE FONT DIALOG BOX

● Select all the text in the document ⌐.
● Drop down the **Format** menu from the menu bar.
● Choose **Font** in the **Format** menu. The **Font** dialog box opens.

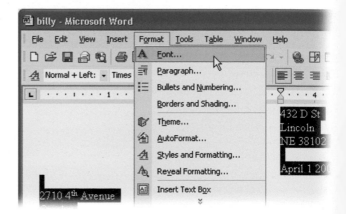

QUICK WAYS TO FORMAT FONTS

B *I* <u>U</u>   You may have noticed that the font, font size, and the buttons for bold, italic, and underline are included in the Formatting toolbar (just above the ruler). To format fonts without using the **Font** dialog box, you can select the text and use these tools to format it. The font and font size are drop-down menus. The font style buttons (shown left) click in or out to show if, say, Bold is on or off in a selected block of text.

2 CHANGING THE FONT

● The **Font** menu is displayed under the **Font** tab in the **Font** dialog box. Scroll up and down it using the scroll bar at the side of the menu. Your text is probably in Times New Roman at the moment.

● As you click on different fonts, the appearance of the selected font is shown in the **Preview** box in the **Font** dialog box.

● Keep scrolling through the fonts until you find one you want to use.

Preview box

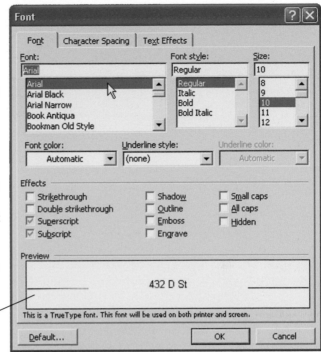

3 CHANGING THE FONT SIZE

● Now check the **Size** menu at top right of the **Font** dialog box.

● The font size is probably set to 10. This is quite small. Try clicking on **12** or any font size you want – 10 and 12 are the most often used in plain text.

● The **Preview** box will show the new font in its new size.

4 APPLYING YOUR CHANGES

● When you are satisfied with the font and font size, click on the **OK** button.

● The **Font** dialog box will close. Your text is now formatted in the new font and font size.

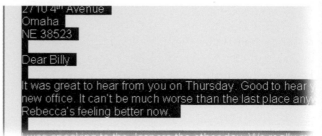

FONT STYLE

In addition to the regular font, there are three other font styles – bold, italic, and underline – that can be used to emphasize individual words, phrases, or any other block of text. They can also be used in combination for extra effect.

1 MAKING YOUR TEXT BOLD

● Select the text you want to make bold.

● Open the **Font** dialog box from the **Format** menu.

● In the **Font style** menu click on **Bold**.

● Click **OK** to close the **Font** dialog box.

● Your selected text now appears in bold.

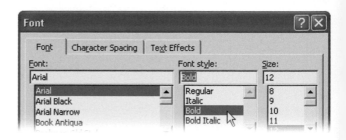

Bold text ●

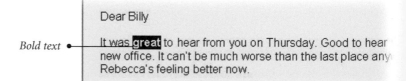

2 MAKING YOUR TEXT ITALIC

● Follow Step 1 (opposite), but click on **Italic** in the **Font Style** menu of the **Font** dialog box.

● Click **OK** to close the **Font** dialog box.

● Your selected text is now displayed in italics.

Italicized text ●

2710 4th Avenue
Omaha
NE 38523

Dear Billy

It was great to hear from you on Thursday. Good to hear y
new office. It can't be much worse than the last place any
Rebecca's feeling better now.

was speaking to the Jaspers the other day. We really mu
catch up on the latest gossip. How about our place? We're
Give us a bell and let me know what you think. I can't wait

3 UNDERLINING YOUR TEXT

● Select the text and open the **Font** dialog box in the usual way.

● Drop down the **Underline style** menu (below the **Font** menu in the dialog box).

● There are many underline options, but the most useful is a single line under the selected text. An alternative is **Words only** – each word is underlined, but not the spaces separating them. Click on your choice.

● Click **OK** to close the **Font** dialog box.

● The selection is now emphasized by underlining.

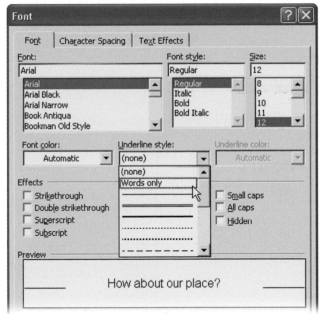

Words only ●
underlined text

Rebecca's feeling better now.

I was speaking to the Jaspers the other day. We really mu
catch up on the latest gossip. How about our place? We're
Give us a bell and let me know what you think. I can't wait

Take care.

LINE SPACING

You may want to increase the spacing between the lines of your letter – some find it easier to read. For example, double line spacing creates a space the height of one line between each line of the text. Other options are also available.

1 SELECT THE ENTIRE LETTER

● Click on **Format** on the menu bar to drop down the **Format** menu.
● Click on **Paragraph** from the **Format** menu to open the **Paragraph** dialog box.

2 LINE SPACING SELECTION

● Click the small down arrow on the right of the **Line spacing** box. The **Line spacing** menu drops down.
● Choose **Double** line spacing from the menu.

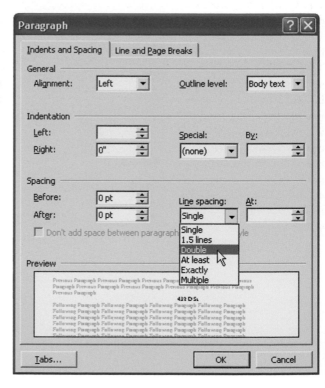

● Click on the **OK** button. Your selected text now appears with the chosen line spacing.

3 MULTIPLE LINE SPACING

You are not limited only to single, 1.5, and double line spacing when using Word.

● Select part of your text and click the down arrow in the **Line spacing** box. The **Line spacing** menu drops down.

● Click on **Multiple** at the foot of the menu.

● In the **At** box the figure **3** appears. Three-line spacing is the default selection for multiple line spacing. If you want a different number, highlight the 3, type the number of line spaces, and click on **OK**.

● The lines of your selected text are now separated by your chosen line spacing.

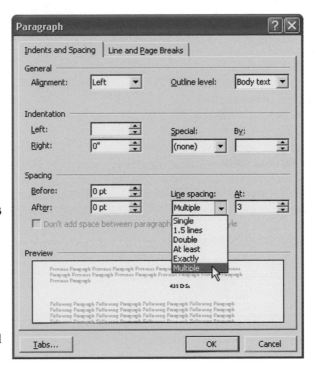

STORING YOUR LETTERS

It is usually essential to save your letters on your hard disk so that you can refer to them at a later date. This chapter provides an overview of how to store and recall your text.

WORKING WITH FILES

A file is what we call any piece of data that is stored on a computer's hard disk. This could be a spreadsheet, a program, or your letter that you have created using Word. Not only can you store (save) your documents when you have completed them, it is important that you also save your files as you work, especially if they are long and you have put a lot of work into them. If your computer suddenly crashes, you could lose everything you have done since you last saved your work.

1 CREATING A NEW FILE

● When you open Word, a new file is automatically created in which you can begin typing.

● You may want to create other new files later on. Drop down the **File** menu and click on **Blank Document** in the pane that appears on the right-hand side of the screen.

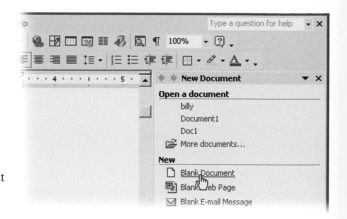

2 SAVING A FILE

● Drop down the **File** menu from the menu bar. Click on **Save**.

● If the file has already been saved, the **Save** command will simply save the new version and you may continue typing. If you are saving the file for the first time, the **Save As** dialog box appears and you can assign the document a name and a location.

3 OPENING A FILE

● Drop down the **File** menu from the menu bar. Click on **Open**. The **Open** dialog box appears.

● The **Open** dialog box shows the files you have already saved. Click on the file you want and then click on **Open**.

● The file opens and you may begin working on it.

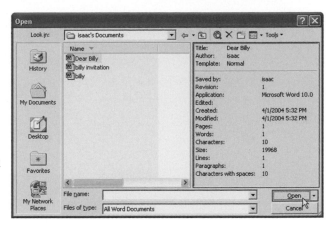

4 CLOSING A FILE

● You usually close a document when you have finished working on it. Drop down the **File** menu and click on **Close**.

● If you have not saved your text, or if you have changed it since you last saved, you are asked if you want to save the file.

● Click on **Yes** if you have forgotten to save your work. Click on **No** if you're absolutely sure that you don't want to save either the document or the changes you have made since you last saved. If in doubt, click on **Cancel** and return to the document.

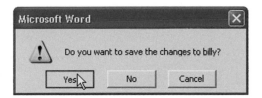

5 SAVING THE FILE TO FLOPPY DISK

● Click on **Save As** in the **File** menu to open the **Save As** dialog box.

● Drop down the **Save in** menu in the dialog box.

● Click on **3½ Floppy (A:)** in the **Save in** menu.

● Click **OK** and your file is saved to the floppy disk.

WORKING WITH FOLDERS

As you create more files, your hard disk may begin to look cluttered. When you want to open a file, you may not be able to find it because the list of files is so long. The way to avoid this is to use folders, which can be given names, such as Personal and Finance, so that you know where to store and find your files.

1 CREATE A NEW FOLDER

● When you want to save a document in a new folder, begin by dropping down the **File** menu and click on **Save As**. The **Save As** dialog box appears.

● Click on the button showing a sparkling folder – this is the **Create New Folder** button.

● The **New Folder** dialog box opens. Type in a name for your new folder and click the **OK** button.

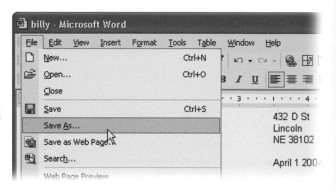

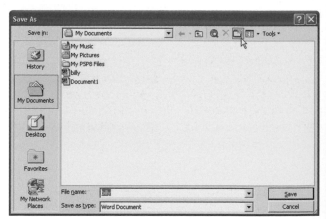

• The **New Folder** dialog box closes. The **Save As** dialog box reappears, this time showing your new, and empty, folder.

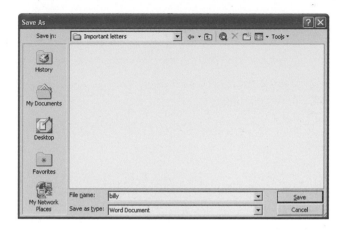

2 SAVING INTO YOUR FOLDER

• Type a name for your file in the **File** name text box and click on **Save**. The **Save As** dialog box closes and your file has been saved in the new folder.

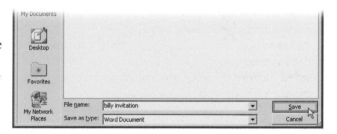

3 MOVING WITHIN FOLDERS

• To move up one level and open the folder that contains the current folder, click on the folder icon that has the right-angled arrow in the **Save As** dialog box – this icon is also in the **Open** dialog box.

So many folders...

You can have as many folders as you want within a single folder, but this may become unwieldy. So it might be better to split your folders according to type. You could have a Work folder with a Customer folder and a Supplier folder to divide two different kinds of letters; and a Personal folder with a Friends folder and a Family folder within it. You can of course further subdivide and create folders within folders within folders, but you may discover you're unable to find anything. Utility is the key – create folders only when you think they'll be helpful.

PRINTING

You will want your letter to appear on paper looking as neat as possible. Word has features that let you preview the printout of your letter, make improvements, and finally print your letter.

PRINT PREVIEW

Print Preview lets you see how the printed version of your letter will appear. This is done by showing each page as a scaled-down version of the specified paper size. The changes you can make in Print Preview include adjusting the margins, but it's not possible to edit the text when previewing. You can preview one page at a time or view several pages at once. Seeing more than one page at a time allows you compare how they look and see how your changes affect your letter.

1 PREVIEW YOUR TEXT

- Open a file that you want to print out.
- Go to the top of the text with the insertion point ⌐.
- Click on **File** in the Menu bar and click on **Print Preview** in the **File** drop-down menu.
- Your screen now shows a print preview of your letter.

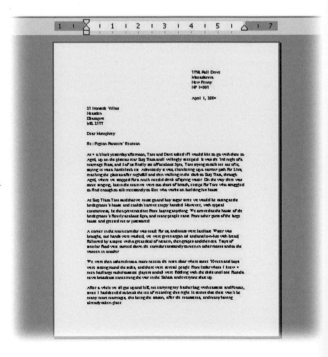

Insertion Point

2 SHOWING MULTIPLE PAGES

● If your letter has more than one page, you may want to see them all on one screen. Look at the Print Preview toolbar (now the only toolbar at the top of the screen). There is a rounded box containing four small rectangles (shown at right). This is the **Multiple Pages** icon.

● Click on the **Multiple Pages** icon, and a menu of gray pages appears.

● Move the mouse pointer over the menu to choose

how many pages you want to view. In the example shown, **1 x 2 Pages** is selected. The first number is the number of rows in which your pages appear, the second number is the number of pages to be shown. The maximum is 3 x 8, which is selected by holding down the left mouse button and moving the mouse pointer right.

● Release the mouse button over the required display.

● You can now see how your letter will appear on the printed page.

1 x 2 Pages

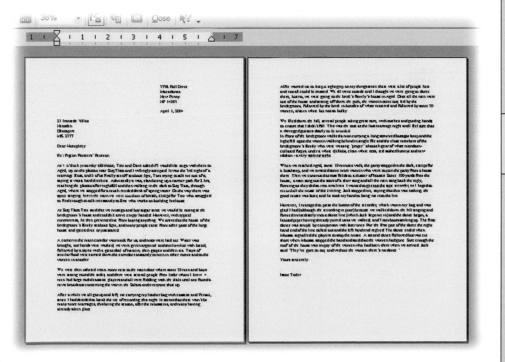

3 PAGE SETUP

● You may want to improve the look of your letter. Perhaps there is not enough room between the text and the edge of the paper, or maybe a couple of lines that could be fitted onto the current page spill over onto a new page. Both these problems can be solved by changing the margins.

● Begin by dropping down the **File** menu and click on **Page Setup**.

● The **Page Setup** dialog box appears.

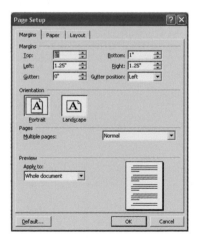

4 CHANGING THE MARGINS

● Four boxes in the **Page Setup** dialog box control the top, bottom, left, and right margins.

● You can increase or decrease the margins by increments of one-tenth of an inch by clicking the up and down arrow buttons to the right of each margin control box. Or click inside a box to enter a size.

● When you have selected the margin sizes, click the **OK** box to see your results.

● When you are satisfied with your changes, click on **Close** in the Print Preview toolbar to return to the normal view of your letter.

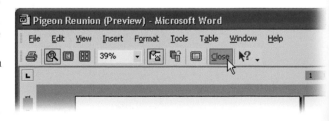

PRINTING YOUR LETTER

The actual process of printing out your letter is very simple. The Print Preview feature makes it unnecessary to print a number of draft versions of your letter because you now know how it will appear on the page. All that is left to do now is to use the very simple **Print** command to produce a hard copy of your letter.

1 THE PRINT DIALOG BOX

● Drop down the **File** menu and click on **Print** to open the **Print** dialog box.
● You can print selected pages of your letter if you want. Enter the numbers of the pages into the **Pages** box under **Page range**.
● You can also print more than one copy of your letter. Enter the number you want into the **Number of copies** box at the right of the **Print** dialog box.
● Check that your printer is connected to your computer and that it is switched on.
● Click on **OK** and your letter begins to be printed.

If you do not wish to print all pages, enter the page numbers required here

PRINTING QUICKLY

In the majority of cases, you will not need to "customize" the printing of your document because you will need only one copy of your letter. Click on the printer icon in the toolbar at the top of the screen. Your letter is printed without using the **Print** dialog box.

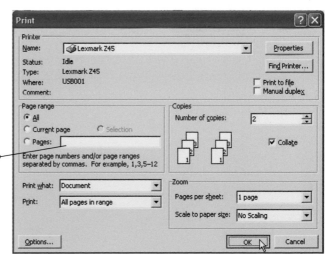

LET WORD HELP

Word has many helpful features including a spelling checker, a grammar checker, a thesaurus, templates on which to base your documents, and wizards that produce customized documents.

SPELLING CHECKER

However good your letter looks on paper, it can be let down by typing errors. Even if your spelling is impeccable, it is inevitable that some incorrect keystrokes are made.

Word can check your spelling for you as you type, or you can have Word check the spelling of your whole document when you've finished writing it.

1 CHECKING AS YOU TYPE

● Try typing a deliberate mistake into your letter.

● A wavy red line appears below the incorrect word.

● Move the mouse pointer over the word containing the error and click with the right mouse button (right click). A pop-up menu appears near the word.

● Word lists alternative words that you could have intended to type instead of the mistake. Left-click on the correct word.

Dear Margaret

Thank you for your leter.

Thank you for your leter.

| letter |
| later |
| leer |
| latter |
| litter |
| Ignore All |
| Add to Dictionary |
| AutoCorrect ▶ |
| Language ▶ |

- The mistake is replaced by the correct word and the pop-up closes.

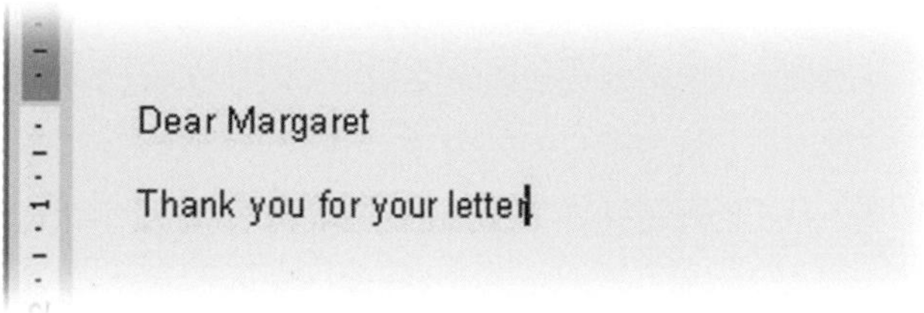

Dear Margaret

Thank you for your letter

2 ADDING WORDS

- Now type something that is correct but obscure and which the spelling checker is unlikely to recognize, such as a foreign word or an unusual name.
- The word, though not a mistake, is underlined by the wavy red line.
- Right-click the word. The menu drops down.
- Click on **Add to Dictionary**. The spelling checker adds the word to its dictionary and will no longer underline the word as a "mistake."
- The wavy red line disappears because the spelling is now accepted as being correct.

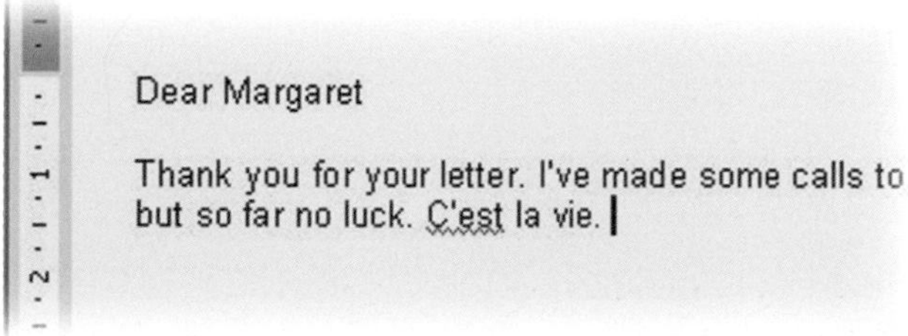

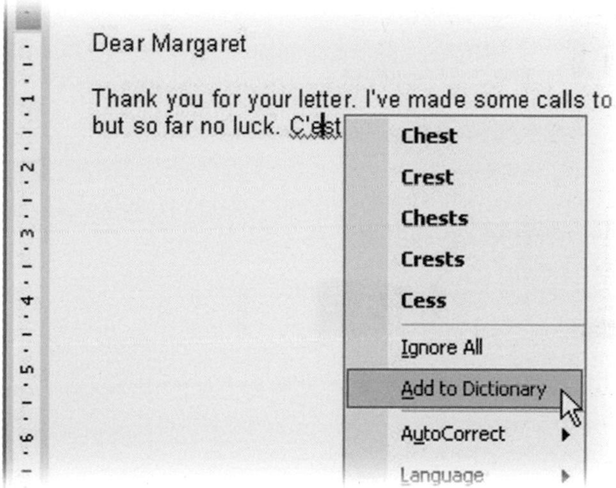

Dear Margaret

Thank you for your letter. I've made some calls to but so far no luck. C'est la vie.

Dear Margaret

Thank you for your letter. I've made some calls to but so far no luck. C'est

Chest
Crest
Chests
Crests
Cess

Ignore All
Add to Dictionary
AutoCorrect ▶
Language ▶

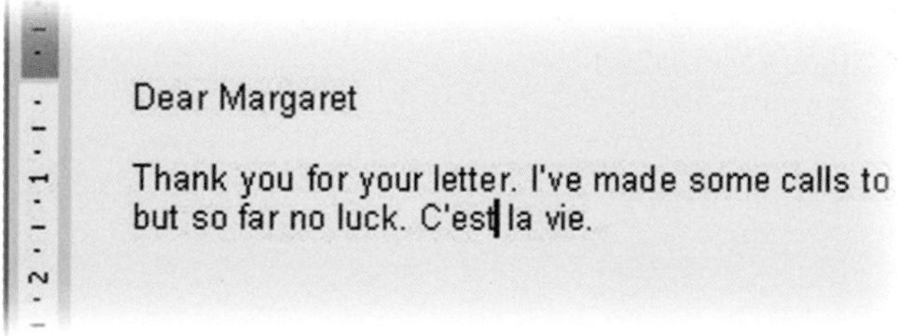

Dear Margaret

Thank you for your letter. I've made some calls to but so far no luck. C'est la vie.

GRAMMAR CHECKER

Word's automatic grammar checker works very much like the spelling checker. The obvious difference is that Word marks what it believes to be grammatical errors with a wavy green line, not a red line. The grammar checker cannot offer perfect advice due to the complexities of English. So accept its suggestions carefully.

CORRECTING GRAMMAR

- Word has detected a clumsy sentence structure.
- Right-click the sentence and a menu pops up.
- Choose the suggestion or click on **About this Sentence** to have the problem explained. Click on **Ignore** if you think the grammar checker is itself making a mistake.
- If you click on **About this Sentence**, the office assistant, which can be switched on by using the **Help** menu, pops up and explains what Word thinks is the problem.
- Click with the mouse button away from the advice to close the panel.

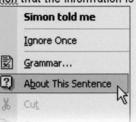

tter. I've made some calls to try to find out what you want est la vie. I was told by Simon that the information is curre

Simon told me

Ignore Once

Grammar...

About This Sentence

Cut

· 1 · 6 · 1 · 7 · 1 · 8 · 1 · 9 · 1 · 10 · 1 · 11 · 1 · 12 · 1 · 13 · 1 · 14 · 1 · 15 · 1 · 16 ·

ade some calls to
was told by Simon

Passive Voice

For a livelier and more persuasive sentence, consider rewriting your sentence using an active verb (the subject performs the action, as in "The ball hit Catherine") rather than a passive verb (the subject receives the action, as in "Catherine was hit by the ball"). If you rewrite with an active verb, consider what the appropriate subject is - "they," "we," or a more specific noun or pronoun.

- Instead of: Juanita was delighted by Michelle.
- Consider: Michelle delighted Juanita.

- Instead of: Eric was given more work.
- Consider: The boss gave Eric more work.

- Instead of: The garbage needs to be taken out.
- Consider: You need to take the garbage out.

- Right-click the sentence again to display the pop up menu and click on the suggested correction.

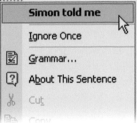

The grammar of the sentence has been revised

THESAURUS

You may want to find an alternative word to express what you mean. The thesaurus feature in Word lists possible words in the same way as the paper-based thesaurus except that it works directly on the word for which you require a synonym.

SYNONYMS

- Place the insertion point in the word for which you want to find a synonym.
- Drop down the **Tools** menu from the menu bar. Click on **Language**.
- A submenu appears, click on **Thesaurus**.

● The **Thesaurus** dialog box opens. The list of available synonyms are listed in the right-hand panel of the dialog box.

● Click on a synonym. It appears in the **Replace with Synonym** box.

● Click on the **Replace** button, and the selected word is replaced with the synonym.

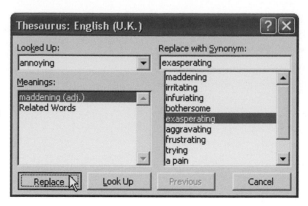

CHECKING AFTER YOU HAVE FINISHED TYPING

Some people find that having Word checking their spelling and grammar as they type is distracting and intrusive.

If you would prefer not to have the wavy red and green underlines appearing below your text, you can turn these functions off.

1 TURNING OFF CHECKING

● To turn off the spelling checker while you type, drop down the **Tools** menu from the toolbar.

● Click on **Options** and the **Options** dialog box opens onscreen.

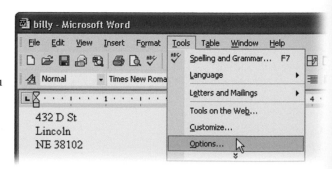

● There are a number of tabs at the top of the **Options** dialog box for altering different aspects of Word. Click on the **Spelling & Grammar** tab to display the available options under **Spelling** and **Grammar**.

● Click once in the **Check spelling as you type** tick box. The tick disappears.

● Click on the **OK** button. Word will now no longer check your spelling as you type. You can still, however, check the spelling of all the text in one pass, after you have finished typing.

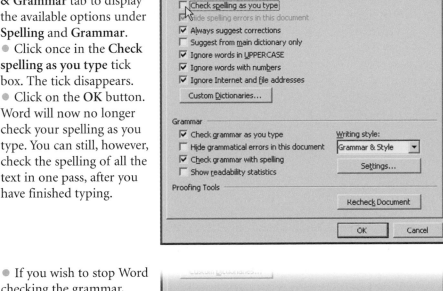

● If you wish to stop Word checking the grammar, click once in the **Check grammar as you type** tick box. The tick disappears and the grammar checker is turned off.

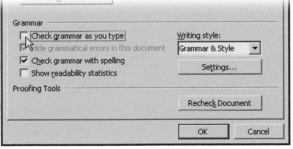

● You can also ask Word to check the grammar without checking the style of your writing. Keep the tick in the **Check grammar as you type** tick box and select **Grammar Only** in the **Writing style** panel.

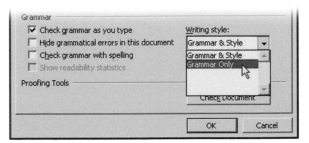

2 CHECKING THE DOCUMENT

● Drop down the **Tools** menu from the menu bar.

● Click on **Spelling and Grammar** from the **Tools** menu. Word will work through your document with the **Spelling and Grammar** dialog box, prompting you at every error that is found.

● If you want to accept a suggested spelling, click on the correct one from the **Suggestions** box and click on the **Change** button.

● If you want to correct the error yourself, click inside the **Not in Dictionary** box and position the insertion point over the error. Make the text correction yourself by using the keyboard and click on the **Change** button.

● If you don't think that there is an error, click on the **Ignore Once** button. If you click on **Ignore All**, Word will ignore all instances of this word.

● Word moves on to the next error in your text until it can find no more and the information box appears telling you that the check is complete. Click on **OK**.

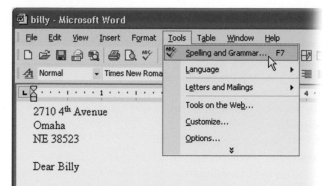

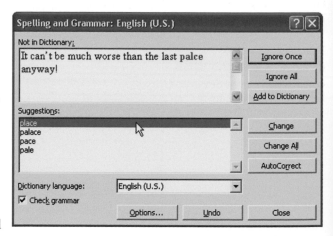

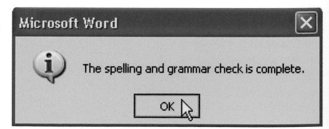

TEMPLATES

Usually when you come to create a new file, either you work from the blank file that Word creates when it is launched, or you create a new blank file by choosing the **Blank Document** option from the **New** dialog box. This time, you can save yourself some of the work involved in laying out a document by creating a preformatted letter and filling in the blanks. As an example of this, follow the steps below to create a letter using the **Elegant Letter** template.

1 CREATING A NEW FILE

- Drop down the **File** menu and click on **New**.
- In the **New Document** pane that opens, click on **General Templates** in the **New from template** section.
- Choose the **Letters & Faxes** tab in the **Templates** dialog box that appears, and click on the icon labeled **Elegant Letter**.
- Click on **OK**.

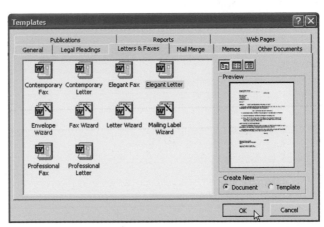

2 FILLING IN THE BLANKS

- Your new file will now be open on the screen.
- Click on the box at the top of the letter marked **Click here and type company name**. The box does not print out – it just shows you where to type.

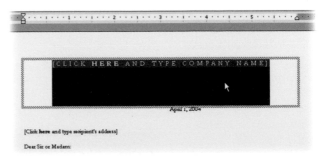

● Click on the line of text that reads **Click here and type recipient's address**. You can begin typing the recipient's address – the line of text vanishes when you begin typing.

April 1, 2004

[Click **here** and type recipient's address]

Dear Sir or Madam:

Type your letter here. For more details on modifying this letter template letter, use the Window menu.

Sincerely,

● Using the insertion point or the mouse pointer, select the text of the paragraph that is already in place and begin typing. The old text disappears as you begin to start typing.

April 1, 2004

[Click **here** and type recipient's address]

Dear Sir or Madam:

Type your letter here. For more details on modifying this letter template letter, use the Window menu.

Sincerely,

● Add your name and job title over the lines of text at the end of the letter. Just click in these lines to select them, and start typing.

Sincerely,

[Click **here** and type your name]
[Click **here** and type job title]

● Your address goes at the foot of the Elegant Letter. Scroll down the page and add your address into the address box.

● You have now created a letter using the Elegant Letter template.

[STREET ADDRESS] · [CITY/STATE] · [ZIP/POSTAL CODE]
PHONE: [PHONE NUMBER] · FAX: [FAX NUMBER]

WIZARDS

Wizards are a simple way of producing formatted letters quickly. There is no need to type names and addresses directly into the letter – Word uses dialog boxes for you to supply the information and then adds this to the letter. You can create the same letter using the Letter Wizard that you did using the template.

1 STARTING THE WIZARD

● Drop down the **File** menu and click on **New**.
● Click on **General Templates**, and choose the **Letters & Faxes** tab in the **Templates** dialog box that appears, and click on the icon marked **Letter Wizard**.
● Click on the **OK** button.
● Click on **Send one letter** in the small dialog box that appears onscreen.

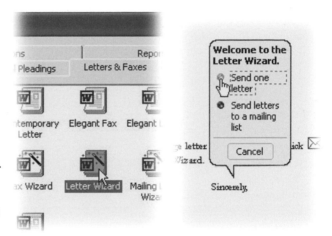

2 LETTER FORMAT

● The **Letter Wizard** dialog box opens. The first step is the **Letter Format**.
● Drop down the **Choose a page design** menu and choose the one you want. You will notice that **Elegant Letter**, the template we used earlier in this section, is one of the designs.
● Drop down the **Choose a letter style** menu and choose from **Full Block** (no indents), **Modified Block**

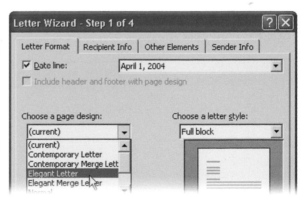

(some indenting), or **Semi-Block** (full, with stylish first line indents).

● Click on the **Next** button to go to the next step in the **Letter Wizard**.

3 RECIPIENT'S INFORMATION

● The **Letter Wizard** dialog box now shows the **Recipient Info** step.

● Enter the recipient's name and address in the relevant text boxes.

● Choose a salutation from the drop-down menu under **Salutation**, or type in your own.

● Click on the **Next** button.

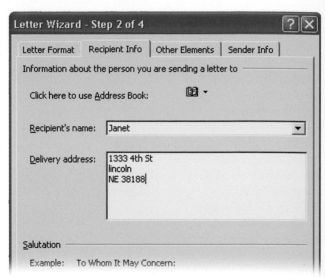

4 OTHER ELEMENTS

● The **Letter Wizard** dialog box now shows the **Other Elements** step.

● If you want to include a reference line, click on the check box to the left of **Reference line.** A tick will appear in the box. You can now drop down the **Reference line** menu and use the available options.

● Do the same for any other features you want: **Mailing instructions, Attention, Subject.**

● If you wish to send a courtesy copy, insert the details into the boxes at the foot of the dialog box.

● Click on the **Next** button.

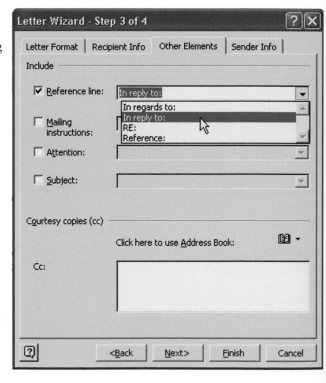

5 SENDER INFORMATION

● The last step of the **Letter Wizard** dialog box is the **Sender Info** step.

● Type your name into the Sender's name box.

● Type your address into the **Return address** box.

● Select a closing from the **Complimentary closing** drop-down menu – or type your own into the box.

● Click on **Finish** to allow the Letter Wizard to create your document.

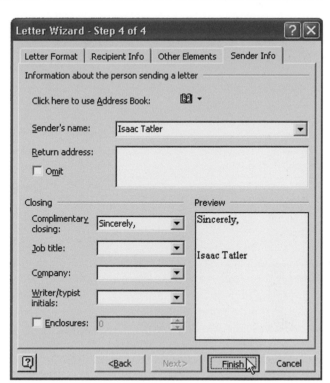

6 START TYPING

● The **Letter Wizard** dialog box vanishes. The office assistant appears and asks you if you want to do any more to your letter.

● Make a selection or click on **Cancel**.

● Your letter is ready. Everything is in place except the paragraphs of main text.

● Start typing as with the Elegant Letter template.

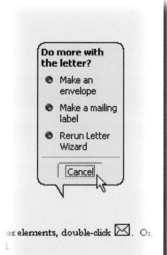

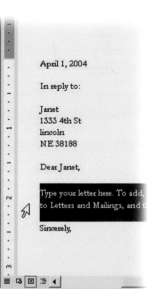

MAIL MERGE

Mail merge is a way of sending personalized letters to a number of people. Although more often used by business, mail merge is also useful for telling people about the large events in our lives.

MAIN DOCUMENTS AND DATA SOURCES

So far you have only been working with letters to individual recipients. You may, however, wish to create a letter to be sent to a number of people – for instance, to notify all your friends that you have moved. You could produce a letter addressed to one person, print it out, change the recipient's name and address, print out the new letter to the next person, and so on. This would, however, be a very tedious and time-consuming process. To save you this trouble you can use a feature called Mail Merge. This allows you to create a standard letter and a list of names and addresses. The letter and the list are then merged to create personalized letters to everyone in the list. The standard letter is called a Main Document – the list is called a Data Source. Let's start by creating a Main Document from scratch.

1 CREATE A MAIN DOCUMENT
● Drop down the **Tools** menu and select the **Letters and Mailings** option. Now select the **Mail Merge Wizard** from the list of options that appears in the drop-down menu. (You will see that you can choose to **Show Mail Merge Toolbar**, and you may wish to do this once you know how to use Mail Merge.)

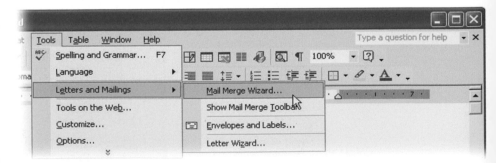

● In the task pane that appears, choose **Letters** if it is not already selected, and click on **Next: Starting document** at the bottom of the screen.

● In the next task pane, select your starting document. Here we are selecting the standard blank Word document that is already open.

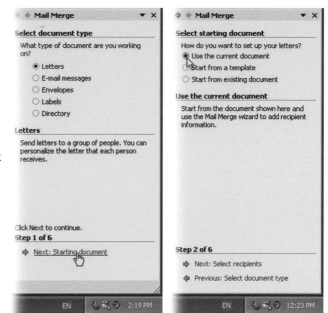

2 CREATING AN ADDRESS LIST

● Before working on your new Main Document, you need to create a structure for your data. You need an Address List to do this.

● Click on **Next: Select recipients** at the bottom of the screen.

● Select **Type a new list** and then click on **Create** in the task pane.

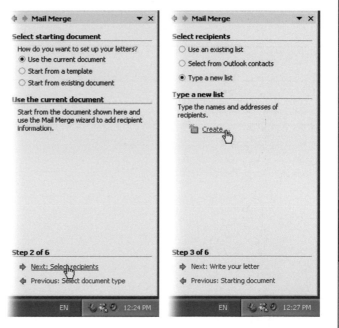

● The **New Address List** box opens.

● Select each field in turn and type in the details of your first recipient.

● You won't need all the fields. Any that are not needed can be left blank.

● When the first entry is complete, click on **New Entry** and complete the address information for another recipient.

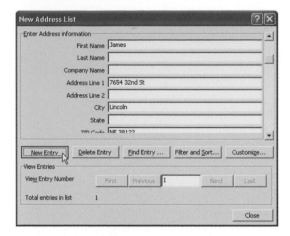

FIELDS AND RECORDS

Each kind of data in the Master Document that is attached to the Data Source (such as the recipient's names, or each line of his or her address) is called a field. Fields are what link the Master Document to the Data Source. The actual data in the fields – such as names in the Name field: James, Doncaster, Mum & Dad – are called records.

● Continue to fill in addresses until all the details of all recipients have been completed.

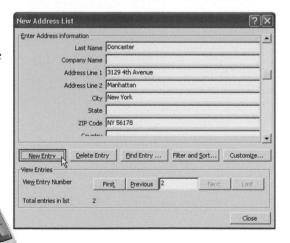

● When you have input all the details for all recipients, click on **Close**.

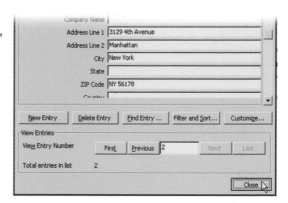

● The **Save Address List** dialog box appears. Type a name for your address list in the **File name** box (in this example we are calling it **List**) and click the **Save** button. You have now created a Data Source.

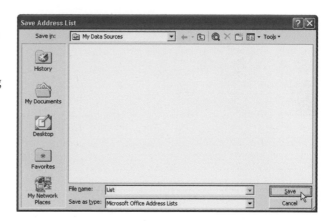

3 CHECK YOUR RECIPIENTS

● Your list of Mail Merge Recipients appears onscreen. Here you can select particular recipients, find specific details within the list, and add or delete entries. If the list is complete and you wish to send to all recipients, click on **OK**.

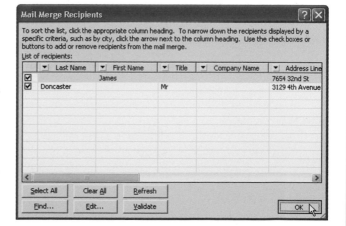

4 WRITING YOUR LETTER

● Select **Next: Write your letter** at the bottom of the task pane.

● With the cursor at the top of your blank document, click on **Address block** in the task pane to define where the address will appear.

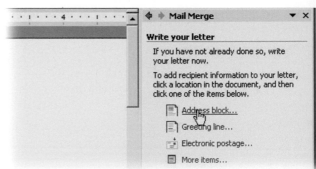

● The **Insert Address Block** dialog box appears, allowing you to choose the format of the recipient's name and to specify the address elements that you wish to include in the address block.

● Choose a format and click on **OK** to include all address elements.

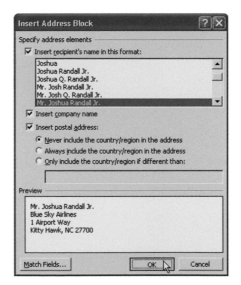

● Move the insertion point down a few lines and click on **Greeting line** to define this as the position in which you want your greeting to appear.

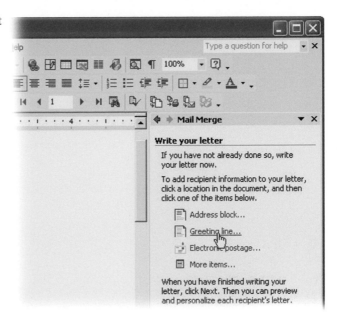

● The **Greeting Line** dialog box opens, allowing you to specify the format of your greeting. Select your choices and click on **OK**.

● Clicking on **More items** offers you the ability to insert particular details from your Data Source at chosen positions within the letter, should you wish to do so.

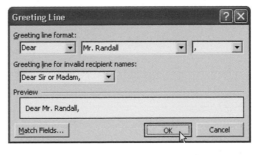

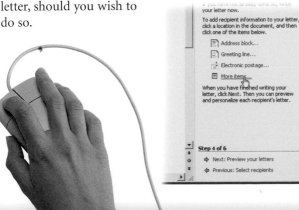

● Type in the text of your letter in the position that you wish it to occupy on the page.

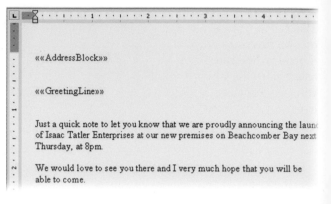

5 PREVIEW YOUR LETTER

● Now click **Next: Preview your letters** at the bottom of the task pane.

● Your letter appears on screen with the details of the first recipient on your list in the positions you have chosen.

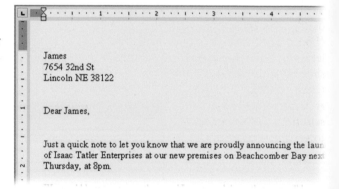

6 COMPLETE THE MAIL MERGE

● Click on the right hand arrow in the task pane to scroll through the letters to each of your recipients.

● If all recipient details are correct and you do not wish to edit the list, click on **Next: Complete the merge** at the bottom of the task bar.

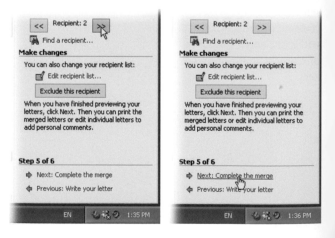

• In the final step of the Mail Merge Wizard you are offered the chance to edit individual letters or to go ahead and print them. If you are satisfied with your letters, click on **Print**.

7 PRINT YOUR MAIL MERGE

• The **Merge to Printer** dialog box appears. You can choose to print all your letters, just the document showing onscreen, or a range of letters from your recipient list. Here we are selecting all. Click on **OK** to print out your mail merge letter.

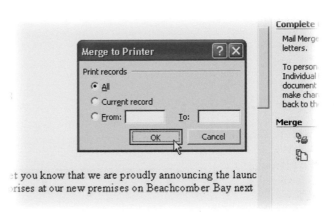

• The **Print** dialog box opens, allowing you to select how many pages of your main document you will print and the number of copies. You may wish to keep a file copy of each letter you send, in which case type **2** in the **Number of copies** panel.
• Click **OK** and a copy of your letter will be printed for each recipient in your address list.

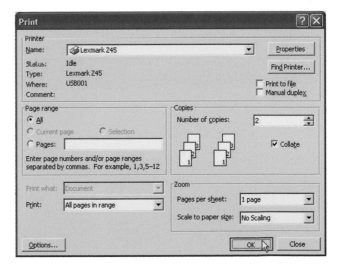

DESIGNING DOCUMENTS

I N THIS SECTION WE CONCENTRATE on the facilities that Word offers to help you design more interesting and professional text documents than those produced by simply using the default settings that Word provides. These facilities include font selection, customizing and manipulating paragraphs, adding colored borders and backgrounds, using tabs, columns, and lists, and creating your own style sheets to save time and effort.

WORKING WITH FONTS

There are several different levels of formatting and styling available in Word. This chapter looks at changing the font, resizing it, and changing the spacing and color of the letters.

CHANGING THE FONT

The default font in Microsoft Word is Times New Roman, which is one of the most popular fonts. There are many other fonts available and, while you can use as many fonts as you wish in a document, it is better to use no more than three in any one section. Increasing the number of fonts can have the effect of fragmenting the text and making it look messy, and certain fonts do not look good together.

THE CHOSEN VIEW

Throughout this book it is recommended that you work in **Print Layout** view, as many of the effects used are only displayed in this view of a document. To do this, click on **View** in the Menu bar and select **Print Layout**, or click on the **Page Layout View** button at the bottom of the screen.

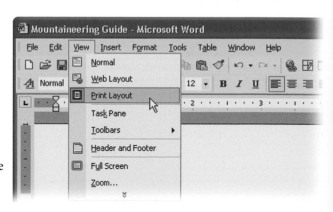

A VARIETY OF FONTS

In the examples of styling and formatting text that are used throughout this book, the text is displayed in a variety of fonts. While Microsoft Word includes a range of the most commonly used fonts, you may not have all the fonts shown here. This will not affect your ability to work your way through the examples, but you will need to choose alternative fonts. An almost limitless number of fonts can be bought from stores or over the internet.

1 CREATING THE TEXT

● In the example used here, we are writing a document for a mountaineering company that offers guided expeditions and more.

● Begin by typing their contact details in a new document, and press [Enter ←] at the end of each line with an extra [Enter ←] after the zip code.

● You'll see that when the email address is typed in, Word recognizes it for what it is and automatically shows it in blue.

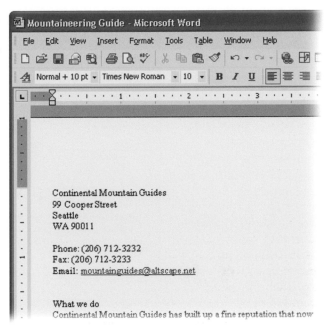

2 SELECTING A NEW FONT

● Although this text is perfectly clear, it lacks any impact. The first change that you can make is to use different fonts to emphasize the different parts of the company's details.

● Highlight the company name, click on **Format** in the Menu bar, and click on **Font** at the top of the drop-down menu.

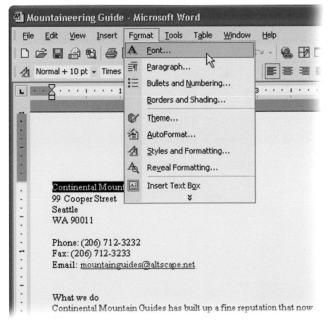

● The **Font** dialog box now opens. In the **Font** selection menu, use the scroll bar to move to another font (we have chosen **Georgia**, and checked the **All caps** box). The **Preview** panel at the foot of the dialog box shows how the text will appear in your document. Click on **OK**.

● For the rest of the contact details, except for the email address, we are going to use another font. Highlight the text, open the **Font** dialog box again, and choose another font (we selected **Century Gothic, Small caps**). Now click on **OK**.

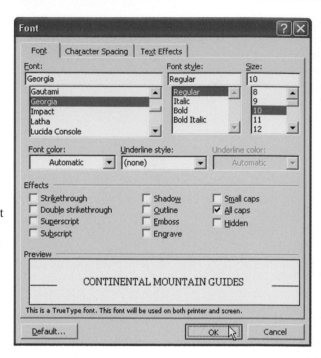

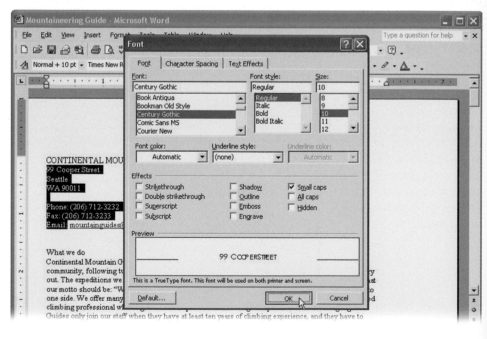

● The fonts have now been changed, and the company name, company address, and email address are each in a different font, which distinguishes the various elements from each other.

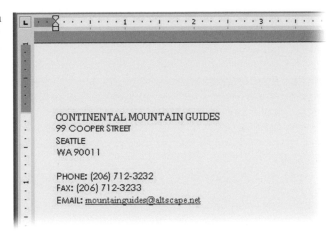

CHANGING THE FONT SIZE

Word's default font size of ten points (a point is one seventy-second of an inch) is fine for the bulk of the text that you are likely to produce, but different parts of your document, such as headings, can benefit from being in a larger font size.

USING THE FONT SIZE SELECTOR BOX

● With the text that you wish to resize already highlighted (in this case the company name), click on the Font size selector box in the Formatting toolbar, scroll to **16** (meaning 16 point), and click on it. The lettering of the selected text is now larger.

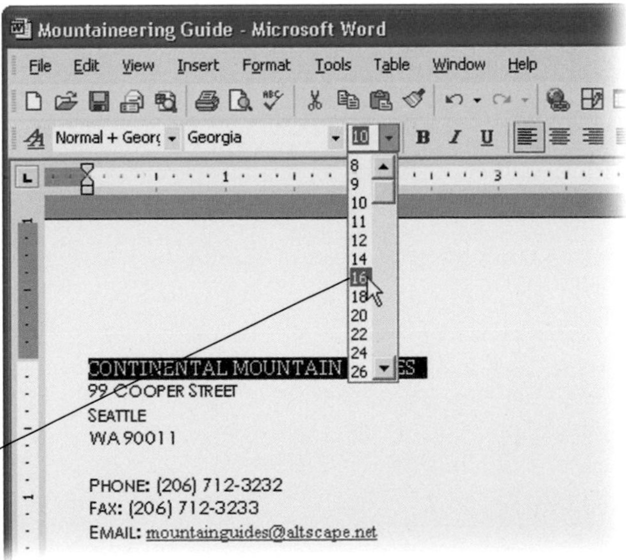

Selected font size ●

㉗ Font Size Selector

● Highlight the next three lines of the address and follow the same sequence to change the font size to 14 pt, and then do the same to change the final three lines to 12 pt. Your text should now appear as shown in this example.

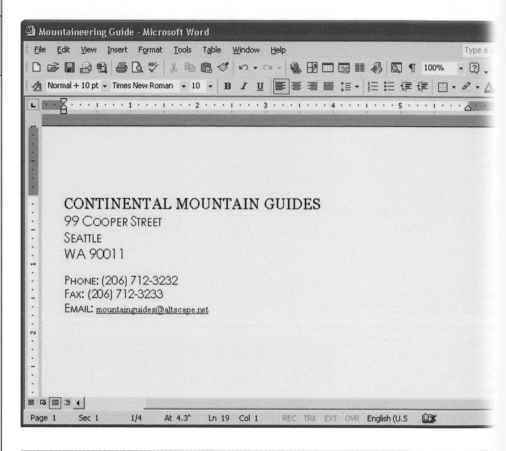

FONT STYLES

You will see that, as well as offering a choice of fonts, the **Font** dialog box also has a **Font style** panel. Choosing different options in this panel will enable you to turn the font from its normal, or regular, form to italic, bold, or italic bold type, providing that all these variations are available in the particular font that you are using. These options can be used to emphasize parts of your text.

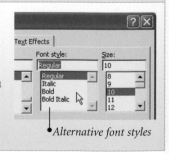

Alternative font styles

CHANGING THE FONT EFFECT

As well as bold, italic, and underline, there are a number of effects available in Word that you can use to change the appearance of your text. For example, shadowed, outlined, embossed, and engraved effects can all be used. Once you have followed this example, try out the other effects, some of which can be very useful.

EMBOSSING TEXT

- Begin by highlighting the company name in the address and open the **Font** dialog box , and click on the **Font** tab at the top of the dialog box.

- In the center of the **Effects** section of the **Font** dialog box, you'll see check boxes for **Shadow**, **Outline**, **Emboss**, and **Engrave** effects. Click in the check box next to **Emboss** and then click on **OK**.

- Click anywhere on your page to remove the highlighting, and the embossed effect on the lettering becomes visible.

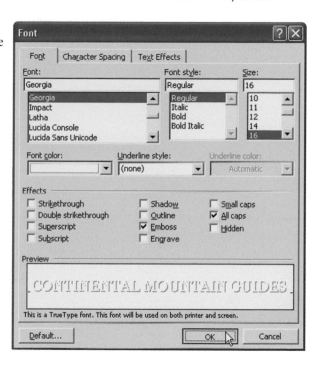

CONTINENTAL MOUNTAIN GUIDES
99 COOPER STREET
SEATTLE
WA 90011

PHONE: (206) 712-3232
FAX: (206) 712-3233
EMAIL: mountainguides@altscape.net

187 **Selecting a New Font**

CHANGING THE LETTER SPACING

Changing the amount of space between individual letters can also be used to emphasize important parts of the text.

In this example, we will space out the letters of the company name to give it greater weight on the page.

INCREASING THE LETTER SPACING

● Highlight the company name again, open the **Font** dialog box 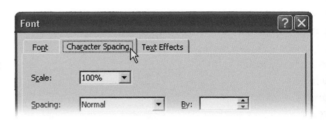, and click on the **Character Spacing** tab.

● In the **Spacing** box, click on the arrow next to **Normal** and select **Expanded**. In the **By** box, enter the figure **3**, meaning 3 pt, and click on **OK**.

● Click on the company name again to see how the name now extends across the page.

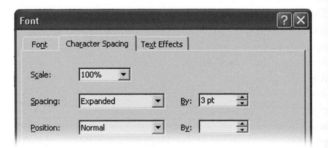

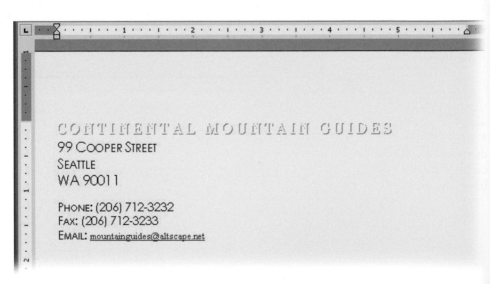

CONTINENTAL MOUNTAIN GUIDES
99 COOPER STREET
SEATTLE
WA 90011

PHONE: (206) 712-3232
FAX: (206) 712-3233
EMAIL: mountainguides@altscape.net

187 Selecting a New Font

CHANGING THE FONT COLOR

With the increasing availability, and falling cost, of color printers, using some of the color options in Word offers a simple and effective way of making selected text stand out. Bear in mind that it's best not to combine too wide a range of colors.

1 SELECTING THE COLOR PALETTE

● Although the snowy-whiteness of the embossed text is appropriate for the company's business, it's a little pale. To change the font color, highlight the company name and then open the **Font** dialog box.

● Click on the **Font** tab, if it is not already selected.

● Click the arrow to the right of the **Font color** selection box and the color palette will appear.

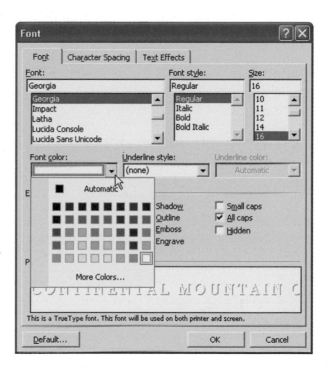

2 CHOOSING THE COLOR

● Move the mouse cursor down to **Blue** and click once. This color has now been selected for the text.

● The text in the **Preview** window now shows you the effect of the color change. If you are happy with this color, click on **OK**.

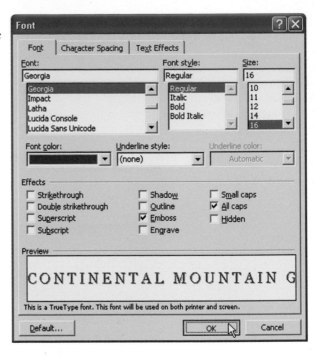

● Click anywhere on your page to remove the highlighting and reveal the text in the new color.

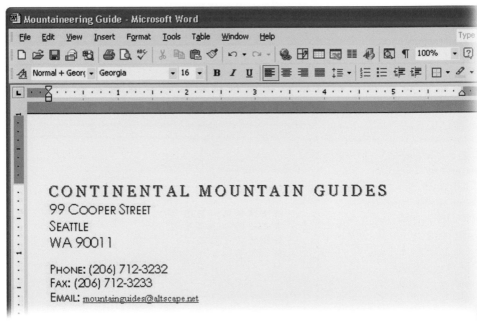

3 CHOOSING FURTHER COLORS

● As Word automatically colors the email address in blue, the contact details above the email address can also have their own colors. Try changing the **Phone** details to orange and the **Fax** line to sea green to achieve the effect shown in the example here.

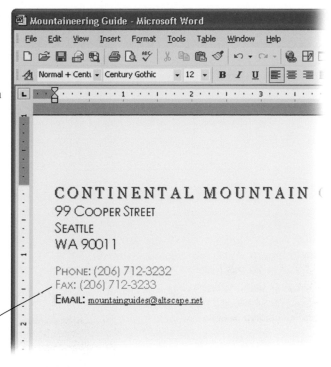

Lines of text stand out from each other ●

Bold, Italic, and Underline

The quickest way to change your text by using these effects is to highlight the text that you want to change and then click on one of these three buttons in the Formatting toolbar. You're not limited to just one of these effects for a piece of text. You can have text that is bold and italic, as well as being underlined, if that's what you want.

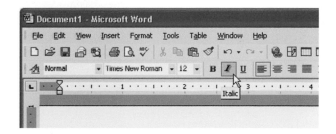

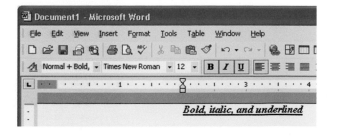

㉘ **Bold,** ㉙ **Italic,** ㉚ **Underline**

STYLING PARAGRAPHS

As far as Word is concerned, a paragraph is any piece of text that ends with a paragraph mark, so the styling shown here can be applied to a single letter or to several pages of text.

ALIGNING PARAGRAPHS

There are four possible ways to align paragraphs in Word: left-aligned, centered, right-aligned, and justified. Left-alignment is the default paragraph alignment in Word. Each line of a paragraph starts against the left margin, and the line endings are "ragged" in the way a typewriter would produce them. Centered alignment has the effect of centering each line of a paragraph on the mid-point between the margins. Right-alignment has the effect of aligning the right-hand end of each line up against the right-hand margin leaving the start of each line ragged, and justified alignment produces a straight edge at both the beginning and the end of each line by adding spaces to make every line of text the same length.

1 SELECTING THE TEXT

● The company's details are going to be the heading of the guide, and a heading frequently benefits from having its own alignment, in order to distinguish it from the text on the rest of the page. Begin by highlighting all of the company's details.

CONTINENTAL MOUNTAIN GUIDES
99 COOPER STREET
SEATTLE
WA 90011

PHONE: (206) 712-3232
FAX: (206) 712-3233
EMAIL: mountainguides@altscape.net

2 ALIGNING TEXT TO THE RIGHT

● First we'll see how right-aligning affects the appearance, so click on the **Align Right** button ⌐ in the Formatting toolbar.

● Click off the highlighted text to see the effect.

● Although the shorter lines are obviously right-aligned, the company name has hardly moved because it almost fills the width of the page, and it sticks out way beyond the other lines.

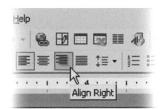

CONTINENTAL MOUNTAIN GUIDES
99 COOPER STREET
SEATTLE
WA 90011

PHONE: (206) 712-3232
FAX: (206) 712-3233
EMAIL: mountainguides@altscape.net

3 CENTERING THE TEXT

● The start of the company name looks as if it's out on a limb, and the whole heading would look better if it were centered, so highlight the company details again and click on the **Center** button ⌐ in the Formatting toolbar.

● Click off the highlighted text to see how the separate lines of the company's details now all appear to be part of a single unit.

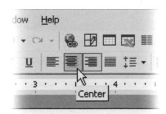

CONTINENTAL MOUNTAIN GUIDES
99 COOPER STREET
SEATTLE
WA 90011

PHONE: (206) 712-3232
FAX: (206) 712-3233
EMAIL: mountainguides@altscape.net

 ❸ Right-Aligned Text 125

 ❷ Centered Text 125

INSERTING A DROPPED CAPITAL

First paragraphs can be made more noticeable by starting them with a large initial capital letter that drops down more than one line. This dropped capital letter is familiarly known as a "drop cap", and it is easily achieved in Word.

WHAT WE DO

Continental Mountain Guides has built up a fine reputation that now extends beyond the climbing community, following two heavily publicized rescues that we were fortunate enough to be called to carry out. The expeditions we lead are always safe and successful, and one enthusiastic climber suggested that our motto should be: "We ain't lost one yet." However, as we never intend to, the suggestion was put to one side. We offer many climbing opportunities for the absolute beginner, as well as for the experienced climbing professional who might need our specialized knowledge of specific mountaineering regions. Guides only join our staff when they have at least ten years of climbing experience, and they have to demonstrate to us that they are dedicated to climbing and to sharing that passion.

1 SELECTING THE DROP CAP BOX

● The Mountaineering Guide has an introductory section with a heading that has been formatted in Century Gothic 16 pt bold, and a paragraph formatted in Trebuchet MS 10 pt. This paragraph would be more interesting if it began with a drop cap.

● Place the cursor over the paragraph and click to position the insertion point within it. Go to **Format** in the Menu bar and select **Drop Cap**. The **Drop Cap** dialog box opens.

● Click on **Dropped** in the **Position** options.

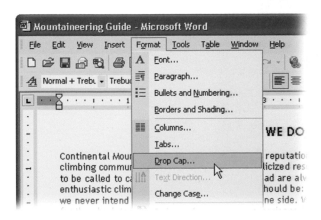

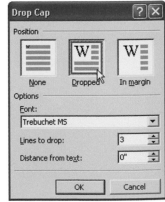

2 CHOOSING THE SIZE

- The **Lines to drop** box shows the default number of lines for the capital letter to drop is **3**. This is too large a drop cap for a short paragraph, so change the figure to **2** and click on **OK**.

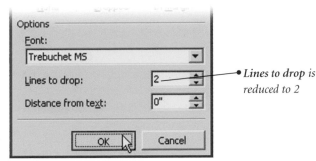

Lines to drop is reduced to 2

- The drop cap is shown surrounded by a frame.
- Click elsewhere on the document and the altered paragraph, with its new dropped capital, appears as it will on the printed page.

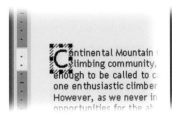

3 CREATING JUSTIFIED TEXT

- Finally, this paragraph would sit better with the company details above it if it were justified.
- Highlight the text and click on the **Justify** button in the Formatting toolbar.
- Both the beginnings and endings of the lines of the

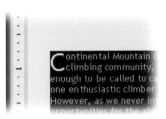

paragraph now align, and the start of the document is beginning to look tidier.

WHAT WE DO

Continental Mountain Guides has built up a fine reputation that now extends beyond the climbing community, following two heavily publicized rescues that we were fortunate enough to be called to carry out. The expeditions we lead are always safe and successful, and one enthusiastic climber suggested that our motto should be: "We ain't lost one yet." However, as we never intend to, the suggestion was put to one side. We offer many climbing opportunities for the absolute beginner, as well as for the experienced climbing professional who might need our specialized knowledge of specific mountaineering regions. Guides only join our staff when they have at least ten years of climbing experience, and they have to demonstrate to us that they are dedicated to climbing and to sharing that passion.

125 ❸❹ Justified Text

ADDING SPACE BETWEEN PARAGRAPHS

Creating space between paragraphs can improve the look of your document. This can be done by simply inserting a number of paragraph returns (⟨Enter ⟵⟩). However, there is a better way of choosing precisely the amount of space you wish to insert.

1 SELECTING THE PARAGRAPH

● In a section of the Mountaineering Guide on seminars and expeditions, the paragraphs have been separated by paragraph returns (you can make these visible using the Standard toolbar ⬚).

● A better method of separating paragraphs, particularly when a large amount of space is required between them, is to select manually how much space there should be.

Extra paragraph returns add a fixed amount of space

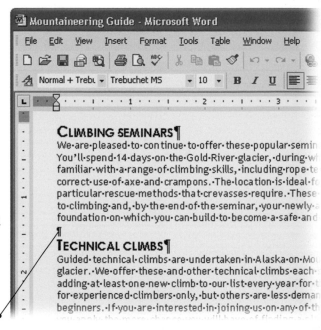

● First delete the paragraph marks separating the paragraphs, and highlight the first paragraph. Then click on **Format** in the Menu bar and choose **Paragraph** from the menu.

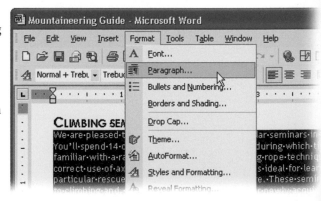

2 DEFINING THE SPACE

● The **Paragraph** dialog box opens. In the **Spacing** section, click on the up arrow in the **After** panel. The entry now reads **6 pt** and the **Preview** panel shows the increased space following the paragraph. Click on **OK**.

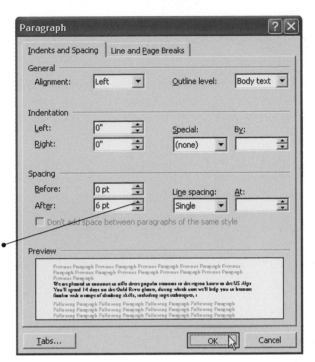

Up arrow increases the spacing after paragraph ●

● The paragraph is now separated from the following paragraph by a 6 pt space without an extra Enter ⏎ being inserted.

*Using the **Paragraph** formatting menu, this space can be made exactly the size you want it* ●

CHANGING THE INDENT

In printing terms, a "displayed" paragraph is one where the beginning and ends of the lines are indented compared to the paragraphs before and after it, producing a narrower column of text. This has the effect of emphasizing the paragraph.

SETTING THE LEFT INDENT

- Highlight the first paragraph, about climbing seminars, and place the mouse cursor over the **Left Indent** box on the ruler.

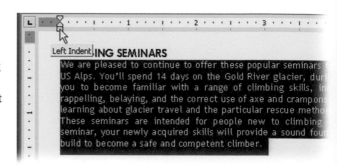

- Holding the mouse button down, drag the cursor to the right until the left indent box and the two indent arrows are over the quarter-inch mark, and release the mouse button. The left-hand edge of the paragraph is now indented.

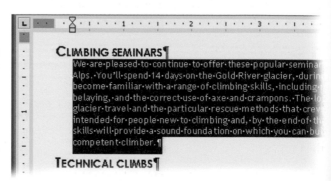

SETTING THE RIGHT INDENT

- Now place the mouse cursor over the **Right Indent** marker, hold down the mouse button, and drag the marker to the 5.5-inch position on the ruler and release the mouse button to set the indent.

● The right-hand line endings of the paragraph are now indented.

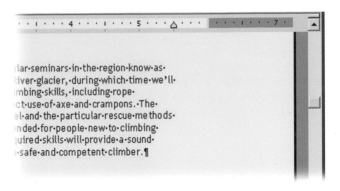

ADDING A BORDER

Word allows you to emphasize a selected paragraph by adding a border in a range of styles and colors. We are going to create a border around the outside of the selected text, but there are other options available in the **Outside Border** menu.

1 OPENING THE BORDER MENU

● Highlight the paragraph, including the paragraph mark, and click on the **Outside Border** button in the Formatting toolbar.

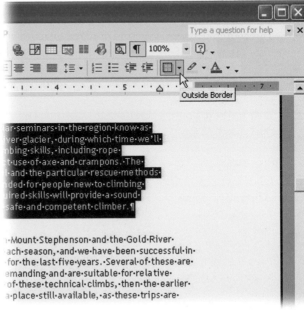

2 SELECTING OUTSIDE BORDER

● A menu of border selections appears. Click on the **Outside Border** option.

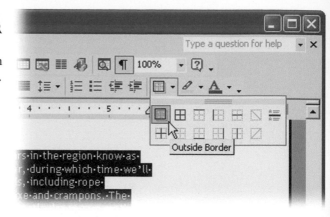

Outside Border

● The paragraph is now enclosed within a border.

CLIMBING SEMINARS¶

We·are·pleased·to·continue·to·offer·these·popular·seminars·in·the·region·know·as· the·US·Alps.·You'll·spend·14·days·on·the·Gold·River·glacier,·during·which·time·we'll· help·you·to·become·familiar·with·a·range·of·climbing·skills,·including·rope· techniques,·rappelling,·belaying,·and·the·correct·use·of·axe·and·crampons.·The· location·is·ideal·for·learning·about·glacier·travel·and·the·particular·rescue·methods· that·crevasses·require.·These·seminars·are·intended·for·people·new·to·climbing· and,·by·the·end·of·the·seminar,·your·newly·acquired·skills·will·provide·a·sound· foundation·on·which·you·can·build·to·become·a·safe·and·competent·climber.¶

TECHNICAL CLIMBS¶

Guided·technical·climbs·are·undertaken·in·Alaska·on·Mount·Stephenson·and·the·Gold·River· glacier.·We·offer·these·and·other·technical·climbs·each·season,·and·we·have·been·successful·in

3 CHANGING THE BORDER STYLE

● With the text within the border highlighted, go to the **Format** menu and click on **Borders and Shading**.

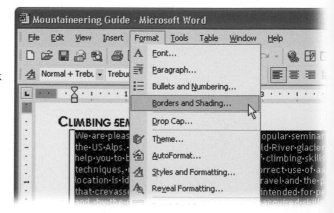

● The **Borders and Shading** dialog box opens. Click on the **Borders** tab if it is not already at the front. In the **Style** panel, click on the down arrow and select one of the selection of borders by clicking on it. Click on **OK**.

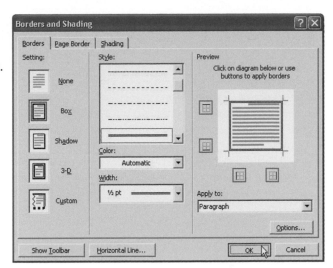

● The border around the paragraph changes to the selected style.

CLIMBING SEMINARS¶

We·are·pleased·to·continue·to·offer·these·popular·seminars·in·the·region·know·as· the·US·Alps.·You'll·spend·14·days·on·the·Gold·River·glacier,·during·which·time·we'll· help·you·to·become·familiar·with·a·range·of·climbing·skills,·including·rope· techniques,·rappelling,·belaying,·and·the·correct·use·of·axe·and·crampons.·The· location·is·ideal·for·learning·about·glacier·travel·and·the·particular·rescue·methods· that·crevasses·require.·These·seminars·are·intended·for·people·new·to·climbing· and,·by·the·end·of·the·seminar,·your·newly·acquired·skills·will·provide·a·sound· foundation·on·which·you·can·build·to·become·a·safe·and·competent·climber.¶

TECHNICAL CLIMBS¶

RESIZING BORDERS MANUALLY

There are two ways in which you can change the distance between the text and the border that encloses it. If you open the **Borders and Shading** dialog box you will see an **Options** button that allows the precise adjustment of the distance between the text and the border. An alternative method is simply to place the cursor against one of the sides of the border, hold down the mouse button, and drag the edge of the border to a new position.

4 ADDING COLOR TO THE BORDER

• With the text within the border highlighted, go to the **Format** menu and click on **Borders and Shading**. Click in the **Color** box to display the color palette.

• Move the mouse cursor down and click on **Tan**.

• Click on **OK** and the border is now colored.

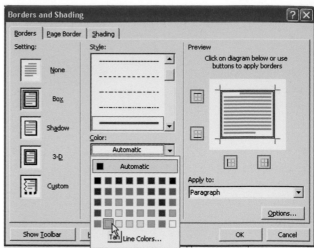

·aspects·of·kit,·travel,·supplies,·team·management,·border·controls,·health,·

CLIMBING SEMINARS¶

We·are·pleased·to·continue·to·offer·these·popular·seminars·in·the·region·know·as·
the·US·Alps.·You'll·spend·14·days·on·the·Gold·River·glacier,·during·which·time·we'll·
help·you·to·become·familiar·with·a·range·of·climbing·skills,·including·rope·
techniques,·rappelling,·belaying,·and·the·correct·use·of·axe·and·crampons.·The·
location·is·ideal·for·learning·about·glacier·travel·and·the·particular·rescue·methods·
that·crevasses·require.·These·seminars·are·intended·for·people·new·to·climbing·
and,·by·the·end·of·the·seminar,·your·newly·acquired·skills·will·provide·a·sound·
foundation·on·which·you·can·build·to·become·a·safe·and·competent·climber.¶

REMOVING A BORDER

• With the text within the border highlighted, click on the **Outside Border** button in the Formatting toolbar. The menu of border selections appears.

• Move the cursor over the **No Border** option and click to remove the border.

SHADING A PARAGRAPH

Whether or not a paragraph has been given a border, the text can be made to stand out by shading or coloring the background. Even if you don't have a color printer, this method can be used to choose a shade of gray, which can be effective.

1 SELECTING THE DIALOG BOX

● Highlight the paragraph, go to the **Format** menu in the toolbar and click on **Borders and Shading**. Now click on the **Shading** tab in the **Borders and Shading** dialog box to bring it to the foreground.

2 CHOOSING A COLOR

● Click on **Light Green** on the bottom row of the color palette, and the preview panel shows what this will look like.

● Click on **OK**, and the paragraph is now colored.

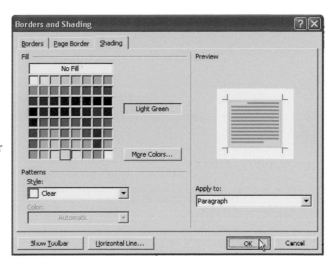

CLIMBING SEMINARS¶

We·are·pleased·to·continue·to·offer·these·popular·seminars·in·the·region·know·as·the·US·Alps.·You'll·spend·14·days·on·the·Gold·River·glacier,·during·which·time·we'll·help·you·to·become·familiar·with·a·range·of·climbing·skills,·including·rope·techniques,·rappelling,·belaying,·and·the·correct·use·of·axe·and·crampons.·The·location·is·ideal·for·learning·about·glacier·travel·and·the·particular·rescue·methods·that·crevasses·require.·These·seminars·are·intended·for·people·new·to·climbing·and,·by·the·end·of·the·seminar,·your·newly·acquired·skills·will·provide·a·sound·foundation·on·which·you·can·build·to·become·a·safe·and·competent·climber.¶

TECHNICAL CLIMBS¶

Guided·technical·climbs·are·undertaken·in·Alaska·on·Mount·Stephenson·and·the·Gold·River·glacier.·We·offer·these·and·other·technical·climbs·each·season,·and·we·have·been·successful·in·

REMOVING SHADING FROM A PARAGRAPH

If you wish to remove shading that you have already created, follow these steps. With the paragraph highlighted, open the **Borders and Shading** dialog box via the **Format** menu, and choose **Shading**. Now click in the **No Fill** box above the color palette, click **OK**, and the shading is removed.

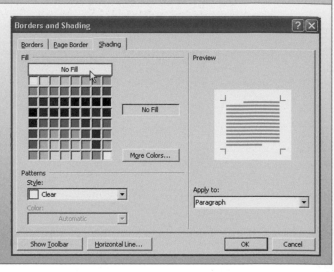

ALIGNING THE TEXT

● When text is within a rectangular border, it can look better being justified 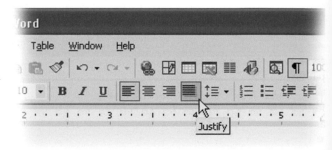. Highlight the paragraph and click on the **Justify** button in the Formatting toolbar. The text now fits neatly within the border.

CLIMBING SEMINARS

We are pleased to continue to offer these popular seminars in the region know as the US Alps. You'll spend 14 days on the Gold River glacier, during which time we'll help you to become familiar with a range of climbing skills, including rope techniques, rappelling, belaying, and the correct use of axe and crampons. The location is ideal for learning about glacier travel and the particular rescue methods that crevasses require. These seminars are intended for people new to climbing and, by the end of the seminar, your newly acquired skills will provide a sound foundation on which you can build to become a safe and competent climber.

TECHNICAL CLIMBS

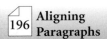

USING FORMAT PAINTER

Once you've decided on a paragraph format that you want to apply to other paragraphs, you can apply the style by using a feature of Word known as **Format Painter**, rather than going through each individual step again for each paragraph.

1 SELECTING THE FORMAT TO COPY

● Select the paragraph whose format you wish to apply to another paragraph. Make sure that the paragraph mark is also selected. Click on the **Format Painter** button on the Standard toolbar.

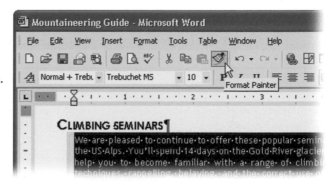

2 SELECTING THE NEW PARAGRAPH

● The cursor changes to a paintbrush icon. Move to the paragraph that is to be formatted in the same way as the selected paragraph.
● Click on the paragraph.

● All the formatting that has been done, including adding space, indenting the paragraph, adding a colored border and shading, and justifying the text, will be applied instantly to the chosen paragraph.

Formatting has been applied ●

MULTIPLE PAINTING

If you want to apply the same format to more than one paragraph by using **Format Painter**, double-click on the **Format Painter** button when you select it. You can then format as many paragraphs with the chosen format as you want by clicking in each one. When you've finished applying the format, either click on the **Format Painter** button to deselect or press the [Esc] key.

LISTS AND COLUMNS

Some data looks neater and more readable when presented as a list or in a column. In this chapter we look at the list and column options available in Word, and how to use them.

USING NUMBERED LISTS

Displaying items line by line, each new entry starting with a number, is probably the most common form of list. Text that has already been typed in can be turned into a list, and Word also has the facility to create a list automatically as you type.

1 SELECT BULLETS AND NUMBERING

● Type in a list of items, starting a new line each time. Now highlight the list, go to the **Format** menu in the toolbar, and select **Bullets and Numbering**.

AUTOMATIC NUMBERING

Word detects when you are manually creating a numbered list. If you type a line of text that begins with a **1** followed by a space, when you press the [Enter ←] key, Word automatically begins the new line with a **2** and inserts a tab.

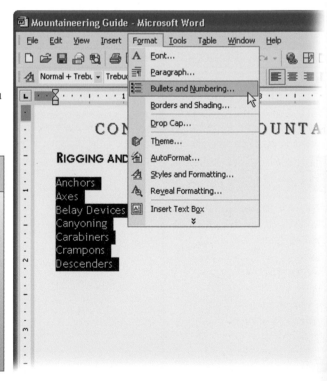

2 CHOOSING THE OPTION

● The **Bullets and Numbering** dialog box opens. Click on the **Numbered** tab to view the numbering options.

● Select the numbering style immediately to the right of the **None** box by clicking on that box. The chosen box is highlighted by a blue rectangle. Now click on **OK**.

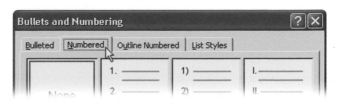

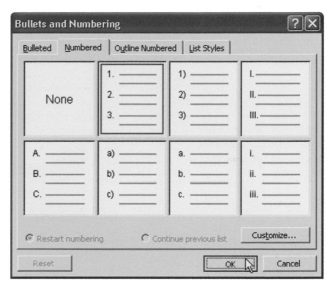

● The list of items is now numbered.

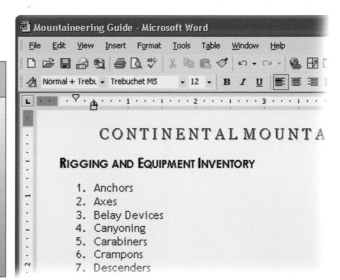

SWITCHING OFF THE NUMBERING

Word's automatic numbering feature can be annoying when you don't want to number every line. To remove a number, press the `← Bksp` backspace key once to delete the number, and again to remove the indent.

CHANGING THE INDENTS

As you have seen on the previous page, when you turn a list into a numbered list, Word automatically indents it. To remove the indent, or indent the list further, follow these steps. This method also works for other kinds of lists and for normal text.

1 SELECTING THE LIST

● If the list is not already highlighted, begin by doing so. Don't worry if the numbers themselves aren't highlighted. This is because Word treats them differently from regular text.

2 CHANGING THE INDENT

● Move the cursor up to the Formatting toolbar and click on the **Decrease Indent** button.

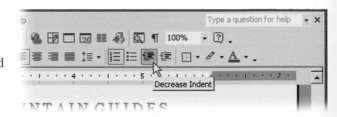

● The whole list moves to the left, aligning with the text above it.
● If you want to increase, rather than decrease, the indent, click on the **Increase Indent** button, which is to the right of the **Decrease Indent** button.

125 ❸❽ Decrease Indent

125 ❸❾ Increase Indent

BULLETED LISTS

Even when the lines in a list do not need to be numbered, you may still wish to emphasize the entries. Word offers a range of bulleted lists suited to different purposes. For example, you might use check marks for a list of completed tasks.

1 SELECTING THE LIST

● Begin by highlighting the list that you wish to bullet.

● Select **Bullets and Numbering** from the **Format** menu in the toolbar □.

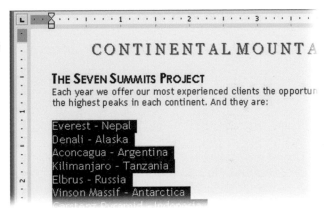

2 SELECTING THE BULLETED TAB

● In the **Bullets and Numbering** menu, click on the **Bulleted** tab to bring it to the front.

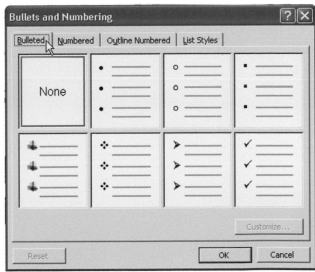

210 **Select Bullets and Numbering**

3 SELECTING THE BULLET STYLE

● There are several bullet styles that you can use, but in this example we are selecting the option next to **None**. Now click on **OK**.

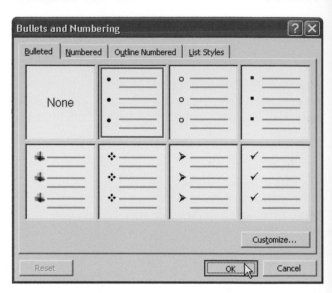

● The list now has a bullet at the start of each line, and you can change the indent, if you want to, as before.

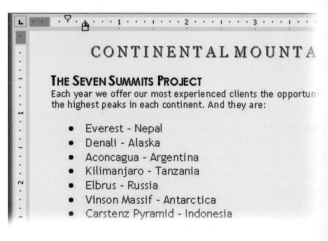

QUICK LISTS

If you are happy with the default style of numbering or bullet size, there is a quick way to produce a numbered or bulleted list. Once you have typed in the list of items, highlight the list, and then click on either the **Numbering** button ⃞ or the **Bullets** button ⃞ in the Formatting toolbar.

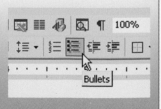

125 **❸⑥ Numbered List**

125 **❸⑦ Bulleted List**

CREATING A TABBED LIST

Microsoft Word includes the facility to set out text or figures in neat tables, but for small amounts of information it can often be easier to create columns by turning the entries into a tabbed list, using the **Tabs** menu to format the page.

1 INSERTING TABS BETWEEN ITEMS

● Type a list of items and press the [Tab⇆] key between each item on each line. With the Formatting Marks turned on, the tab mark (the right-pointing arrow) shows where each tab has been inserted.

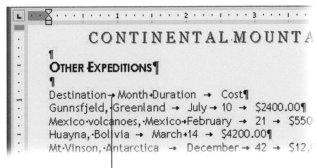

●Tab marks indicate where a tab has been inserted

2 BRINGING UP THE TABS DIALOG BOX

● Take a look at the list and decide which is the longest left-hand entry. In this case it is the entry for Mexico, at just over 1.5 inches wide.

● Ignoring the line of headings for the moment, highlight the rest of the list.

● Click on **Format** in the Menu bar, and choose **Tabs**.

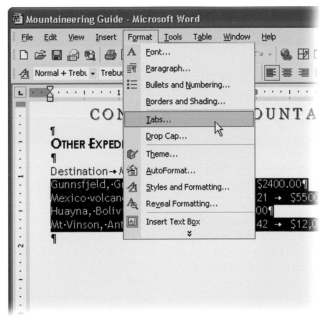

3 SETTING A TAB STOP POSITION

● The **Tabs** dialog box opens. Given the length of the Mexico destination, we are going to set the first column at 2.25 inches, so in the **Tab stop position** box type **2.25**. Now click on **Set**, and then click on **OK**.

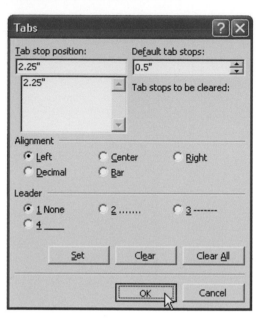

● A tab stop appears in the ruler at the 2.25-inch position, and the left-hand edges of the months are now lined up in a column.

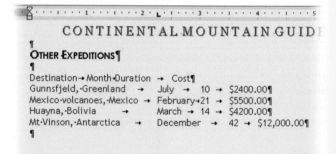

4 SETTING THE NEXT TAB STOP

● With the list still highlighted, follow the same steps to set another tab at 3.25 inches. The numbers of the duration are now lined up.

5 SETTING A DECIMAL TAB

● So far we've only used a left tab, that is, the items are lined up down their left-hand side. The cost figures would look better lined up down their right-hand side, so we will use a decimal tab.

● With the list highlighted, open the **Tabs** dialog box again. Set a tab at 4.5 inches and click on the **Decimal** radio button.

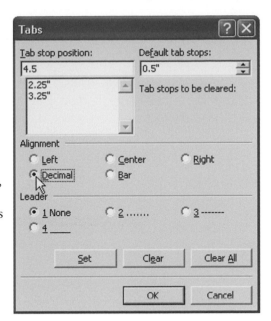

● Click on **Set** and then on **OK**. A decimal tab stop appears on the ruler, and the prices are now aligned down the decimal point at the 4.5-inch position.

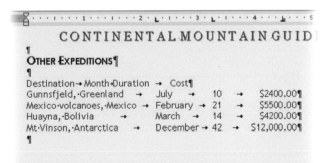

REMOVING A TAB SETTING FROM THE RULER

A quick way to remove a tab setting is first to highlight the text that contains the tab. Place the mouse cursor on the ruler tab setting that you want to remove, and hold the mouse button down. The vertical alignment line appears, but all you need to do is to drag the tab symbol down off the ruler and release the mouse button. The tab disappears.

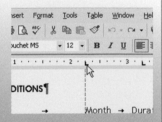

SETTING TABS BY THE RULER

As is the case with many of the functions in Microsoft® Word, there is more than one way of setting tabs. Using the ruler provides a more visual method than the **Tabs** dialog box, and allows you to make quick adjustments until you are satisfied.

1 SETTING THE FIRST TAB IN THE RULER

● The headings above the list still need aligning over their respective columns. Highlight that line and click on the ruler at the 2.25-inch mark. A left tab appears on the ruler.

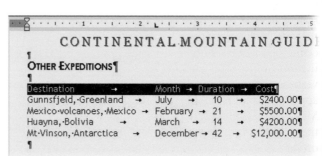

● The **Destination** heading remains aligned to the left, but the **Month** heading now lines up with the months below it.

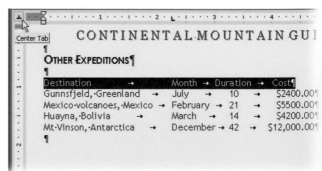

2 SELECTING A CENTER TAB

● With the line of headings still highlighted, click on the **Left Tab** symbol at the left-hand end of the ruler. The symbol for a **Center Tab** appears. This tab has the effect of centering text on the tab.

3 SETTING THE CENTER TAB

● Click on the ruler at the 3.25-inch mark. A center tab is set and the word **Duration** is almost centered above the list of the numbers of days.

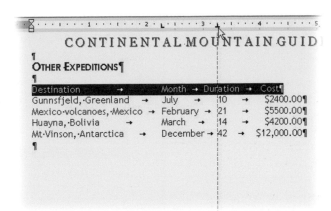

4 FINE TUNING THE SETTING

● The word **Duration** looks slightly left of center, so move the cursor up to the ruler, place it over the center tab, and hold down the mouse button. A dotted vertical alignment line now appears down the screen. Move the cursor slightly to the right until this line falls on the second digit column.

● Release the mouse button, and the heading now looks centered over the column of numbers.

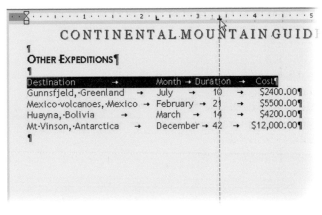

5 SELECTING A RIGHT TAB

- Finally, click through the options of the tab button at the left-hand end of the ruler until the **Right Tab** symbol appears.

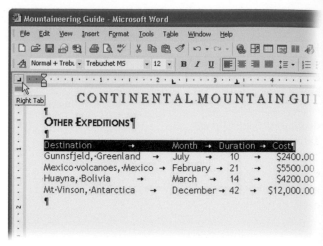

6 SETTING THE RIGHT TAB

- Click on the ruler at about the 4.75-inch mark. The end of the word **Cost** is now aligned with the trailing zeroes of the amounts in the column.

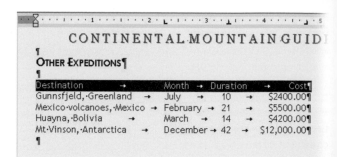

7 CHECKING THE EFFECT

- The right tab lines up the right-hand end of the text. To see the effect, change **Cost** to **Cost/person**. The words move to the left as you type, and the end of "person" is aligned with the zeroes. The effect is clearer with the formatting marks turned off ⌐.

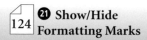

8 ADDING LEADERS BETWEEN ITEMS

● One way of making it easier to read across tabbed columns is to add a leader between each one.

● Highlight the list of destinations and click on **Tabs** in the **Format** menu. The **Tabs** dialog box opens. Click on the radio button next to 2......., and then click on **Set**.

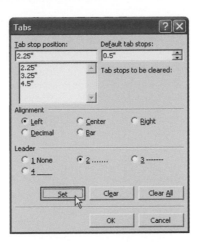

● Now highlight **3.25"** in the **Tab stop position** list of tabs, click on the radio button next to 2....... again, and then click on **Set**.

● Repeat this process for the 4.5" tab position and click on **OK**. The list of expeditions now has rows of leaders to make the list more readable.

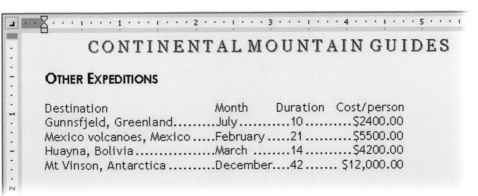

USING MULTIPLE COLUMNS

We have looked at ways of turning lists into columns, but there are times when continuous text benefits from being set in columns, too. This can give the page a newspaper like appearance, and can be useful in newsletters and pamphlets.

1 CHOOSING THE COLUMNS OPTION

● In this example, the Mountain Guides brochure includes a section on rented accommodation, which we are going to set in columns.

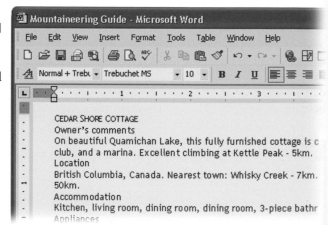

● Begin by highlighting the text that you want to be laid out in columns.
● Then click on **Format** in the Menu bar and choose **Columns** from the drop-down menu.

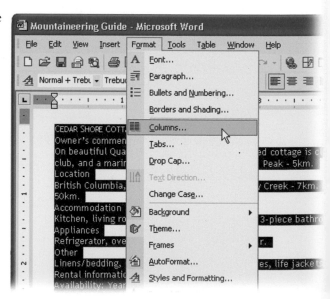

2 SET THE NUMBER OF COLUMNS

● The **Columns** dialog box opens. Click on box **Three** in the **Presets** section of the dialog box to select three columns.

● The preview panel shows how the text will look.

● Click on **OK**, and the selected text is now set out in three columns, with the default space of 0.5 inches between them.

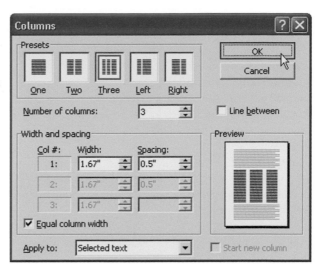

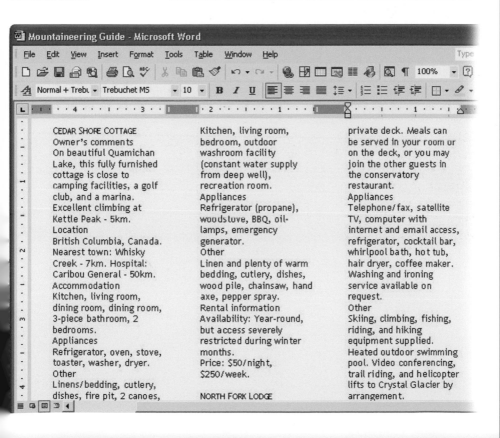

CEDAR SHORE COTTAGE
Owner's comments
On beautiful Quamichan
Lake, this fully furnished
cottage is close to
camping facilities, a golf
club, and a marina.
Excellent climbing at
Kettle Peak - 5km.
Location
British Columbia, Canada.
Nearest town: Whisky
Creek - 7km. Hospital:
Caribou General - 50km.
Accommodation
Kitchen, living room,
dining room, dining room,
3-piece bathroom, 2
bedrooms.
Appliances
Refrigerator, oven, stove,
toaster, washer, dryer.
Other
Linens/bedding, cutlery,
dishes, fire pit, 2 canoes,

Kitchen, living room,
bedroom, outdoor
washroom facility
(constant water supply
from deep well),
recreation room.
Appliances
Refrigerator (propane),
woodstove, BBQ, oil-
lamps, emergency
generator.
Other
Linen and plenty of warm
bedding, cutlery, dishes,
wood pile, chainsaw, hand
axe, pepper spray.
Rental information
Availability: Year-round,
but access severely
restricted during winter
months.
Price: $50/night,
$250/week.

NORTH FORK LODGE

private deck. Meals can
be served in your room or
on the deck, or you may
join the other guests in
the conservatory
restaurant.
Appliances
Telephone/fax, satellite
TV, computer with
internet and email access,
refrigerator, cocktail bar,
whirlpool bath, hot tub,
hair dryer, coffee maker.
Washing and ironing
service available on
request.
Other
Skiing, climbing, fishing,
riding, and hiking
equipment supplied.
Heated outdoor swimming
pool. Video conferencing,
trail riding, and helicopter
lifts to Crystal Glacier by
arrangement.

3 INSERTING COLUMN BREAKS

● The information would be clearer if each column began with a new entry. This can be done by using column breaks.

● Place the cursor at the point in the text where you would like to start a new column, click on **Insert** in the Menu bar, and choose **Break** from the menu.

● The **Break** dialog box opens. Click on the radio button next to **Column break** and click on **OK**.

● By using this method, each column can begin with a new entry.

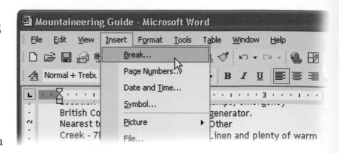

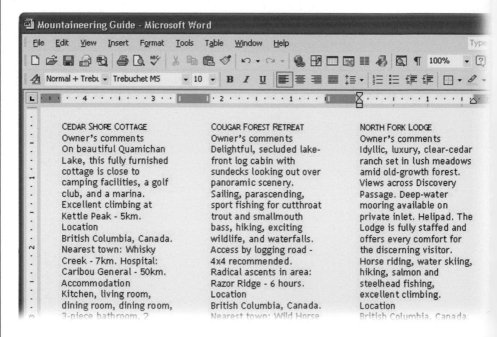

CEDAR SHORE COTTAGE
Owner's comments
On beautiful Quamichan Lake, this fully furnished cottage is close to camping facilities, a golf club, and a marina. Excellent climbing at Kettle Peak - 5km.
Location
British Columbia, Canada. Nearest town: Whisky Creek - 7km. Hospital: Caribou General - 50km.
Accommodation
Kitchen, living room, dining room, dining room, 3-piece bathroom, 2

COUGAR FOREST RETREAT
Owner's comments
Delightful, secluded lake-front log cabin with sundecks looking out over panoramic scenery. Sailing, parascending, sport fishing for cutthroat trout and smallmouth bass, hiking, exciting wildlife, and waterfalls. Access by logging road - 4x4 recommended. Radical ascents in area: Razor Ridge - 6 hours.
Location
British Columbia, Canada. Nearest town: Wild Horse

NORTH FORK LODGE
Owner's comments
Idyllic, luxury, clear-cedar ranch set in lush meadows amid old-growth forest. Views across Discovery Passage. Deep-water mooring available on private inlet. Helipad. The Lodge is fully staffed and offers every comfort for the discerning visitor. Horse riding, water skiing, hiking, salmon and steelhead fishing, excellent climbing.
Location
British Columbia, Canada.

4 INSERTING VERTICAL LINES

● Rather than having blank spaces between columns, you can insert a vertical line between them. Place the cursor anywhere in the columns, open the **Columns** dialog box 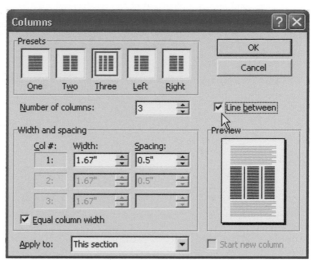, and click in the **Line between** check box.

● Click on **OK** and the columns are now separated by a vertical line, which helps lead the eye in the same way that we saw earlier with tab leaders.

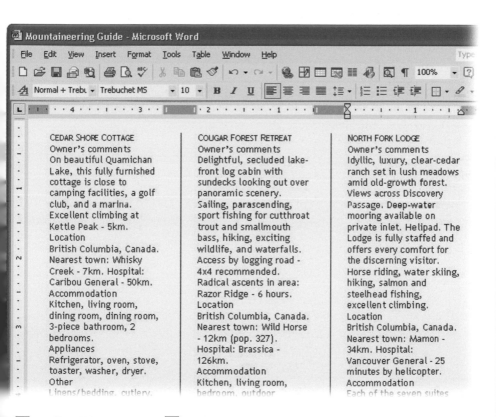

CEDAR SHORE COTTAGE
Owner's comments
On beautiful Quamichan Lake, this fully furnished cottage is close to camping facilities, a golf club, and a marina. Excellent climbing at Kettle Peak - 5km.
Location
British Columbia, Canada. Nearest town: Whisky Creek - 7km. Hospital: Caribou General - 50km.
Accommodation
Kitchen, living room, dining room, dining room, 3-piece bathroom, 2 bedrooms.
Appliances
Refrigerator, oven, stove, toaster, washer, dryer.
Other
Linens/bedding, cutlery,

COUGAR FOREST RETREAT
Owner's comments
Delightful, secluded lake-front log cabin with sundecks looking out over panoramic scenery. Sailing, parascending, sport fishing for cutthroat trout and smallmouth bass, hiking, exciting wildlife, and waterfalls. Access by logging road - 4x4 recommended. Radical ascents in area: Razor Ridge - 6 hours.
Location
British Columbia, Canada. Nearest town: Wild Horse - 12km (pop. 327). Hospital: Brassica - 126km.
Accommodation
Kitchen, living room, bedroom, outdoor

NORTH FORK LODGE
Owner's comments
Idyllic, luxury, clear-cedar ranch set in lush meadows amid old-growth forest. Views across Discovery Passage. Deep-water mooring available on private inlet. Helipad. The Lodge is fully staffed and offers every comfort for the discerning visitor. Horse riding, water skiing, hiking, salmon and steelhead fishing, excellent climbing.
Location
British Columbia, Canada. Nearest town: Mamon - 34km. Hospital: Vancouver General - 25 minutes by helicopter.
Accommodation
Each of the seven suites

222 **Choosing the Columns Option**

221 **Adding Leaders Between Items**

USING STYLE SHEETS

This chapter deals with style sheets, a feature of Word that enables you to define many aspects of the style of each kind of text and apply the defined styles throughout your document.

THE POWER OF THE STYLE SHEET

Style sheets are one of the most powerful – and least understood – features of Word. Each style sheet is a list of formatting instructions, or styles, that can be applied to text. Every document is based on a style sheet. When you open a new document by clicking on the **New Blank Document** button in the Standard toolbar, Word automatically bases it on the normal style sheet, which is why the word **Normal** appears in the **Style** box at the end of the Formatting toolbar.

DEFINING FEATURES
A style sheet can define many features of a section of text. These include the font, and its size, color, and effects; the shape of a paragraph as determined by indents, spacing, and how page breaks are controlled; the position and alignment of tabs; what borders and shading are used, if any; and how bullets and numbering are styled. The smallest unit to which a style sheet can be applied is a paragraph, which need only be one line that ends with a paragraph mark.

CHOOSING ELEMENTS
To apply styles sensibly to a document, first identify the various parts of the text that play different roles. For example in a book, the title, the table of contents, main text, captions, and index all play different roles, and can all be styled differently. The styles can be set in separate style sheets and applied.

SAVING TIME
Once a style sheet has been created, any changes that you make to that sheet are automatically applied to all parts of your document that are based on that style.

CEDAR SHORE COTTAGE

Owner's comments
On beautiful Quamichan Lake, this fully furnished cottage is close to camping facilities, a golf club, and a marina. Excellent climbing at Kettle Peak - 5km.

Location
British Columbia, Canada. Nearest town: Whisky Creek - 7km. Hospital: Caribou General - 50km.

Accommodation
Kitchen, living room, dining

Styled text
Using a style sheet, a defined font, type size, and indent has been applied to every instance of this kind of text each time it appears in the document.

CREATING A NEW STYLE SHEET

Style sheets come into their own when applied to a document in which the information falls into various categories, and in which these categories are used repeatedly. In the example below, each entry in the directory contains the same categories of information, such as **Owner's comments**, **Location**, and **Accommodation**.

1 SELECTING THE TEXT

● The list of cabins and their details has all been formatted in Trebuchet 10 pt. Now, new styles are going to be designed for each part of the details of the properties, starting with the name of the property.
● Highlight the name of the first property and click on **Styles and Formatting** in the **Format** drop-down menu on the toolbar.

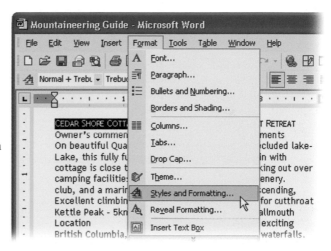

2 OPENING A NEW STYLE OPTION

● The **Styles and Formatting** task pane appears at the right-hand side of your screen.
● Any formatting previously created in the document will be listed, but we are going to create a new style so click on the **New Style** button.

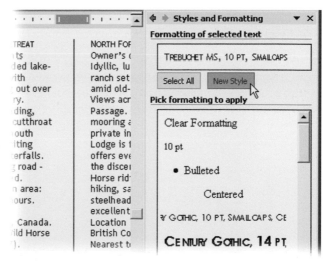

3 NAMING THE STYLE

● The **New Style** dialog box now opens. The first task is to name the new style that we are creating, so type **Accommodation Name** in the **Name** box. A descriptive name will help you to know which style to choose when styling text at a later date.

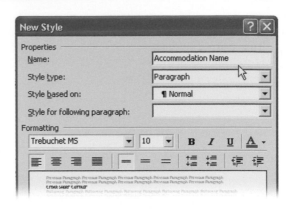

4 CHOOSING THE FONT

● Now click on **Format** at the bottom left-hand corner of the **New Style** dialog box, and click on **Font** in the pop-up menu that appears.

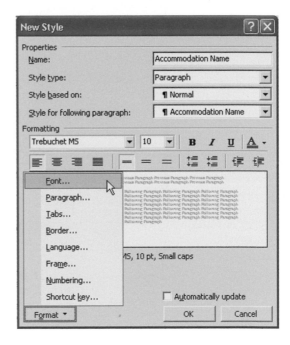

● The **Font** dialog box opens. This box offers you a range of possibilities for changing the appearance of the font, including the font itself, its style (Italic etc.), and its size.

● In the **Font** selection box choose **Century Gothic**, and then select **Bold** in the **Font style** selection box. You will see that the text is now shown in this font in the **Preview** panel.

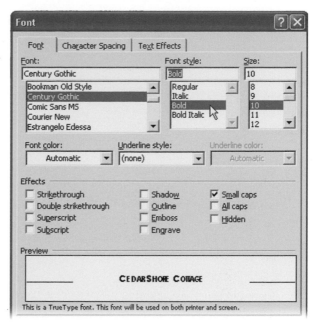

5 CHANGING THE FONT SIZE

● In the **Size** selection box choose **12**. Again, the text in the preview panel now reflects this change.

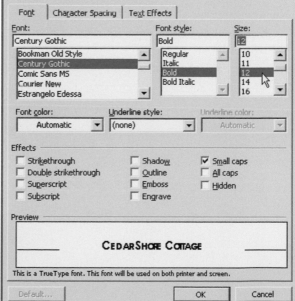

● Our Accommodation Name was already set as small caps in the original document, but if you wish to make this change at this stage, simply click on the **Small caps** check box of the **Effects** section. This has the effect of turning all the lower-case letters into small capital letters. Any of the Effects can be applied to the text you have selected.

● Click on **OK**.

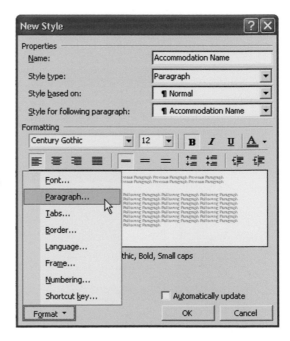

6 INTRODUCING SPACE AFTER

● The appearance of the text on the page would be improved if there were a small space between the name and the text that follows it.

● Click on **Format** in the **New Style** dialog box and then click on **Paragraph** in the pop-up menu.

● The **Paragraph** dialog box opens. In the **Spacing** section, click once on the up arrow to the right of the **After** box. The figure of **6 pt** appears in the panel, meaning that a 6 point space will be inserted after the property name.

● Click on **OK** to close the **Paragraph** dialog box.

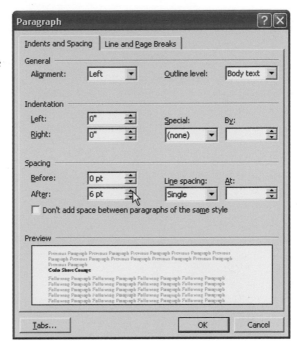

● The **New Style** dialog box now reappears. A description of the new formatting that has been chosen is shown beneath the preview panel.

● Click on **OK** to close the **New Style** dialog box and save this new style.

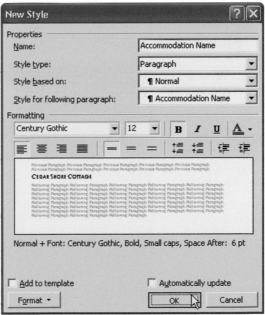

7 APPLYING THE NEW STYLE

● Click on **Accommodation Name**, which has now appeared in the formatting list in the **Styles and Formatting** task pane.

● The new style is now applied to the name of the property, and the **Style** panel at the top left of the screen indicates the name of the text style.

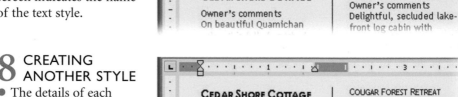

8 CREATING ANOTHER STYLE

● The details of each property are divided into sections, and a style is needed for the section heads. Highlight the words **Owner's comments**. Choose **Styles and Formatting** from the **Format** menu and click on **New Style** in the **Styles and Formatting** task pane to open the **New Style** dialog box. We are going to call this style **Section Head**.

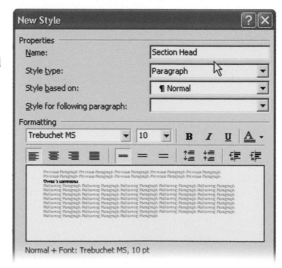

● Click on **Format** in the bottom left corner of the **New Style** dialog box, and again click on **Font** to open the **Font** dialog box.
● Keep **Trebuchet MS** as the font and choose **Bold Italic** in the **Font style** selection box. Click on **OK**.

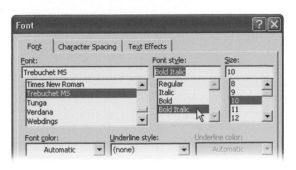

● The **New Style** dialog box reappears. Click on **Format**, select **Paragraph** to open the **Paragraph** dialog box, and in the **Spacing After** box type **2**. This will introduce a small space after the heading. Click on **OK** to close the **Paragraph** dialog box.

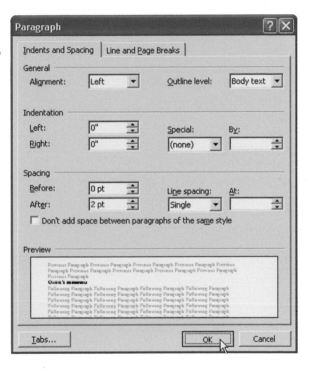

● Click on **OK** in the **New Style** dialog box and click on **Section Head** in the **Styles and Formatting** task pane. The section heading now has the required style.

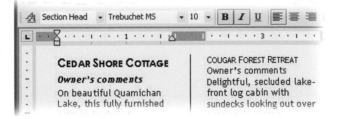

9 STYLING THE MAIN TEXT

● The text of each section needs its own style, so click in the paragraph below the newly styled **Owner's comments** to position the insertion point in this text. From the **Format** menu in the toolbar choose **Styles and Formatting** and then click on **New Style** in the **Styles and Formatting** Task Pane to open the **New Style** dialog box. Call this style **Section Details**.

● Click on **Format** and select **Font** to open the **Font** dialog box. This time choose **Trebuchet MS** and make it **9** pt. Click on **OK** to return to the **New Style** box.

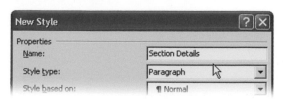

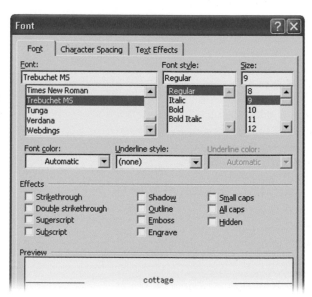

INDENTING THE TEXT

● The text will stand out more if it is indented. From the **Format** pop-up menu choose **Paragraph** and in the **Indentation** section of the **Paragraph** dialog box click on the up arrow of the **Left** box. The figure of **0.1"** appears.

● To add space between this text and the next paragraph, in the **Spacing** section change the **After** box to **4pt**. Click on **OK**.

● Click **OK** again in the **New Style** box, click on **Section Details** in the **Styles and Formatting** task pane to apply the style, and the selected text, in the chosen font and size, is now indented. Close the task pane by clicking on the **X** in the top right corner.

APPLYING YOUR STYLE SHEETS

● Highlight the name of the second property at the top of the second column.
● Click on the arrow to the right of the **Style** selection box at the top left corner of the screen, and move the cursor down to **Accommodation Name** in the drop-down menu that appears. (The other styles in the **Style** menu shown here may not be identical to those in your **Style** menu.

● Click on **Accommodation Name** and that style is applied to the second accommodation name.

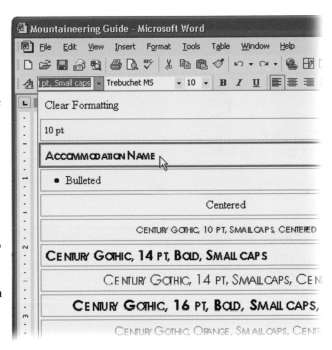

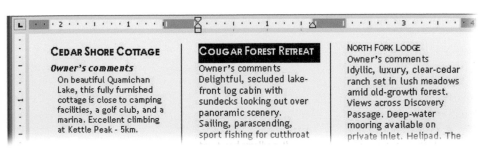

● Highlight **Owner's comments** beneath it, and select **Section Head** from the **Style** selection box.

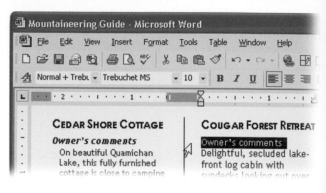

● Click on **Section Head** and the style is applied to the heading.

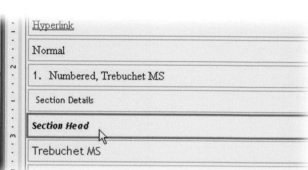

Text now changes to Section Head style

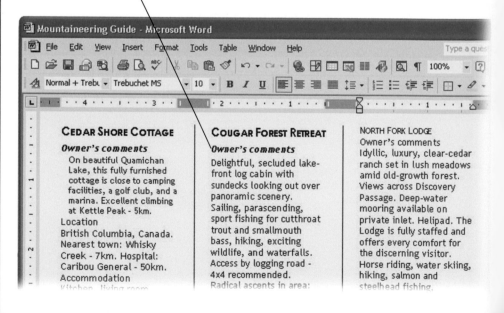

● Highlight the text beneath that heading and select **Section Details** from the style list.

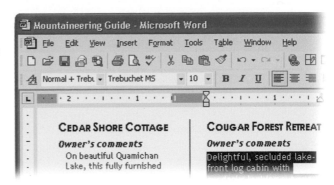

● Click on this panel and the style is applied to the selected text.
● Follow these steps to apply the style sheets to all the text throughout your document.

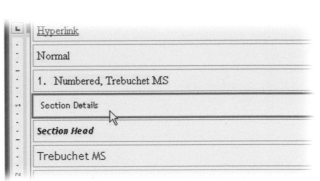

Text now changes to Section Details style ●

USING FORMAT PAINTER TO APPLY STYLES

We have seen how to create style sheets and apply them to all the text throughout a document, but this last process can be laborious if the text is extensive. Luckily, Word offers a solution – Format Painter enables you to do the job much faster.

1 STYLING THE PROPERTY NAME

● Highlight the property name at the top of the second column and make sure that you include the paragraph mark because this contains all the style details for the paragraph. (You can turn on the Formatting Marks to ensure that the paragraph mark is highlighted ⌐.)

● Click on the **Format Painter** icon in the Standard toolbar ⌐.

● Your cursor now has a paintbrush icon next to it. Go to the property name at the top of the third column and highlight it.

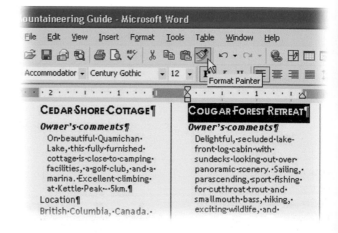

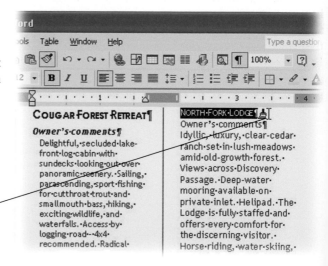

Paintbrush icon ●

● Release the mouse button, and the text is now styled in the selected style.

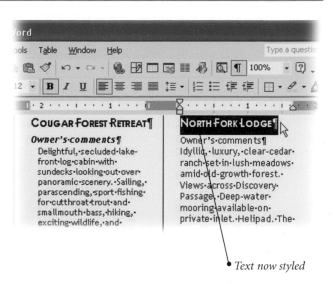

Text now styled

2 STYLING THE SECTION HEADS

● Select **Owner's comments** near the top of the first paragraph and double-click on the **Format Painter** button. You can now "paint" all the section heads in the text with the **Section Head** style ⌐. Press the [Esc] key, or click on the **Format Painter** button again when you have produced this result.

Styled Section Head

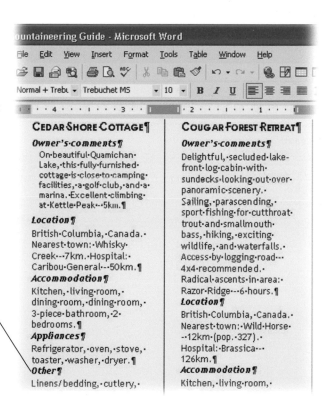

3 STYLING THE SECTION DETAILS

- Finally, highlight the first paragraph in the first column that has been formatted with the **Section Details** style, double-click on the **Format Painter** button and apply the style to all the remaining unstyled paragraphs.

- The document should now look like the one below, with all text in the chosen styles.

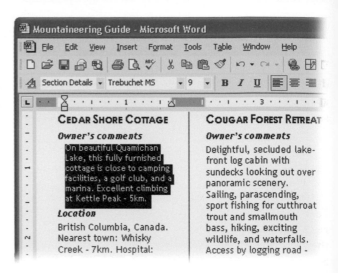

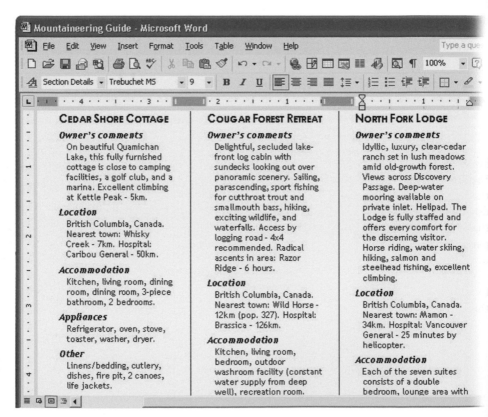

MAKING ONE STYLE FOLLOW ANOTHER

Once you have decided that one style is always to be followed by a second specific style, you can instruct Word always to follow the first style with the second. Begin by clicking on **Format** in the Menu bar and selecting **Styles and Formatting**.

1 SELECTING THE FIRST STYLE

● In the **Styles and Formatting** task pane, right-click on the first of the two styles, in this case **Section Head**, and select **Modify** from the drop-down menu that appears.

Chosen style

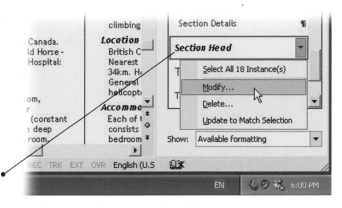

2 SELECTING THE SECOND STYLE

● The **Modify Style** dialog box opens. The first style, **Section Head**, appears in the **Name** box. Click on the down arrow to the right of the **Style for following paragraph** box to drop down the list of styles.
● Click on the style that is to follow the first style, in this case **Section Details**.

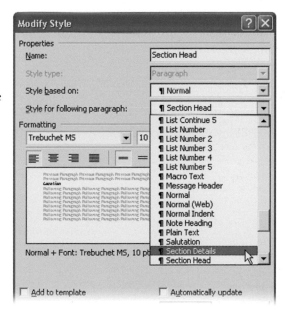

3 SAVING THE CHANGES

- **Section Details** appears in the **Style for following paragraph** box.
- Click on **OK**, and the **Modify Style** dialog box closes. Close the task pane to complete the changes.
- On each occasion now when **Section Head** is used as a style and the Enter← key is pressed, the following text will be formatted with the **Section Details** style.

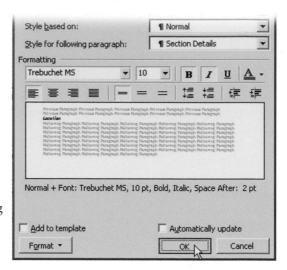

STYLING FROM A TEXT SELECTION

So far we have created styles by choosing each of the features for the style through the **Styles and Formatting** task pane.

Another method is to begin by formatting a paragraph with all the style features that you want to put into a style sheet.

1 FORMATTING THE TEXT

- In this example, the following formatting has been applied to the text:

Font: *Comic Sans MS, Bold*
Font size: *18 pt*
Font color: *Red*
Space after: *12 pt*
Border setting: *Shadow*
Border style: *Thin-thick*
Border color: *Tan*
Shading: *Light Yellow*
Text: *Centered*
Right indent: *3.77 inches*

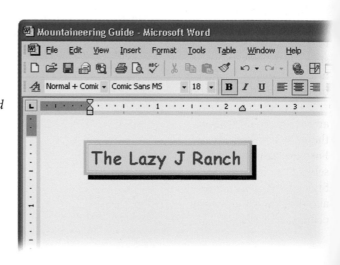

2 FROM A FORMAT TO A STYLE

● Highlight the text that you have formatted, click on **Format** in the Menu bar, select **Styles and Formatting** to open the Style box, and click on **New Style** in the Task Pane.

● Word has picked up the formatting specifications of the selected text and these are shown in the description section of this dialog box. Certain elements are not shown only because the box is too small for them all. Enter a name for the new style (here the name **Lazy J** has been chosen). Click on **OK** to close the **New Style** dialog box.

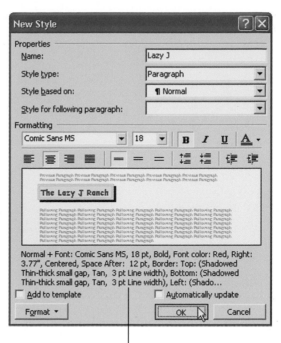

Formatting specifications •

3 USING THE NEW STYLE

● The **Styles and Formatting** Task Pane reappears with the new style listed. This style is now available to be applied quickly to any chosen text.

● To modify this style or any other, right-click on the style in the **Styles and Formatting** task pane and select **Modify**. The **Modify Style** dialog box opens, allowing you to make any changes you wish.

USING EXCEL

THE ESSENTIAL FEATURES of Excel are presented in this section in separate chapters to allow easy understanding of their functions. Before you can do anything sophisticated with Excel, you need to know how to enter data correctly into worksheet cells. You also need to know how to change or correct this data; how to copy and move data within the worksheet; and how to insert, clear, and delete cells. The majority of this section consists of instructions for performing these essential, simple tasks. Some basic examples run through the book, and it may be difficult to keep track of these if you skip any sections. Please note that the examples we have shown are designed to illustrate various specific techniques, and do not necessarily reflect typical worksheet uses or design.

MICROSOFT EXCEL

Excel belongs to the group of computer applications known as spreadsheets, and the first spreadsheet program started the process of making computers an indispensable business tool.

WHAT CAN EXCEL DO?

Storing spreadsheet data is only the beginning as far as Excel is concerned. The wide range of features it contains let you manipulate and present your data in almost any way you choose. Excel can be an accounts program; it can be used as a sophisticated calculator capable of utilizing complex mathematical formulas; it can also be a diary, a scheduler, and more. Used in combination with

Microsoft Word, Excel's database features make creating mailing lists and personalized letters very easy. Excel's presentation facilities use color, borders, and different fonts to emphasize data. A variety of charts is available, which can be selected to suit the kind of data being presented. For storing, manipulating, and presenting data, Microsoft Excel offers an unrivaled range of possibilities.

WHAT IS A WORKSHEET?

At the heart of Excel is a two-dimensional grid of data storage spaces called a worksheet (right). This is where you input the data that you want to store, manipulate, or analyze. The individual spaces are called worksheet cells. To begin with, all the cells are empty. As you put data into the cells, you build and develop the individual worksheets.

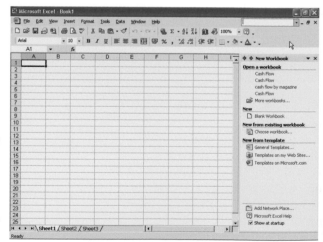

LAUNCHING EXCEL

Approaching a new program for the first time can be a daunting experience because you don't know what to expect. However, new programs are learned one step at a time and the first step is the simple one of launching Excel from your desktop.

1 LAUNCHING WITH THE START MENU

● So, let's get going. First you need to launch Excel.
● If you are running Windows XP, click on the **Start** button at bottom left, and then choose **All Programs** from the pop-up list. **Microsoft Excel** should appear in the submenu to the right (or it may be within a Microsoft Office Program group). Highlight the Excel bar and click with the mouse.
● The Excel window appears onscreen ◌.

2 LAUNCHING WITH A SHORTCUT

● If there is already a shortcut to Excel on your Desktop, just double-click on the shortcut icon.
● The Excel window appears onscreen ◌.

THE EXCEL WINDOW

Soon after you launch Microsoft Excel, a window called **Microsoft Excel – Book1** appears. At the center of the window is a worksheet – a grid of blank rectangular cells. Letters and numbers label the columns and rows of the grid. Each cell has an address (such as E3), which is the column and row in which it is found.

THE EXCEL WINDOW

1 Title bar
Title of the active workbook.
2 Menu bar
Contains the main menus for frequently used commands.
3 Formula bar
What you enter in the active cell also appears here.
4 Standard toolbar
These buttons carry out frequently used actions.
5 Formatting toolbar
Options for changing data presentation.
6 Column header buttons
Click on the header button to select the whole column.
7 Row header buttons
Click on the row header to select the entire row.
8 Active cell
Whatever you type appears in the active cell.
9 Worksheet tabs
Workbooks contain worksheets – click to select one.

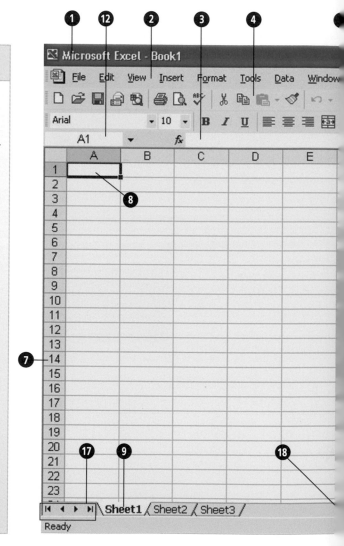

256 Selecting Worksheet Cells

258 Selecting a Single Row

270 Formulas and Calculations

THE EXCEL TASK PANE

20 Task Pane arrow
Scrolls through the various task pane commands.
21 Open tasks
Opens recent workbooks.

22 "New from" task
Base new workbook on existing.
23 Templates
Load ready-made worksheets from your PC or the internet.

To hide the Task Pane and increase the usable screen area, click on **View** in the toolbar and uncheck the box next to **Task Pane**.

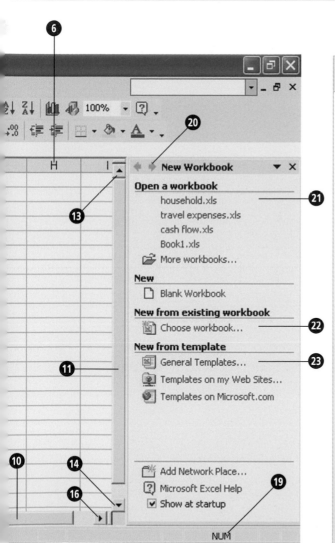

THE EXCEL WINDOW

10 Horizontal scroll bar
To scroll horizontally through the worksheet.
11 Vertical scroll bar
To scroll vertically through the worksheet.
12 Name box
Gives the address of the active cell.
13 Scroll-up arrow
Moves up the worksheet.
14 Scroll-down arrow
Moves down the worksheet.
15 Left-scroll arrow
Scrolls the sheet to the left.
16 Right-scroll arrow
Scrolls the sheet to the right.
17 Tab scrolling buttons
Scroll through the sheets if they cannot all be displayed.
18 Tab split box
Click and drag to show tabs or to increase the scroll bar.
19 NUM lock
Shows that the numeric keypad on the right of the keyboard is on.

THE TWO MAIN EXCEL TOOLBARS

Many of the actions, or commands, that you want to perform on data can be carried out by clicking on toolbar buttons. When you launch Excel, the Standard toolbar and the Formatting toolbar are the usual toolbars displayed. They contain buttons whose actions are described below. The Standard toolbar contains buttons for actions as diverse as opening a new workbook or undoing an action. The Formatting toolbar contains buttons for changing the worksheet's appearance.

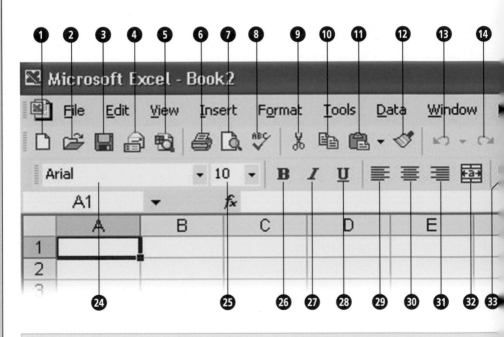

BUTTON FUNCTIONS

- ❶ New workbook
- ❷ Open file
- ❸ Save workbook
- ❹ Email workbook/sheet
- ❺ Search
- ❻ Print
- ❼ Print preview
- ❽ Spelling checker
- ❾ Cut
- ❿ Copy
- ⓫ Paste
- ⓬ Format painter
- ⓭ Undo action(s)
- ⓮ Redo action(s)
- ⓯ Insert hyperlink
- ⓰ AutoSum
- ⓱ Sort ascending
- ⓲ Sort descending
- ⓳ Chart wizard
- ⓴ Drawing toolbar
- ㉑ Zoom view
- ㉒ Help
- ㉓ Help box
- ㉔ Font selector

254 | Opening a New Workbook

281 | Copying and Pasting

296 | Checking Spelling

CUSTOMIZING A TOOLBAR

Click the arrow at far right of the Formatting toolbar then on the arrow on the **Add or Remove Buttons** box that appears. A drop-down menu opens from which you can add or remove toolbar buttons.

ScreenTips

It isn't necessary to memorize all these buttons. Roll the cursor over a button, wait for a second, and a ScreenTip appears telling you the function of the button.

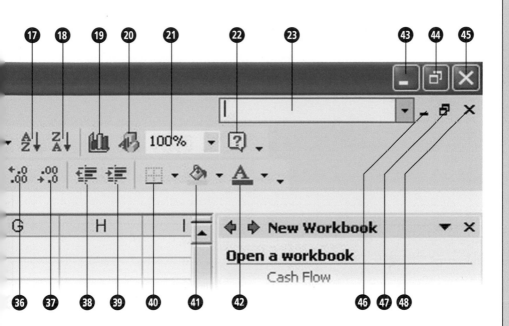

BUTTON FUNCTIONS

25 Font size selector	**33** Currency style	**41** Fill color
26 Bold	**34** Percent style	**42** Font color
27 Italic	**35** Comma style	**43** Minimize Excel
28 Underline	**36** Increase decimals	**44** Restore Excel
29 Align left	**37** Decrease decimals	**45** Close Excel
30 Center	**38** Decrease indent	**46** Minimize worksheet
31 Align right	**39** Increase indent	**47** Restore worksheet
32 Merge and center	**40** Add/remove borders	**48** Close worksheet

265 Entering Decimals

274 Adding a Border

275 Highlighting Information

NAMING, SAVING, AND FINDING WORKBOOKS

Anything you create using Microsoft Excel is stored on your computer as a file called a workbook. A workbook contains one or more separate worksheets. When you first start up Excel, you are presented with an unused workbook called Book1. This contains from three to 10 blank worksheets, depending on the version of Excel. The blank worksheets are initially called Sheet1, Sheet2, and so on.

1 RENAMING A WORKSHEET

● You can switch between worksheets by clicking on the tabs at the bottom of the workbook window. To begin with, the worksheets are all blank.

● Once you put data into a worksheet, you should give the worksheet a short name to indicate what it contains. Because all worksheets start with a default name (such as **Sheet1**), you are actually renaming the worksheet. Here's how to do it.

● Double-click on the existing name, so that it becomes highlighted.

● Type the new name and press Enter ↵.

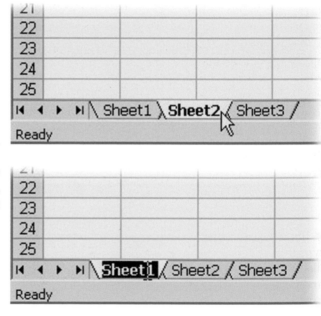

2 SAVING AND NAMING

• You should save your work frequently to your hard disk. When you save in Excel, you save the whole workbook containing the worksheet(s) that you have been developing.

• The first time you save a workbook, you should name it (actually rename it) at the same time.

• Choose **Save As** from the **File** menu.

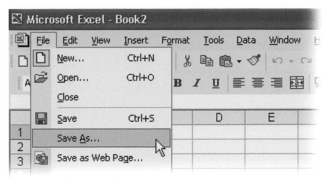

• The **Save As** dialog box appears. Your workbook will be saved in the folder displayed in the **Save in** box. In this instance, just accept the displayed folder. Remember the name of the folder in which you've saved the workbook.

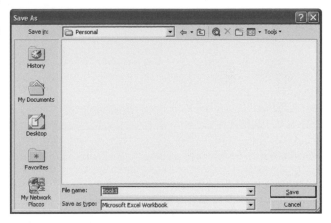

• In the **File name** box, type the name you would like to give your workbook, and then click on the **Save** button.

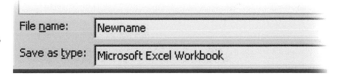

• On subsequent occasions when you want to save the workbook, just click the **Save** button on the Standard toolbar.

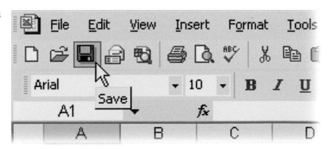

3 CLOSING A WORKBOOK

● Click the close button at top right.

● If you have made any changes since your last save, a box appears asking whether you want to save changes. Click **Yes** (or **No** if you do not wish to save any changes you've made).

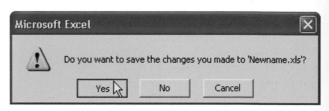

4 OPENING A NEW WORKBOOK

● Just click the **New** workbook button on the Standard toolbar.

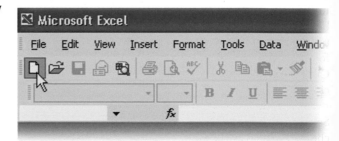

5 OPENING A SAVED WORKBOOK

● Click the **Open** button on the Standard toolbar

● In the **Open** dialog box, click on the workbook you want to open.

● Click on the **Open** button at the bottom right of the box.

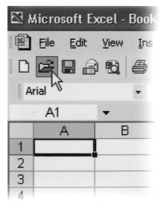

6 FINDING A SAVED WORKBOOK

- There will be occasions when you cannot find the workbook you want. Excel includes its own Search facility to help you when this happens.

- To find a workbook, begin by clicking on the **Search** button in the Standard toolbar.

- The **Basic Search** task pane opens. Click the arrow next to **Selected locations** and choose **My Documents** from the list. Click on the box next to **My Documents** until it appears as a pile of boxes with a tick on the top, to search all the sub-folders within the folder. Click the arrow again to close the menu.

- Click the arrow next to **Selected file types** and choose **Excel Files**.

- Click the **Search** button. All your Excel workbooks will appear in the **Search Results**. Double-click on the one you want to open.

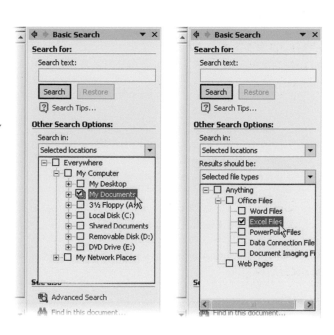

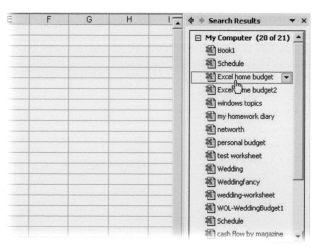

ENTERING DATA

The Excel program is based on the worksheet – a grid of individual boxes, or "cells," into which you enter data. You can then manipulate that data in various ways.

SELECTING WORKSHEET CELLS

Before performing any operation in Excel – for example, typing data into cells, coloring cells, or deleting them – you need to choose which cells you are going to perform the action on. This process is called cell selection and is a fundamental Excel skill. You can select a single cell, a block of cells, a horizontal row or vertical column, or several rows or columns at the same time. You can also select several groups of cells. When a group of cells is selected, they will appear in black, except for one cell, the "active cell" (see box below), which remains white. Try practicing these techniques following the instructions below.

1 SELECTING A SINGLE CELL
● Move the mouse pointer over your chosen cell and click the left mouse button.
● The thick black border that now appears around the cell indicates that it is selected, and this is now the active cell.

Active cell

ACTIVE CELLS

The significance of the active cell is that once you have made a selection, anything you type will appear only in the active cell. Other actions that you perform after selection (such as coloring cells or deleting them) will apply to all the cells in the selected area.

WHY SELECT MULTIPLE CELLS?

You select multiple cells most often to perform "block" activities such as formatting 🗋, inserting new columns, rows, and cells 🗋, clearing cells, or duplicating existing data 🗋 from a single cell to several cells. New data can be typed into cells only one cell at a time (in the outlined or "active" cell), but it sometimes saves time to select all the cells into which you are going to enter data before you start typing. You can easily move the active cell around in the selected area one cell at a time using the Tab⇆ key.

2 SELECTING A BLOCK OF CELLS

● A block can range from a few adjacent cells in a single row or column to a large rectangular area.
● Click on a cell at one end (or at one corner) of the block you wish to select.
● Hold down the ⇧ Shift key, and then click on the cell at the opposite end (or corner) of the block.

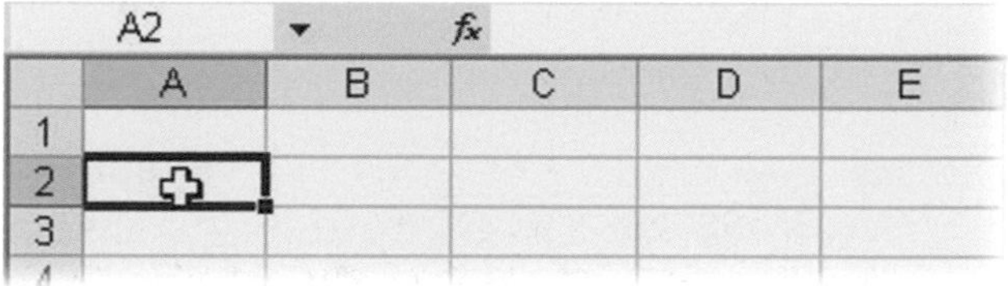

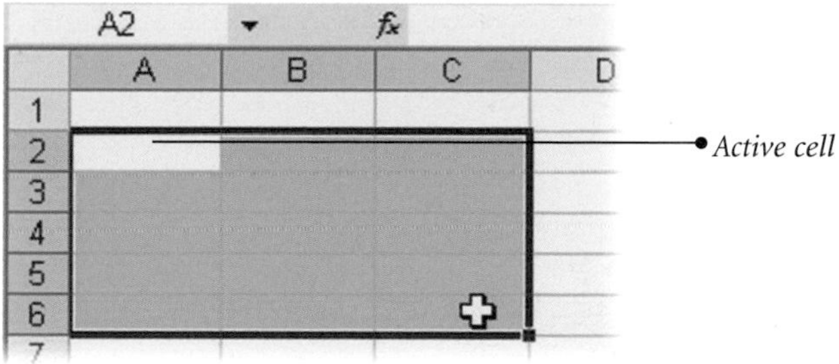

Active cell

3 SELECTING A SINGLE COLUMN

● Click on the column header button at the top of your chosen column.

Column header button

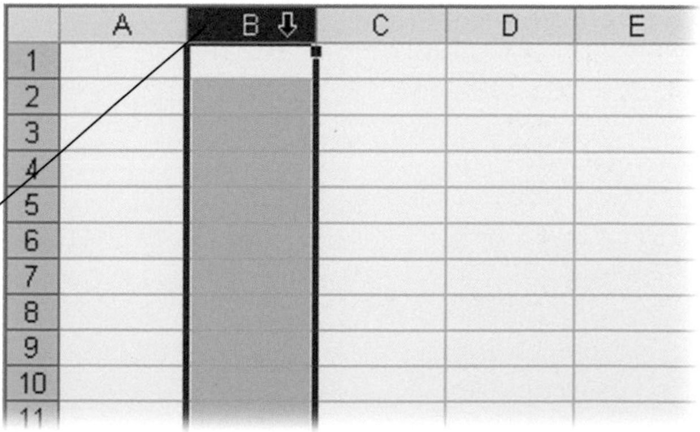

4 SELECTING A SINGLE ROW

● Click on the row header button to the left of your chosen row. This row will then be highlighted.

Row header button

5 SELECTING ROWS OR COLUMNS

● While holding down the left-hand mouse button, drag the mouse pointer across the header buttons for the columns or rows you wish to include, and then release the button.

6 SELECTING SEVERAL BLOCKS

● Select the first cell or block, hold down the [Ctrl] key, select the next cell or block, then select a third cell or block, and so on. Release the [Ctrl] key only when you have completed your selections.

Active cell

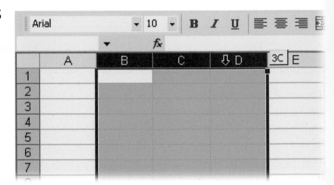

7 SELECTING ALL THE WORKSHEET

● Click on the top left corner of the border of the worksheet. This is called the **Select All** button. The whole of the worksheet will now be highlighted, and the top left cell is the active cell.

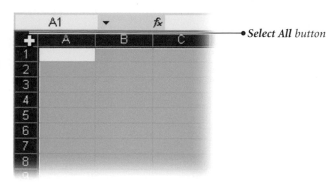

• *Select All button*

ENTERING TEXT

There are three categories of data that you can put into a worksheet – text, numbers, and formulas. Worksheets usually take a tabular form, and text is used most often as labels for the table's rows and columns. It makes sense to enter these text labels first, in order to provide a structure for the numerical data and formulas. To learn the techniques for entering data, you may find it helpful to follow a worked example. The example given here involves creating a sales worksheet for a small business, Fantasy Ices, that makes ice cream products. Alternatively, you can use the same methods for any worksheet you choose. To follow the example, open a new workbook and save it as **fantasyices.xls** 🗎. Rename Sheet1 in the workbook **Sales** 🗎.

1 SELECT THE FIRST CELL FOR TEXT

● Click on cell A2 to select this cell. Cell A2 is now the active cell and anything you type on the keyboard will appear in this cell. Note that **A2** appears in the name box to the top left of the worksheet.

• *Name box*

• *Active cell*

2 TYPING IN THE TEXT

● For the worked example, type the word **Product**. Note that a flashing bar, called the insertion point, stays just to the right of the last letter you typed, marking where the next letter you type will appear. Don't worry for now if you make typing mistakes.

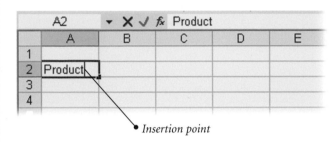

Insertion point

Oops... typing error

If you mistype a letter, press the ← Bksp key on your keyboard to delete the last letter you typed. If you want to start data entry into a cell from scratch, press the Esc key. Even if you have completed entering data, it's easy to change data later ⌐.

3 COMPLETE THE ENTRY

● Once you have typed your text, press Enter ←. This completes the data entry into the cell, and the active cell now moves down a single cell to A3.

A3	▼	ƒx		
	A	B	C	D	E
1					
2	Product				
3					
4					
5					
6					
7					

4 LABELS FOR ROW HEADINGS

● Into cell A3, type **Twizzlesticks** – this is the company's biggest product. Press Enter ←.
● Repeat the process by typing **Chokky bars**, **Orange sorbet**, and **Raspberry surprise** into cells A4, A5, and A6. These are the company's other three products. Press Enter ← after typing each of these text labels.

A3	▼ X ✓ ƒx Twizzlesticks
	A	B	C	D	E
1					
2	Product				
3	Twizzlesticks				

A6	▼ X ✓ ƒx Raspberry surprise
	A	B	C	D	E
1					
2	Product				
3	Twizzlesticks				
4	Chokky bars				
5	Orange sorbet				
6	Raspberry surprise				
7					

292 Changing Cell Contents

5 COLUMN HEADING TEXT

● Now add some further text labels as column headers for the numerical data you are going to enter into the worksheet.

● Select cells B2 to D2 (see page 256 to remind yourself how to select). Type **Sales (boxes)**, which appears in the active cell, B2.

● Complete the entry by pressing the Tab⇆ key. This time, the active cell moves one cell to the right.

● Type **Price ($)** into C2, press the Tab⇆ key, and type **Sales Revenue** into D2.

B2		▾ ✕ ✓ fx	Sales (boxes		
	A	B	C	D	E
1					
2	Product	Sales (boxes			
3	Twizzlesticks				
4	Chokky bars				
5	Orange sorbet				
6	Raspberry surprise				
7					

C2		▾	fx	Price ($)	
	A	B	C	D	E
1					
2	Product	Sales (box	Price ($)		
3	Twizzlesticks				
4	Chokky bars				
5	Orange sorbet				
6	Raspberry surprise				
7					
8					

Overflowing text

When you type a long text label into a cell, it may appear to overflow into the next cell on the right – and when you type into that next cell, your long text label appears to have been cut off. Don't worry – it's easy to fix. There are several ways of adjusting the width of columns so that all the text fits 🔲.

TEXT ALIGNMENT

Note that Excel will automatically start any text label at the left-hand end of the cell (the text is said to be ranged left) whereas numerical values are ranged right. Excel classifies anything typed into a cell as text unless it specifically recognizes it as a numerical value. You can change the alignment of data in a cell using toolbar buttons 🔲.

🔲 **Adjust the Column Widths** 263

🔲 **The Two Main Excel Toolbars** 250

6 ADD FURTHER TEXT LABELS

- Select cell C7 and type **Total Revenue**. Press Enter↵ when finished.
- Select cell B10 and type **Last Updated**. Press Enter↵, type **Date** into cell B11, press Enter↵, and type **Time** into the B12 cell.
- Select cell A14 and type **Proportion of our products that are**. Press Enter↵ and type the text labels shown at bottom right into cells A15 to A17. When you type **Ice milk** in cell A17, Excel may suggest that you want to enter the label **Ice cream** in this cell. Ignore this and just keep typing.

COMPLETION KEYS

There are various keyboard methods for completing the entry of data into a cell. In addition to the Enter↵ and Tab⇄ keys (which move the active cell down or to the right, respectively, on completing the entry), you can use the cursor arrow keys for moving the active cell in various directions as you complete an entry.

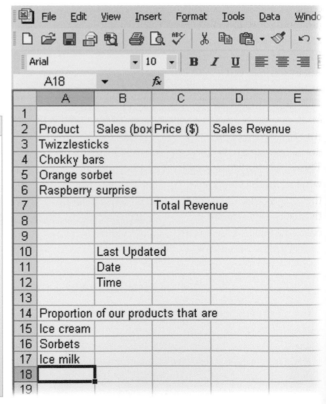

7 ADJUST THE COLUMN WIDTHS

● There are some quick methods for adjusting the widths of columns to fit cell data. For this example:

● Move the mouse pointer over the line that divides column headers A and B. The pointer should form a bar with arrows pointing to either side.

● Press down on the left mouse button, and drag the mouse pointer to the right. A dotted vertical line shows the position of the new column divider. Release the mouse button when it is to the right of the words **Raspberry surprise** in cell A6, and the column widens to that extent.

● With the mouse pointer on the line that divides column headers B and C, double-click the mouse. This method automatically widens column B to display the longest line of text in that column. Now widen columns C and D.

	A	B	C	D	E
1					
2	Product	Sales (box	Price ($)	Sales Revenue	
3	Twizzlesticks				
4	Chokky bars				
5	Orange sorbet				
6	Raspberry surprise				
7			Total Revenue		

A18

Width: 16.14 (118 pixels)

	A	B	C	D
1				
2	Product	Sales (box	Price ($)	Sales Revenue
3	Twizzlesticks			
4	Chokky bars			
5	Orange sorbet			
6	Raspberry surprise			
7			Total Revenue	

A18

	A	B	C	D
1				
2	Product	Sales (box	Price ($)	Sales Reven
3	Twizzlesticks			
4	Chokky bars			
5	Orange sorbet			
6	Raspberry surprise			
7			Total Revenue	
8				

AUTOCOMPLETE

You will often need to enter the same text label more than once into a worksheet. If Excel detects that you have started typing a text label for the second time into the same column, the handy Autocomplete feature supplies the text for you, highlighted in black. To accept the autocompleted text, press Enter↵ (or Tab⇆). To ignore it, just carry on typing.

ENTERING NUMBERS

Numerical values include integers (whole numbers), decimal numbers (such as 3.25), fractions, monetary amounts, percentages, dates, and times. Excel applies various rules to detect whether a string of characters typed into a cell constitute a numerical value and, if so, what types (integer, date, time etc). If Excel recognizes the typed-in expression as a numerical value, it will align it ranged right in the cell. Excel can perform a calculation on the contents of a cell only if it has been entered and recognized as a numerical value.

1 ENTERING WHOLE NUMBERS

● Just click on the cell that you wish to hold the number and then type.
● In the case of our worked example, click on cell B3 and type in any whole number between 1,000 and 10,000. These are the sales of boxes of Twizzlesticks. You can choose whether or not to type commas in numbers above 1,000. Press (Enter ↵) to complete the entry once you have typed your number.
● Now enter further whole numbers (less than 1,000) into cells B4 to B6, pressing (Enter ↵) after each entry. These numbers represent the sales of boxes of the company's other products.

B3	▾	✕ ✓	*fx* 3467	
	A	B	C	
1				
2	Product	Sales (boxes)	Price ($)	Sal
3	Twizzlesticks	3467		
4	Chokky bars			
5	Orange sorbet			
6	Raspberry surprise			

B6	▾		*fx* 345	
	A	B	C	
1				
2	Product	Sales (boxes)	Price ($)	Sale
3	Twizzlesticks	3467		
4	Chokky bars	893		
5	Orange sorbet	98		
6	Raspberry surprise	345		

IS IT A NUMBER?

Excel interprets various sorts of expression (not just strings of digits) as numerical values. For example $43, or 43%, or 4.3, or 4,300, or 4.3E+7 (standing for 43,000,000) are all recognized as numerical values. Both −43 and (43) would be recognized as negative or debit numbers.

NUMBER FORMATS

The way in which a number or numerical expression is displayed in a cell is affected by what format that cell has. By default, cells have a "general" number format. When you type any numerical expression into a cell that has this "general" number format, Excel analyzes what type of expression it is and then displays it in an appropriate standard way, usually (though not always exactly) as it is typed. For example, an integer will be displayed as an integer, a date will be given a date format, and so on.

2 ENTERING DECIMALS

● You enter decimal numbers into cells just as you would write them. Simply type a period to represent the decimal point.

● For the worked example, select cell C3 in the Price column, and type a decimal number, such as **6.25**. This is the price of a box of Twizzlesticks, with cents after the decimal point (you'll apply a $ sign later). Press Enter.

● A box of Chokky bars is priced at only 74 cents, so enter **0.74** in cell C4 and press Enter. Orange sorbet is a big ticket item at $21.33 a box, so type **21.33** in cell C5.

C3		✕ ✓ ƒx 6.25		
	A	B	C	
1				
2	Product	Sales (boxes)	Price ($)	Sal
3	Twizzlesticks	3467	6.25	
4	Chokky bars	893		
5	Orange sorbet	98		
6	Raspberry surprise	345		
7			Total Revenue	
8				

C4		✕ ✓ ƒx 0.74		
	A	B	C	
1				
2	Product	Sales (boxes)	Price ($)	Sal
3	Twizzlesticks	3467	6.25	
4	Chokky bars	893	0.74	
5	Orange sorbet	98		
6	Raspberry surprise	345		
7			Total Revenue	
8				
9				
10		Last Updated		
11		Date		
12				

3 ENTERING FRACTIONS

- For fractions, you type the two parts of the fraction divided by a / (forward slash).
- A box of Raspberry surprise ices has the rather curious price tag of $12¾. In cell C6, type the fraction **12 3/4**, i.e., type a 1, a 2, a space, a 3, then a forward slash, and finally a 4. Then press Enter ⏎.

C6	▼ ✗ ✓ ƒx	12 3/4	
	A	B	C
1				
2	Product	Sales (boxes)	Price ($)	Sal
3	Twizzlesticks	3467	6.25	
4	Chokky bars	893	0.74	
5	Orange sorbet	98	21.33	
6	Raspberry surprise	345	12 3/4	
7			Total Revenue	
8				
9				
10		Last Updated		
11		Date		
12		Time		

MORE NUMBER FORMATS

Excel supports a wide number of number formats and you can access them from the **Format Cells** dialog box. Click on the **Format** menu and choose **Cells**. When the dialog box opens, click the **Number** tab at the top. You will see a list of the different number formats in the left-hand column. For example, if you select **Fraction**, a list of the various ways in which you can choose to express fractions appears in the right-hand window.

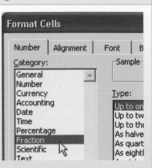

ENTERING CURRENCY AND DATES

You can enter monetary amounts into cells by typing the appropriate currency symbol ($ or £) before the number representing the amount. Alternatively, it can save time to enter all the amounts without symbols, and then apply the currency style to all the appropriate cells. A Style is a set of formats (attributes that define how the contents of a cell look or behave). In the case of the currency style, this is a very simple set of formats that can be applied with one click of a toolbar button, as you will see. To enter dates and times, you should follow certain conventions to make sure what you type is recorded correctly as a date or time.

1 ENTERING CURRENCY

● In the worked example, you have already entered the product prices in column C. Here's how to apply the currency style.

● Select ⌐ cells C3 to C6.

● Click on the **Currency** button on the Formatting toolbar.

● A $ sign is added before each product price.

C3	▼	fx 6.25	
	A	B	C
1			
2	Product	Sales (boxes)	Price ($)
3	Twizzlesticks	3467	6.25
4	Chokky bars	893	0.74
5	Orange sorbet	98	21.33
6	Raspberry surprise	345	12 3/4
7			Total Revenue
8			

syices

t Format Tools Data Window Help

B *I* <u>U</u> ≣ ≣ ≣ 国 | % , +.0 .00 |

6.25

B	C	D Currency	E
les (boxes)	Price ($)	Sales Revenue	
3467	6.25		
893	0.74		
98	21.33		
345	12 3/4		
	Total Revenue		

C3	▼	fx 6.25	
	A	B	C
1			
2	Product	Sales (boxes)	Price ($)
3	Twizzlesticks	3467	$ 6.25
4	Chokky bars	893	$ 0.74
5	Orange sorbet	98	$ 21.33
6	Raspberry surprise	345	$ 12.75
7			Total Revenue
8			
9			
10		Last Updated	
11		Date	
12		Time	

SINGLE CURRENCY

For Excel to recognize a monetary amount as a number, you are limited to using the currency defined under Regional Settings in your system's Control Panel (normally $ in the US and £ in the UK). If the default symbol is $, typing £35, for example, will not be recognized as a numerical value (but you can change the default if you wish). Cell entries that are not recognized as numerical values cannot be used in Excel calculations.

256 **Selecting Worksheet Cells**

2 ENTERING DATES

● A standard way for entering a date into a cell so that it will be recognized as a date is to type the day, a space, the first three letters of the month, a space, then the year in full.

● Select cell C11, type **7 Jun 2003** and press Enter ↵ .

● The entry is displayed in the cell as 7-Jun-03, ranged right indicating that it has been recognized as a date.

	A	B	C	
1				
2	Product	Sales (boxes)	Price ($)	Sal
3	Twizzlesticks	3467	$ 6.25	
4	Chokky bars	893	$ 0.74	
5	Orange sorbet	98	$ 21.33	
6	Raspberry surprise	345	$ 12.75	
7			Total Revenue	
8				
9				
10		Last Updated		
11		Date	7 Jun 2003	
12		Time		

Today's the Day

There is a quick way of entering today's date (as held by your PC's internal clock) into a cell. Select the cell and then, holding the Ctrl key down, press the ; (semicolon) key.

C12			fx	
	A	B	C	
1				
2	Product	Sales (boxes)	Price ($)	Sal
3	Twizzlesticks	3467	$ 6.25	
4	Chokky bars	893	$ 0.74	
5	Orange sorbet	98	$ 21.33	
6	Raspberry surprise	345	$ 12.75	
7			Total Revenue	
8				
9				
10		Last Updated		
11		Date	07-Jun-03	
12		Time		
13				

MAKE A DATE!

An alternative way of entering a date is to type the month as a number, the day, then the year, separated by forward slashes, i.e. 6/7/2003 to indicate 7 June 2003. If you were to type June 7 2003, on the other hand, it would not be recognized as a date or, in fact, as any type of numerical expression. Note also that what is displayed in the cells is not always exactly what you typed. Once Excel has recognized what category a numerical value falls into, it sometimes displays it in a standard format for that category rather than showing the figures exactly as typed.

3 ENTERING TIMES

● To enter a time in Excel, type the hour (using the 24-hour clock), a colon, then the minutes past the hour. Alternatively type the hour (using the 12-hour clock), a colon, the minutes past the hour, a space, and then either AM or PM.

● Into cell C12, type **15:45** and then press [Enter ←].

● Excel displays the time in the cell exactly as you have typed it in.

9			
10		Last Updated	
11		Date	07-Jun-03
12		Time	15:45
13			
14	Proportion of our products that are		
15	Ice cream		
16	Sorbets		

9			
10		Last Updated	
11		Date	07-Jun-03
12		Time	15:45
13			
14	Proportion of our products that are		
15	Ice cream		
16	Sorbets		

4 ENTERING PERCENTAGES

● To enter a percentage, just type a number followed by the percentage sign. You can also convert a decimal number in a cell to a percentage by applying the **Percent Style** to a cell.

● Type **50%** into cell B15 and press [Enter ←].

● Type **0.25** into cell B16 and press [Enter ←].

● Click on B16 again, then click on the **Percent Style** button on the Formatting toolbar to convert the decimal to a percentage. Press [Enter ←]. Type **25%** into cell B17, and then save the workbook 🗋.

9			
10		Last Updated	
11		Date	07-Jun-03
12		Time	15:45
13			
14	Proportion of our products that are		
15	Ice cream	50%	
16	Sorbets		
17	Ice milk		
18			

9			
10		Last Updated	
11		Date	07-Jun-03
12		Time	15:45
13			
14	Proportion of our products that are		
15	Ice cream	50%	
16	Sorbets	0.25	
17	Ice milk		
18			
19			
20			

253 **Saving and Naming**

FORMULAS AND CALCULATIONS

For even the simplest Excel worksheets, you will soon want to use formulas. A formula returns (calculates and displays) a value in a cell based on numbers you supply it with, arithmetic operators (such as plus or multiply), and cell references (the numerical values held in other worksheet cells). Much of the power of Excel derives from the use of cell references in formulas, because if you decide later on to change a value in a referenced cell, all formulas in the worksheet that depend on that reference are automatically recalculated.

1 MULTIPLYING TWO CELL VALUES

● If you want a cell to contain the result of multiplying the values of two other cells, you can type an = sign into the cell followed by the addresses of the two referenced cells, separated by the multiplication operator: *.

● In the ice cream sales worksheet, you want cell D3 to contain the revenue from Twizzlestick sales. This is the sales figure (cell B3) multiplied by the price per box (cell C3). So, select cell D3 and type: = **B3*C3**. Press Enter↵.

● Select cell D3 again and look at the Formula bar. Note that there is a distinction between what D3 actually contains (a formula, as shown in the Formula bar) and what it displays (the value that is calculated by that formula).

COUNTIF		▼ X ✓ *fx* =B3*C3	
	A	B	C	D
1				
2	Product	Sales (boxes)	Price ($)	Sales Revenue
3	Twizzlesticks	3467	$ 6.25	=B3*C3
4	Chokky bars	893	$ 0.74	
5	Orange sorbet	98	$ 21.33	
6	Raspberry surprise	345	$ 12.75	
7			Total Revenue	
8				
9				
10		Last Updated		
11		Date	07-Jun-03	
12		Time	15:45	
13				
14	Proportion of our products that are			
15	Ice cream	50%		
16	Sorbets	25%		

D3	▼	*fx* =B3*C3	
	A	B	C	D
1				
2	Product	Sales (boxes)	Price ($)	Sales Revenue
3	Twizzlesticks	3467	$ 6.25	$ 21,668.75
4	Chokky bars	893	$ 0.74	
5	Orange sorbet	98	$ 21.33	
6	Raspberry surprise	345	$ 12.75	
7			Total Revenue	
8				
9				
10		Last Updated		
11		Date	07-Jun-03	
12		Time	15:45	
13				
14	Proportion of our products that are			
15	Ice cream	50%		

2 FORMULAS USING THE MOUSE

● Instead of typing, you can use the mouse to help you construct formulas. Try this method for entering the formula: =B4*C4 into cell D4.

● Select cell D4 and type the = sign.

● Now click on cell B4. D4 now contains the expression: **=B4**.

| COUNTIF | ▼ X ✔ *fx* = |
A	B	C	D
1			
2 Product	Sales (boxes)	Price ($)	Sales Revenue
3 Twizzlesticks	3467 $	6.25	$ 21,668.75
4 Chokky bars	893 $	0.74	=
5 Orange sorbet	98 $	21.33	
6 Raspberry surprise	345 $	12.75	
7		Total Revenue	
8			
9			

| COUNTIF | ▼ X ✔ *fx* =B4 |
A	B	C	D
1			
2 Product	Sales (boxes)	Price ($)	Sales Revenue
3 Twizzlesticks	3467 $	6.25	$ 21,668.75
4 Chokky bars	893 $	0.74	=B4
5 Orange sorbet	98 $	21.33	
6 Raspberry surprise	345 $	12.75	
7		Total Revenue	
8			
9			

● Type an asterisk (*) and then click on cell C4. Finally, press Enter ↵.

| COUNTIF | ▼ X ✔ *fx* =B4*C4 |
A	B	C	D
1			
2 Product	Sales (boxes)	Price ($)	Sales Revenue
3 Twizzlesticks	3467 $	6.25	$ 21,668.75
4 Chokky bars	893 $	0.74	=B4*C4
5 Orange sorbet	98 $	21.33	
6 Raspberry surprise	345 $	12.75	
7		Total Revenue	
8			
9			

3 COMPLETING THE FORMULAS

● Now use either entry method to enter the formulas: =B5*C5 into cell D5 and: =B6*C6 into cell D6.

| COUNTIF | ▼ X ✔ *fx* =B5*C5 |
A	B	C	D
1			
2 Product	Sales (boxes)	Price ($)	Sales Revenue
3 Twizzlesticks	3467 $	6.25	$ 21,668.75
4 Chokky bars	893 $	0.74	$ 660.82
5 Orange sorbet	98 $	21.33	=B5*C5
6 Raspberry surprise	345 $	12.75	
7		Total Revenue	
8			
9			
10	Last Updated		
11	Date	07-Jun-03	
12	Time	15:45	
13			

4 ADDING VALUES IN SEVERAL CELLS

● To add the values in several cells, you can type an addition formula. For example, to add together the sums in cells D3 to D6, you could use the formula: =D3+D4+D5+D6.

● However, when (as here) all the cells you want to add are adjacent in the same row or column, there is a quicker method – called AutoSum.

● In cell D7, you want to put the sum of the revenues generated by the individual products, held in cells D3 to D6. To do so, select cell D7, and then click the AutoSum button on the Standard toolbar.

● A flashing border appears around cells D3 to D6, and the term: =SUM(D3:D6) appears in cell D7 and in the formula bar. This indicates that a function (a special type of formula) called SUM, which adds the values in cells D3 to D6, is ready to be used in cell D7.

B	C	D	E	F	G
Sales (boxes)	Price ($)	Sales Revenue			
3467	$ 6.25	$ 21,668.75			
893	$ 0.74	$ 660.82			
98	$ 21.33	$ 2,090.34			
345	$ 12.75	$ 4,398.75			
	Total Revenue				

THE EXPONENTIAL OPERATOR

The exponential operator, $\wedge$, raises a value to a given power. For example, if you type: =A3^2 into a cell, Excel will take the value in cell A3 and square it. If you type: =A3^3, Excel will cube the value in cell A3. The exponential operator takes precedence over all other operators in Excel.

B	C	D	E	F	G
Sales (boxes)	Price ($)	Sales Revenue			
3467	$ 6.25	$ 21,668.75			
893	$ 0.74	$ 660.82			
98	$ 21.33	$ 2,090.34			
345	$ 12.75	$ 4,398.75			
	Total Revenue	=SUM(D3:D6)			

SUM(**number1**, [number2], ...)

ARITHMETIC OPERATORS

The five arithmetic operators available are: + (addition), - (subtraction), * (multiplication), / (division), and $\wedge$ (raising to the power). These follow the standard order of operations, which can be overruled only by using brackets. For example, if you want to subtract A2 from 5, and then multiply the result by B2, you should type: =(5-A2)*B2.

● Press Enter↵, and the figure for total revenue appears in cell D7.

	B	C	D	E	F	G
	Sales (boxes)	Price ($)	Sales Revenue			
	3467	$ 6.25	$ 21,668.75			
	893	$ 0.74	$ 660.82			
	98	$ 21.33	$ 2,090.34			
ise	345	$ 12.75	$ 4,398.75			
		Total Revenue	$ 28,818.66			
	Last Updated					
	Date	07-Jun-03				

QUICK CALCULATIONS

Excel can be used for one-off calculations. If you want to perform a quick calculation and you don't have a calculator, you can use any cell in Excel instead. Suppose you want to add 23 to 31 and multiply the result by 27. Select a blank cell and type: =(23+31)*27, then press Enter↵. If you don't want to leave your calculation on display, you should then clear the cell ⌐.

SIMPLE FORMATTING

Even the most elementary worksheets may benefit from some basic formatting to help clarify which parts are headings and which are data, and to improve the visual attractiveness of the worksheet. The full range of Excel's formatting features could be the subject of a book in itself. The examples given below are some simple formatting ideas that can be applied with buttons on the Formatting toolbar.

1 EMPHASIZING HEADINGS

● It is common to distinguish column and row labels. One way of doing this is to emphasize them by using a bold, colored typeface.
● Select cells A2 to D2. Hold down the Ctrl key, and then click on cell B10.

B10	▼	ƒx Last Updated		
	A	B	C	D
1				
2	Product	Sales (boxes)	Price ($)	Sales Revenue
3	Twizzlesticks	3467	$ 6.25	$ 21,668.75
4	Chokky bars	893	$ 0.74	$ 660.82
5	Orange sorbet	98	$ 21.33	$ 2,090.34
6	Raspberry surprise	345	$ 12.75	$ 4,398.75
7			Total Revenue	$ 28,818.66
8				
9				
10		Last Updated		
11		Date	07-Jun-03	

Clearing Cells

- Click the **Bold** button on the Formatting toolbar.
- Now click the arrow next to the **Font Color** button.
- Choose a shade of blue from the palette.
- Now select cells A3 to A6 and A15 to A17, and also make them bold, but using a different color.

Font Color button •

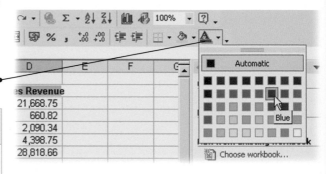

READY-MADE FORMATS

For some formatting ideas, select the whole table and choose the **AutoFormat** command from the **Format** menu. In the **AutoFormat** dialog box, browse through the options. If you like one, choose it and then click on **OK**.

	A	B	C	D
1				
2	Product	Sales (boxes)	Price ($)	Sales Revenue
3	Twizzlesticks	3467	$ 6.25	$ 21,668.75
4	Chokky bars	893	$ 0.74	$ 660.82
5	Orange sorbet	98	$ 21.33	$ 2,090.34
6	Raspberry surprise	345	$ 12.75	$ 4,398.75
7			Total Revenue	$ 28,818.66
8				
9				
10		Last Updated		

A17 ▾ *fx* Ice milk

2 ADDING A BORDER

- You can separate off distinct parts of a worksheet with a border. Here it would make sense to put a line under the main product sales data.
- Select cells B6 to D6.
- Click the small arrow next to the **Borders** button.
- Choose a thick bottom border from the palette.

B6 ▾ *fx* 345

	A	B	C	D
1				
2	Product	Sales (boxes)	Price ($)	Sales Revenue
3	Twizzlesticks	3467	$ 6.25	$ 21,668.75
4	Chokky bars	893	$ 0.74	$ 660.82
5	Orange sorbet	98	$ 21.33	$ 2,090.34
6	Raspberry surprise	345	$ 12.75	$ 4,398.75
7			Total Revenue	$ 28,818.66
8				
9				
10		Last Updated		
11		Date	07-Jun-03	
12		Time	15:45	
13				
14	Proportion of our products that are			

TRANSFERRING FORMATS

You can copy a format from one cell to another without affecting the cell's contents. Select the cell whose format you want to copy, click the **Format Painter** button (a paintbrush) on the Standard toolbar, then click in the cell to which you want the copied format transferred.

Fill Color button

3 HIGHLIGHTING INFORMATION

● It is often worth highlighting important information with a background color.

● Select cell D7, which represents Fantasy Ices' revenue to date.

● Click the small down arrow to the right of the **Fill Color** button.

● Choose a light shade from the palette.

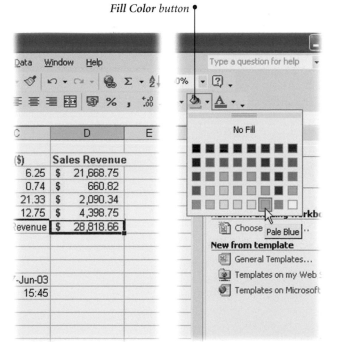

BUILDING WORKSHEETS

To build Excel worksheets fast and easily, you need to know about methods for copying data, creating simple data series, and adding new rows, columns, and cells to your worksheet.

COPYING DATA BY FILLING

Putting the same data into adjacent cells is a common Excel task. Instead of typing the data into every cell, you can type it once, and then copy it by using methods called **Fill** and **AutoFill**. To practice these techniques, here's an example, which consists of setting up an appointment diary for the directors of Fantasy Ices. Open the "fantasyices.xls" workbook, click on Sheet2 and rename this sheet **Diary**.

1 ENTER SOME TEXT LABELS

● Into cell A1, type **Morning Appointments July 31-August 4**. Type **Director** into cell A2, **Mr Twizz** into cell A4, and **Mrs Stick** into cell A11.

2 SELECT A RANGE OF CELLS TO FILL

● To perform a fill, select the cell(s) you want to copy, then extend the selection into the cells where you want the copied data to appear. In this case, you want to copy Mr Twizz into cells A5 to A8, so select the whole range A4 to A8.

NO MULTIPLE SELECTIONS

You cannot use **Fill** or **AutoFill** to copy data from a single cell (or range of cells) to multiple nonadjacent cells or ranges of cells. You can only fill data into groups of adjacent cells.

3 USE THE FILL COMMAND

● Choose **Fill** from the **Edit** menu. A submenu now appears to the right of the **Fill** command. Choose **Down** from the **Fill** submenu.

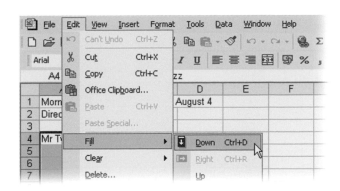

● The range of cells from A4 to A8 now fills with the name of Mr Twizz.

4 SELECT A CELL FOR AUTOFILL

● An alternative to **Fill** is **AutoFill**, a method that involves dragging the mouse rather than using a menu command.

● Select the cell or cells that you want to copy, in this example, cell A11 (Mrs Stick).

● At the bottom right-hand corner of the selected cell is a square called the fill handle. Move the mouse pointer over the fill handle until it becomes a cross. Now hold down the mouse button.

Fill handle

FILLING A BLOCK OF CELLS

You cannot fill from a single cell into a block of cells (2 cells wide x 2 cells deep or bigger) in a single operation. Two operations are required to do this. First select the range into which data is to be copied, making sure that the cell containing the data to be copied is at one corner. Then choose a sequence of commands, such as **Fill Down** followed by **Fill Right**.

5 DEFINE THE FILL RANGE

● Move the mouse pointer around the worksheet. You will see that different ranges of adjacent cells are surrounded by a border. This is the range into which your cell selection will be copied. Drag the mouse until the border surrounds the range A11 to A15.

6 COMPLETE THE AUTOFILL

● Now release the mouse button. The label Mrs Stick is copied from cell A11 into cells A12 to A15.

FILLING IN ALL DIRECTIONS

The **Fill** command allows you to fill data into a range in any direction (down, right, left, and up). Choosing **Fill Down** in the submenu will copy the values in the cells on the top edge of the selected range into the rest of the range; choosing **Fill Right** will copy the values on the left-hand edge of the selected range into the rest of the range; and so on.

CREATING DATA SERIES

The AutoFill feature is one of Excel's "smart" features and can be used for more than just copying data into cell ranges. It can also be used to create data series across cell ranges, for example series of dates (Jan 1, Jan 2, Jan 3...), months (Jan, Feb, Mar...), days of the week (Mon, Tue, Wed...), and number series (1, 2, 3... or 5, 10, 15... etc). This can be time-saving when building certain types of worksheet.

1 CREATING A SERIES OF DAYS

● Into the Diary worksheet, type **Week Day** into cell B3, press Enter↵, then type **Mon** (or **Monday**) into cell B4 and press Enter↵ again.

● Now select cell B4 again, put your mouse pointer over the fill handle, and drag the mouse pointer so that the gray AutoFill border surrounds the whole range B4 to B8.

● Release the mouse button. Instead of copying Mon into cells B5 to B8, AutoFill has filled these cells with the other days of the week (Tue, Wed, etc), which is what you want.

	A	B	C	D	E
1	Morning Appointments July 31 - August 4				
2	Director				
3		Week Day			
4	Mr Twizz	Mon			
5	Mr Twizz				
6	Mr Twizz				
7	Mr Twizz				
8	Mr Twizz				
9			Fri		
10					

	A	B	C	D	E
1	Morning Appointments July 31 - August 4				
2	Director				
3		Week Day			
4	Mr Twizz	Mon			
5	Mr Twizz	Tue			
6	Mr Twizz	Wed			
7	Mr Twizz	Thu			
8	Mr Twizz	Fri			
9					
10					
11	Mrs Stick				

Don't want a series?

If you want to AutoFill a value like Jan, Tuesday, 9:00, or 12 Apr 2000, into a range of cells without producing a series, hold down the [Ctrl] key on the keyboard as you drag the fill handle. Doing this guarantees that you will get a simple fill instead of a series.

OTHER SERIES

You can also use AutoFill to produce series of months (Jan, Feb, Mar... , or January, February, March...), number series (for example, 1, 2, 3, 4... , or 10, 20, 30, 40...) and general series such as Period 1, Period 2, Period 3 etc. For all series except months, dates, days of the week, and hour series, you must type the first two items in the series that you want to create into adjacent cells, select them, and then drag the fill handle in order for the series to be incremented in the selected cells.

2 CREATING A SERIES OF DATES

● Type **Date** into cell C3 and 31 July 2000 into cell C4. Press Enter ←.

● Select cell C4 again. Drag the fill handle to encompass the range C4 to C8.

● On releasing the mouse button, cells C5 to C8 fill with dates from 1 August to 4 August – again, exactly what you want.

	A	B	C	D	E	F
1	Morning Appointments July 31 - August 4					
2	Director					
3		Week Day	Date			
4	Mr Twizz	Mon	31 July 2003			
5	Mr Twizz	Tue				
6	Mr Twizz	Wed				
7	Mr Twizz	Thu				

	A	B	C	D	E	F
1	Morning Appointments July 31 - August 4					
2	Director					
3		Week Day	Date			
4	Mr Twizz	Mon	31-Jul-03			
5	Mr Twizz	Tue				
6	Mr Twizz	Wed				
7	Mr Twizz	Thu				
8	Mr Twizz	Fri				
9				04-Aug-03		
10						

3 CREATING A SERIES OF TIMES

● Sometimes you need to provide AutoFill with the first two values in a series in order to end up with the series that you want.

● Type **9:00 AM** into cell D3 and **9:30 AM** into cell E3, then select both cells.

● Drag the fill handle across to G3 and release.

● The time series is extended into F3 and G3.

	A	B	C	D	E	F
1	Morning Appointments July 31 - August 4					
2	Director					
3		Week Day	Date	9:00 AM	9:30 AM	
4	Mr Twizz	Mon	31-Jul-03			
5	Mr Twizz	Tue	01-Aug-03			
6	Mr Twizz	Wed	02-Aug-03			
7	Mr Twizz	Thu	03-Aug-03			

B	C	D	E	F	G	H
intments July 31 - August 4						
eek Day	Date		9:00 AM	9:30 AM		
on	31-Jul-03					
e	01-Aug-03				10:30 AM	
ed	02-Aug-03					
u	03-Aug-03					

D3	▼	*fx* 09:00:00							
	A	B	C	D	E	F	G	H	I	J
1	Morning Appointments July 31 - August 4									
2	Director									
3		Week Day	Date	9:00 AM	9:30 AM	10:00 AM	10:30 AM			
4	Mr Twizz	Mon	31-Jul-03							
5	Mr Twizz	Tue	01-Aug-03							
6	Mr Twizz	Wed	02-Aug-03							
7	Mr Twizz	Thu	03-Aug-03							

COPYING AND PASTING

Copying and pasting is a technique used in many computer applications, not simply in Excel worksheets. All copy and paste operations work in the same way. You choose some data that you want to copy, and then use the **Copy** command. The original data stays where it is and the copy of the data is placed in a particular part of your computer's memory called the Clipboard. You then select where you would like the copied data to appear in your worksheet, and use the **Paste** command. The data is now copied from the Clipboard and placed in the chosen target area. You can repeat the **Paste** command to place the copied data over several different target areas if you wish. **Copy** and **Paste** commands can be carried out either via drop-down menus, toolbar buttons, or keyboard shortcuts.

1 COPYING A SINGLE CELL

● In your Fantasy Ices Diary worksheet, you want to set up three appointments for a Ms Black to meet with Mr Twizz.

● Type **Ms Black** into cell E4 and press Enter ↵.

● Select cell E4 again, and then choose **Copy** from the **Edit** menu.

● You will see a flashing outline appear around cell E4, indicating that its contents have been copied to the Clipboard.

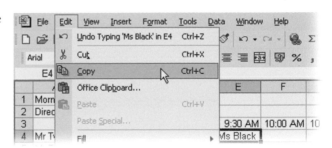

2 PASTING THE DATA

● Select cell E7 and then choose **Paste** from the **Edit** menu. Ms Black is pasted into cell E7.
● Select cell F8 and repeat the **Paste** command. Press the Esc key to complete the copy/paste operation.

	File	Edit	View	Insert	Format	Tools	Data	Window	Help
	↶	Undo Typing 'Ms Black' in E4	Ctrl+Z						Σ
	Arial	✂ Cut		Ctrl+X					% ,
	E7	🗐 Copy		Ctrl+C					
		🗐 Office Clipboard...					E	F
1	Morn	📋 Paste		Ctrl+V				
2	Direc							
3		Paste Special...				9:30 AM	10:00 AM	10
4	Mr Tv	Fill	▶		Ms Black		
5	Mr Tv						
6	Mr Tv	Clear	▶				

	A	B	C	D	E	F
1	Morning Appointments July 31 - August 4					
2	Director					
3		Week Day	Date	9:00 AM	9:30 AM	10:00 AM	10
4	Mr Twizz	Mon	31-Jul-03		Ms Black	
5	Mr Twizz	Tue	01-Aug-03			
6	Mr Twizz	Wed	02-Aug-03			
7	Mr Twizz	Thu	03-Aug-03		Ms Black	
8	Mr Twizz	Fri	04-Aug-03			Ms Black
9						
10						

Want to move, not copy?

If you want to move data in a worksheet, that is, you want to place it in a new location without leaving a copy in the original location, this can be carried out by an operation called cut and paste 🔲.

3 COPYING A BLOCK OF CELLS

● You now want to copy and paste the whole of Mr Twizz's diary to Mrs Stick's part of the diary. When pasting a block of data, you need only select the top left-hand cell of the target area for the paste.
● Select the block B3 to G8 and click the **Copy** button on the Standard toolbar.

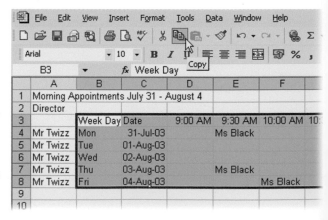

4 PASTING THE COPIED BLOCK

● Select cell B10 – the top left-hand cell of your target area – and click the **Paste** button on the Standard toolbar.

● The copied data is pasted over the range B10 to G15. Your "fantasyices.xls" workbook can now be saved.

Paste button •

	A	B	C	D	E	F
1	Morning Appointments July 31 - August 4					
2	Director					
3		Week Day	Date	9:00 AM	9:30 AM	10:00 AM	10:
4	Mr Twizz	Mon	31-Jul-03		Ms Black	
5	Mr Twizz	Tue	01-Aug-03			
6	Mr Twizz	Wed	02-Aug-03			
7	Mr Twizz	Thu	03-Aug-03		Ms Black	
8	Mr Twizz	Fri	04-Aug-03			Ms Black
9						
10						
11	Mrs Stick					

Pasted cells •

	A	B	C	D	E	F
1	Morning Appointments July 31 - August 4					
2	Director					
3		Week Day	Date	9:00 AM	9:30 AM	10:00 AM	10:
4	Mr Twizz	Mon	31-Jul-03		Ms Black	
5	Mr Twizz	Tue	01-Aug-03			
6	Mr Twizz	Wed	02-Aug-03			
7	Mr Twizz	Thu	03-Aug-03		Ms Black	
8	Mr Twizz	Fri	04-Aug-03			Ms Black
9						
10		Week Day	Date	9:00 AM	9:30 AM	10:00 AM	10:
11	Mrs Stick	Mon	31-Jul-03		Ms Black	
12	Mrs Stick	Tue	01-Aug-03			
13	Mrs Stick	Wed	02-Aug-03			
14	Mrs Stick	Thu	03-Aug-03		Ms Black	
15	Mrs Stick	Fri	04-Aug-03			Ms Black
16						
17						
18						

MULTIPLE PASTES

To carry out multiple pastes after a **Copy** command, hold down the [Ctrl] key and then select, one by one, the various target cells for your pastes. You then simply choose **Paste** from the **Edit** menu. Alternatively, click the **Paste** button on the Standard toolbar.

Pasting Care

When copying and pasting a block of cells, if you try to select the whole target area for the paste but get the size wrong, Excel will come up with an onscreen error message, saying that the Copy and Paste areas don't match. It is better to select just the top left-hand cell of the target area. However, always be careful when pasting blocks of cells – there is a risk of overpasting existing data in the worksheet, and you get no warning if this is about to happen.

COPYING BY DRAG AND DROP

Drag and drop is another very useful method for copying data from one cell or block of cells to another part of the worksheet. It is a quick method, because it is performed by dragging with the mouse rather than by choosing menu commands or toolbar buttons. However, it does require a little practice.

1 COPYING A SINGLE CELL

● In the Diary sheet of the "fantasyices.xls" workbook, you can practice some drags and drops after filling in some more dates for the directors of Fantasy Ices.

● Type **Dr Green** into cell D6. Position your mouse pointer over the bottom border of cell D6, and it turns into an arrow. Hold down the mouse button.

● Hold down the Ctrl key. A small + sign appears next to the mouse pointer.

● Drag the mouse so that the mouse pointer moves down the worksheet. A gray rectangular outline, the same size as a cell, moves down the screen following the mouse pointer and the + sign. A yellow label with a cell address (such as D8) on it also travels with the mouse pointer. This continually updates and indicates which cell the gray outline has reached.

	A	B	C	D	E
1	Morning Appointments July 31 - August 4				
2	Director				
3		Week Day	Date	9:00 AM	9:30 AM
4	Mr Twizz	Mon	31-Jul-03		Ms Black
5	Mr Twizz	Tue	01-Aug-03		
6	Mr Twizz	Wed	02-Aug-03	Dr Green	
7	Mr Twizz	Thu	03-Aug-03		Ms Black
8	Mr Twizz	Fri	04-Aug-03		
9					

2	Director				
3		Week Day	Date	9:00 AM	9:30 AM
4	Mr Twizz	Mon	31-Jul-03		Ms Black
5	Mr Twizz	Tue	01-Aug-03		
6	Mr Twizz	Wed	02-Aug-03	Dr Green	
7	Mr Twizz	Thu	03-Aug-03		Ms Black
8	Mr Twizz	Fri	04-Aug-03		
9					

	A	B	C	D	E
1	Morning Appointments July 31 - August 4				
2	Director				
3		Week Day	Date	9:00 AM	9:30 AM
4	Mr Twizz	Mon	31-Jul-03		Ms Black
5	Mr Twizz	Tue	01-Aug-03		
6	Mr Twizz	Wed	02-Aug-03	Dr Green	
7	Mr Twizz	Thu	03-Aug-03		Ms Black
8	Mr Twizz	Fri	04-Aug-03		
9					
10			Week Day	Date	9:00 AM	9:30 AM
11	Mrs Stick	Mon	31-Jul-03		Ms Black

● Drag until the gray outline reaches cell D13. Now for the "drop." Release the mouse button and finally the Ctrl key. Dr Green is copied to cell D13.

10		Week Day	Date	9:00 AM	9:30 AM	10:00 AM	10:
11	Mrs Stick	Mon	31-Jul-03		Ms Black		
12	Mrs Stick	Tue	01-Aug-03				
13	Mrs Stick	Wed	02-Aug-03	Dr Green			
14	Mrs Stick	Thu	03-Aug-03		Ms Black		
15	Mrs Stick	Fri	04-Aug-03			Ms Black	
16							

2 COPYING A BLOCK OF CELLS

● You can drag and drop blocks of cells just as easily as single cells. Try this simple exercise.

● Select the range D4 to E6, and move the mouse pointer over the bottom border of the selection until you see the pointer turn into an arrow.

● Hold down the mouse button and the Ctrl key, and drag the mouse to the right until the gray rectangular outline surrounds the range F4 to G6. Then release the mouse button and Ctrl key.

● The dragged range gets pasted into cells F4 to G6.

	A	B	C	D	E	F	G	H
1	Morning Appointments July 31 - August 4							
2	Director							
3		Week Day	Date	9:00 AM	9:30 AM	10:00 AM	10:30 AM	
4	Mr Twizz	Mon	31-Jul-03		Ms Black			
5	Mr Twizz	Tue	01-Aug-03					
6	Mr Twizz	Wed	02-Aug-03	Dr Green				
7	Mr Twizz	Thu	03-Aug-03		Ms Black			
8	Mr Twizz	Fri	04-Aug-03			Ms Black		
9								

	A	B	C	D	E	F	G	H
1	Morning Appointments July 31 - August 4							
2	Director							
3		Week Day	Date	9:00 AM	9:30 AM	10:00 AM	10:30 AM	
4	Mr Twizz	Mon	31-Jul-03		Ms Black			
5	Mr Twizz	Tue	01-Aug-03					
6	Mr Twizz	Wed	02-Aug-03	Dr Green				
7	Mr Twizz	Thu	03-Aug-03		Ms F4:G6			
8	Mr Twizz	Fri	04-Aug-03			Ms Black		
9								

	A	B	C	D	E	F	G	H
1	Morning Appointments July 31 - August 4							
2	Director							
3		Week Day	Date	9:00 AM	9:30 AM	10:00 AM	10:30 AM	
4	Mr Twizz	Mon	31-Jul-03		Ms Black		Ms Black	
5	Mr Twizz	Tue	01-Aug-03					
6	Mr Twizz	Wed	02-Aug-03	Dr Green		Dr Green		
7	Mr Twizz	Thu	03-Aug-03		Ms Black			
8	Mr Twizz	Fri	04-Aug-03			Ms Black		
9								

Control to Copy

If you forget to hold down the Ctrl key during a drag and drop operation, you will find that you move the dragged data instead of copying it.

WHEN TO DRAG AND DROP

Drag and drop is just one way of copying data. The drag and drop technique in Excel is most useful for copying data over short distances on a worksheet. For copying data over longer distances, or from one worksheet to another, use the copy and paste technique. For copying from a cell to an adjacent cell (or cells), it is better to use **Fill** or **AutoFill**.

INSERTING NEW COLUMNS, ROWS, AND CELLS

It is in the nature of worksheets for them to grow and evolve over time, and it is common to extend them by adding new columns, rows, or individual cells as the need arises. When you do this, you have to shift some of the existing cells, together with their contents, to the right or further down in the worksheet in order to create room for the new cells. This usually causes no problems, although it does require some thought, especially when inserting individual cells or groups of cells.

1 INSERTING A COLUMN

● The directors of Fantasy Ices want to make some 8:30 am appointments to meet up with each other. This requires the creation of a new column in the Diary worksheet.

● Select column D by clicking on the column D header button. This is where you want the new column to appear.

● Choose **Columns** from the **Insert** menu.

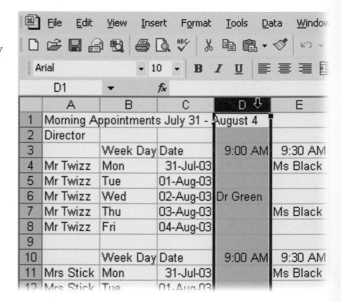

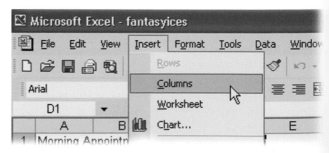

- A new blank column is inserted and the original contents of column D, and the contents of columns to the right of column D, are all automatically shifted one column to the right.
- Now type **8:30 AM** into cell D3 and copy this time to cell D10.
- Add some appropriate appointments to column D.

	A	B	C	D	E
1	Morning Appointments July 31 - August 4				
2	Director				
3		Week Day	Date		9:00 AM
4	Mr Twizz	Mon	31-Jul-03		
5	Mr Twizz	Tue	01-Aug-03		
6	Mr Twizz	Wed	02-Aug-03		Dr Green
7	Mr Twizz	Thu	03-Aug-03		
8	Mr Twizz	Fri	04-Aug-03		

	A	B	C	D	E
5	Mr Twizz	Tue	01-Aug-03		
6	Mr Twizz	Wed	02-Aug-03		Dr Green
7	Mr Twizz	Thu	03-Aug-03		
8	Mr Twizz	Fri	04-Aug-03		
9					
10		Week Day	Date	8:30 AM	9:00 AM
11	Mrs Stick	Mon	31-Jul-03		
12	Mrs Stick	Tue	01-Aug-03		
13	Mrs Stick	Wed	02-Aug-03		Dr Green

CONTEXT SENSITIVE MENUS

Note that Excel's drop-down menus are context-sensitive. After you have selected a column in a worksheet, the **Insert Rows** command is not a feasible command, and so it is grayed out on the **Insert** menu. When a row or rows is selected, the **Insert Columns** command is similarly grayed out.

	A	B	C	D	E
1	Morning Appointments July 31 - August 4				
2	Director				
3		Week Day	Date	8:30 AM	9:00 AM
4	Mr Twizz	Mon	31-Jul-03		
5	Mr Twizz	Tue	01-Aug-03		
6	Mr Twizz	Wed	02-Aug-03	Mrs Stick	Dr Green
7	Mr Twizz	Thu	03-Aug-03	Mrs Stick	
8	Mr Twizz	Fri	04-Aug-03		
9					
10		Week Day	Date	8:30 AM	9:00 AM

WHAT SHIFTS WHERE?

Remember that when you choose to insert a new column or columns, they are inserted at the left-hand side of the column(s) that you selected on the worksheet before choosing **Insert Columns**. When you insert some new row(s) they are inserted above the row(s) that you selected on the worksheet. There is no choice as to the direction in which columns or rows get shifted – this choice only appears when you insert one or more cells.

2 INSERTING TWO ROWS

● Mr Twizz wants to make some Saturday and Sunday appointments. This means adding two more rows to the worksheet.

● Select rows 9 and 10. This is where you want the new rows to appear.

● Choose **Rows** from the **Insert** menu.

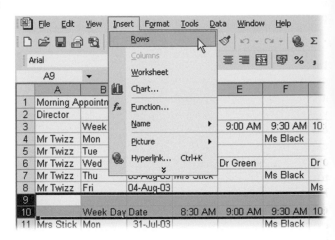

● New blank rows are inserted and the original contents of rows 9, 10, 11 etc, are all automatically shifted two rows down.

● Select the range A8 to C8 and AutoFill these cells down to A10-C10. Enter some weekend appointments for Mr Twizz by typing **Mr Brown** into cells E9 and F10.

AutoFilled cells

3 INSERTING A FEW CELLS

● Mr Twizz wants to make some extra appointments for 9:15, but Mrs Stick doesn't need to. You want to add some individual cells, but not a whole row or column, to Mr Twizz's part of the worksheet.

● Select the range F3-F10.

● Choose **Cells** from the **Insert** menu.

● The **Insert** dialog box appears. To create room for your new cells, you have the choice of shifting the existing range F3-F10 (and all cells to the right) further to the right; or to shift F3-F10 (and all cells below) down. You want to shift the existing cells to the right, so just click on **OK**.

● Now type **9:15 AM** into cell F3, and fill in some 9:15 appointments with Ms Orange in cells F6 and F7 for Mr Twizz. Save your "fantasyices.xls" workbook.

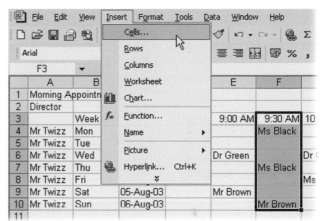

	A	B	C	D	E	F	
1	Morning Appointments July 31 - August 4						
2	Director						
3		Week Day	Date	8:30 AM	9:00 AM	9:30 AM	10
4	Mr Twizz	Mon	31-Jul-03			Ms Black	
5	Mr Twizz	Tue	01-Aug-03				
6	Mr Twizz	Wed	02-Aug-03	Mrs Stick	Dr Green		Dr
7	Mr Twizz	Thu	03-Aug-03	Mrs Stick		Ms Black	
8	Mr Twizz	Fri	04-Aug-03				Ms
9	Mr Twizz	Sat	05-Aug-03		Mr Brown		
10	Mr Twizz	Sun	06-Aug-03			Mr Brown	
11							
12		Week Day	Date	8:30 AM	9:00 AM	9:30 AM	10
13	Mrs Stick	Mon	31-Jul-03			Ms Black	
14	Mrs Stick	Tue	01-Aug-03				
15	Mrs Stick	Wed	02-Aug-03	Mr Twizz	Dr Green		
16	Mrs Stick	Thu	03-Aug-03	Mr Twizz		Ms Black	
17	Mrs Stick	Fri	04-Aug-03				Ms
18							
19							

File Edit View Insert Format Tools Data Window Help

Cells...
Rows
Columns
Worksheet
Chart...
Function...
Name
Picture
Hyperlink... Ctrl+K

Arial

F3

	A	B		E	F	
1	Morning Appointm					
2	Director					
3		Week		9:00 AM	9:30 AM	10
4	Mr Twizz	Mon			Ms Black	
5	Mr Twizz	Tue				
6	Mr Twizz	Wed		Dr Green		Dr
7	Mr Twizz	Thu			Ms Black	
8	Mr Twizz	Fri				Ms
9	Mr Twizz	Sat	05-Aug-03		Mr Brown	
10	Mr Twizz	Sun	06-Aug-03		Mr Brown	
11						

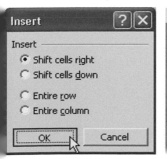

Insert

Insert
- ● Shift cells right
- ○ Shift cells down
- ○ Entire row
- ○ Entire column

OK   Cancel

F7   X √ fx Mrs Orange

	A	B	C	D	E	F	
1	Morning Appointments July 31 - August 4						
2	Director						
3		Week Day	Date	8:30 AM	9:00 AM	9:15 AM	9
4	Mr Twizz	Mon	31-Jul-03				Ms
5	Mr Twizz	Tue	01-Aug-03				
6	Mr Twizz	Wed	02-Aug-03	Mrs Stick	Dr Green	Mrs Orange	
7	Mr Twizz	Thu	03-Aug-03	Mrs Stick		Mrs Orange	
8	Mr Twizz	Fri	04-Aug-03				
9	Mr Twizz	Sat	05-Aug-03		Mr Brown		
10	Mr Twizz	Sun	06-Aug-03				Mr

COPYING AND INSERTING

Copying and inserting consists of a combination of an insert operation and a copy and paste operation. On occasions, you will want to make a copy of a cell or a whole range of cells and place this copy on the worksheet but without pasting over and losing existing contents. So you need to create some extra room in the worksheet to take the copy. You could create this extra space with an Insert command, and then do a copy and paste. However, a copy and insert operation is quicker, as it achieves the same result with a smaller number of actions.

1 COPY/INSERT IN SEVERAL ROWS

● A new Director, Mr Bloggs, has joined Fantasy Ices. He needs a space for his own appointments in the Diary sheet of "fantasyices.xls," and his first appointments will be the same as Mr Twizz's.

● Select the rows you want to copy and insert – in this case, rows 3 to 11. Then click on the **Copy** button.

● Select a row where you would like the copied data to be inserted – in this case row 12.

● Choose **Copied Cells** from the **Insert** menu. The copied data is inserted into the worksheet.

● Now type **Mr Bloggs** into cell A13 and AutoFill down to cell A19. Mr Bloggs now has his own section of the appointments diary.

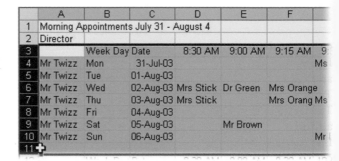

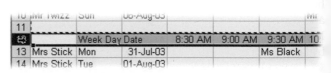

COPY, DRAG, AND INSERT!

It is possible to copy, drag, and insert cells through a technique similar to copy, drag, and drop ⌐. To copy, drag, and insert, select the cell or cells to copy, and then hold down both [Ctrl] and [⇧ Shift]. Drag your selection to the insert/paste target area. You will see a gray outline shape follow the mouse pointer. If you want existing cells in the worksheet to move right when the insert happens, place this gray outline to the left of the target area. If you want existing cells to move down, place the gray outline above the target area. Then release the mouse button and both keyboard keys.

2 COPY/INSERT A SINGLE CELL

● At the other extreme, try copy/inserting a single cell. Dr Green needs an extra appointment with Mr Twizz at 9:30 AM on Thursday. This time slot is already taken up by Ms Black. No matter – with a copy/insert, Dr Green can have the 9:30 AM time slot and the appointment with Ms Black can be put back by half an hour.

● Select cell E6 and click on the **Copy** button.

● Click on cell G7 (the intended time slot) and choose **Copied Cells** from the **Insert** menu.

● When the **Insert Paste** dialog appears, choose **Shift cells right** and click on **OK**.

● Dr Green now gets her 9:30 AM appointment with Mr Twizz and Ms Black's appointment is put back to 10:00 AM.

	A	B	C	D	E	F
1	Morning Appointments July 31 - August 4					
2	Director					
3		Week Day	Date	8:30 AM	9:00 AM	9:15 AM	9:
4	Mr Twizz	Mon	31-Jul-03				Ms
5	Mr Twizz	Tue	01-Aug-03				
6	Mr Twizz	Wed	02-Aug-03	Mrs Stick	Dr Green	Mrs Orange	
7	Mr Twizz	Thu	03-Aug-03	Mrs Stick		Mrs Orang	Ms
8	Mr Twizz	Fri	04-Aug-03		✛		
9	Mr Twizz	Sat	05-Aug-03		Mr Brown		
10	Mr Twizz	Sun	06-Aug-03				Mr
11							

31-Jul-03				Ms Black		Ms Bl
01-Aug-03						
02-Aug-03	Mrs Stick	Dr Green	Mrs Orange		Dr Green	
03-Aug-03	Mrs Stick		Mrs Orang	Ms Black		
04-Aug-03					Ms Black	
05-Aug-03						
06-Aug-03				Mr Brown		

Insert Paste [?][X]

Insert
- ● Shift cells right
- ○ Shift cells down

[OK] [Cancel]

Date				9:30 AM	10:00 AM	10:30
31-Jul-03				Ms Black		Ms Bl
01-Aug-03						
02-Aug-03	M		ge	Dr Green		
03-Aug-03	Mrs Stick		Mrs Orang	Ms Black		
04-Aug-03				Ms Black		

Date	8:30 AM	9:00 AM	9:15 AM	9:30 AM	10:00 AM	10:30
31-Jul-03				Ms Black		Ms Bl
01-Aug-03						
02-Aug-03	Mrs Stick	Dr Green	Mrs Orange		Dr Green	
03-Aug-03	Mrs Stick		Mrs Orang	Dr Green	Ms Black	
04-Aug-03					Ms Black	
05-Aug-03		Mr Brown				
06-Aug-03				Mr Brown		

Copying by Drag and Drop

EDITING WORKSHEETS

This chapter is about editing existing worksheets. You can change the contents of cells, check spellings, move cells, add comments, remove cell contents, or delete the cells altogether.

CHANGING CELL CONTENTS

You can change the contents of a cell in its entirety or only part of the contents. For example, you can shorten a text label, or change the month but keep the original day. There is a single straightforward method for changing all of a cell's contents, and there are two distinct methods for making partial changes. These two methods are called "in-cell editing", and "editing in the formula bar." The examples given below are applied to the Sales worksheet of "fantasyices.xls."

1 CHANGING A TEXT LABEL

● The directors of Fantasy Ices have decided to relaunch Twizzlesticks under a new name.

● Select cell A3 – the cell that contains the Twizzlesticks label.

● Type the new name – **Kooltwists**. Press Enter↵. Note that the new label takes on the same format as the old label – when you change a cell's contents, it retains its format.

A3	▼	*fx* Twizzlesticks	
	A	B	C
1			
2	Product	Sales (boxes)	Price ($)	Sal
3	Twizzlesticks	3467	$ 6.25	$
4	Chokky bars	893	$ 0.74	$
5	Orange sorbet	98	$ 21.33	$
6	Raspberry surprise	345	$ 12.75	$
7			Total Revenue	$

A4	▼	*fx* Chokky bars	
	A	B	C
1			
2	Product	Sales (boxes)	Price ($)	Sal
3	Kooltwists	3467	$ 6.25	$
4	Chokky bars	893	$ 0.74	$
5	Orange sorbet	98	$ 21.33	$
6	Raspberry surprise	345	$ 12.75	$
7			Total Revenue	$
8				

2 ALTERING FORMULA VALUES

- There's an update required to the sales data for orange sorbets – that is, to the value held in cell B5.
- Select cell B5 and revise the number for the sales of boxes of orange sorbets.
- Press `Enter←`. Note that when you confirm the change to cell B5, the value in cell D5 (the sales revenue from orange sorbets) and D7 (total revenue) also change. This makes sense, but how has it happened?
- Click on cell D5 and look in the Formula bar. When there is a formula in the active cell, it shows in the Formula bar. Cell D5 contains the formula: **=B5*C5**. When you change any cell value referenced by a formula, Excel automatically updates the value in the cell containing that formula. Because you changed B5, Excel has automatically updated D5, which contains a formula referencing B5.
- Click on cell D7. It contains the formula: **=SUM(D3:D6)**. Because cell D5 (which is contained in the referenced range D3:D6) changed, the value in D7 updated as well.

B5 ▾ X ✓ *fx* 145

	A	B	C	D
1				
2	Product	Sales (boxes)	Price ($)	Sales Revenue
3	Kooltwists	3467	$ 6.25	$ 21,668.75
4	Chokky bars	893	$ 0.74	$ 660.82
5	Orange sorbet	145	$ 21.33	$ 2,090.34
6	Raspberry surprise	345	$ 12.75	$ 4,398.75
7			Total Revenue	$ 28,818.66
8				
9				

B6 ▾ *fx* 345

	A	B	C	D
1				
2	Product	Sales (boxes)	Price ($)	Sales Revenue
3	Kooltwists	3467	$ 6.25	$ 21,668.75
4	Chokky bars	893	$ 0.74	$ 660.82
5	Orange sorbet	145	$ 21.33	$ 3,092.85
6	Raspberry surprise	345	$ 12.75	$ 4,398.75
7			Total Revenue	$ 29,821.17
8				
9				
10		Last Updated		

D5 ▾ *fx* =B5*C5

	A	B	C	D
1				
2	Product	Sales (boxes)	Price ($)	Sales Revenue
3	Kooltwists	3467	$ 6.25	$ 21,668.75
4	Chokky bars	893	$ 0.74	$ 660.82
5	Orange sorbet	145	$ 21.33	$ 3,092.85
6	Raspberry surprise	345	$ 12.75	$ 4,398.75
7			Total Revenue	$ 29,821.17
8				
9				
10		Last Updated		

D7 ▾ *fx* =SUM(D3:D6)

	A	B	C	D
1				
2	Product	Sales (boxes)	Price ($)	Sales Revenue
3	Kooltwists	3467	$ 6.25	$ 21,668.75
4	Chokky bars	893	$ 0.74	$ 660.82
5	Orange sorbet	145	$ 21.33	$ 3,092.85
6	Raspberry surprise	345	$ 12.75	$ 4,398.75
7			Total Revenue	$ 29,821.17
8				
9				
10		Last Updated		

3 IN-CELL EDITING OF TEXT LABELS

● Chokky bars are getting a name-change to plain "Chocolate bars." You can make this change by means of an in-cell edit.

● Double-click in the middle of cell A4. This prepares the cell for in-cell editing. The cell is ready to edit if you see an insertion point (small vertical bar) flashing between two letters in the cell.

● Click the mouse pointer before the first **k** in **Chokky**, then hold down the mouse button and drag the mouse to the right to highlight the string of letters **kky**. This is the part of the label that you want to replace. Now release the mouse button.

● Type **clate** and press Enter ↵ to leave **Choclate bars** (don't worry that you've introduced a deliberate spelling mistake! – you'll see why shortly).

● Now change **Raspberry surprise** to **Raspberry sundar** (again don't worry about the spelling mistake).

	A	B	C	
	Arial ▾ 10 ▾ **B** *I* U			
	A4 ▾ ✗ ✓ *fx* Chokky bars			
	A	B	C	
1				
2	Product	Sales (boxes)	Price ($)	Sal
3	Kooltwists	3467	$ 6.25	$
4	Chokky bars	893	$ 0.74	$
5	Orange sorbet	145	$ 21.33	$
6	Raspberry surprise	345	$ 12.75	$

	A	B	C	
	Arial ▾ 10 ▾ **B** *I* U			
	▾ ✗ ✓ *fx* Chokky bars			
	A	B	C	
1				
2	Product	Sales (boxes)	Price ($)	Sal
3	Kooltwists	3467	$ 6.25	$
4	Chokky bars	893	$ 0.74	$
5	Orange sorbet	145	$ 21.33	$
6	Raspberry surprise	345	$ 12.75	$

	A	B	C	
	▾ ✗ ✓ *fx* Choclate bars			
	A	B	C	
1				
2	Product	Sales (boxes)	Price ($)	Sa
3	Kooltwists	3467	$ 6.25	$
4	Choclate bars	893	$ 0.74	$
5	Orange sorbet	145	$ 21.33	$
6	Raspberry surprise	345	$ 12.75	$
7			Total Revenue	$

	A	B	C	
	A6 ▾ ✗ ✓ *fx* Raspberry sundar			
	A	B	C	
1				
2	Product	Sales (boxes)	Price ($)	Sal
3	Kooltwists	3467	$ 6.25	$
4	Choclate bars	893	$ 0.74	$
5	Orange sorbet	145	$ 21.33	$
6	Raspberry sundar		$ 12.75	$
7			Total Revenue	$

4 EDITING IN THE FORMULA BAR

● Now click on cell C11, which contains the date 7 June 2000. You want to change this date to 15 August 2000.

● Place your mouse pointer in the Formula bar and you will see that it changes into an I-shaped cursor.

● Click to the right of the figure **7**, press down on the mouse button, and drag the pointer to the left to highlight the string of characters **6/7**. This is the part that you want to change. Now release the mouse button.

● Type **8/15** and finally press Enter ↵.

On Second Thoughts...

If, while making a change to a cell, you decide not to make the change after all, you can abort the change by pressing the Esc key.

	A	B	C	D
1				
2	Product	Sales (boxes)	Price ($)	Sales Revenue
3	Kooltwists	3467	$ 6.25	$ 21,668.75
4	Choclate bars	893	$ 0.74	$ 660.82
5	Orange sorbet	145	$ 21.33	$ 3,092.85
6	Raspberry sundar	345	$ 12.75	$ 4,398.75
7			Total Revenue	$ 29,821.17
8				
9				
10		Last Updated		
11		Date	7-Jun-03	

C11   *fx* 6/7/2003

C11   × ✓ *fx* 6/7/2003

C11   × ✓ *fx* 8/15/2003

CHECKING SPELLING

Excel provides a tool for checking the spelling of the text in your worksheets. The Spelling tool works by checking the spelling of each word against a built-in dictionary. When the Spelling tool finds a mistake, it offers you the choice of correcting the error or not, and in most cases will suggest the correct spelling. You have the opportunity to add specialist words, which Excel doesn't recognize, to your own custom dictionary so that the Spelling tool doesn't query them again.

1 STARTING THE SPELLING TOOL

● The Spelling tool checks each word in each cell, row by row, starting from the active cell. Unless a range of cells is selected when you check spelling, the tool checks the entire work-sheet, including both cell values and comments ⬦.
● To check the whole worksheet, select its top left-hand cell. In this case, select cell A1 of the Sales worksheets in "fantasyices.xls." Click the **Spelling** button on the Standard toolbar.

Habitual Misspeller
If there is a particular word that you habitually mistype or misspell, try putting it on an **AutoCorrect** list. This feature automatically corrects specified misspellings whenever you make them. To add to the AutoCorrect list, click on **Tools** in the menu bar, and choose **AutoCorrect** from the drop-down menu. Type your habitual misspell in the **Replace** box, and then type the correct spelling in the **With** box, and click on **OK**.

DON'T EXPECT THE IMPOSSIBLE

Bear in mind that the Spelling tool cannot pick up a typing error if the mistype gives rise to another, correctly spelled, word. For example, if you mistype "product" as "produce," the Spelling tool will not see this as an error! So you should do a visual check after using the Spelling tool.

2 ADDING TO YOUR DICTIONARY

● The Spelling tool displays the **Spelling** dialog box when a word is found that it doesn't recognize. If you want to add this word to your own custom dictionary so that it is not queried again, click on the **Add to Dictionary** button.

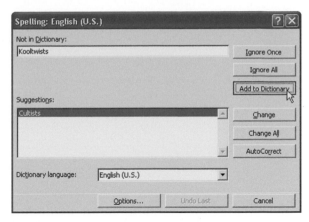

3 SPELLING TOOL SUGGESTIONS

● When the Spelling tool comes across **Choclate**, it suggests that this should be changed to **Chocolate**. You agree, so click on the **Change** button.

4 ACCEPTING A SPELLING

● When the Spelling tool comes across **sundar**, it provides various spelling suggestions of what you meant to type. In this case, click on **sundae** in the **Suggestions** box, and then click on the **Change** button.

● Once the Spelling tool has checked the entire sheet for misspellings, it comes up with a task completion message. Just click on **OK**.

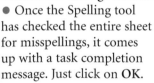

MOVING AND SWAPPING DATA

Moving data is similar to copying data, except that you leave no copy of the data behind in its original location. You can move data by cut and paste, or by drag and drop. These techniques are similar to copy and paste ⬜ and copying by drag and drop ⬜. You can also carry out cut/inserts, which are similar to copy/inserts ⬜ but, again, they leave no copy of your original data on the worksheet.

MOVING BY CUT AND PASTE

● For a cut and paste, you first select a cell or cells that you want to move and then carry out a **Cut** command. You then choose a target area for the move and carry out a **Paste** command.

● In the Diary Sheet of your "fantasyices.xls" workbook, select cell E6 (Dr Green), and then click the **Cut** button on the Standard toolbar.

● An outline flashes around cell E6. Select cell E8 and click on the **Paste** button.

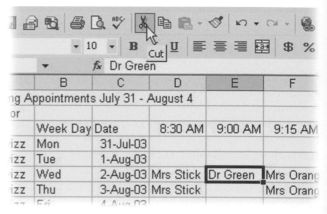

● Dr Green appears in cell E8 and disappears from E6. The data has moved from E6 to E8.

	B	C	D	E	F
	ng Appointments July 31 - August 4				
or					
	Week Day	Date	8:30 AM	9:00 AM	9:15 AM
izz	Mon	31-Jul-03			
izz	Tue	1-Aug-03			
izz	Wed	2-Aug-03	Mrs Stick		Mrs Orang
izz	Thu	3-Aug-03	Mrs Stick		Mrs Orang
izz	Fri	4-Aug-03		Dr Green	
izz	Sat	5-Aug-03		Mr Brown	

MOVING BY DRAG AND DROP

● Moving by drag and drop is identical to copying by drag and drop, except that you don't need to hold down the [Ctrl] key.

● Select cells F6 and F7 (which both contain Ms Orange). Place the mouse pointer over the bottom border of F7 and see that it turns into an arrow.

● Hold down the mouse button and drag the mouse to the left. Once you have positioned the gray outline over cells E6 and E7, release the mouse button.

● The data in cells F6 and F7 moves across.

Date	8:30 AM	9:00 AM	9:15 AM	9:30 AM	10:0
31-Jul-03				Ms Black	
1-Aug-03					
2-Aug-03	Mrs Stick		Mrs Orange		Dr G
3-Aug-03	Mrs Stick		Mrs Orange	Dr Green	Ms
4-Aug-03		Dr Green			Ms
5-Aug-03		Mr Brown			

Date	8:30 AM	9:00 AM	9:15 AM	9:30 AM	10:
31-Jul-03				Ms Black	
1-Aug-03					
2-Aug-03	Mrs Stick	Mrs Orange			Dr G
3-Aug-03	Mrs Stick	Mrs Orange		Dr Green	Ms
4-Aug-03		Dr Green			Ms
5-Aug-03		Mr Brown			

SWAPPING ROWS AND COLUMNS

To swap two adjacent columns, click the right-hand column and click on the **Cut** button. Now click the left-hand column and choose **Cut Cells** from the **Insert** menu. To swap two adjacent rows, select and cut the lower row, then select the upper row and choose **Cut Cells** from the **Insert** menu.

CUTTING AND INSERTING

- When you cut and insert, the cut data is removed from one part of the worksheet and placed into new cell(s) inserted elsewhere in the worksheet. Normally, you have to specify where existing cells should move to accommodate the new cells.
- Select cell G4 (Ms Black). Click on the **Cut** button.
- Select cell E9 and choose **Cut Cells** from the **Insert** menu on the Menu bar.
- In the **Insert Paste** dialog box, choose **Shift cells right**.
- Ms Black moves from cell G4 to cell E9. Other cells in row 9 are shifted to the right to accommodate the new insertion.

How Does Moving Affect Formulas?

Special repercussions arise from moving (or copying) formulas, cells containing formulas, or cells referenced by formulas within a worksheet. However, Excel generally arranges for formulas to continue working wherever they are moved, or wherever data referenced by the formulas is moved.

KEYBOARD SHORTCUT

There is a quick keyboard shortcut for the Cut command. Hold down the Ctrl key and then press the x key. Remember that Ctrl plus c can be used for the Copy command, and Ctrl plus v for the Paste command.

SWAPPING CELLS BY CUTTING AND INSERTING

● If you cut some data and then attempt to insert it elsewhere in the same row or column, Excel manages the operation differently from other cut/insert operations. Instead of creating new cells, it moves the actual cells containing the data, and you are given no choice as to the direction in which other cells should be shifted. The positions of the moved and displaced cells are swapped, which is usually what you want to happen.

● In your Sales worksheet, you want to swap the data in rows 5 (Orange sorbet) and 4 (Chocolate bars). First select the range of cells A5 to D5, and click on the **Cut** button.

● Now select cells A4 to D4 and choose **Cut Cells** from the **Insert** menu.

● The cells that were previously A5 to D5 are moved to A4 to D4, and the cells that were previously A4 to D4 automatically drop down to occupy A5 to D5.

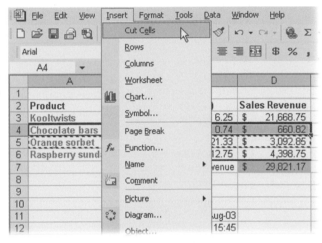

ADDING AND EDITING COMMENTS

So far, you have seen that a cell can contain text, numerical values, and formulas. A cell also has a format associated with it and every cell has a name. A further property that can be associated with a cell is a comment. This is like a note attached to the cell. You can easily add comments to cells and they can be displayed, changed, edited, or deleted at any time in the future.

1 ADDING A COMMENT

● Select a cell to which you would like to add a comment. For this example, select cell A15 in the Sales sheet of the "fantasyices.xls" workbook. Choose **Comment** from the **Insert** menu.

● A pale-yellow comment box appears, joined by a short arrow to the cell it refers to. At the top of the box, Microsoft Excel automatically inserts the name of the licensed user, which it assumes is the "commentator." Below this is a flashing insertion point.

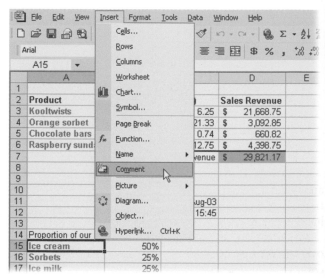

- Type your comment.
- If you are someone different from the recorded licensed user and you wish to register this, double-click on the person's name to highlight it. Then type your own name in its place.
- To close the comment, click on a blank cell outside the comment box.

9			
10		**Last Updated**	
11		Date	15-Aug-03
12		Time	15:45
13			
14	Proportion of our prod	**Dick Twizz:**	
15	Ice cream	I think we can classify	
16	Sorbets	the chocolate bars as ice	
17	Ice milk	cream, for now at least.	
18			
19			
20			
21			
22			
23			
24			
25			

Sales / Diary / Sheet3 /

2 DISPLAY AND EDIT COMMENTS

- Cells with comments attached have a small red triangle at their top right-hand corners.
- Move the mouse pointer over cell A15, and the comment is displayed automatically.
- To edit the comment, move the mouse pointer over the cell and click the right mouse button. A shortcut menu appears. Choose **Edit Comment** from the shortcut menu.
- You can now type in some more text or edit the existing text.

4	Orange sorbet	Page Break	21.33	$
5	Chocolate bars	*fx* Function...	0.74	$
6	Raspberry sund		12.75	$
7		Name ▶	venue	$
8		Edit Comment		
9				
10		Picture ▶		
11		Diagram...	ug-03	
12		Object...	15:45	
13				
14	Proportion of our	Hyperlink... Ctrl+K		
15	Ice cream	50%		
16	Sorbets	25%		
17	Ice milk	25%		
18				

12		Time	15.45
13			
14	Proportion of our prod	the chocolate bars as ice	
15	Ice cream	cream, for now at least.	
16	Sorbets	Even though they	
17	Ice milk	contain only about 35	
18		percent ice	
19			
20			

3 RESIZING A COMMENT BOX

- If the amount of text in a comment box becomes too long for the box, you can resize the box.
- Place your mouse pointer over the bottom right-hand corner of the comment attached to cell A15. You will see it turn into a double-headed arrow.
- Hold down the left mouse button and drag the corner of the comment box to resize it. You will see an outline preview of the new box size.
- Release the mouse button once you are happy with the new size of the box.

11		Date	07-Jun-03
12		Time	15:45
13			
14	Proportion of our prod	Even though they	
15	Ice cream	contain only about 35	
16	Sorbets	percent ice cream, the	
17	Ice milk	rest is toffee and	
18		chocolate.	
19			
20			
21			

Double-headed arrow ●

11		Date	15-Aug-03
12		Time	15:45
13			
14	Proportion of our prod	**Susan Stick:**	
15	Ice cream	I think we can classify	
16	Sorbets	the chocolate bars as ice	
17	Ice milk	cream, for now at least.	
18		Even though they	
19			
20			
21			
22			

LOTS OF COMMENTS

To display all comments on a worksheet at the same time, choose **Options** from the **Tools** menu and click on the **View** tab at the top of the dialog box. Choose **Comment & indicator**, and then click on **OK**. Change the option back to **Comment indicator only** to hide comments.

11		Date	07-Jun-03
12		Time	15:45
13			
14	Proportion of our prod	**Susan Stick:**	
15	Ice cream	I think we can classify the	
16	Sorbets	chocolate bars as ice cream, for	
17	Ice milk	now at least. Even though they	
18		contain only about 35 percent ice	
19		cream, the rest is toffee and	
20		chocolate.	
21			
22			
23			
24			
25			

H ◄ ► H \ Sales / Diary / Sheet3 /

CLEARING CELLS

Occasionally you'll want to remove some worksheet data. You can either clear or delete relevant cells. Of these, clearing is the less drastic maneuver. When you clear a cell, you remove some (or all) of the items associated with the cell without removing the cell itself. You have to choose whether you want to remove the cell's contents, its format, comments attached to the cell, or all of these at once.

1 CLEARING A FORMAT

● You can clear the format from a cell without changing its contents (values or formulas it contains). The cell then reverts to a "general" format – the standard format that all cells have before they are given any special format.

● In the Sales worksheet, choose cell B10, which reads "Last Updated."

● Choose **Clear** from the **Edit** menu, and **Formats** from the submenu.

● Cell B10 reverts to a standard format.

Clearing a Comment
To clear a comment (but not content or format) from a cell, right-click the cell and choose **Delete Comment** from the pop-up menu.

2 CLEARING CELL CONTENTS

● It is common practice to clear cell contents, but you must remember that clearing contents alone does not remove formats and comments.

● Select cells A15 and B15 in the Sales worksheet.

● With the mouse pointer over cell B15, click the right mouse button and a pop-up shortcut menu appears. Choose **Clear Contents**.

● The cells' contents have been removed, but the little red triangle indicates that there is still a comment attached to cell A15.

● Cell A15 has also retained its special format. Type **Ice cream** back into the cell and the continuing presence of both the comment and special format becomes apparent.

12		Time		15:45
13				
14	Proportion of our products that are			
15	Ice cream	50%		
16	Sorbets	25%		
17	Ice milk	25%		
18				
19				

3	Kooltwists	3467	Insert...	21,668
4	Orange sorbet	145	Delete...	3,092
5	Chocolate bars	893		660
6	Raspberry sundae	345	Clear Contents	4,398
7				29,821
8			Edit Comment	
9			Delete Comment	
10		Last Updated	Show Comment	
11		Date		
12		Time	Format Cells...	
13			Pick From List...	
14	Proportion of our products that are		Hyperlink...	
15	Ice cream	50%		
16	Sorbets	25%		
17	Ice milk	25%		

14	Proportion of our products that are		
15			
16	Sorbets	25%	
17	Ice milk	25%	
18			
19			

CLEARING BY FILLING

An alternative method for clearing cells is to use the Fill Handle to duplicate empty, blank cells over the area you wish to clear. This method clears the contents and formats but not the comments.

10		Last Updated	
11		Date	07-Jun-03
12		Time	15:45
13			
14	Proportion of our produ		
15	Ice cream		
16	Sorbets		
17	Ice milk		
18			
19			
20			
21			
22			

Susan Stick:
I think we can classify the chocolate bars as ice cream, for now at least. Even though

3 CLEARING ALL FROM CELLS

● If you want to clear out a cell completely, returning it to a pristine state, use the Clear All command.

● Select the range A14 to B17 in the Sales worksheet.

● Choose **Clear** from the **Edit** menu and then choose **All** from the submenu.

● Everything – contents, formats, and comments – has now been removed.

CLEARING WITH THE KEYBOARD

You can clear contents (not formats and comments) from a cell, or a range of cells, by selecting the cell(s) and then hitting the ← Bksp or Del. Never try to clear a cell by typing a space into it (using the keyboard spacebar). The cell may look empty, but it actually contains a space character that could cause problems later on.

DELETING COLUMNS, ROWS, AND CELLS

Deleting columns, rows, and cells means removing the actual cells from the worksheet and not just the cell contents. Just as nature abhors a vacuum, similarly Excel cannot tolerate "holes" in worksheets. So, when cells, rows, or columns are deleted, other cells in the worksheet have to be shifted in order to plug the gap. Deletions are thus the diametric opposite of insertions ⌐.

1 DELETING A COLUMN

● Try practicing some deletions on the Diary worksheet you have created in the "fantasyices.xls" workbook.

● Mr Twizz and Mrs Stick decide they don't want to meet up for any 8:30 am appointments after all. Select column D, and then choose **Delete** from the **Edit** menu.

● Column D is deleted, and all columns to the right of column D shift one column to the left.

2 DELETING A FEW ROWS

● Mr Bloggs leaves, so he no longer requires space in the Diary worksheet.

● Select rows 12 to 20, click on the right mouse button, and choose **Delete** from the pop-up menu.

286 **Inserting New Columns, Rows, and Cells**

- Rows 12 to 20 disappear, and the rows below row 20 move up to fill the gap that the deletion created.

3 DELETING SOME CELLS

- Mr Twizz decides to cancel his 9:15 am appointments. Select cells E3 to E10, and then choose **Delete** from the **Edit** menu.

- A dialog box appears asking whether you want to shift cells left or shift cells up. Choose **Shift cells left** and click on **OK**.

- Cells E3 to E10 are removed, and cells to the right are shifted left.

SURE YOU WANT TO DELETE?

Before deleting cells, ask yourself whether you really just want to clear them ⃞. Deleting cells removes the cells from the worksheet and moves other worksheet cells. If all you want to do is to "blank out" some cells, use the **Clear** command instead.

305 **Clearing Cells**

USING THE INTERNET

USING THE INTERNET is an easy-to-follow guide to exploring the internet through your PC. In this section, you will find explanations on everything from understanding the toolbars to using email and choosing a search provider, helping you to make the most of what the internet has to offer. It takes you through simple and advanced searching techniques, explains how to use different search commands; and gives you an overview of the major search engines and directories, as well as telling you the differences between the two. It also provides you with details about specialized search providers that can help you to find people, news, and software.

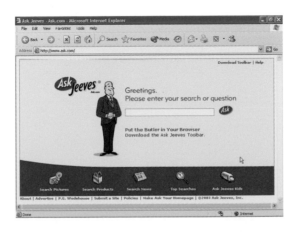

INTERNET AND EMAIL

Just a few years ago, the idea that people around the world would soon be talking, shopping, and working by using the internet and email appeared very far-fetched indeed.

GETTING CONNECTED

Windows XP makes it very easy to connect to the internet through wizard-driven help screens. Once connected, you can launch Internet Explorer, known as your "internet browser," to log on at the start of each session on the internet.

WHAT YOU WILL NEED

Internet Explorer is there to let you browse the worldwide web, but there are a couple of extra items that are needed before you can connect. All modern PCs will have an internal modem installed, but you will also need a telephone cable connected to this. The other end of the cable needs to be attached to the telephone line. High speed, or broadband, internet connections are becomingly increasingly popular with home users, allowing you to download large files much more quickly.

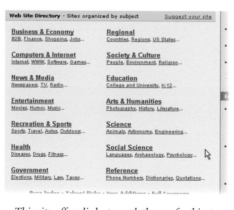

This site offers links to a plethora of subjects. Each of the links contains its own links.

WHAT'S ON THE INTERNET?

Perhaps the question should really be, "What isn't on the internet?" Whether you are using it for research on American Transcendentalism and need details on the life and works of Emerson, or whether you need details on the latest space launch from Cape Canaveral, the answers will be online. Text and images can be selected and pasted into Wordpad for later use. Pages can be bookmarked for revisiting at a later date, and you may even build a website of your own where you can share your news and views.

THE INTERNET CONNECTION WIZARD

The first time that you use Internet Explorer, you will be presented with the Internet Connection Wizard. This will help you to set up a new internet account and should make getting online a pain-free experience. By default, your homepage and the first website that you see will be Microsoft's site (**MSN.com**).

CONNECTION WIZARD

- Double-click on the **Internet Explorer** icon on the desktop.
- The **New Connection Wizard** opens. Click the **Next** button. By default, the **Connect to the Internet** radio button is selected.
- Follow the sequence of the Internet Connection Wizard's screens, and you will establish your internet connection.

Internet Service Provider (ISP)
The Internet Connection Wizard will put you in touch with an ISP. An ISP provides your gateway to the internet, with a local telephone number that gives you access to its servers.

<table>
<tr><td>

OTHER WAYS TO CONNECT

The Internet Connection Wizard can be opened via its own menu entry. Click on the **Start** button, select **All Programs**, then **Accessories**, move to **Communications**, and then select **New Connection Wizard**.

</td></tr>
</table>

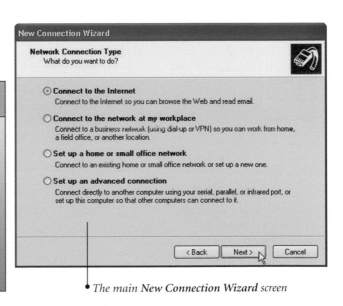

New Connection Wizard

Network Connection Type
What do you want to do?

- ⦿ **Connect to the Internet**
  Connect to the Internet so you can browse the Web and read email.

- ○ **Connect to the network at my workplace**
  Connect to a business network (using dial-up or VPN) so you can work from home, a field office, or another location.

- ○ **Set up a home or small office network**
  Connect to an existing home or small office network or set up a new one.

- ○ **Set up an advanced connection**
  Connect directly to another computer using your serial, parallel, or infrared port, or set up this computer so that other computers can connect to it.

[< Back] [Next >] [Cancel]

• *The main **New Connection Wizard** screen*

INTERNET EXPLORER

Internet Explorer heads a suite of programs produced by Microsoft dedicated to everything internet-related, from browsing the web, to writing and sending emails, to building and publishing your own web pages. Internet Explorer is a web browser, and it is the most popular program for exploring the internet.

WHAT DOES EXPLORER DO?

Internet Explorer is the web-browsing program that enables you to connect to websites and view them, surf the web using hypertext links, and download (copy) files from the internet to your own computer. By default, its email features operate through Outlook Express.

SEARCH WITH INTERNET EXPLORER

Once you are connected to the internet, you can start to discover just what Internet Explorer can do. You can navigate the internet with Explorer using just a small number of buttons, but searching can be made much more efficient by using a range of tools and techniques. These are covered in detail in the following chapters ◻.

*Type in a keyword here, and then click on the **Search** button below to start viewing a website; note that there are other options for obtaining different search results by clicking on one of the radio buttons above*

324 **Searching Efficiently**

THE STANDARD TOOLBAR

1 Back
2 Forward
The Back and Forward buttons take you through the web pages you have visited.
3 Address bar
Enter the address of a website and go directly to that site.
4 Stop
Stops a page downloading.
5 Refresh
Refreshes the current page.

6 Home
Loads the default home page.
7 Search
Opens the Search panel in the Explorer window. This gives you access to features that help you connect to search engines.
8 Favorites
Save, access, and manage your favorite sites on the web.
9 Media
Find and play video and music.

10 History
Opens the History panel.
11 Mail
A menu of email options.
12 Print
Prints the current page.
13 Edit
Edit and save a version of the current web page.
14 Messenger
Find out who's online and sending messages.

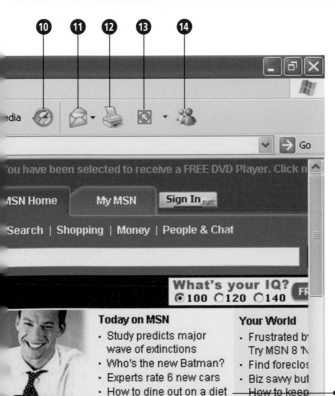

www.msn.com
The website shown here, **www.msn. com**, is Microsoft's main website. Each of the links down the left-hand side opens up a page containing hundreds of links to other pages related to that topic.

• *This is the main window where everything that you choose to view is displayed*

GETTING ONLINE HELP AND SUPPORT

Windows XP **Help and Support** is an invaluable source of answers to questions that will help you make the most of your computer. You can take tours that provide overviews of given topics, follow step-by-step instructions to achieve a desired result, find troubleshooting tips, and link to the internet for up-to-date information.

1 HELP BY TOPIC

● Clicking on **Help and Support** in the **Start** menu opens the **Help and Support** center.

● Type a keyword in the **Search** panel, or choose a topic from the list to have Windows look for you.

Type in a keyword here, or select a help topic from the list below

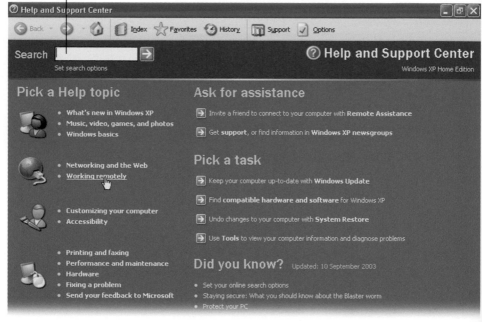

2 TYPE IN THE KEYWORD

- In this example, we have typed the keyword **Music** into the **Search** field.
- Click on the green arrow.

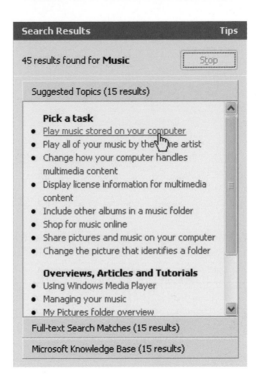

3 THE SEARCH RESULTS

- As you can see, there is an astonishing number of results returned. Clicking on one of the topics will take you to that subject.

Using the index
An alternative method of finding help on the subject area that's puzzling you is to click on **the Index** icon in the toolbar at the top of the screen. You can then enter the precise term describing what you need help with.

4 NARROWING THE SEARCH

- Once a topic has been selected, the instructions are displayed in the right-hand panel. For more information on other, similar subjects, click the **Related Topics** command and select an option from the menu.

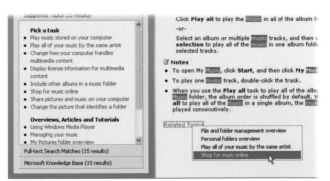

MICROSOFT OUTLOOK EXPRESS

Email is simply the electronic equivalent of the postal service. From your address, you send mail to your ISP 📄, which sends the mail via the worldwide network of servers to the recipient's ISP, from which he or she can get mail addressed to them.

EMAIL

Outlook Express is an application for sending, receiving, and managing your email. It has the facility for storing all your email addresses and personal contact details in an electronic address book, which is easy to edit and keep up-to-date.

With Outlook Express, you can send and receive emails that contain, not only text elements, but also images, separate documents, and links to websites that you want to share with friends. Images and documents can easily be sent as "attachments" that the recipient can open and view.

THE ELEMENTS THAT MAKE UP AN EMAIL ADDRESS

When you signed up with your ISP, you will have been asked to give details for your email address. This address is unique to you and is made up from several pieces of information, including your name and country code.

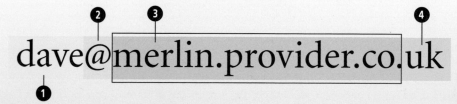

❶ User Name
Identifies the addressee.
❷ Separator
An @ ("at") symbol separates the user and domain names.

❸ Domain name
The computer address, with dots (periods) as separators.
❹ Country code
All countries except the US use a

two-letter suffix as the last part of the address. For example, uk stands for the United Kingdom, il for Israel, and nz for New Zealand.

LAUNCHING OUTLOOK EXPRESS

You can launch the application, Outlook Express, in three principal ways: from the Windows Start Menu, from the Windows desktop (if the Outlook Express shortcut is there), or from within Microsoft Internet Explorer itself.

FROM THE START MENU

● To launch Outlook Express from the Start menu, click on the **Start** button and select **Outlook Express** from the program icons in the left-hand list.

FROM THE DESKTOP

● To launch Outlook Express from the desktop, locate the **Outlook Express** shortcut icon and double-click on it with the left mouse button.

FROM INTERNET EXPLORER

● Open Internet Explorer and click on the **Mail** button on the main toolbar.
● Select the option that you require from the drop-down menu.

● Outlook Express is launched, showing either the **Inbox**, in which you can read your mail, or a new message window, in which to write an email, depending on the option that you selected.

THE OUTLOOK EXPRESS WINDOW

The Outlook Express window is divided into different sections, some of which are visible only when you perform the actions they relate to. You can personalize the Outlook Express window to display as many of these elements as you wish.

WINDOW PANELS

1 Outlook bar
The Outlook bar provides handy shortcuts to some of the key folders. You can customize the Outlook bar to include the folders that you use most frequently.

2 Contacts panel
This panel displays a list of all the contacts that are stored in the current user's Address Book.

3 Folders panel
A folder can be selected in this panel to become the currently active folder whose contents are displayed in the main area of the window.

4 Folders list
This shows all the folders and subfolders in which the current user's email and newsgroup messages have been saved.

5 Views bar
The Views bar allows you to show or hide different categories of messages according to your choice.

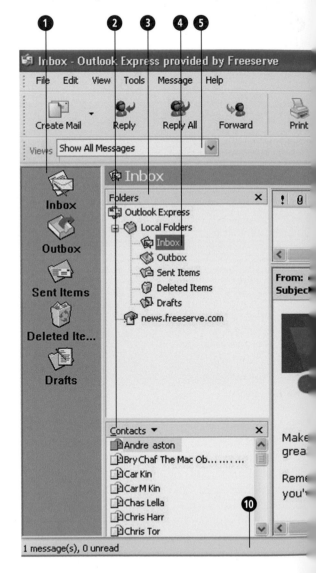

THE MENU BAR

The menu bar at the top of the screen, just below the title bar, contains menu options, such as **File** and **Edit**, that are shared with other Microsoft programs and may be familiar. However, the **Message** option, through which messages are controlled, is unique to Outlook Express.

Subject

Better Bidding and Simpler Selling with eBay!

.co.uk
impler Selling with eBay!

r **bidding** and simpler **sellir**

eBay.co.uk's **Helpf**

ig at **eBay.co.uk** more fun with our helpful hints
site to help you, but here's a selection to get yc

your username, robbeattie and your password tc
password simply **click here** and we'll help you ot

Working Online

WINDOW PANELS

6 Message list
This shows a list of all the messages that are contained in the active folder (the folder that has been selected from the Folder list or Outlook bar).
7 Preview panel header
Contains summary information about the currently selected message.
8 Preview panel
The contents of the selected message in the Message list can be read here.
9 Toolbar
The bar at the top of your screen displays buttons that enable you to access Outlook's main features quickly and easily. The items on the toolbar change depending on which part of the program you are using.
10 Status bar
Displays information about activities that you perform and the status of your internet connection.

THE MESSAGE WINDOW

Once the **Create Mail** button has been clicked on the toolbar, an email can be composed in the Message window. Email messages are made from several parts. The message header contains the sender's and the recipient's address details, and the subject of the message. The message body contains the message itself. A message may also contain other elements, such as file attachments.

COMPOSING A NEW MESSAGE

● Select a mail folder, such as the **Inbox**, by clicking on it in the Folder list or Outlook bar.

● Click the **Create Mail** button on the toolbar. This opens a new Outlook Express message window.

● Click the left mouse button in the message body area of the window and type in the text of your message.

● Address the message.

● Add a subject line.

● Add any file attachments to send with the message.

● Send the message.

*When you have finished composing your message and have addressed the mail, click on the **Send** button.*

ELEMENTS OF THE MESSAGE WINDOW

❶ The To: field
This contains the email address of the recipient of the message. Every message must contain the address.

❷ The Cc: field
This contains the email addresses of people to whom you would like to send "carbon copies" of the message.

❸ The Subject: field
This contains the subject of the message. Filling in the subject is optional, but it is good practice to use a subject so that people can tell at a glance what your message is about.

❹ Message Body
This is where you type the text of the message. It acts as a normal word-processing window.

❺ Toolbar
This provides access to the main activities you will want to carry out when typing a message. There are buttons for editing text (cut, copy, and paste); for checking spelling; and for sending and prioritizing the message when it is finished.

❻ Formatting Toolbar
This offers some of the standard word-processing features to enable you to align text, choose

the font and style, manage paragraphs, and add bullet points. Formatting can only be applied to text that has been selected (by clicking and dragging the mouse). Not all email programs have the sophisticated word-processing features that Outlook Express contains. If you do not know which program the addressee has on his computer, it is advisable not to add complex formatting to your email message because his email program may not have the facilities to display it.

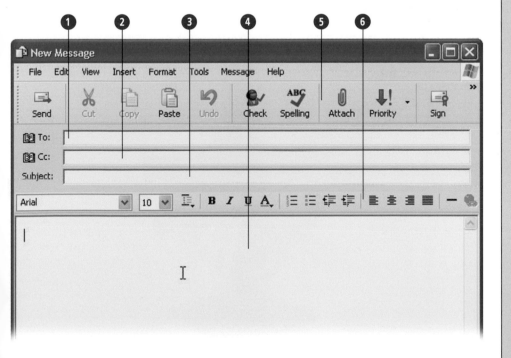

WINDOW ON THE WEB

The web browser program installed on your PC is the window through which you view the web. As well as taking you straight to known web addresses, it is the starting point for any search.

SEARCHING EFFICIENTLY

For millions of people around the world, the internet has become an invaluable treasure house of information, a vast source of software, music, games, pictures, and data. Over the last few years, it has also become a global online shopping mall. Whatever you're looking for, it's probably available via the net.

SAVING VALUABLE TIME

Surprisingly, very few people think about how to make their internet searching as efficient as possible. As a newcomer to the internet, you may enjoy "surfing" through endless websites in the course of your quest but, as you may already have discovered, a search in its simplest form can return many thousands of suggested websites that would take hours to sift through. As the novelty wears off and the internet becomes an increasingly essential tool, rather than a new toy, this section of the book will help you to search quickly and efficiently. By following the step-by-step instructions and learning how a variety of search tools work, you will soon be able to:

1 Choose the right search tool for the job.

2 Structure your search queries efficiently.

3 Become a power user of search tools.

Order out of chaos

The internet has been described as the new Wild West and, because of its nature, imposing any order is almost impossible. You can, however, impose your own order on this chaos by knowing how to search it.

STARTING FROM THE BROWSER

A web browser is a piece of software installed on your PC that lets you look at (or "browse") different websites. It also enables you to start a search, and will connect you to the search engines that can help you find what you're looking for. Although a number of different browsers are available, Microsoft's Internet Explorer is far and away the most popular, and it is the program we have used in the examples shown in this section. You can have more than one browser installed on your PC at the same time, and it is a matter of personal preference which one you use.

WHAT IS EXPLORER?

Microsoft Internet Explorer comes as a standard part of Windows software and was probably already installed on your computer when it arrived. A suite of internet-related programs that includes Outlook Express and FrontPage, Internet Explorer enables you to connect to websites and view them, surf the web using hypertext links, and download programs and files from the internet

Seen through Explorer
The web browser interprets the code that makes up a web page, and presents the page on your computer screen.

to your own computer. By default, its email features operate through Outlook Express, and its edit feature is directly linked to FrontPage, which can be used to create and publish your own web pages.

DIFFERENCES IN APPEARANCE

Most websites look the same whatever browser you use. But you might notice small changes if you view the same page using different browsers. This is because the language used for web pages (called Hypertext Markup Language, or HTML) describes how a page appears, and different browsers may interpret the HTML instructions differently.

THE EXPLORER TOOLBAR

It is perfectly possible to use Internet Explorer using only the features provided on the standard buttons toolbar. This toolbar is at the top of the Explorer window and comprises a row of graphically styled buttons. These buttons are shortcuts to features that will help you find your way round the web quickly, so it is worth spending time familiarizing yourself with the toolbar and learning what each symbol means. Each item on the toolbar is also in the main menus.

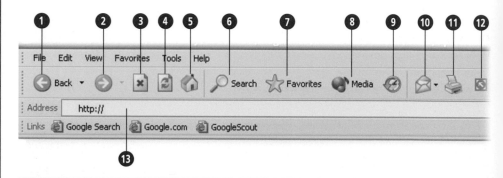

THE STANDARD TOOLBAR

1 Back
Takes you back through web pages you have already visited.

2 Forward
Once you have used the Back button, takes you forward through the web pages again.

3 Stop
If you change your mind or your browser is having a problem downloading a page, click this button to stop the page downloading.

4 Refresh
Refreshes the current page by downloading it again.

5 Home
Loads the default home page,
or the web page that you have chosen as your home page, such as a search engine 📄.

6 Search
Opens the Search panel in the Explorer window. This gives you access to features that help you connect to search engines.

7 Favorites
Opens the Favorites panel, where you can create and manage a list of your favorite sites on the web, giving you easy access to these sites.

8 Media
Helps you find and play back music and video clips through WindowsMedia.com.

9 History
Opens the History panel, where you can store a list of all the websites you have visited.

10 Mail
Provides a menu of options relating to email, such as reading your email or creating a new message.

11 Print
Prints the current page.

12 Edit
Allows you to edit the HTML code of the current web page.

13 Address bar
Allows you to type in the address of a known website and go directly to that site.

337 Search Engines

RUNNING A SIMPLE SEARCH

In the very simplest form of search carried out using Internet Explorer, the search term is typed in, and a designated search engine returns a list of sites. The problem is that there may be thousands of sites with varying degrees of relevance.

1 CHOOSING THE SEARCH BUTTON

● With Internet Explorer running, click the **Search** button on the toolbar. This will create a frame on the left of the browser window.

2 KEYING IN THE SEARCH TERM

● Type a search term in the search text box and click on **Search.** The search begins.
● Note that there is a **Customize** button in this frame. Clicking on this allows you to change the way Explorer searches for items, and which search engine is used. In this case the search engine is MSN.

3 VIEWING THE LIST OF HITS

● When the list of hits appears in the left-hand frame, click any entry to display that site in the main part of the browser window. MSN also displays a helpful preview of the most likely websites in the right-hand window.

4 SEARCHING FROM THE DESKTOP

● You can also use the Search Companion to locate the information you need on the internet.

● Click the **Start** button and then choose **Search** from the pop-up menu.

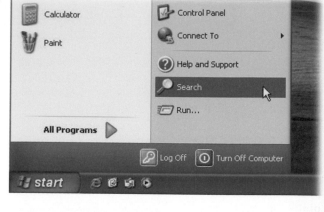

● When the Search Companion window opens, look down the list of options in the left-hand panel and click on **Search the Internet**.

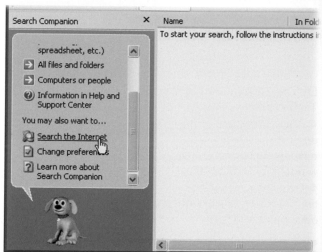

STARTING THE SEARCH

● Type your search query into the panel below **Find a Web page containing**, and then click on **Search**.

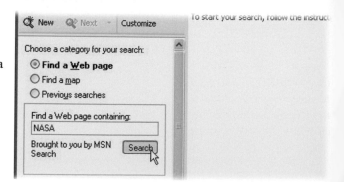

ANALYZING THE RESULTS

● The search engine will return a list of suggested websites.

● You can click on any of the topics in the left-hand panel to jump directly to that website.

● Note that in this example we are using the MSN search engine, which also previews a small selection of the suggested windows in the right-hand panel.

● Click on the website you want to visit.

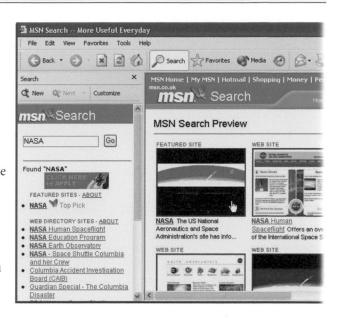

DISPLAYING THE WEB PAGE

● The selection we clicked on in the previous step is now displayed in the main window.

● Clicking on hyperlinked text 🖰 on the web page will open further pages.

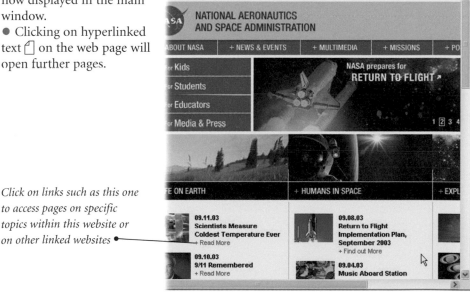

Click on links such as this one to access pages on specific topics within this website or on other linked websites ●

464 **What Is a Hyperlink?**

SEARCH TOOLS

Web searching is made possible through the services of search providers, who offer software and databases that are accessed through the web browser or through the provider's website.

WHAT DO SEARCH TOOLS DO?

When you use a search engine, web directory, or internet search program of any kind, you are never running a "live" search of what is on the internet at that moment. You are really using a program to interrogate a database owned by the search provider, and which may contain information from millions of pages.

DIFFERENT WAYS OF WORKING

Despite the similarity between the "portal" interfaces of the most visited search tools, you will soon find that search providers return widely differing search results and present them in different ways. This is because the databases on which these engines and directories are based are built and managed in very different ways. The first reason for this is the differing information on the search providers' databases. This information has to be collected, collated, and organized before it is ready for public use, and every search provider carries out these stages in a different way.

Some databases are more current than others, or are larger and contain more data. Some search providers can deliver results more quickly than others, and some have more user-friendly or more easily customized interfaces. Some providers are selective in what they collect and may provide site reviews. Others process all the data on a web page regardless of its content or quality, and although the database may therefore look as though it is more comprehensive, it may actually be less efficient and offer less useful search results.

Accessing information
The way in which data is collected, stored, and organized in a database will affect the quality of the results it provides.

DIFFERENT RESULTS

These differences explain why the same search query can produce very different outcomes. Search results from different providers vary in terms of:

- speed of response
- total number of hits
- number of relevant hits
- position of relevant hits
- presentation of hits.

The factors that tend to make us favor one search provider over another relate to the efficiency and usability of the interface. In the end, your choice will usually be determined partly from personal preference for the interface and partly because you want to pick the right tool for a particular type of search. However, there are other important considerations, and these are explained in the following pages.

DIRECTORIES AND ENGINES

One important element that distinguishes one search provider from another is the way they make the information stored in their databases available. Yahoo and Lycos are directory-based , classifying the data like a table of contents, whereas AlltheWeb and Google are search engines that rely on their powerful search software.

WEB DIRECTORY OR SEARCH ENGINE?

A web directory is essentially a list of links, usually accompanied by a site description and sometimes a review. The user starts at a top level category, or classification, and then drills down through a series of deeper subcategories until reaching the specific subject area and the required site. A search engine enables a user to search a database created by the search provider.

Speed of search
How long does it take to give useful results?

A search engine provides pages of hits – often thousands of them – arranged by relevance to the query. In either case, the speed with which a particular search tool produces the results you need and the ease with which you can use its tools and access the results are key factors in determining whether or not you use it for your search.

Ease of use
Only using a search tool will show you how easy it is to access its features and the search results.

332 **Web Directories**

337 **Search Engines**

WEB DIRECTORIES

Web page author submits URL to the web directory.

Web site owners submit their site's address, or URL (standing for "Uniform Resource Locator"), to the search engine 🗋. Most search engines and web directories provide a "Submit Your Site" option on their main web page to allow the authors of web pages to do this. A reviewer then assesses the page and decides whether to include it in the directory. This process can take several weeks, or even months for some directories.

Web directory reviewer/editor assesses the submission.

Search Provider's Database
If the web reviewer passes the page for inclusion, it will be categorized before being placed in the web directory.

Some web pages are rejected by the reviewer and do not make it into the directory.

Searching the web
A description and URL for the web page will now appear in the appropriate category.

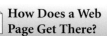

How Does a Web
333 Page Get There?

How Does a Web Page Get There?

Information for web directories is compiled and collated (and often rejected) by reviewers and editors employed by search providers. Most providers offer a step-by-step method for submitting web pages for scrutiny, so this process can best be understood by looking at it from a web page author's point of view. For example, if you had just completed an illustrated history of backgammon, you might want to make it available through the search provider Yahoo! Using the web browser, you would first go to the Yahoo! home page and find the category in which the page should be placed by starting at one of the 14 top-level categories and drilling down to find the most appropriate subcategory for the page.

SUBMITTING THE WEB PAGE

For our backgammon example, this is fairly straightforward as there is a specific Backgammon subcategory within the Recreation>Games>Board Games section of the directory. Having located the appropriate page, all you need to do is click the **Suggest a Site** link at the top of the screen. It is very important to follow this procedure carefully when registering a site with a search provider, such as Yahoo!, because by giving the site reviewer the most useful information regarding the content and category of your site, you give it the best chance of inclusion in the directory. Directory users are very likely to do precisely what you have just done when looking for sites on backgammon. So your time and effort at this stage will be well-spent to make your site available to users.

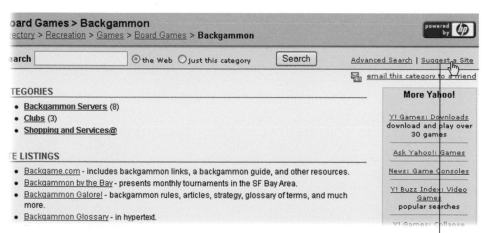

The first step in "posting" your site

MAKING THE LINK

● After clicking **Suggest a Site** in Yahoo! you are taken through a step-by-step sequence.

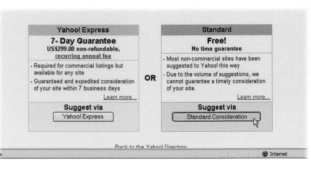

● At the next screen, click the **Continue** button.

● In the online form that appears, type in the details of your web page following the bulleted advice below each box.

● This information helps the reviewer to decide whether you have chosen the correct category for your web page.

● The reviewer will then look at your web page and apply the search provider's acceptance criteria before deciding whether or not your page makes it into the directory's database.

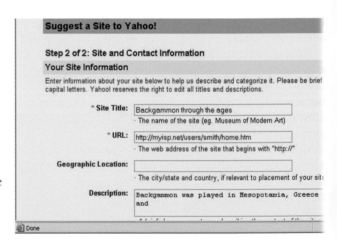

Always read the Help file...
Always read the search provider's Help files before submitting a site. As well as helping web authors to promote their sites more efficiently, the Help files will also provide all users with useful information about how the search engine or web directory works. Reading these, in conjunction with the advanced search documentation, will quickly give you an understanding of the directory and make you a power user, which is never a bad thing!

CHANGING A WEB PAGE'S DIRECTORY LISTING

● If you add pages to a website that are likely to change its listing (for example, if your history of backgammon becomes a history of backgammon *and* checkers) you need to inform the directory provider. In the case of Yahoo! you would use the online **change form** option in the **Suggest a Site** page. Web directory reviewers need to be warned when a web page changes so that they can reassess the site and recategorize it.

● As you will see 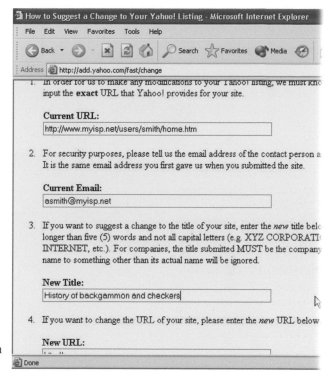, search engines need no input from the web page author because they operate almost completely automatically. If you change your site, most search engines will pick up these changes and amend their databases.

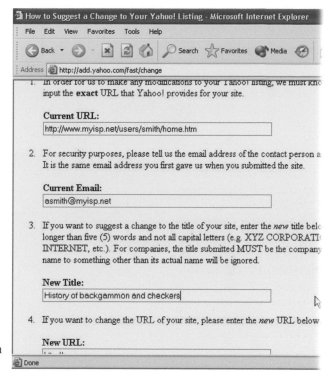

How to Suggest a Change to Your Yahoo! Listing - Microsoft Internet Explorer

File   Edit   View   Favorites   Tools   Help

Back · ⊙ · ⊠ ⊡ ⚑   Search ⚡ Favorites ⚑ Media ⚑

Address 🔲 http://add.yahoo.com/fast/change

1. In order for us to make any modifications to your Yahoo! listing, we must know input the **exact** URL that Yahoo! provides for your site.

    Current URL:
    http://www.myisp.net/users/smith/home.htm

2. For security purposes, please tell us the email address of the contact person a It is the same email address you first gave us when you submitted the site.

    Current Email:
    asmith@myisp.net

3. If you want to suggest a change to the title of your site, enter the *new* title belo longer than five (5) words and not all capital letters (e.g. XYZ CORPORATI INTERNET, etc.). For companies, the title submitted MUST be the company name to something other than its actual name will be ignored.

    New Title:
    History of backgammon and checkers

4. If you want to change the URL of your site, please enter the *new* URL below

    New URL:

🔲 Done

CONVERGING SERVICES

Yahoo! is, of course, only one of many web directories available free to users on the web. Many search engine providers now include a web directory on their websites, though on a far more modest scale than the Yahoo! directory. Many directory services now also offer a search engine. Rather than developing these additional services in-house, search providers are now commonly striking up partnership deals with each other, and it is not uncommon for several "rival" web directories to draw on the same database. However, the results are usually processed and presented in different ways, so that it is difficult for most of us to spot the shared connections.

SHARED DIRECTORIES

The directories featured here are evidence that databases are becoming more and more thorough in their coverage of the contents of the internet, and that these databases are being shared by an ever-growing number of search providers.

THE OPEN DIRECTORY PROJECT

This initiative aims to build a comprehensive directory of the web using mainly volunteer editors. In fact, at the ODP website **dmoz.org** you are encouraged to "Become an Editor." You can choose a topic and, by using the tools provided, add, delete, and update links. The Open Directory Project's data is used by a very large number of search providers including Google, AltaVista, Lycos, AOL Search, and HotBot.

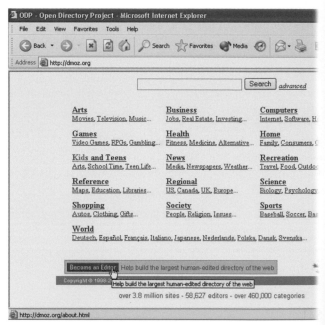

LEADING DIRECTORY PROVIDERS

One powerful directory provider is LookSmart (**www.looksmart.com**), which claims to have a directory of 2 million sites indexed into 200,000 categories. It has some of the major players as partners, such as MSN, About.com, and Lycos.

SEARCH ENGINES

A search engine consists of a database of sites on the internet, and software (known as spiders, crawlers, worms, or web robots) that endlessly trawl the internet collecting data to feed back to the database for processing and possible inclusion. Spiders also check out websites submitted to the search engine.

*Author's new page
is made available
on the internet*

The internet

*Author submits the
same page to the
search engine*

*The internet comprises the web,
Usenet, newsgroups, databases,
Newsfeeds etc.*

*Spiders visit web pages that
have been submitted by
authors and return data to
the database*

*Spiders, unlike their organic
counterparts, are searching
the web 24 hours a day
locating new data*

Search Provider's database

*Using the data returned by
spiders, the search provider's
database accumulates vast
records of URLs related to
their keywords*

*Users search the database by
submitting search queries to
the search engine*

SEARCHING THE LINKS

Search engines collect information for their databases by using software called robots – which are more usually known as spiders or crawlers. Spiders trawl websites collecting information for the search providers' databases.

The information collected will usually vary between search providers. Most spiders find new web pages by following links within documents, and then links within the linked documents, and so on. It obviously doesn't take long to build up a collection of many thousands of URLs based on this simple principle. Different spiders collect different kinds of data from the web pages (and other information sources) they visit. Spiders are usually programmed to collect all or some of the following elements:

TITLES
The titles of individual web pages as defined by the web-page author.

CONTENT (INITIAL PARAGRAPHS)
The first few paragraphs of any web page.

META TAGS (SEE BELOW)
Hidden content, as defined in META tags.

CONTENT (ENTIRE)
The entire contents of a web page.

META TAGS

META tags are lines of text hidden within a web page's HTML code. The META tags most commonly collected by spiders relate to keywords and description. By default, when a search engine give a description of a website in its list of hits, it shows the opening paragraphs of a web page. However, some search engines will replace this with the description you have specified within the Description META tag.

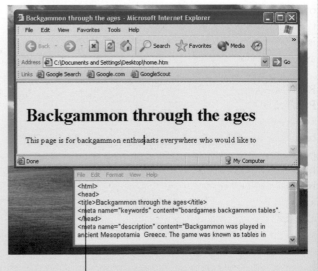

The title tag is the part of an HTML page that is most commonly collected by spiders

PROCESSING THE INFORMATION

- Having spidered a website, a search engine processes the information to ensure that searches return relevant hits.
- Some concentrate on the frequency and position of these keywords. Nearly all search engines look for keywords in the pages' titles, heads, subheads, and text in the first paragraphs.

FREQUENCY RATING

- These calculations help give the page a frequency rating for a term. Pages with a high frequency rating are at the top of lists of hits of searches for that term. The rating of pages is usually performed automatically.

RATING BY POPULARITY

- Services such as Google base their ratings on a popularity system. A site linked to by many others is judged to be important, and if it is linked to by already important sites, the site is rated even higher.
- As the ranking of sites has no direct human involvement, Google can claim to be both spam- and bias-resistant.

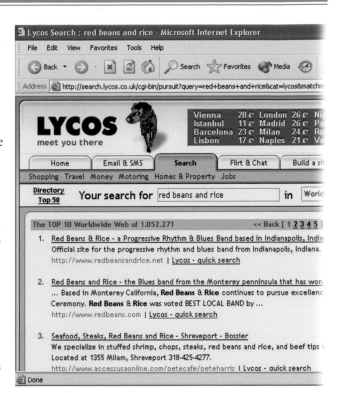

METASEARCH PROGRAMS

Metasearch programs enable you to interrogate a number of search providers simultaneously, and offer both search engines and web directories. The providers of metasearch programs do not usually own or produce their own databases of websites and URLs. They provide the gateway for simultaneous searches to be carried out on the services with which they deal.

BROAD SEARCHES

● Metasearch programs can be extremely useful if you need to find out how much exists on the web on a particular topic. For broad searches, they are extremely useful.

● The Metacrawler engine (**www.metacrawler.com**) searches a large number of search engines and web directories, and ranks its findings by their relevance to your initial search term.

DEEP WEB SEARCH

● The "deep web", which includes dynamic pages that are inaccessible to crawler-based search engines, may be the new cyberspace frontier.

● Turbo 10 (**turbo10.com**) works by selecting the ten search engines best suited to your query to produce an up-to-date listing of live pages. Control buttons allow you to flick through the results.

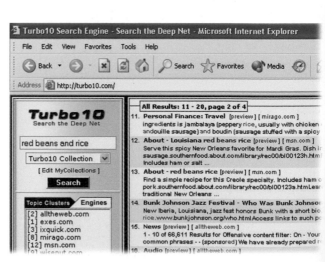

STANDALONE SEARCH PROGRAMS

As an alternative to one of the web-based search engines, an increasing number of people now use a standalone search agent – in other words a program that you install on your PC and use as your main (or possibly your only) search tool.

COPERNIC AGENT BASIC

● The example shown here, Copernic Agent Basic ▢, functions in many ways as a metasearch engine. Search terms are highlighted in the hits list. Previous searches are saved, if required, in the top frame. This program also enables you to download documents or images for offline browsing.

● Updates are carried out automatically including information about engines and categories. Programs like Copernic do not necessarily offer anything that the best web-based search providers cannot offer. However, their offline capabilities and the fact that they can connect directly to a wide range of information sources make them a very interesting alternative for many users.

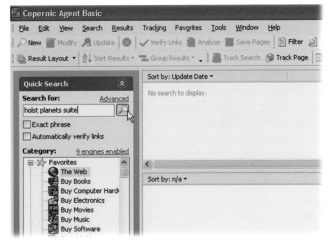

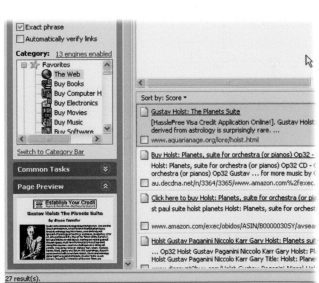

Software Selection

USING SEARCH ENGINES

Ask a bookseller for a book on "entertainment" and you will get, at best, a perplexed frown. Similarly, search engines need a reasonably well-defined query to provide a useful response.

A BASIC SEARCH

Despite some similarities, search engines differ in the way they gather, handle, and deliver information. Nearly all search sites provide advanced search options – usually on separate *advanced search* pages. If you only intend to make a quick search, however, there are ways to modify your query so that you can type it into a standard search box and expect accurate results. In fact, many advanced menus are based on the few simple techniques described over the next few pages.

THE COMMONSENSE APPROACH

The first technique is not really a technique at all – just common sense. If you run a search and get results that are irrelevant, look at what went wrong with your search, then revise your query and resubmit it. You can make use of a first search to gather sufficient information to put together a second search simply by finding out what to include or exclude.

VAGUE SEARCH TERMS

Imagine someone would like to learn more about a piece of music, but all they know is that it comes from the orchestral work *The Planets*. A simple search for **the planets** is not likely to be very successful because the search term is way too broad and vague, but let's try anyway.

IRRELEVANT HITS

A search for **the planets** on Google (**www.google. com**) returned over three million hits, but without anything relevant in the first pages of hits. The searcher needs to narrow down the search.

RELATED TERMS

Usually a shot-in-the-dark search can be useful in providing a new angle for a second search. The first failed search could suggest using a synonym for the search term, or new words to be added to the initial search term. In this case, adding a related term such as **orchestra** to the search pays off immediately.

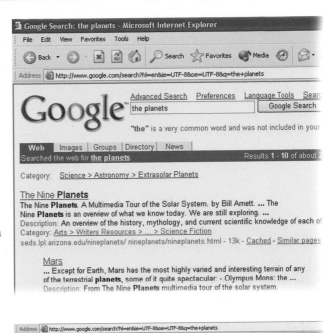

GETTING CLOSER

The search for **the planets** and **orchestra** not only reduces the number of hits but, more importantly, it brings some relevant results to the top of the list. To narrow the search further, the searcher can now, if necessary, compile further searches using extra terms, such as **Gustav Holst**, as part of the search query.

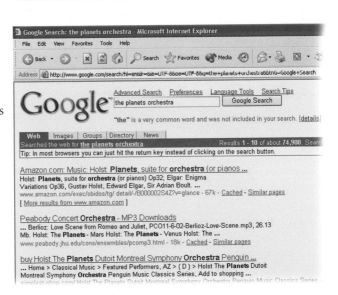

ADVANCED SEARCHING

Basic searches can be adequate for straightforward queries. However, you can greatly increase your chances of finding what you want on the web by knowing how to carry out more sophisticated searches. By learning some simple "grammar," you can have greater control over the way a search service responds to your requests. The majority of search services let you specify your search criteria in very precise ways, but different services provide these features in different ways.

SEARCH ENGINE MATH

Using math symbols can be the simplest and most effective way to broaden or, more importantly, narrow your search. They are accepted at almost every search engine on the web.

The three main symbols that you can use as search modifiers are:
+ (plus symbol); - (minus symbol); and "..." (double quotation marks surrounding the search term).

- SYMBOL

Use the - symbol to exclude words from your search, for example: **the planets - astronomy**. This searches for sites containing *the planets* but excludes those containing the word *astronomy*, and it reduces the number of hits returned dramatically. Remember to leave a space between the search term and any symbol.

+ SYMBOL

Use the + symbol to introduce additional search terms to your query. Place the + immediately before the additional search term (leaving a space between them). In this example, **the planets + holst** will search for web pages that contain the words *the planets* and *holst*. This simple device reduces the number of hits by more than ten percent, with the most relevant appearing at the beginning.

COMBINING SEARCH MATH

You can use search math queries in a variety of combinations. This will probably produce your most effective searches. For example: **the planets+holst -astronomy** reduces the number of hits even further, with nearly all of them completely relevant.

EXPERIMENT WITH LETTER SPACES

As each search engine has its own way of handling queries, it is often worth experimenting with the use of letter spaces in your search terms. In this example, removing the letter spaces from the same sequence of terms produced no results at all.

READ THE README

Search engine math, wildcards, and/or Boolean modifiers may not be universally accepted by search sites, but it is extremely rare for a search engine not to accept either + or AND or - or NOT. At least three search engines will not handle double quotations, and several more only accept wildcards and other options via their drop-down menu systems. If you don't get the results that these modifiers should provide, either read the advanced instructions for that provider, or simply move to a search engine that accepts them.

Double Quotes

Use the double quote marks around words to be grouped. If your query contains **"the planets suite"** then the search engine will look for pages containing those words as a phrase.

MORE SEARCH OPTIONS

Many search engines allow you to use an asterisk as a wildcard option in a search. This is useful if your search term has variant spellings. For example, you can type **mandol***** to cater for the two spellings: mandolin and mandoline, as well as including pages devoted to the mandola and mandolinists. It will also return hits for occurrences of the plural form, although most search engines automatically anticipate that you will be interested in plurals for your search terms.

BOOLEAN EXPRESSIONS

You will often encounter the phrase *Boolean modifiers* or *Boolean expressions*. These are essentially a technical way of describing the words AND, OR, NOT, and a few others when used as search modifiers. Boolean expressions are also commonly accepted by search engines, but on the whole you are safer using + (plus) rather than **AND**, and - (minus) rather than the modifier **NOT**. Some, but not all, search engines require you to use upper case when using Boolean logic. To be on the safe side, always use capital letters when entering Boolean expressions.

THE MODIFIERS: AND, NOT, OR, NEAR

AND: All search terms connected by **AND** will appear (i.e., bread **AND** cheese).

NOT: To exclude certain words (i.e., bread **NOT** cheese).

OR: Pages that contain either of two search terms (i.e., bread **OR** cheese)

NEAR Lets you specify (in numbers of characters) how near one search term is to another on a web page. This term is not widely accepted unless it is submitted as a menu option. Parentheses allow you to group elements in your search. For example, **NOT** bread **AND** cheese means that pages with bread will be rejected but pages containing the word cheese will be returned. **NOT** (bread **AND** cheese) will avoid pages that contain both words.

Upper and lower case

By default, search engines look for your search query as upper case or lower case words. If you want to search specifically for upper case words, capitalize them in your search query. But the overwhelming majority of search engines will then look only for upper case occurrences of the search terms you have entered and ignore lower case variants.

DOMAIN NAME SEARCH

With this type of query you can specify that only a certain domain name is searched. For example, if you want to find out more about Windows Me straight from the developers, limit your search to the websites of microsoft.com by using the following syntax: **"windows me" domain: microsoft.com.**

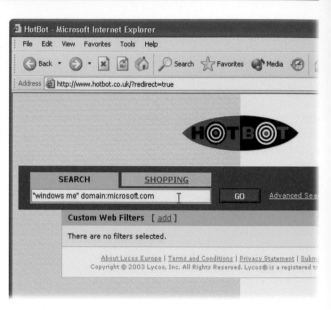

EXCLUSIVE LIST OF HITS

The resulting list of hits is confined exclusively to the numerous websites produced by Microsoft.

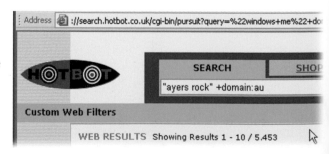

You can also search for parts of the domain name. For example, to limit your search to sites that have the Australian identifier, type **"your search term" +domain:au.**

USE THE ADVANCED OPTIONS

The following pages show how some of the leading search engines and web directories offer advanced features on their main search pages. These features achieve the same or similar results to using search engine math and Boolean operators, and often much more. The main search page of HotBot (**www.hotbot. com**) offers all the features described so far. It also has an **Advanced Search** option that allows you to carry out an even more detailed search by refining it further.

EASIER SEARCHING

It is unlikely that you will need to remember too many of these advanced search terms, other than ones we have looked at so far. Search sites are increasingly making life easier for users by providing useful drop-down menus, help files, check boxes, and other useful tools for users.

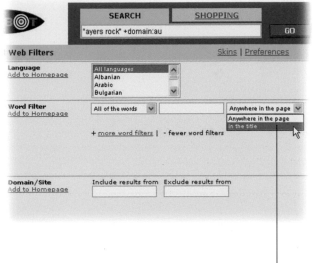

Many advanced features are made available through drop-down menus. In this example, a menu is conveniently placed near the search box

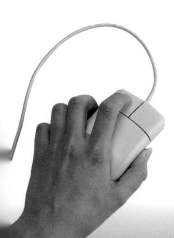

TITLE SEARCH

The title of a web page is determined by the words between the TITLE tags in the code of a web page. These words appear in the title bar at the top of the web browser. To search for web pages by title, use the following syntax: **title:your search term.** This option is unavailable in some search engines.

FORMAT-SPECIFIC SEARCHES

Many search providers supply useful radio buttons and check boxes near the main search box that enable you to specify the format for your search. For example, HotBot (address **www.hotbot.lycos.com**) has a check box that allows you to specify an images-only search. Here, a search is being carried out for royalty-free images.

Preferences - Microsoft Internet Explorer

Favorites   Tools   Help

Search   Favorites   Media

//www.hotbot.lycos.com/prefs_filters.asp?prov=Inktomi&filter=web

Word Filter	Exact Phrase ▾ Anywhere in the Page ▾	Limit resul... containing the words ...
	royalty free	
	Any of the Words ▾ Anywhere in the Page ▾	
		Limit your specific pa...
	+More Word Filters | -Fewer Word Filters	
		Create mo... clicking m... filters.
Date	⦿ Anytime ▾	Limit resul... published...
	○ After ▾ or on January ▾ 2003 ▾	specified p... time.
Page Content	☐ Audio ☐ MS PowerPoint ☐ Shockwave/Flash	Return onl... containing...
	☑ Image ☐ MS Word ☐ Video	specified m... of technolo...
	☐ Java ☐ PDF (Acrobat) ☐ WinMedia	
	☐ MP3 ☐ RealAudio/Video	
	☐ MS Excel ☐ Script	
	☐ Specific Extension: [ ] (e.g. .gif)	
Block Offensive Content	○ Always	Prevent pa... containing...

*The **Image** check box* •

LINKS SEARCH

A links search locates all web pages that contain hyperlinks to the specified web page. This is useful if you are interested in finding out how many people have linked their web pages to your own. The search syntax is: **link:yourwebpage.com**. As with title and domain searches, this advanced search is not accepted by all search engines.

The blue search box at the top of the AltaVista web page (**www.altavista.com**) provides tabs that open pages for **Images, MP3/ Audio, Video, Directory,** and **News** options. The page also features a list of tools that includes **Advanced Search.** This facility allows you to specify, for example, a date range in order to limit your search results.

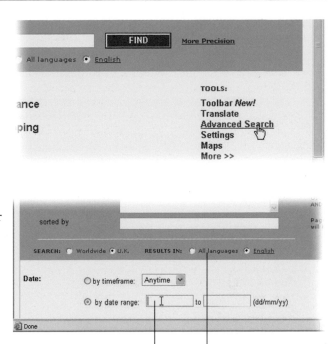

*The **date range** boxes •*   *• The **language** options*

The **Images, MP3/Audio,** and **Video** tabs at the top of the search box are useful for finding material in a particular format. Simply click the tab, type in your search term, check any relevant choices, and then click on the **Find** button.

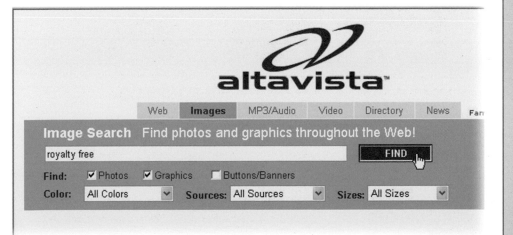

When presenting the results of a search for images, AltaVista doesn't only return a list of hits – it provides thumbnails (miniature versions of the original picture) of all the relevant images, too. Click on a thumbnail or on the link beneath it to go to the web page from which the image was retrieved.

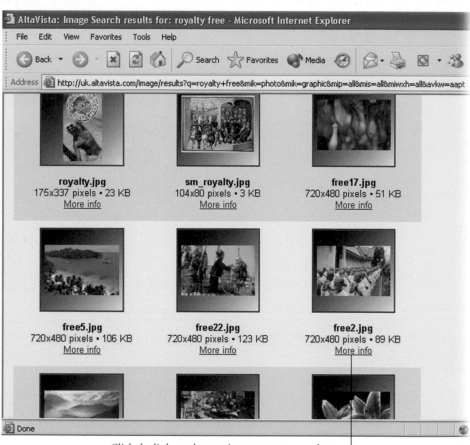

Click the links under any image to go to a web page

PICTURE FILE FORMATS

The letters .jpg after the images above show that they are JPEG files. This compressed graphics file format is useful for images containing a lot of color. The GIF format, which you will also come across, is primarily used for displaying images from online sources such as the internet. It only supports 256 colors, but the files are small and can be used for animating web pages.

From Engines to Directories

The difference between search engines and web directories is becoming less distinct. It is now usual for search providers to offer a web directory as well as a search box on their main web page. To find information as quickly as possible, the search box and search menus are usually the place to begin. However, if you have a little more time to explore a subject, or you want results that have passed some kind of quality control, a directory can be preferable to a search engine.

This example shows one of the most popular web directories of all – Yahoo! (**www.yahoo.com**) – and we are again looking for information on Holst. The first stage involves some commonsense choices about the categories in which the composer or piece of music are likely to be found.

Business & Economy	Regional
B2B, Finance, Shopping, Jobs...	Countries, Regions, US States...
Computers & Internet	Society & Culture
Internet, WWW, Software, Games...	People, Environment, Religion...
News & Media	Education
Newspapers, TV, Radio...	College and University, K-12...
Entertainment	Arts & Humanities
Movies, Humor, Music...	Photography, History, Literature...
Recreation & Sports	Science
Sports, Travel, Autos, Outdoors...	Animals, Astronomy, Engineering...
Health	Social Science
Diseases, Drugs, Fitness...	Languages, Archaeology, Psychology...
Government	Reference

After choosing a category, such as **Music**, you can begin to refine your search by drilling down to a suitable subcategory. In this example, you might choose **Composition**, and then select **Composers**.

- Charts (48)
- Chats and Forums (150)
- Classifieds@
- Collecting@
- Composition (580) NEW!
- Computer Generated (207)
- Contests, Surveys, Polls (28)
- Copyrights@
- Cultures and Groups (10)
- Disc Jockeys (42)
- Musicology (56)
- New Release Lists (2)
- News and Media (315)
- Organizations (227)
- Photography (38)
- Producers (5)
- Production@
- Recording (109)
- Reference (55)
- Reviews (102)

http://dir.yahoo.com/Entertainment/Music/Composition/

CATEGORIES

- Composers@
- Computer Generated@
- Interactive Operas@
- Lyrics and Notation@
- Organizations (22)
- Songwriting (535) NEW!
- Theory@
- FAQs (1)
- Usenet (4)

SITE LISTINGS

http://dir.yahoo.com/Entertainment/Music/Artists/Composers/

As you drill down further, the appropriate headings become more obvious. Holst is most likely to be found under the heading **Classical**. Eventually, you will find a list of websites that match your search requirements.

Search [   ] ⊙ the Web ○ just this category   [Search]

CATEGORIES

- Books@
- Classical@
- Film Music@
- Jazz@

- Microtonal@
- Songwriters@
- Web Directories (3)

SITE LISTINGS

- Abbott, Titus - film music composer/sound designer based in Montreal and Portland,
- Adams, John Luther - includes biography, calendar, writings, and recordings.
- Allaman, Eric - composes for television and film

- Classical Composer Biographies - a list of biographical information about a variety of classical composers. Includes information about selected pieces.
- Early Music Women Composers 👀 - contains links for medieval, renaissance and baroque women composers along with an annotated discography.
- Classical Composers Database 👀 - provides information on many composers.
- Dr. Estrella's Incredibly Abridged Dictionary Of Composers 👀 - contains biographical information on hundreds of composers of western art music, music history essays and timelines, and links.

http://srd.yahoo.com/S=538952:D0/R=3/CS=538952/SS=2309474/*http://utopia.knoware.nl/users/jsmeets/inde

Here, the search has reached the end of the directory entries and has reached a website dedicated to classical composers.

Classical Composers Database (www.classical-composers.org) 2089 composers!

New Calendar Timeline Wanted Search Links About Help Mail/Submit
A B C D E F G H I J K L M N O P Q R S T U V W X Y Z

...ys/dying days for today (15 September). Anniversaries for 2003, 2004, 2005, 2006, 2007, 2008.

Website style: [vanilla] [clear] [contrast]

Welcome to the Classical Composers Database

An ever-growing list of composers
Already 2089 entries!
Links and contributions accepted!

Last updated: Saturday 13 September 2003, 20h 43m 13s GMT
(This site is under construction by definition!)
© Jos Smeets, 1995-2003

New. Latest contributions and changes

The list of classical composers available on this website confirms that you have reached what you are looking for: a large database of composers that contains an entry for **Holst, Gustav.**

90. Holliger, Heinz (1939-)
91. Holmboe, Vagn (1909-1996)
92. Holst, Gustav (1874-1934)
93. ten Holt, Simon (1923-)
94. Holt, Simon (1958-)
95. Holter, Iver (1850-1941)
96. Holzbauer, Ignaz (1711-1783)
97. Homilius, Gottfried August (1714-1785)
98. Honegger, Arthur (1892-1955)
99. Hönigsberg, David (1959-)

http://www.classical-composers.org/cgi-bin/ccd.cgi?comp=holst

Finally, you have arrived at a biography of Gustav Holst. The principal advantage of using a directory search rather than entering keywords in a search box is that you are presented with many more related options that you can examine during the search. This may lead you to information related to your areas of interest that a straightforward keyword search may not.

Gustav Holst

Born: 21 September 1874, Cheltenham (England)
Died: 25 May 1934, London (England)

Music

(contributed by Kenric Taylor <ktaylor(at)wso.williams.edu>)

Works include

Chorus

- Choral Hymns from the Rig Veda: 1st-4th Groups (1908-1912)
- First Choral Symphony (1923-1924)

STANDALONE SEARCH PROGRAMS

Search software is available that runs directly from your computer rather than via a website. The free search program Copernic Agent Basic  (available from **www. copernic.com**), is a powerful metasearch tool with some very useful customizable features. For example, it can update automatically its list of search engines while you are browsing. It also enables you to download search results for offline browsing, and will remove duplicates for you.

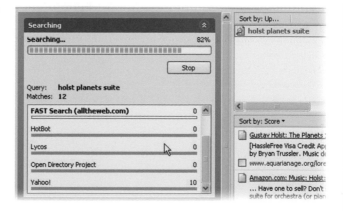

WHICH SEARCH ENGINE?

This chapter looks at nine of today's most popular search providers describing the main features and showing the web page layout and the results format for each.

WHICH SEARCH TOOL?

You might wonder if there is any need to go looking for another search provider once you have found one that suits your needs. The simple answer is no – as long as you are happy with the accuracy, quality, and currency of the results that the provider returns, and the speed of delivery and the ease of use.

SEVERAL PROVIDERS

However, it is advisable to bookmark several web directories and search engines. First, different search providers never return an identical set of results. Second, search engines present results in a variety of very different ways and this will reveal information differently.

Different results
As the examples opposite show, the same query (in this case, **"gustav holst"** + **"the planets suite"** + **orchestra** - **astronomy**) *submitted to two search engines (AlltheWeb and Google) can return different lists of hits. The next chapter explains why these differences in the order and content of the results occur, by looking at how search engines and web directories work.*

WHY SEARCHES GO WRONG

The roots of this problem lie in the two methods used to compile databases – by keyword or by concept. Keyword searches collect words in a site that are thought to be important. The problem arises when you enter a word with more than one meaning. If you enter the word "groom," you will be offered sites on horse care and weddings. Concept searches try to work out the meaning of the text rather than just using the specific words. Problems arise when the software working out the meaning of an article containing the word "heart" places it in a medical category when the subject is love.

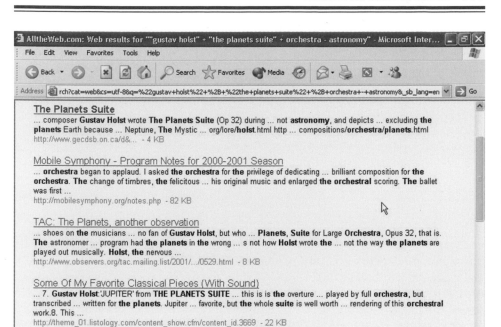

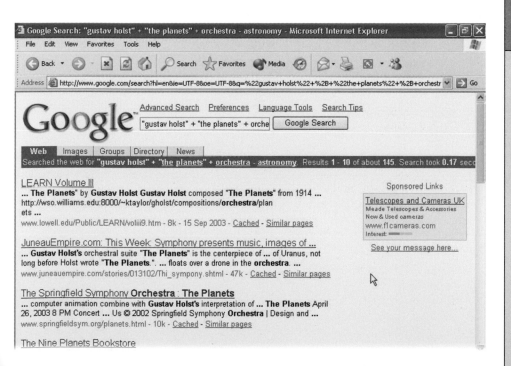

ALLTHEWEB

This is a well respected crawler-based search engine that indexes billions of web pages and also allows you to search specifically – and easily – for everything from news stories to multimedia files. It shares a number of characteristics with Google, particularly its clean interface, and its fast, comprehensive searches.

RESULTS FORMAT

By default, AlltheWeb displays results 10 at a time. Each entry includes the title, a brief description, and the actual web address itself. It will also "cluster" results at the foot of each page into groups of similar results. In this example the clusters of results include recipes, preparation, and cookbooks.

Displays more pages from the same site

Click the title to visit the web page

ALLTHEWEB FEATURES

- www.alltheweb.com
- Indexes more than three billion web pages and millions of multimedia files.
- Scans the web every seven to 11 days.
- Supports searches in 49 languages.
- AlltheWeb indexes hundreds of news stories every minute.

Search box

Advanced search options

Language options

Click here to filter out offensive content

Multimedia search features

Web page title

Web page description

Web address

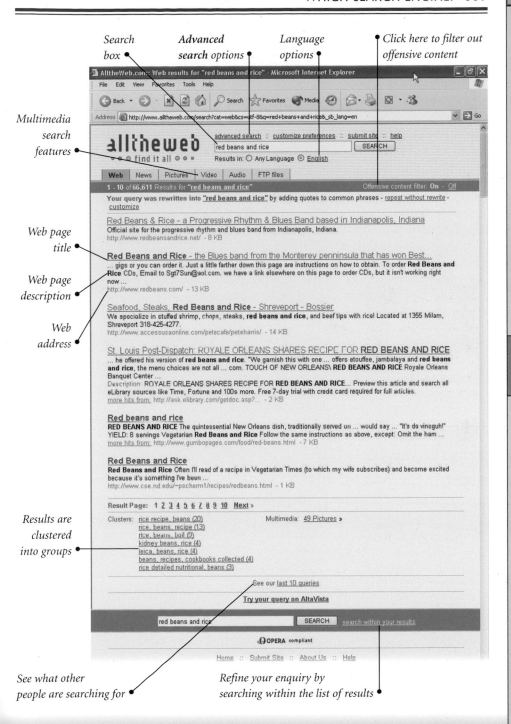

Results are clustered into groups

See what other people are searching for

Refine your enquiry by searching within the list of results

ALTAVISTA

AltaVista opened for business in 1995 and remains one of the top web crawlers. It has a particularly good search facility for picture, as well as audio and video files.

Its machine translation service *Babel Fish* was the first of its kind and can translate words, phrases, and entire websites from a wide range of foreign languages.

RESULTS FORMAT

Results include the page title, description and web address of each site. The total number of sites matching the search query is listed at the top and the results are displayed in batches of 10 per page.

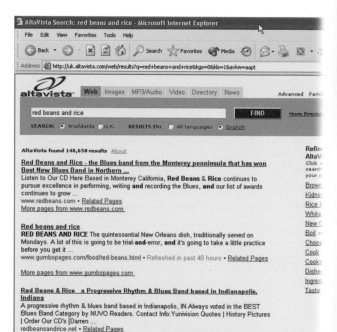

Displays more pages from the same site

Displays similar, related sites

ALTAVISTA FEATURES

● **www.altavista.com**
● Supports multilingual searches.
● Runs more than 20 local country sites.
● Prisma technology allows speedy refining of search queries.

Search box

Multimedia search features (images, audio, and video tabs)

Language options

Advanced search options

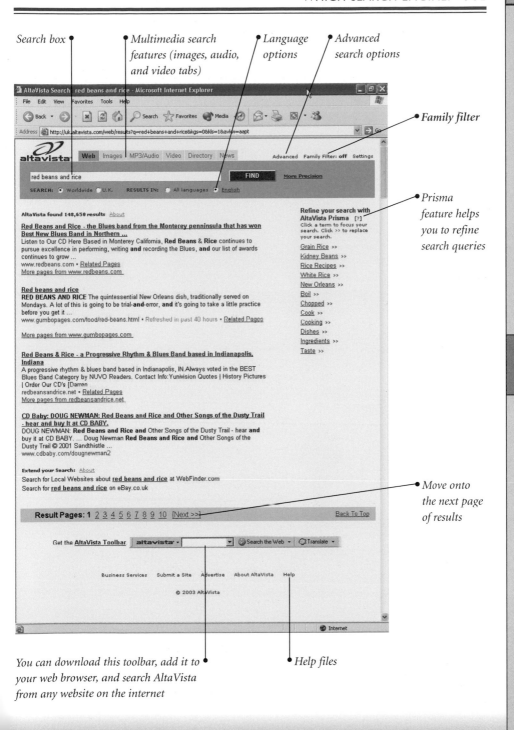

Family filter

Prisma feature helps you to refine search queries

Move onto the next page of results

You can download this toolbar, add it to your web browser, and search AltaVista from any website on the internet

Help files

ASK JEEVES

Ask Jeeves rose to fame as a so-called "natural language" search engine that allowed you to type in your search queries in plain English. Originally, Ask Jeeves returned its answers in the form of questions, in the hope of finding exactly what you are looking for by refining your query. In fact, Ask Jeeves had a large team of editors working on the results – which was why they were so effective. Ask Jeeves now relies on Teoma's crawler-based technology (www.teoma.com).

Type your query here as a plain English question (or simply a word, or a string of words)

If you download and install this toolbar, you can search Ask Jeeves from anywhere on the internet

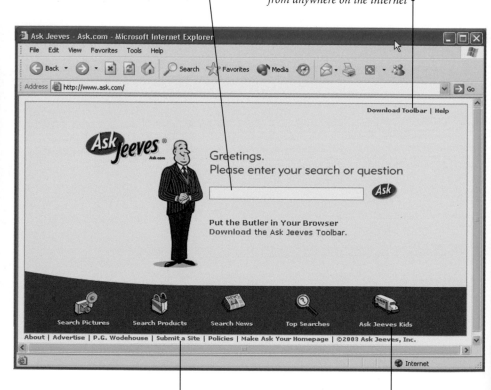

Click here to submit your own website to Ask Jeeves

This allows you to search specifically selected kid-friendly websites

ASK JEEVES FEATURES

- www.askjeeves.com
- Queries can be made in natural language.
- Main search provided by Ask Jeeves directory.

- Unknown spellings are queried and a spell check facility is offered.
- Secondary search (a *metasearch* feature)

interrogates leading search engines.
- **Personal Jeeves** feature offers customized information and services.

RESULTS FORMAT

When Ask Jeeves returns the answers to a query it divides them into two. First, you will see Sponsored Web Results. These are actually provided by Google, which allows advertisers to bid for placement in this area based on relevant keywords. Second, you will see Web Results, which are provided by the Teoma search engine and are listed in order of relevance.

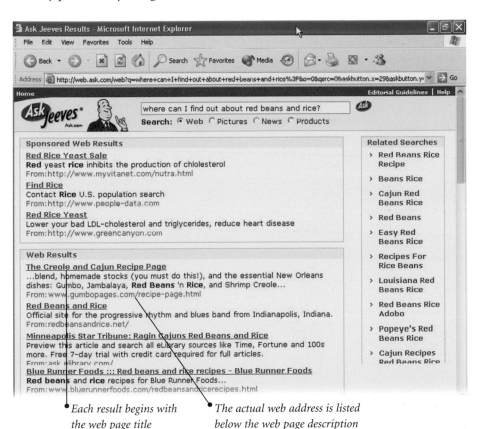

Each result begins with the web page title

The actual web address is listed below the web page description

DOGPILE

Opened in 1996, Dogpile is one of the most popular metasearch engines on the internet – an engine that sequentially queries other search engines and web directories. It currently gathers information from sites including Google, Yahoo, AltaVista, Ask Jeeves, About, AlltheWeb, FindWhat, and LookSmart.

RESULTS FORMAT

By default, Dogpile returns the results to any search query ordered by relevance. In each case, the entry has a title and description; the actual web address is then listed underneath. Alternatively, you can tell Dogpile to list the results "by Search Engine" so that the suggested websites are divided into sections that indicate the search engine that has produced the results, such as Yahoo or Google. If you choose to list the search results in this fashion, you can click on the link to go through to an individual website or go straight to the search engine itself to see more results.

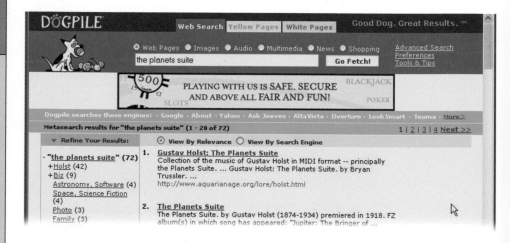

DOGPILE FEATURES

- **www.dogpile.com**
- Easily customized.
- Searches through a large number and wide variety of different information sources.
- Displays results listed by relevance or by the individual search engine that produced them.
- Also offers Yahoo-style directory listings.

Type in your
search term here ●

View results by relevance or
list them by search engine ●

● Multimedia
search features

● *Advanced Search*
command

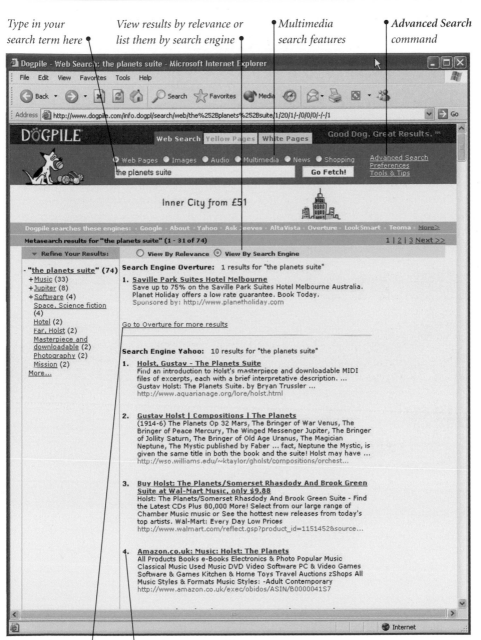

Go directly to the ●
search engine and view
other, similar results

● Results are ordered by
relevance within each
search engine category

GOOGLE

Google's main search page is in stark contrast to the busy portal interface favored by many top search providers.

However, behind the simple, uncluttered interface a very powerful search engine using unique software is at work.

PAGE RANKING

Google's search engine is based on an automated method that ranks web pages according to their relationship with other web pages – with special attention being paid to the links between pages that share common subjects or themes. Google analyzes the relevance of a page by looking at the pages that link to it. Each link is regarded as a "vote" for that page, and the more votes a page receives, the more highly it is ranked.

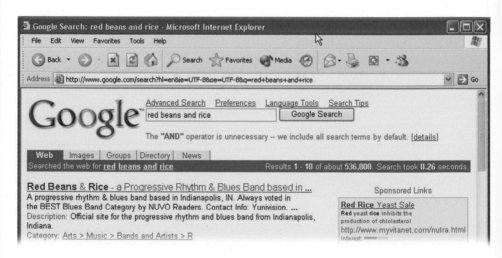

SEARCH TERMS AND PROXIMITY

Google only produces results that match all your search terms. It also notes the proximity of the search terms on a page, and prioritizes those hits that place the search terms close to each other.

"I'm feeling lucky"

The developers at Google are very confident of the effectiveness of Google's search capabilities, and they have incorporated a unique feature in their **I'm Feeling Lucky** button.

If you click on this button after entering your search terms, Google will send you straight to the website that emerges at the top of its search results, and many times it is uncannily accurate.

Google's *I'm Feeling Lucky* button runs your search and then takes you straight to the web page of the number one hit – which may be just the one you're looking for •

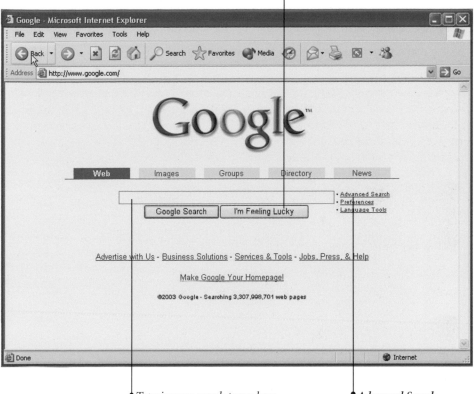

• Type in your search terms here and click on **Google Search**

• **Advanced Search** command

GOOGLE FEATURES

- **www.google.com**
- Minimalist, uncluttered search screen.
- Features a unique **I'm Feeling Lucky** button for fast results.

- Has its own software for rating pages.
- Matches all terms used.
- Widely regarded by users as the best all-round search engine.

HOTBOT

HotBot has been one of the leading search engines since its launch by Wired Digital in 1996. It has, however, undergone a number of changes, and in its latest incarnation it has switched to providing a multiple search engine service where you can choose between searching Lycos, Google, Ask Jeeves, or HotBot itself with a single mouse click. HotBot mixes sponsored links (which appear at the top of the results page) with general web results provided by the Inktomi search engine. If a particular set of results proves unsatisfactory, you can simply search again using one of the other supported search engines.

THE LYCOS NETWORK

Since October 1998 HotBot has been part of the Lycos network and is run as a separate service on this network, which offers numerous net-based services including free email, clubs, chat, a shopping center, and entertainment.

Search term panel

Advanced Search command

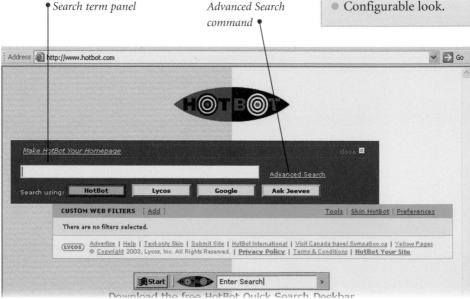

Choose which search engine to use

Open HotBot's advanced search options

Click on the Skins command to change the look and feel of HotBot

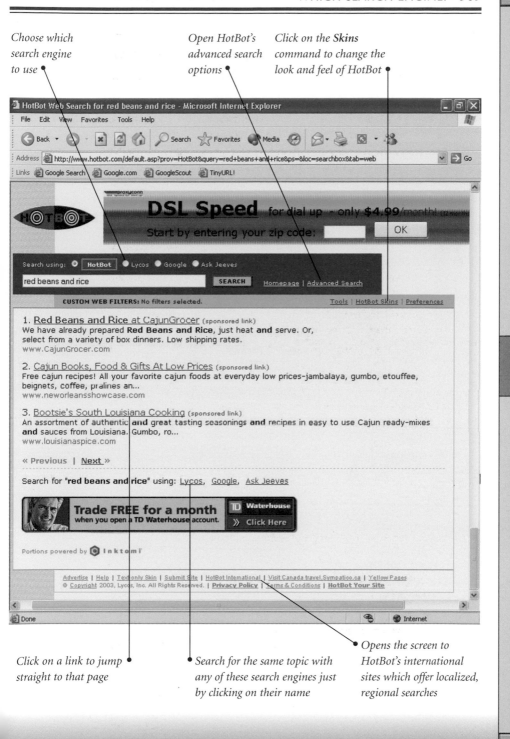

Click on a link to jump straight to that page

Search for the same topic with any of these search engines just by clicking on their name

Opens the screen to HotBot's international sites which offer localized, regional searches

LYCOS

Although Lycos looks like a portal – a sort of gateway to other websites and services – it also offers crawler-style web searching and Yahoo-like directory listings. This combination makes it one of the most flexible search sites on the internet. From the main Lycos screen you can set up a free email account, organize free internet access, play online games, chat online, build your own home page, read news headlines, and much more. Alternatively, you can type a query into the search panel or click on the Directory link, which takes you to a list of main topics such as Cars, Entertainment, Finance, and Gardening. From these you can "drill down" into various sub-topics until you find the subject you are looking for.

DOMAIN NAME

Lycos also offers a domain registration service that allows you to choose a unique address for yourself or your business in the following format – **www.yourname.com/net/ org/biz/info**. For a small annual fee you can set up multiple email addresses, and use the web space that is provided as part of the package for your website.

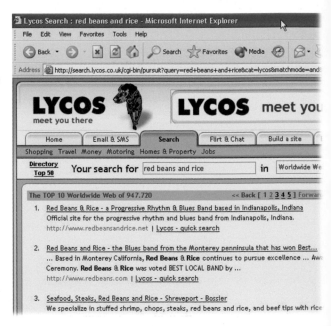

IMAGE GALLERY

The excellent searchable image gallery contains thousands of picture files, viewable initially as thumbnails. You can also use Lycos to search the web specifically for image, audio, or video files.

LYCOS FEATURES

- **www.lycos.com**
- Powerful search site with many features that can be customized to suit the user's needs.
- Combines search engine with directory and portal features.
- Excellent image and multimedia search feature.

*Type in your
search query here* •

*Search for
images here*

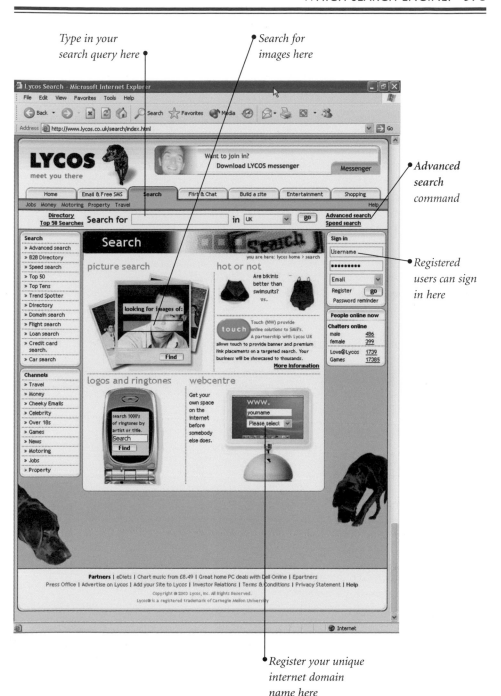

• *Advanced
search
command*

• *Registered
users can sign
in here*

• *Register your unique
internet domain
name here*

METACRAWLER

Metacrawler allows you to search a number of search engines at once, including Google, Yahoo, AltaVista, Ask Jeeves, About, LookSmart, Overture, and FindWhat. The site makes it easy to search for images or other kinds of multimedia as well as news; there's even a shopping-only search option. Metacrawler will correct your spelling and includes useful features for finding addresses in the United States. You can also tell it only to return results in a specified language.

RESULTS FORMAT

Metacrawler can list the results by relevance or by search engine. The main results list gives the source of each entry, a brief description of the site, and its web address. Metacrawler also groups the results into categories to help you refine your search. Sponsored web links (i.e. those that have been paid for) are indicated with a "Sponsored by:" tag.

Metacrawler breaks the search results down into categories so that you can refine your search

Click here to move on to the next page of results

Click on this radio button to search for images

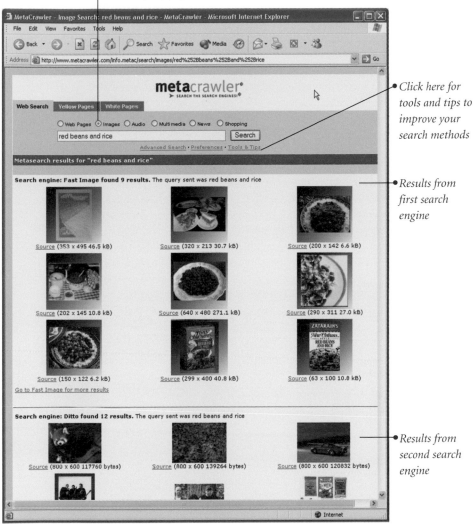

Click here for tools and tips to improve your search methods

Results from first search engine

Results from second search engine

METACRAWLER FEATURES

- **www.metacrawler.com**
- Gather results from multiple search engines.
- Offers news, image, and shopping searches.
- Finds addresses – private and business – in the US.
- MetaSpy feature shows other users' queries.

MSN SEARCH

MSN Search is an important component of the main MSN portal. It offers the powerful combination of directory listings from LookSmart with crawler results from Inktomi. One of the keys to its success, however, is the team of editors who monitor popular searches and then seek out those sites they believe to be the most relevant. This combination of sound, automated crawler technology and hands-on human editing makes MSN one of the most useful search engines around.

RESULTS FORMAT

MSN returns results in two main sections. Depending on the type of search, the main list may contain results from sites held within MSN's own directory, followed by web pages gathered from the internet – some of these may be paid-for pages. There will also be a section of sponsored links (again, paid for) as well as a popular topics section, designed to help you refine your search by suggesting related topics.

Search term panel •———

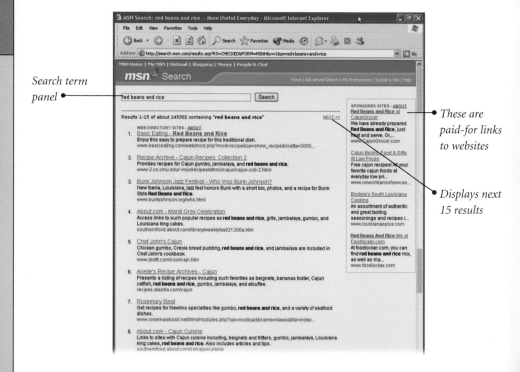

These are paid-for links to websites

Displays next 15 results

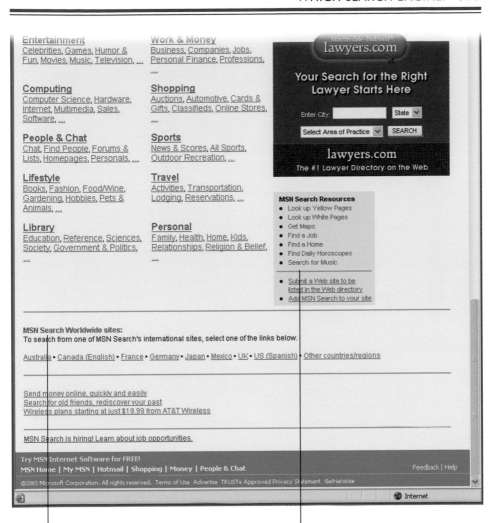

Entertainment
Celebrities, Games, Humor & Fun, Movies, Music, Television, ...

Computing
Computer Science, Hardware, Internet, Multimedia, Sales, Software, ...

People & Chat
Chat, Find People, Forums & Lists, Homepages, Personals, ...

Lifestyle
Books, Fashion, Food/Wine, Gardening, Hobbies, Pets & Animals, ...

Library
Education, Reference, Sciences, Society, Government & Politics, ...

Work & Money
Business, Companies, Jobs, Personal Finance, Professions, ...

Shopping
Auctions, Automotive, Cards & Gifts, Classifieds, Online Stores, ...

Sports
News & Scores, All Sports, Outdoor Recreation, ...

Travel
Activities, Transportation, Lodging, Reservations, ...

Personal
Family, Health, Home, Kids, Relationships, Religion & Belief, ...

lawyers.com

Your Search for the Right Lawyer Starts Here

Enter City: [   ] State [v]

Select Area of Practice [v] SEARCH

lawyers.com
The #1 Lawyer Directory on the Web

MSN Search Resources
- Look up Yellow Pages
- Look up White Pages
- Get Maps
- Find a Job
- Find a Home
- Find Daily Horoscopes
- Search for Music

- Submit a Web site to be listed in the Web directory
- Add MSN Search to your site

MSN Search Worldwide sites:
To search from one of MSN Search's international sites, select one of the links below.

Australia • Canada (English) • France • Germany • Japan • Mexico • UK • US (Spanish) • Other countries/regions

Send money online, quickly and easily
Search for old friends, rediscover your past
Wireless plans starting at just $19.99 from AT&T Wireless

MSN Search is hiring! Learn about job opportunities.

Try MSN Internet Software for FREE!
MSN Home | My MSN | Hotmail | Shopping | Money | People & Chat   Feedback | Help
©2003 Microsoft Corporation. All rights reserved. Terms of Use Advertise TRUSTe Approved Privacy Statement GetNetWise

Internet

• *Search for local information from any one of MSN Search's international sites*

• *Additional search options*

MSN FEATURES

- www.search.msn.com
- Mixes directory listings and automated web crawler results.

- Many sites suggested by team of human editors.
- Main MSN site contains many portal-style features.

- Can locate businesses and individuals in the US.
- Has many international sites for local searches.

SPECIALIZED SEARCHES

The availability of information and products on the web has led to the development of countless sites where you can find people, services, news, and software.

ADVANCED OPTIONS

As we have seen in previous chapters, all the most popular search engines provide much more than the basic tools for searching the web. Nearly all offer advanced options that enable you to search specifically for email addresses, Usenet newsgroup postings, information from news feeds, white and yellow pages, shopping databases, software collections, maps, online shopping, and auctions.

DATABASE INTERROGATION

Since all this information is held on databases owned and maintained by search providers, the source of the material – whether web, Usenet newsgroup, or commercial telephone listings – is irrelevant. When you run a search from your web browser you are not running a live search of what is on the internet at that moment, but rather interrogating a database owned by that particular search provider. Some search providers, however, specialize in certain types of information, which we look at in the next few pages.

SEARCHING FOR PEOPLE

Email directories and white pages services are still in their infancy and are not yet fully comprehensive. This means that there is no guarantee you'll find that long-lost neighbor who moved away years ago.

However, if your old neighbor signed up for a free email account and, while doing so, left the box that says **include me in your email directory** checked, he/she may certainly be listed in at least one email directory.

Other providers

Email addresses and white pages data are available as search options from many search providers. You can also run a people search from Microsoft Outlook or Outlook Express.

OUTLOOK EXPRESS

Although Microsoft's email program, Outlook Express, is not primarily a tool for searching the web, it does include a **Find People** feature. You can use it to find people either locally in your own address book or globally on the internet.

1 OUTLOOK EXPRESS
● In Outlook Express, click on the **Addresses** button in the toolbar.

2 FIND PEOPLE
● In the **Address Book** window, click on the **Find People** button.

3 SEARCH PROVIDER
● Choose a search provider from the drop-down menu. In this example, the VeriSign **Internet Directory Service** is being used.

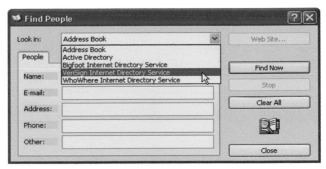

4 FIND NOW
● Type the name of the person you are searching for and click on **Find Now**.

5 BROWSE THE NAMES

● After a short wait, a list of names is compiled for you to browse.

BIGFOOT

Bigfoot (**www.bigfoot.com**) is renowned for its simplicity for finding people, primarily in the US. Just enter the first and last names of the person you're looking for. It also offers a number of options to narrow down the search.

1 KEYING IN THE SEARCH NAME

● Type the name of the person you're looking for, and specify a city if you want to make the search more specific.

2 PICKING A STATE

● Click the arrow next to **Pick a State** and choose the relevant state from the menu that appears.

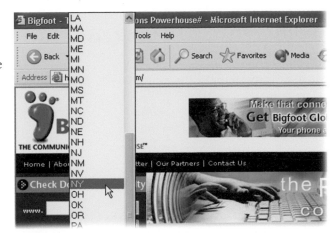

3 STARTING THE SEARCH

● Click the **Go** button, and Bigfoot will try to find the person you are looking for.

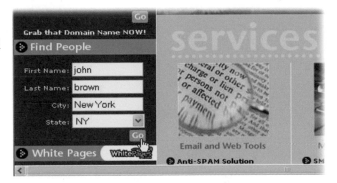

4 DISPLAYING THE RESULTS

● Results appear in the Bigfoot screen grouped under email addresses.

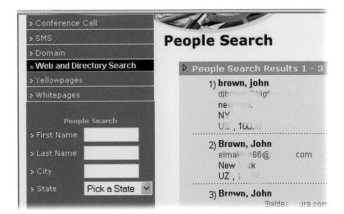

YELLOW PAGES

With the vast explosion in commercial websites – from one-person startups right up to multinationals – and the rise of e-commerce, there has been a corresponding growth on the web of search sites devoted to finding businesses, their products and services, and the people who make them work.

COMMERCIAL SEARCHES

Once again, many of the main search services provide a perfectly adequate method of searching for such material. All you have to do is choose the yellow pages or white pages (or people or businesses) options and then run your search as usual via the search box.

However, if your favorite search service doesn't give you this option, you could go straight to a search provider who specializes in commercial searches. GTE Superpages.com (**www.superpages.com**) offers an immensely wide range of search options for people, companies, services, products, and much more. For UK addresses, try **search.yell.com**. In this example we are using South Western Bell Yellow Pages, Inc.'s **smartpages.com** to find out where we can go out to dinner during our forthcoming trip to Seattle, USA.

1 APPROPRIATE CATEGORY

● Enter **restaurant** in the **Business Type** box, **Seattle** in the **City** box, select **WA** (for Washington) from the **State** drop-down menu, and finally click on **Go!**

If you know the name of the restaurant, click the Business Name radio button first and then type the name into the box

2 FINISHING YOUR SEARCH

● To complete the search, you are offered a list of further categories. Click the appropriate category – in this case, **Restaurants**.

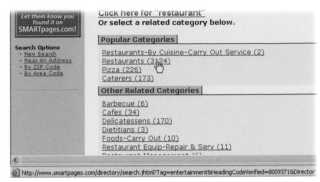

3 CHOOSING AN ENTRY

● Click on any restaurant in the list for further information and a map.

Click here to see a map showing the location of the restaurant

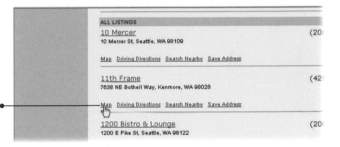

SEARCHING FOR NEWGROUPS

To search for postings to Usenet news-groups, use the Usenet option in your favorite search service, if available. This is sometimes accessed via the Advanced search settings, but different search services use different locations.

SIMPLY DOGPILE
In the case of Dogpile, (**www.dogpile.com**), click the **News** option before clicking on **Go Fetch** to run your search.

USENET GROUPS SEARCH

Along with a number of other search services, product details, and a web index, Google.com offers a vast searchable database of Usenet newsgroup messages including archive material going back several years. Results are clearly organized, making it easy to follow discussion threads within and across the tens of thousands of available newsgroups. Using this kind of facility, searching for Usenet messages can be as easy as searching the web.

1 POWER SEARCH

● Google's usenet service is available on **groups.google. com**. On this web page, key in your search term and then click on the Search button. Clicking on **Advanced Groups Search** instead will offer a range of further options.

Advanced Groups Search option ●

2 ENTER KEYWORDS

● On the **Advanced Groups Search** page, explore the options in the drop-down menus under the **Sort by** panel and choose between **relevance** and **date**. Fill in any other relevant panels that might help the search, and then click on **Google Search**.

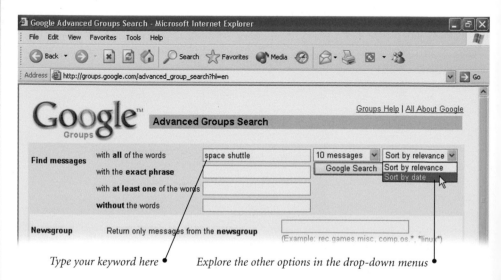

Type your keyword here ● *Explore the other options in the drop-down menus* ●

3 READ THE MESSAGE

● When the list of hits appears, click on the message you wish to read. The date of posting, the name of the newsgroup, and the name of the author appear at the bottom of each entry.

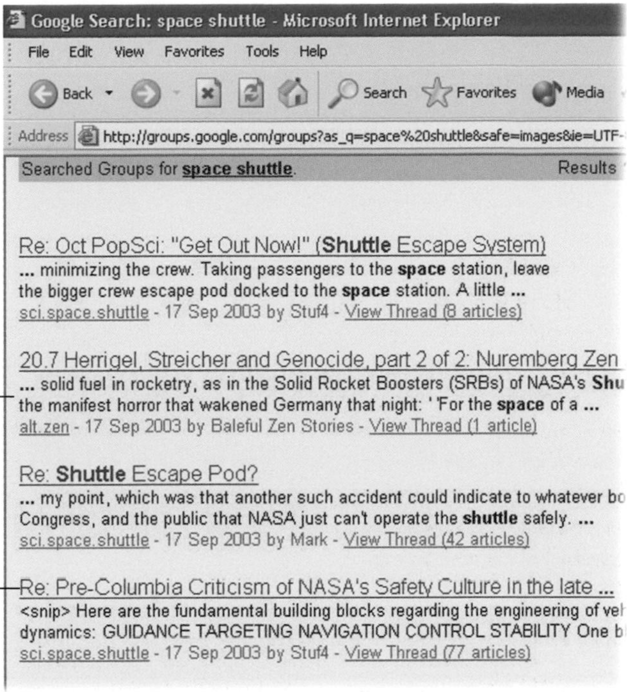

List of hits

Click on an entry to open the message

4 OPENING THE MESSAGE

● The message will then open on your screen, together with information about the writer and the date on which the message was posted.

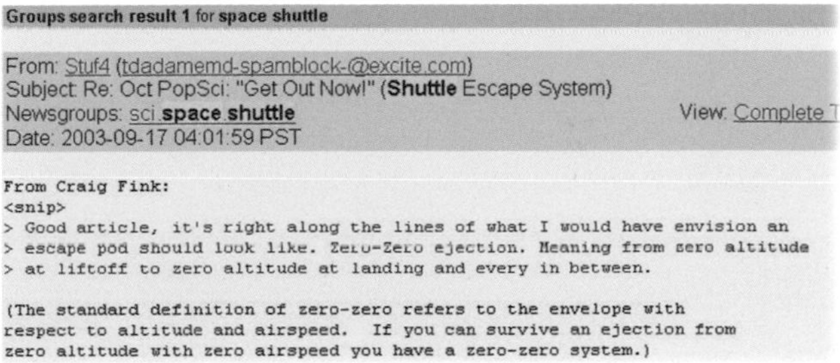

CLASSIFICATIONS OF POSTINGS

Usenet postings can fall into one of the following classifications:
alt. Anything goes
rec. Recreational topics

comp. Computer subjects
soc. Social issues
sci. Science subjects
news. Usenet information
biz. Business matters

humanities. The arts
talk. Current debates
regional. Local subjects
k12. Educational issues
misc. The unclassifiable.

SEARCHING FOR SOFTWARE

If you are interested in searching for software or simply browsing for that essential utility, patch, or game, there are many excellent shareware and freeware sites on the web that will almost certainly have what you are looking for. Most of these are as simple to use as any standard search engine, and contain a search box and/or a directory structure to take you to the kind of software you need.

1 CHOOSING A CATEGORY

● If, for example, you are interested in checking out the latest internet search software for Windows, you can browse the relevant section of a software download site such as **www.download.com**.

● On the home page of the site, click on the **Internet** category heading.

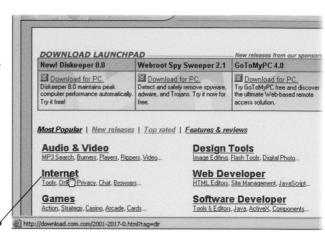

Choose a category ●

2 CHOOSING THE NEXT LEVEL

● The next window contains subdivisions of that category, so click on **Tools & Utilities**.

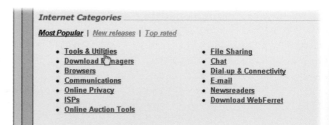

3 DRILLING DOWN

● Continuing down through the categories, click on **Search Tools** to see the selection available on this website.

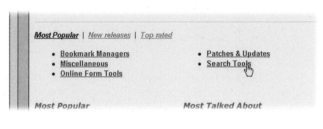

4 SOFTWARE SELECTION

● Here we are choosing to find out more about the **Copernic Agent Basic** program by clicking on the title. This page already tells us that this is free, available to download at no cost.

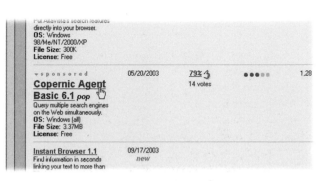

5 SOFTWARE SELECTION

● The **Copernic Agent Basic** page opens. There is a thorough description of the software and what it does, and it seems to be what we are looking for.

● To download **Copernic Agent Basic**, simply click on **Download Now**, and follow the onscreen instructions.

● You will find that the steps we have shown here work for many different kinds of software available on the internet.

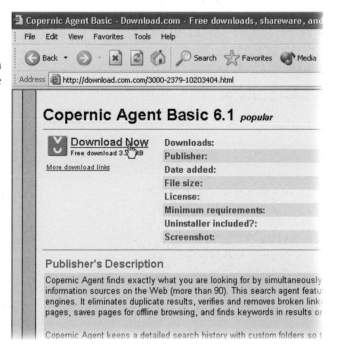

USING THE SEARCH BOX

If you know the name of the piece of software you want to download, use the search box provided at the software site.

For example, to find and download the popular email client, Eudora, from the Tucows software site, do the following:

1 THE OPERATING SYSTEM

● Go to Tucows' website (**www.tucows.com**), and click to specify your operating system, in this case **Windows**.

Specify your operating system ●

2 SPECIFYING THE SOFTWARE

● In the **Search our site** window, type the search term – in this case, **Eudora** – and click the **Go** button.

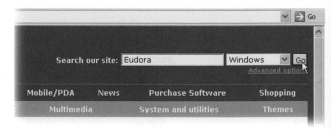

3 CHOOSING THE SOFTWARE

● The page that opens may offer several choices that correspond to the specified software. Choose the one you want by clicking on it.

4 CHOOSING TO DOWNLOAD

● Details of the software and the size of the file are shown. Choose the version of Windows you are running by clicking on it.

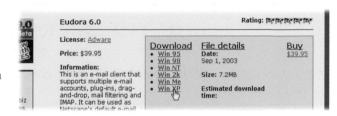

5 CHOOSING A REGION

● From the panels on the page that then opens, choose the region or country in which you live, and click the **Go** command.

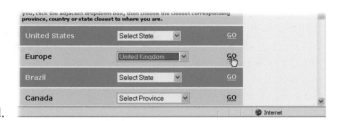

6 CHOOSING A DOWNLOAD SITE

● Choose a site from which to download the software you are searching for by clicking on it.

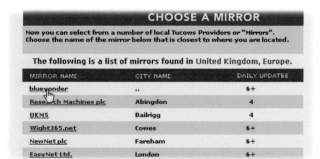

7 SAVING THE FILE TO DISK

● You will be asked if you want to open the file or save it to your PC. Click on the **Save** button, and the selected software starts to download.

SCANNERS & PRINTERS

EVEN THE MOST NOVICE OF PC USERS, or those on a tight budget, now have the chance to scan images into a computer, manipulate them into their own designs, and print out the results in color at near-photographic quality. With cheap and easy-to-use scanners and inkjet printers, the creative possibilities are endless. Yet the whole process can seem daunting to the uninitiated.

This section provides straightforward guidance on all aspects of scanning and printing, taking you through the whole process, from choosing and installing the hardware, to scanning, correcting, and printing your images. By the end of the section, you will have received a thorough grounding in using these two vital pieces of PC hardware, and will be ready to let your imagination run wild.

THE HARDWARE

A scanner and printer are probably the first things you should consider buying in addition to the computer itself. If you are lucky, they may have even been included in your PC package.

DISCOVERING THE POSSIBILITIES

Your PC really isn't proving its worth if you haven't yet discovered the possibilities open to you by adding a scanner and color printer to the setup. Being able to transfer images into your computer opens up an exciting new world of creativity, as the PC is a very powerful tool when it comes to manipulating and editing them.

THE HOME PC SETUP
With the right peripherals, your PC can become a truly creative workstation.

Your computer is used to treat the images in any way you like; and with the right software you can manipulate your pictures beyond recognition.

Pictures and photographs enter your computer via the scanner and are saved on your hard drive.

MANIPULATING YOUR IMAGES

At first you will just be thrilled to see your pictures and photographs appear on your monitor screen. You might apply them to your Windows XP desktop as a "wallpaper," or simply treat your color printer as a copier, and make duplicates of photographs for your friends. The next step is to create your own designs for cards, invitations, or magazine pages by inserting scanned images into desktop publishing (DTP) and word processing programs.

From here, the really exciting stuff begins. With graphics and image editing software, you can manipulate your images, perhaps combining two or three pictures into a montage. Have you ever wanted to be pictured standing on an exotic beach? Now you can, without ever going there!

Your printer can add to the creativity, too. Many have the facility to print long banners, or transfers that you can apply to T-shirts. The possibilities really are endless – you just need plenty of imagination.

PERIPHERALS

An external piece of hardware that is connected to your computer (such as a scanner or printer) is known as a peripheral. Peripherals are connected via cables to ports at the back of your computer, and require software "drivers" that are installed onto your computer's hard drive in order to operate.

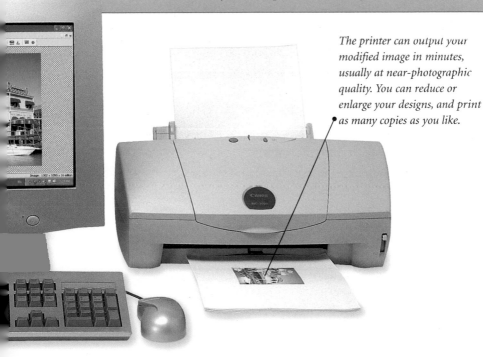

The printer can output your modified image in minutes, usually at near-photographic quality. You can reduce or enlarge your designs, and print as many copies as you like.

WHAT DOES A SCANNER DO?

A scanner is used to transfer pictures, patterns, and images from printed material or photographs into your computer. A lamp passes over the item you are scanning, transferring the information back to the PC as digital data through a light sensitive chip called a CCD (see box below).

A DESKTOP REFLECTIVE SCANNER

The item that you want to scan is placed faced down on the glass of the scanner, also known as the scanner bed.

The lid of the scanner is closed during a scan to prevent external light from entering the scanner and affecting the quality of the scan.

The scanner lamp passes over the picture, reflecting light back into the CCD chip. The scan is then converted into digital data and displayed on your PC.

Rulers and guides are printed around the scanner bed to help position items accurately.

Some scanners have a button that launches the scanning software, or even performs the scan itself.

THE CCD CHIP

Most of the technology involved in scanning the image is centered around the CCD chip *(charge-coupled device)*. Put simply, the sensors on the CCD measure the light being reflected from your picture by the three primary colors (red, green, and blue). This is enough information for your image to be reconstituted in full color on your computer screen.

WHAT DOES A PRINTER DO?

Without a printer, you are unable to output any images or designs from your computer. While there are several different types available, as a home PC user you are most likely to own a color inkjet printer. These printers transfer dots of ink onto the paper by firing it from a cartridge through small nozzles or crystals contained in a print-head. Although you may see the picture you have printed in full glorious technicolor, in actual fact the printer – like the scanner – has only used a small range of different colors to recreate the image, overlapping the various inks to produce millions of colors.

A COLOR INKJET PRINTER

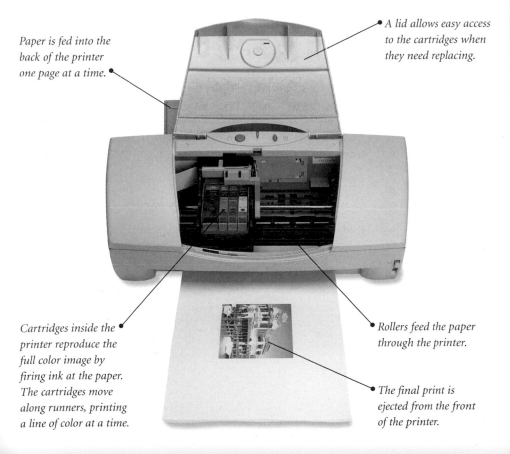

Paper is fed into the back of the printer one page at a time.

A lid allows easy access to the cartridges when they need replacing.

Cartridges inside the printer reproduce the full color image by firing ink at the paper. The cartridges move along runners, printing a line of color at a time.

Rollers feed the paper through the printer.

The final print is ejected from the front of the printer.

THE RIGHT PURCHASE

It is important to consider carefully what you will be using your scanner and printer for, and the results you expect from them, before making a decision at the computer store.

DIFFERENT TYPES OF SCANNER

On the face of it, most of the scanners you see in the computer store will look very similar. The differences are primarily hidden in the technology, with some scanners offering far higher resolution than others ⌐. An important physical difference to be aware of, however, is that most scanners only scan reflective material (items that reflect light from their surface, such as photographs). There are some scanners available that can also scan transparent items (objects through which the light passes, such as slides and photographic negatives).

FLATBED REFLECTIVE SCANNERS
The most common type of scanner is one that scans reflective material such as printed pictures and photographs. There is a huge range to choose from and most are quite compact in size.

ALL-IN-ONE

There are some printers available that can also scan, fax, and copy all in one ⌐. If convenience and space-saving are your goals, then this might be the solution. However, don't expect them to offer the same range of functions or quality as a scanner that is dedicated to the task.

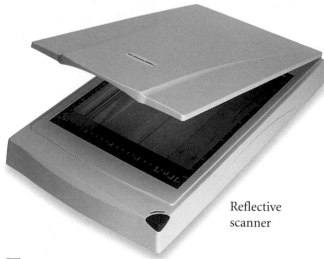

Reflective scanner

428 **What Does Resolution Mean?**

397 **Black and White Laser Printers**

USING A DIGITAL CAMERA INSTEAD OF A SCANNER

A scanner is simply a means of turning graphic information into a digital file and getting it into your computer. If you have a digital camera, this, in effect, performs a very similar task. Assess your needs and think about using your camera to transfer simple graphics or low-quality pictures onto your PC – you may not need a scanner at all. For example, you could very easily photograph a piece of artwork, such as a hand-drawn logo, and then retouch it or trace it in a graphics program.

FLATBED SCANNERS WITH A TRANSPARENCY HOOD

If you want to scan transparencies and photographic slides into your computer, you will need a scanner that is fitted with a transparency hood. The hood contains a second lamp and replaces the usual flat lid covering the scanner bed.

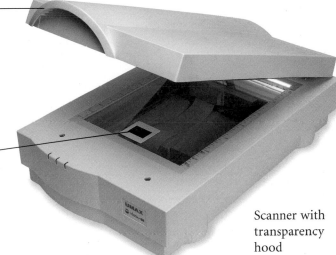

In addition to the standard lamp in the bottom of the scanner, the transparency hood also contains a lamp so that light can pass through the slide or transparency.

Transparencies and slides are positioned on the scanner glass like a conventional picture. Depending on your scanning software, you can sometimes scan many into your computer at once.

Scanner with transparency hood

DRUM SCANNERS

Drum scanners are way beyond the budget, and needs, of the average PC user. However, if you ever require a particularly good quality scan for a professional job then you can send your picture to a bureau. They will use a drum scanner (so-called because the picture is attached to a rotating cylindrical drum) and provide you with a high resolution image on disk.

DIFFERENT TYPES OF PRINTER

Dot matrix printers, which used long rolls of perforated paper and offered very poor print quality, are now rarely seen; and although there are other good quality printers around – dye sublimation printers, for example – their use is usually restricted to professional proofing. For the average user, printer choice has now really fallen between inkjet printers and laser printers, and you will see an abundance of these available at the computer store.

COLOR INKJET PRINTERS

These have fast become the most suitable printer for the home user. The cost of the printer and the quality of the prints themselves seems dispropor-tionate, as most inkjets are capable of near-photographic quality yet many cost very little to buy.

What does Bubble Jet mean?

You may see the term "Bubble Jet" used in relation to an inkjet printer. Don't let this confuse you – Bubble Jet is simply a trademark of Canon, and although the technology may differ slightly, a Bubble Jet printer is still an inkjet printer.

Inkjet printer

INK CARTRIDGES

Color inkjet printers use replaceable ink cartridges that usually contain three inks – yellow, magenta, and cyan, and sometimes also black. If you have a lot of pages to print that consist of only text, then some models provide the option of replacing the color cartridge with one that contains only black ink.

BLACK AND WHITE LASER PRINTERS

Although more expensive than color inkjets, laser printers provide high-quality, black-and-white prints that are particularly suited to lengthy text documents. Because they print at a very fast rate, they are also especially useful if you want to print multiple copies. The most common models take US letter and 8½ x 11in (A4) paper, and some can take pages of twice these sizes.

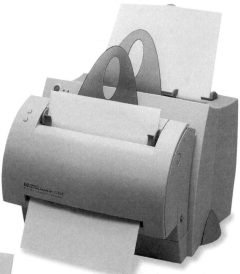

Laser printers
Many of the laser printers aimed at the home and small business user, such as the printers shown here, can carry out a multitude of tasks. As well as printing, they can also scan black and white images and act as a fax machine. There are models that can scan color images and some will operate as a photocopier.

TONER CARTRIDGES

Like photocopiers, laser printers use a cartridge containing heat-sensitive black toner. The toner in a cartridge goes a very long way and should provide a few thousand prints before it needs replacing.

CHOOSING A SCANNER AND PRINTER

There is a scanner and printer available to suit every need and budget. However, with so much choice, you should carefully consider what results you expect before buying. Unlike printers, the availability of different types of desktop scanner is limited, so choice is really dictated by the technical specification of each one. Your choice of printer falls realistically between a color inkjet printer or a black-and-white laser printer, and you need to be familiar with their advantages and disadvantages. Generally speaking, an inkjet printer will provide the most flexibility and, most importantly, color. The choice of color inkjets can still be overwhelming though, with the price range being vast, so look carefully at the functions each one offers.

THINGS TO CONSIDER WHEN BUYING A SCANNER

RESOLUTION
Probably the most crucial aspect of choosing a scanner is the resolution that it offers ⌐. Resolution affects the final quality of your scanned image, so you need to assess what you need and compare your requirements to the scanners on offer. Look for a scanner that offers at least 600 x 1200dpi resolution (you may also see 300 x 600dpi on offer – which is lower – and 1200 x 2400dpi, which is higher).

COLOR DEPTH
Color depth affects the color of your image and is measured in bits. The higher bit-depth your scanner boasts, the better represented the color will be in the final scan. Look for a scanner with 36-bit color depth.

WHAT YOU ARE SCANNING
Remember that if you want to scan photographic slides into your computer, then the scanner you choose will need a transparency hood. Unfortunately, however, this facility comes with a higher price.

SOFTWARE
Take extra care to study what software is provided with each scanner. This can vary dramatically from model to model, but even the most basic scanners should come with a simple scanning program. You don't have to pay very much more, however, to find scanners that are bundled with image editing software as well, sometimes even scaled-down versions of professional packages. These are invaluable if you want to start retouching your images and correcting them to improve their quality ⌐. Another useful application to find included is optical character recognition software, which scans text into your computer as an editable document ⌐.

428   **What Does Resolution Mean?**

434   **Improving Your Scan**

433   **Optical Character Recognition**

THINGS TO CONSIDER WHEN BUYING A PRINTER

PRINT QUALITY

Although laser printers have always offered the best quality prints (you should expect a minimum of 300dpi–600dpi), inkjets are improving rapidly. Photographic quality is now common-place on even the budget models, and you should expect a resolution of 600dpi–1200dpi on the inkjet printer that you buy.

COLOR OR BLACK AND WHITE?

This is simple. Unless you really do need to output many black and white documents (in which case a laser printer may suit you better), buy a color inkjet for maximum flexibility.

SPEED

Inkjets can be notoriously slow, especially if your computer doesn't have much processing power ⌐, but this is a small price to pay for photo-quality prints. Unfortunately, an inkjet can be just as slow even when it only has one color to print. For printing many pages of black text, a laser printer will be more suitable – the speed of printing is unsurpassed when it comes to desktop printers.

PAPER SIZE

Affordable inkjet printers accommodate letter-sized paper, although some offer the facility to print banners on a roll. Although laser printers also commonly take US letter and A4 sheets, there are models available with an extra tray for sheets of twice these sizes.

RUNNING COSTS

Although inkjets have fairly high running costs when you take into consideration the price of replacement ink cartridges and the special paper required, for short runs and infrequent printing they are perfect. Laser printers provide many more prints from their toner cartridges and use standard copy paper that is cheap to buy.

SIZE

Inkjet printers are particularly compact, as the component parts, including the ink cartridge, are small. Also, the paper is usually fed into the printer from above, sometimes one sheet at a time. Laser printers have to accommodate a reasonably large toner cartridge and sometimes a removable paper tray, usually situated at the bottom of the printer where you can stack many sheets of paper. Therefore, a laser printer will take up more desk space – far more if you opt for a model that also takes the larger paper sizes.

Hardware Checklist

COMPATIBILITY

Before rushing out to purchase any scanner or printer, you will need to determine what can feasibly be connected and used with your own computer.

CABLE CONNECTIONS AND PORTS

If you have recently bought a home computer package that included a scanner and printer, as well as all the cables required to connect everything, you should not encounter any compatibility problems. However, not all scanners and printers are compatible with every PC on the market, and this issue can become even more complicated if you are trying to connect a new scanner or printer to an old PC, or attaching many different external hardware devices.

WHAT CONNECTION DO I HAVE?

Before choosing a scanner or printer, you need to determine exactly what connection sockets (known as ports) are available at the back of your computer, so that you can purchase devices that are compatible. The three main types of connection are parallel, SCSI, and USB. Each has its advantages concerning the rate of data transfer, but some also have many disadvantages when it comes to ease of installation.

SCSI computer cable and port.

SCSI PORTS

SCSI (*Small Computer System Interface*) devices require a card to be inserted into the inside of your computer that incorporates the SCSI port. SCSI ports provide a fast rate of data transfer, but also create the most work when it comes to installation. Unless your PC already has a SCSI port, you will have to start tinkering about inside your computer to install one, so SCSI is probably best left alone.

PARALLEL PORTS

Most computers have a parallel port, which has been the standard for connecting a printer to a PC for some time. Installation of parallel devices is reasonably straightforward, but the down side is that using a parallel scanner along with a parallel printer can create a few compatibility problems. The printer shown also has a USB port (see below).

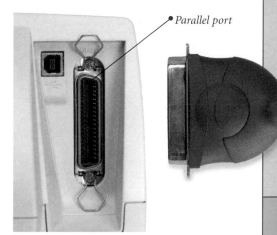
Parallel port

Parallel printer port and cable.

USB PORTS

On the other hand, USB *(Universal Serial Bus)* ports have started to become the new standard on modern computers, and both parallel and SCSI ports are being super-ceded by USB technology. USB provides huge advantages in connecting peripherals to your computer as, in theory, devices that you connect are "plug and play." In other words, you can plug in the device and start using it with minimum fuss. The message here is that if you are buying a new PC package, look for USB compatibility throughout all of your devices. **We will be concentrating on connecting USB devices in this book.**

USB computer port and cable.

USB peripheral port and cable.

USB HUBS

The main advantage of USB, apart from the ease in which you can simply "plug-and-play," is the number of different peripherals you can connect to your PC in a chain. However unlikely it may be for you to need such versatility, you are actually able to connect up to 127 USB devices to your computer. Normally, you would only expect to connect half a dozen at most, but to keep things neat you may want to consider investing in a USB hub. This device sits next to your computer and plugs into one of the USB ports. The hub itself is basically a multiadaptor containing a number of USB ports that enable you to plug all your peripherals into a port of their own. This keeps the cable connections accessible on your desk, rather than behind the computer.

HARDWARE REQUIREMENTS

The whole issue of your PC's processing power, and its suitability for your external devices, can soon spiral down into indecipherable technical jargon. However, if you have recently bought a new PC, it will most probably have enough power to operate your scanner and printer, and allow you to run a few top-end graphics and photo retouching programs as well. If you are concerned, perhaps because you are still running an old PC with a slow processor, then just check on a couple of things before attempting to attach a new scanner and printer. The hardware checklist on this page gives a list of ideal requirements.

CHECKING YOUR SYSTEM SPEC

If you have kept the packaging from your computer, the chances are that there will be a sticker on the box listing specifications such as processor speed, RAM, and hard drive capacity. However, if you have upgraded your computer, these details may now be inaccurate. If you have no written details available, you can obtain some of the information by right-clicking on the icons for **My Computer** and the hard drive (**C:**) and selecting **Properties**.

HARDWARE CHECKLIST

By ensuring that your PC has the following recommended minimum specifications, you should not have any difficulty using a scanner and printer. You will also have enough disk space and processing power to use image editing software and save high resolution scans.

- 300MHz processor
- 32Mb of RAM
- 3Gb of hard drive space
- 24-bit graphics card
- Color monitor
- Two free USB 🗎 ports or a USB hub 🗎.

PRINTER CONSIDERATIONS

Inkjet printers use the PC's memory to process the print job. Therefore, the more memory you have available on your PC, the less likely you are to have a problem with painfully slow printing. It also means that printing won't interfere with other tasks you want to perform on your computer in the meantime. Laser printers usually have their own built-in memory to control the printing, but GDI laser printers – also sometimes called Windows printers – are able to use the computer's memory in the same way that an inkjet printer does.

| 401 | USB Ports |

| 401 | USB Hubs |

CHANGING THE MONITOR SETTINGS

● To ensure your scanned images appear at a good quality onscreen, you should optimize your monitor settings.

● Click on the **Start** button, and select **Control Panel** from the menu.

● In the **Control Panel** window, double-click on the **Display** icon.

● The **Display Properties** window will appear.

● In the **Colors** panel, select the highest possible setting (usually **24-bit** or **32-bit**). A lower setting can produce a poor quality image onscreen.

● Click on **OK**.

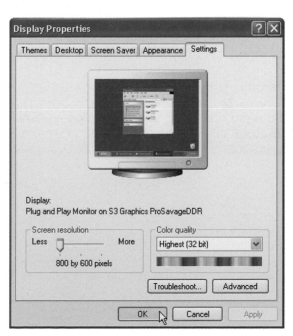

What is the monitor resolution?

A monitor always displays an image at 72dpi, meaning there are 72 dots, or pixels, of information in every inch of the screen.

INSTALLING A SCANNER

Before you can start scanning any images, you need to ensure that your computer recognizes the scanner, and that you have installed the software required to operate it.

UNPACKING YOUR NEW SCANNER

It is worth taking time during the whole installation process to ensure that everything goes according to plan. Although the process should be straightforward enough, a simple error early on can mean you have to spend a frustrating couple of hours trying to work out why your scanner isn't working. We are going to take you through the whole process, starting at the beginning with unpacking the scanner from its box. This may seem trivial, but there are a few important points here that are fundamental to the installation process.

Before you start...
It is important to check that everything that should have been supplied with your scanner is in the box. There should be a power cord, a cable to connect the scanner to the computer, a CD-ROM or disk containing software and drivers, and an installation/user manual. If any of these is missing, it will be impossible to install your scanner.

1 REMOVING THE PACKAGING
● Take care when handling your scanner. Although a scanner is fairly sturdy, the glass top and lamp demand some respect!

● There is probably some kind of label, tape, or other device securing the scanner lid. Begin by removing this and any other residual packaging, and unwrap any cables that were supplied.

2 UNLOCKING THE SCANNER

● The scanner's moving parts are held in place during transit by a locking mechanism. This varies depending on the make and model, but there should be a switch, bolt/nut, or screw that is usually located on the underside of the scanner.

● Release the mechanism. Keep any screws or bolts in a safe place as you should replace them whenever you transport your scanner in the future.

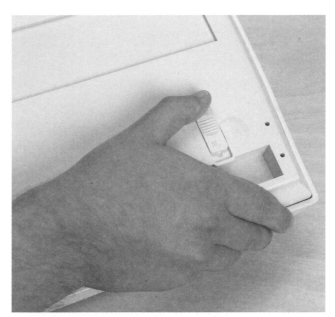

3 LOCATING THE SCANNER

● Place the scanner on a flat, level surface within easy reach of your PC.

● Check that the cables will reach both the power supply and the back of the computer.

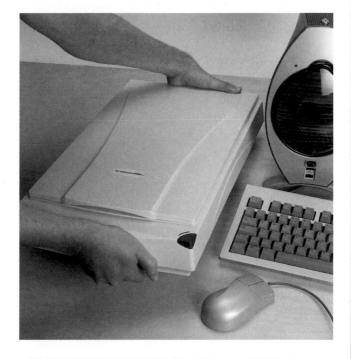

CONNECTING THE SCANNER CABLES

The majority of modern scanners and printers come with USB connections . USB is designed to make the connection and installation of these external devices relatively straightforward. As you are more than likely to be using this form of connection, the following steps, and those in the next chapter, concentrate on installing hardware with USB support. If your computer does not support USB, and is reliant on a parallel or SCSI connection 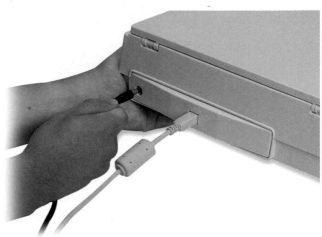, then things can be slightly more complicated and you should refer to the installation manuals that came with your scanner.

1 CONNECTING THE USB CABLE

- First, connect the USB cable to the port at the rear of the scanner.
- Important: don't connect the other end of the cable to the computer just yet.

2 CONNECTING THE POWER

- Next, connect the power cord into the jack socket on the scanner.
- Connect the other end of the cable to an electrical outlet and ensure that both the power and the scanner are turned on.

| 401 | USB Ports |

| 400 | What Connection Do I have? |

SCANNER INSTALLATION

Installing the scanner and software is always best done in conjunction with the manual supplied, as there are always differences between manufacturers. The following sequence is therefore intended as an example only, although the steps that we take you through should be very close to those you will encounter for any scanner. The program that we have chosen to show (Microtek ScanWizard) requires the software to be installed before the scanner. For an example of installing hardware before software, turn to the printer installation .

1 LAUNCHING THE CD-ROM

● Insert the CD-ROM that was supplied with the scanner into your computer's CD drive.
● The disk should start to run automatically and an introductory screen will appear.

● If this doesn't happen, double-click on the **My Computer** icon on the desktop and launch the disk by double-clicking on the (**D:**) drive icon in the **My Computer** window.

Printer Installation

● The CD may include a range of programs that you may wish to install. Take the time to find out what each of them can do before deciding whether or not to install them.

● Click on the relevant icons to read about each program.

Take the opportunity to find out about the software you are about to install

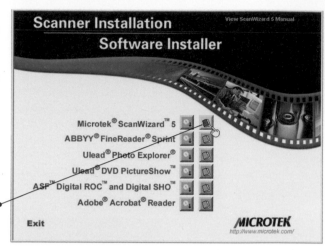

● As well as a description of the program's features, the onscreen pages also include instructions on how to use the software.

● Close the page to return to the main screen.

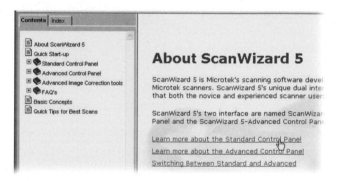

2 INSTALLING THE SOFTWARE

● For now, we are only going to install the software required to make the scanner work. Our scanner has been supplied with a program called ScanWizard.

● Click on the disk icon next to **ScanWizard** to begin the installation.

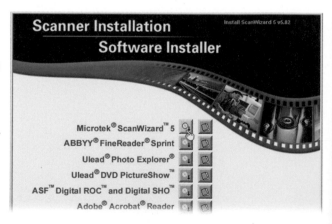

• The installation window opens and the installation program starts. A series of screens will lead you through the process.

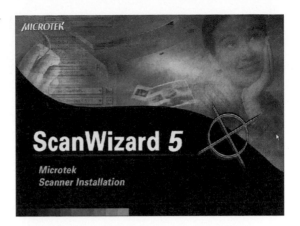

3 REGISTERING THE PRODUCT

• At some point during the installation you will need to read and accept a license agreement.

• You may also be asked to register the product in your name.
• Enter the relevant details, and then click **Next**.

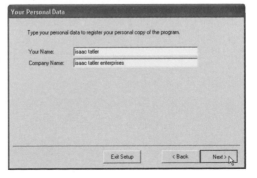

4 SELECTING A LOCATION

● There may be a choice of what type of setup you require. The default setup, already checked in this example, is likely to be the one you need.

● When prompted, select the location in which you want the software to be installed on your computer. These fields are usually filled in automatically and direct the software to the default Programs folder.
● Click on **Next**.

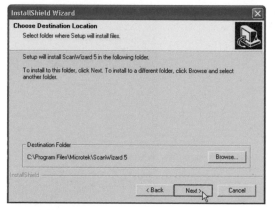

● The installation program will ask you to select a program folder. Again, the proposed default choice is probably the one to accept.
● Click on **Next**.

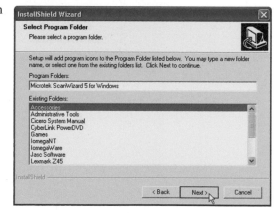

5 COMPLETING THE INSTALLATION

• A progress bar should appear to indicate that the files are being copied from the disk to your hard drive.

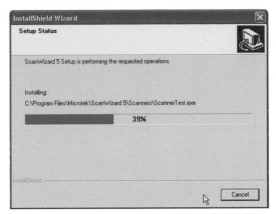

• Windows XP will confirm that the installation was successful and ask you to restart your computer.
• You will not be able to use the new software until the computer has restarted, but if you wish to install further software, choose to restart your computer later.

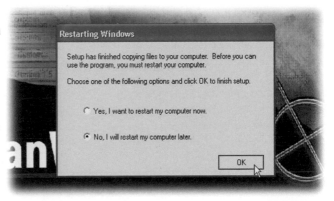

• When you have installed all the programs that you wish to, click on **Exit**.

- You will be reminded that your computer must be restarted before the software can be used.
- Click on **Yes** to reboot.
- Your computer should automatically shut down and boot up again. If it fails to do so, refer to "Restarting Your Computer" below.

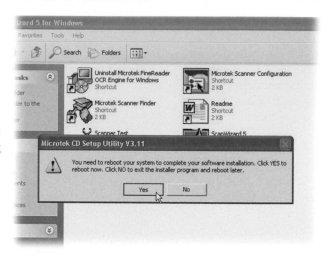

RESTARTING YOUR COMPUTER

It is usually necessary to restart your computer before you can use newly installed software. If the installation process does not provide you with the option, or it doesn't work, you can do it manually. Exit the installer CD and quit any other programs. Click on the **Start** button on the desktop, and choose **Turn off computer** from the pop-up menu. In the **Turn off computer** window, click on the **Restart** option button, and your computer will turn itself off and then boot up again.

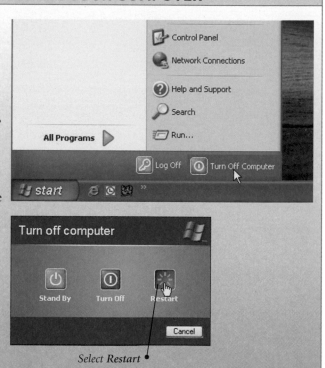

Select Restart

6 CONNECTING THE SCANNER

- Once the computer has restarted and the software is fully installed, it is time to connect the scanner to the computer.
- Plug the USB cable from the scanner into the USB port on your computer.
- Windows will detect the new hardware and will immediately install it.

Locate an available USB port on the back of your computer

- To confirm that your scanner is installed, click on **Start** and then select **Control Panel** from the pop-up menu.

- In the **Control Panel** window, click on **Scanners and Cameras**.

- An icon for your scanner should be present in the **Scanners and Cameras** window.

INSTALLING A PRINTER

The installation process for a USB printer should be no more complicated than for a USB scanner. However, this chapter deals with a couple of techniques just in case you encounter problems.

CONNECTING THE PRINTER CABLES

As discussed in a previous chapter 🗋, we are concentrating on installing hardware with USB compatibility. If your printer does not have a USB port and relies on a parallel connection instead, refer to your instruction manual.

1 CONNECTING THE CABLES

● Connect the USB and power cables to the ports at the back of your printer, then connect the power cord to an outlet and ensure the power is turned on.
● As with the scanner, don't plug the USB cable into the computer until you begin the installation process.
● Switch on the printer.

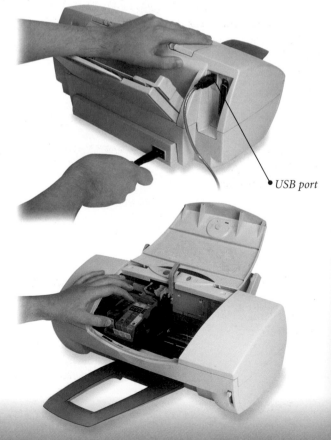

● *USB port*

2 INSERTING THE INK CARTRIDGE

● Depending on your printer, you may also need to insert the ink cartridge at this stage. Refer to the manual that came with your printer for advice.

401 USB Ports

PRINTER INSTALLATION

This example demonstrates an installation using a Lexmark Inkjet printer. Here, we are installing the printer before the software but, as before, use the steps just as a guide and refer to the manual supplied. The next example demonstrates a printer being installed in a different way. Refer to both examples, along with your manual, before you begin to decide which method is relevant to you – both may be relevant.

1 ADDING NEW HARDWARE

• Plug the USB cable from the printer into the USB port on your computer.

• When you insert the cable, Windows recognizes that you have connected new hardware and opens the **Found New Hardware Wizard**.

• Insert the CD-ROM into your computer.

• The wizard will search the CD-ROM for the necessary software.

• It will then begin copying the files from the CD-ROM to your computer's hard disk.

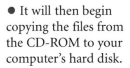
418 Using the Add Printer Wizard

2 ACCEPTING THE LICENSE TERMS

● At some point during the installation, you will be required to accept the terms and conditions of the software license agreement.

● Read the agreement and click **Yes** to continue with the installation.

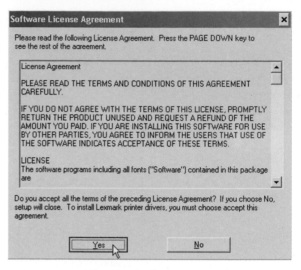

3 ALIGNING THE PRINTHEAD

● For the printer to work properly, the printhead needs to be correctly aligned, and the option for automatic alignment will probably be available. Make sure this checkbox is ticked.

● Click on **Continue**.

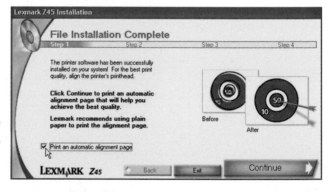

● When the test page has been printed and is correct, click again on **Continue**.

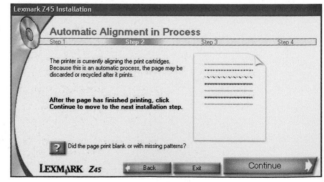

● The installation process may give you the chance to print out a test page of your own, which you can choose to do, or you may click on **Continue** to complete the installation.

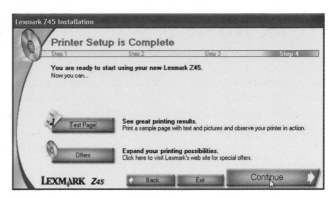

4 COMPLETING THE INSTALLATION

● If your computer is connected to the internet, you may wish to register your printer with the manufacturer, giving you access to technical support and information.

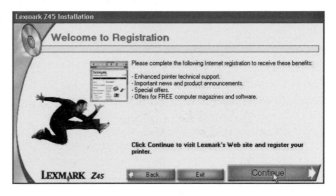

● When the installation is complete, quit the CD-ROM by clicking on **Finish**, and restart your computer ⌐|.

USING THE ADD PRINTER WIZARD

If the previous installation example using the manufacturer's CD-ROM worked correctly, the following steps should have been implemented automatically and your printer will be ready to use. However, if you find that something didn't quite go to plan you may have to carry out this task as well. The following sequence can also be used as a completely alternative installation technique to the previous example, and you may want to follow this route if the CD-ROM installer is not available, or if it does not seem to be installing the printer drivers correctly. Here, we are installing a Lexmark inkjet printer using the Windows XP Add Printer Wizard.

1 OPENING THE CONTROL PANEL

● Click on the **Start** button at the bottom left of the taskbar and choose **Control Panel** from pop-up menu.

2 OPENING THE WIZARD

● In the **Control Panel** window, click on **Printers and Faxes**.
● If you see an icon for your printer already located in this window, then you can go straight to step 6, as the necessary software has already been installed.
● If there is no icon, double-click on **Add a printer** to launch the **Add Printer Wizard**.

3 SELECTING THE CONNECTION

● The **Add Printer Wizard** window opens.

● To begin installing your printer using the Wizard, click on **Next**.

● The Wizard will ask you how your printer is connected to the computer.

● We will assume that you are connecting the printer directly to your computer, rather than on a network, so select the radio button next to **Local printer attached to this computer**.

● Check the box next to **Automatically detect and install my Plug and Play printer**, and click on **Next**.

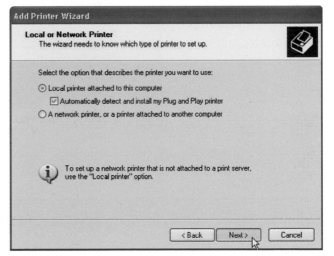

● The Wizard will now search for your printer.

4 SELECTING THE CORRECT PORT

● You will now be asked to select which port to use.
● Identify the port from the list and select it. It should be obvious which port to select.
● Click on **Next**.

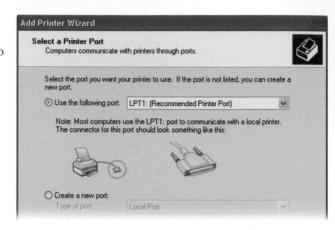

5 SELECTING THE PRINTER

● Select the make and model of your printer and click on **Next**.

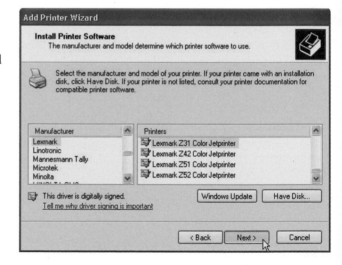

● You will then be asked to confirm the name of the printer. This field will be filled in automatically and need not be changed.
● Click on **Next**.
● The next screen allows you to share your printer on a network. Choose not to, and click on **Next**.

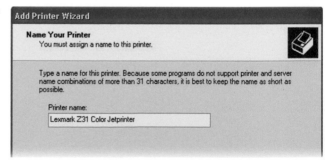

● You are returned to the main **Add Printer Wizard** window.

● Click on **Finish** to close the wizard.

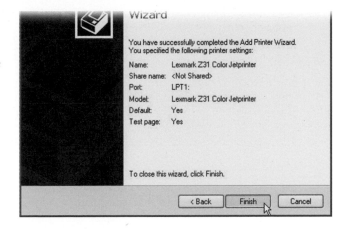

6 CHECKING THE PROPERTIES

● An icon for your new printer has been added in the **Printers** window.

● To check that everything has installed correctly, right-click on the icon and select **Properties** from the pop up menu.

● A window displaying the properties for the printer will open.

● Click on the **Ports** tab.

● Ensure that your printer is listed and that it is printing to the correct port (check this against the port you selected in Step 4).

● If the port is not selected, click on the down arrow and highlight the correct port in the list.

● Click on **OK** when you have finished.

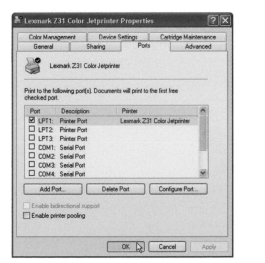

SCANNING AN IMAGE

Scanning a picture into your computer is really very simple, but you need to understand some basic terms and settings to ensure you get the best results from your scanner.

USING THE SCANNING SOFTWARE

At this point, you could quite easily place a picture on your scanner, launch the software, and press the scan button. The chances are that an image would indeed appear on the screen, and to the untrained eye the quality of the scan would seem to be sufficient. So what's the problem? Well, it's not quite as simple as all that – your computer needs to be given some directions for it to provide you with a scanned image that truly meets your needs. The software that was supplied with your scanner will vary depending on the make and quality of the product you bought, but the basic look and operation of each one is similar to the example shown here.

1 LAUNCHING THE SOFTWARE
● With your scanner connected to the computer and turned on, click on the **Start** button on the desktop and select the scanning software from the **All Programs** menu.

Alternatively…
You can launch by clicking on the program icon if the software installation has created one on your desktop.

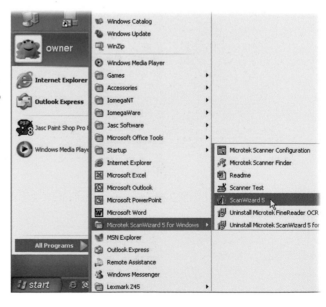

2 THE SCANNING CONTROL PANEL

● The program will launch, and a screen similar to the one below will appear.

● It is from this window that you will define all aspects of the scan, using menus to tell the program what you are scanning, whether you want the scan in color or black and white, what the scan will be used for (and hence what resolution you require), and the size at which the image will be output.

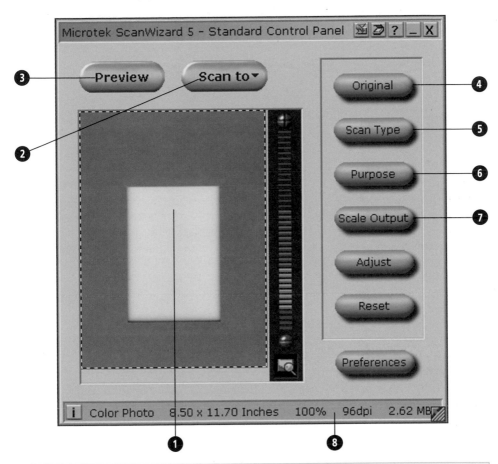

THE SCANNING INTERFACE

❶ The item you are scanning appears here once you perform a prescan (or preview)

❷ Scan to ⌐|
❸ Preview ⌐|
❹ Original ⌐|
❺ Scan Type

❻ Purpose ⌐|
❼ Scale output ⌐|
❽ Details of the last scan performed

 430 Starting the Scan

424 Previewing the Image

 427 Selecting Original

428 Selecting Resolution

 429 Selecting Output Size

PERFORMING A PRESCAN

Unless you are scanning a particularly large picture, scanning the entire area of the scanner bed would result in an image that had a lot of unnecessary space around the edges, which in turn would increase its file size. To scan a more specific area, you need to preview the image by performing a prescan.

1 POSITIONING THE PICTURE

● Position the picture that you are going to scan face down on the scanner bed.
● There are often some rulers or guides around the edges of the glass to help you position the item accurately. Generally, the top of the picture should be nearest to you.
● Close the scanner lid.

Keeping the scanner bed clean
It is important to clean the glass plate on your scanner regularly. Even the smallest specks of dust and dirt will be picked up by the scanner and will appear on your image. Use a special glass cleaner and a soft cloth to remove any grime.

2 PREVIEWING THE IMAGE

● Ignoring the other settings, click on **Preview**.
● You will hear the scanner operate and it will perform a quick pass over your picture, which will appear in the preview screen.
● A prescan is exactly what it suggests – the scanner has not yet done a proper scan or passed any information about the image to your computer.

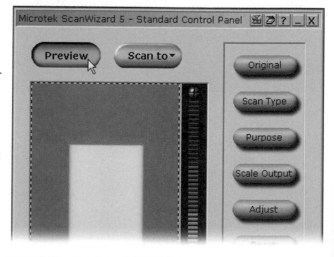

SELECTING THE SCAN AREA

Now that you can see the contents of your scanner bed accurately, you can tell whether your picture is positioned correctly, or whether any of the image is being cut off at the sides. If you do need to make any adjustments to the positioning of your picture, do so now and then perform another prescan 🗏. Next, you need to select only the area of the preview that you want to scan.

1 DRAWING A MARQUEE

The preview scan •

● The preview area of the screen represents the entire surface of the scanner bed.
● You can tell the scanner which part of the preview to scan properly by drawing a marquee (a square made up of flashing dotted lines) around the relevant area.
● Either there will be an existing marquee onscreen, or you will have to draw one by clicking in one corner of the preview and dragging the cursor across to the opposite corner.

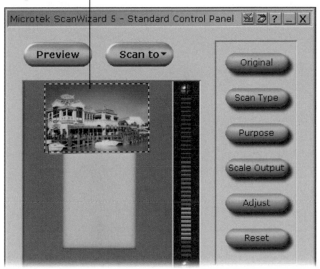

2 MOVING THE SIDE OF THE MARQUEE

● To adjust the side of the marquee, position your cursor over one edge.
● The cursor turns into a double-headed arrow. Hold down the left mouse button and drag to move the side of the marquee.

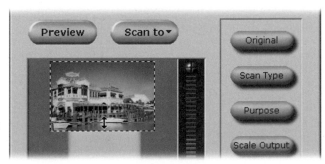

3 MOVING THE CORNER

● To move a corner of the marquee, position the cursor over the corner.

● The cursor turns into a double-headed arrow. Hold down the left mouse button and drag diagonally.

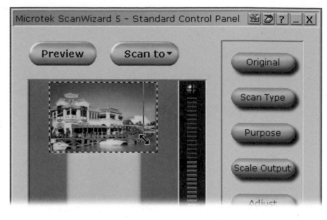

4 CREATING A NEW MARQUEE

● Move the cursor into a new position.

● Hold the left mouse button down and drag diagonally to create a new marquee, for example for a second picture on the scanner bed.

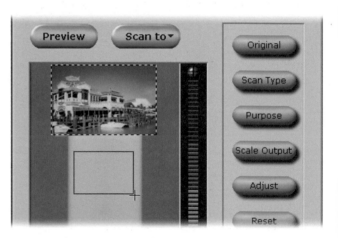

MOVING AN ENTIRE MARQUEE

To move the entire marquee, place the cursor inside it and the cursor changes to a four-way arrow. Hold down the left mouse button and drag the marquee to enclose the area of the image that you want to be scanned.

SELECTING THE INPUT AND OUTPUT

You are likely to see the following choices available in some form within your scanning software. In order to create the type of scan that you require, you need to define the kind of image being scanned and how the image will be output.

1 SELECTING THE TYPE OF ORIGINAL

● Click on the **Original** button and select the type of original being scanned.
● In this case the original is a photograph.

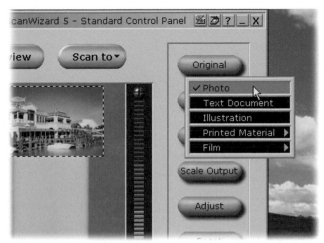

2 SELECTING THE TYPE OF SCAN

● To select the type of scan required, click on the **Scan Type** button, and select the scan that you require.
● In this case we want the scan to be in **True Color**. Images for printing are made up of cyan, magenta, yellow, and black (known as CMYK), whereas images for the web are made up of red, green, and blue (or RGB) – the colors that computer monitors use.

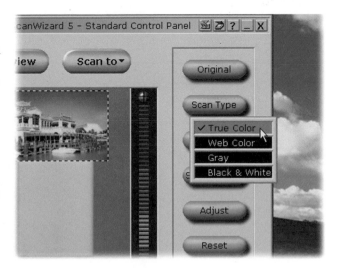

CHOOSING THE CORRECT RESOLUTION

Resolution is possibly the most important aspect of scanning an image, and yet it is also the one area that most people don't understand. The resolution that you scan at directly affects the quality, file size, and usability of the image you are scanning.

WHAT DOES RESOLUTION MEAN?
You will see the resolution setting in your scanning software referred to as dpi. This stands for dots per inch. Basically, if an image is scanned at 100% size at 100dpi then it will contain 100 dots, or pixels, of information in every inch. The same image scanned at 100% size at 600dpi will contain six times the amount of information in an inch. A low resolution means that the image contains less information overall, and will be of a poorer quality than that of an image scanned at a high resolution.

1 SELECTING THE RESOLUTION

● This particular software links the resolution of the scan to the purpose for which it to be used. To print the image on an inkjet printer, click on the **Purpose** button and select **Ink-Jet Printing**.
● The panel at the bottom of the drop-down menu shows that the scan will be at a resolution of 200dpi.
● Each purpose requires a different resolution. For onscreen viewing, the resolution of the scan is set at 96dpi.

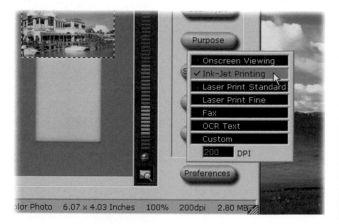

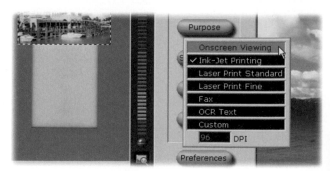

- For standard laser printing, the corresponding resolution is set at 100dpi.
- Each of the remaining **Purpose** options has its own corresponding setting.

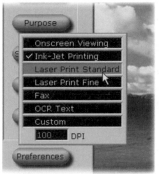

2 ENTERING A SPECIFIC VALUE

- If your software doesn't provide a list of optional resolutions, or if you want to enter a more specific value, select the **Custom** option and then click in the **DPI** panel.
- Type in your new resolution value, for example **500**dpi.

Type the resolution value here •

3 SELECTING THE OUTPUT SIZE

- If you wish to print the image larger or smaller than the original, select a **Scale Output** option.
- This will adjust the scanning resolution so that the printed image has the resolution you selected ⌐.

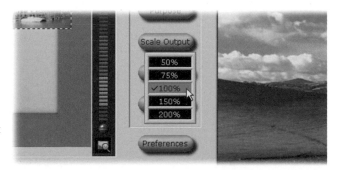

SCANNING THE PICTURE

After selecting the scan area, the mode, and the resolution, the final step in turning your picture into a digital file on your computer is for the scanner to carry out a scan using the information and settings that you have provided it with.

1 STARTING THE SCAN

● Move your cursor over the **Scan to** button and hold down the left mouse button to view the menu choices, which include OCR 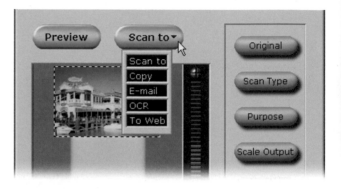.

● We are selecting the default option of **Scan to**.

● Click on the **Scan to** button to begin the scanning process.

CONSIDER THE LEGAL ISSUES BEFORE YOU SCAN

Bear in mind that to reproduce another person's work without their specific consent is breaking copyright law. If you are planning to scan a photo, drawing, or image from any source other than your own (from a magazine or a book, for example) and then use it in any commercial sense (such as in a brochure or poster), then you must gain written permission from the owner of the image before doing so. For example, the copyright owner of any photograph is usually the person who took the picture. If permission is granted, it usually comes at a price and you will have to pay the copyright owner what is known as a royalty fee for the privilege. Scanning such things as money, postage stamps, and corporation trademarks is illegal and out of the question.

433 **Optical Character Recognition**

2 SAVING THE IMAGE

● The **Save As** window now appears.

● Select the **Save in** drop-down menu and navigate to the folder in which you want to save the scan.

● Select the **Save as type** drop-down menu and choose the format in which you want to save the image file (see "File Formats" below).

● Click on **Save**.

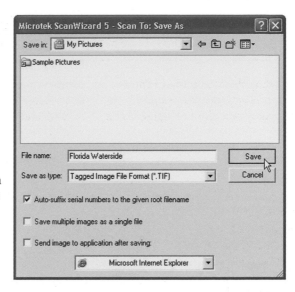

● The progress of the scan is charted at the bottom of the screen.

● When the scan is complete, close the scanner interface, unless you want to perform further scans.

● Your scanned image will have been saved in the specified location.

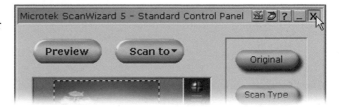

FILE FORMATS

When you save images, consider their final use and select an appropriate file format (or *type*) from the **Save as type** drop-down menu in the **Save As** window. The following two examples of file formats are the most commonly used and are available in most scanning and image editing software.

● **JPEG** (*Joint Photographic Experts Group*): Compresses the file but loses detail from the image. This makes it ideal for use in web graphics and email.

● **TIFF** (*Tagged Image File Format*): Retains detail in the image and is widely recognized. Use this format for images that you are going to print.

SCANNING AN OBJECT

You are not limited to scanning flat, two-dimensional pictures into your computer. Within reason, you can also use your scanner to create an image of real three-dimensional objects – just like taking a photograph. Obviously there is a limit to what you can place on to the scanner bed, but you can get some very impressive results from most small items. To get the best possible quality, you need to restrict the amount of external light that naturally enters the scanner from around the object.

1 POSITIONING THE OBJECT

● Place the item that you want to scan on the scanner bed, in this case a toy car.
● The height of the object may mean that the scanner lid will not close properly, and additional light will enter the scanning area. This will decrease the quality of your scan.
● To reduce this intrusion of light, place something around the sides of the scanner. Some books, for example, would be ideal.

2 PREVIEWING THE OBJECT

● Prescan and scan your object in the usual way, just as if it were a picture ◗.

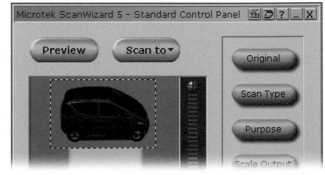

3 SCANNING THE OBJECT

● The final scan will be of a reasonable quality, but it will be necessary to do some corrective work to the image to improve it ⬚.

The Final Image
Once corrected, the quality of a scanned object – such as this toy car – can be remarkably high.

Don't stop there...

If it will fit on the scanner bed, then the chances are that you will get a perfectly good result from any item. Try scanning fabric or wood for example. Beware though – the glass plate on your scanner can easily get scratched, so position heavy or sharp objects carefully.

OPTICAL CHARACTER RECOGNITION

Your scanner can be very versatile, and there are many features at your disposal in addition to simply scanning pictures and objects. Optical Character Recognition (OCR) software enables you to scan printed text into your computer, which, rather than becoming an image file, is saved as an editable text file. The software recognizes each individual character and, although it provides the occasional minor error, it pieces together a document that can be treated like any other text file, in Microsoft Word for example. The main advantage of this is the time saved by not having to key in text that already exists.

IMPROVING YOUR SCAN

No matter how good your scanner is, the quality of your image can usually be greatly improved by applying some minor corrective tweaks using image editing software.

IMAGE EDITING SOFTWARE

Your picture is now scanned into your computer, but that isn't necessarily the end of the story. Your image probably requires some minor adjustment to ensure that it's looking its best when you come to use it. The software packages that come supplied with some scanners can actually have some advanced image editing functions built-in. However, to really get the most out of your scanned images, you should think about using a retouching program designed for the job.

PAINT SHOP PRO

Paint Shop Pro™ is a relatively inexpensive image editing program with some quite advanced features, and we will be using this program here. However, there are many software packages available that can do the same things. If you are using a different program, use the steps outlined here as a guide and look for the same options within the menus of your own image editing software.

OPENING THE IMAGE
● Launch Paint Shop Pro and select **Open** from the **File** menu.

● Locate and highlight your scanned file, and click on the **Open** button to open the image.

ADJUSTING BRIGHTNESS AND CONTRAST

Scanned images can often look a little dull compared with the original picture. It is a good idea, therefore, to get into the habit of adding a bit of life to every picture that you scan. You can do this by using the **Brightness/Contrast** command.

1 BRIGHTNESS/ CONTRAST

● Click on **Adjust**, and select **Brightness and Contrast**, followed by **Brightness/Contrast** from the submenu.

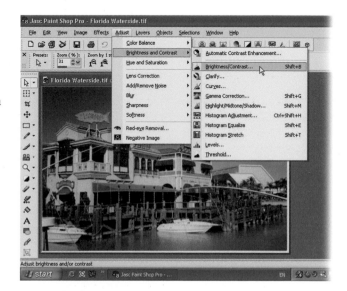

For more advanced correction options...

Instead of choosing **Brightness/Contrast** to correct your image, you can also make more subtle changes by using some of the other functions. Click on **Adjust** and select **Color Balance** or **Hue and Saturation**. Experiment by adjusting your image using **Highlight/ Midtone/Shadow**. The possibilities are endless.

THE BRIGHTNESS/CONTRAST COMMAND

Adjusting brightness and contrast is one of the easiest ways to correct an image. The brightness function controls how light or how dark your image appears, and the contrast function alters the degree of shading. When you apply a change with either command, the highlights, midtones, and shadows in the entire image are all affected at once. For this reason, the command is ideal for the home user who, generally, only needs to make changes suitable for low resolution output. If you were adjusting the image for professional use, you would be advised to use more advanced functions.

2 SELECTING AUTO PROOF

● The **Brightness/Contrast** window will open.

● Click the **Auto Proof** button and this will automatically update the preview image in the background as you make adjustments, so you can see the overall effect of the changes that you make.

● These changes won't actually be implemented until you finally close the **Brightness/Contrast** window.

Click on the Auto Proof button

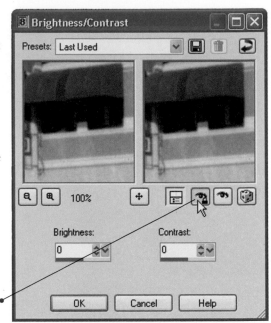

3 CHANGING THE PREVIEW AREA

● The preview boxes in the window display close-ups of the existing image (in the left-hand box) and the effect of any adjustments that you make (in the right-hand box).

● When you first open the **Brightness/Contrast** window, the close-up is automatically set to the center of the image, but this may not be the best part of the image to use to preview your adjustments.

● Position the cursor over the left-hand panel so that a hand appears.

● Click and hold the mouse button and drag the image preview to an area with sufficient detail.

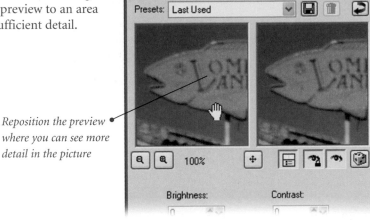

Reposition the preview where you can see more detail in the picture

4 ADJUSTING THE BRIGHTNESS

● Assess whether your image needs to be lighter or darker (scanned images tend to need lightening).

● To brighten the image, click on the upward pointing arrow in the **Brightness** box. To darken the image, click on the downward pointing arrow.

● You will see the change take place to the preview images. Only minor adjustment is usually required, as too much will lose detail from your image.

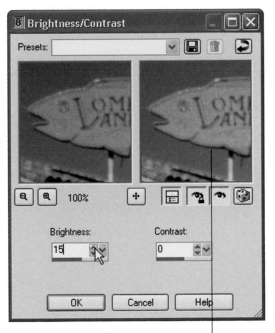

The brightness of the image will change in the right-hand preview box

5 ADJUSTING THE CONTRAST

● Now do the same with the **Contrast**.

● Click on the up and down arrows until the level of contrast in the image is as you want it.

View the change in contrast in the right-hand preview box

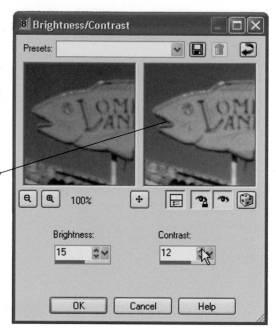

● Once you are happy with the adjustment of the brightness and the contrast, click on **OK**.

● Your picture will be updated with the changes that you have made.

SHARPENING THE IMAGE

Blurring is a common problem in scanned images. Even if at first glance the picture seems fine, you will be surprised at just how much of an improvement can be made by a subtle adjustment to the sharpness. Sharpening the image can also help to compensate for any blurring that results from inkjet printing.

1 SELECTING UNSHARP MASK

● Click on **Adjust** and select **Sharpness**, followed by **Unsharp Mask** from the drop-down menu.

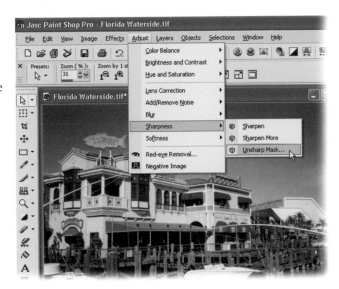

Using the Sharpen and Sharpen More functions

You will also find these two commands available in the **Sharpen** menu alongside **Unsharp Mask**. They apply an overall adjustment to the image, which helps to focus blurred edges; but while they may provide enough of a sharpening effect to improve your image, they do not offer the same level of control as **Unsharp Mask**.

THE UNSHARP MASK COMMAND

When you apply **Unsharp Mask**, the contrast of the pixels that make up the image is increased, so that there is more difference between adjoining pixels – thus sharpening the image. You adjust the sharpness of the image by entering values into three fields: Radius, Strength, and Clipping. To fully explain how these work in conjunction with one another is unnecessary here, and experimentation is really the key until you achieve the desired result. You will only need to make minor adjustments, as too much will make the image look unnatural.

2 ADJUSTING THE SHARPNESS

● As before ⌐, position the preview so that it displays an area of the image with sufficient detail, and turn on the **Auto Proof** function so that you can see the overall effect of your changes on the picture.

● By clicking on the up and down arrows next to the **Radius**, **Strength**, and **Clipping** boxes, you can increase or decrease the sharpening effect.

● Each time you make a change, Auto Proof will take a few moments to implement it.

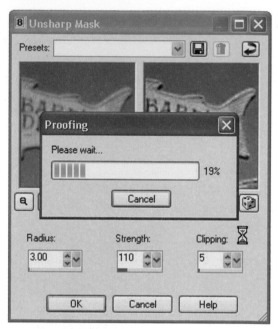

● When you are satisfied that you have improved the image sufficiently, click on **OK**.

● Your corrected image will be displayed onscreen.

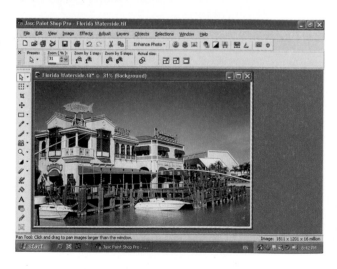

CROPPING THE IMAGE

It may be that you are not happy with the overall shape of your image, or you may want to lose part of a picture that you wish wasn't in shot – a person or building, for example. Cropping your picture simply means cutting off unwanted information from around the edges. This also helps to reduce the file size.

1 SELECTING THE CROPPING TOOL

● Select the cropping tool from the toolbar on the left of your screen.

The cropping tool ●

2 POSITIONING THE CROP

● When you place the cursor over the image window it will take on the shape of the cropping tool.
● Position the cursor at the point where you would like the top left corner of your picture to start.

This position will become the top left corner of your picture when it is cropped

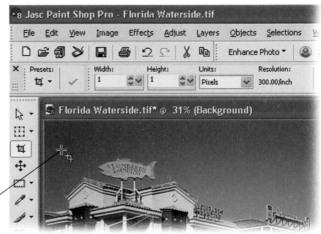

● While holding down the mouse button, drag a rectangle over the image until you reach the point that you would like to be the bottom right corner of your picture.

● Everything outside the rectangle will be deleted when you confirm the crop, so ensure that the selected area is precisely the part of the image that you want.

This position will become the bottom right corner of your picture when it is cropped ●

3 **ADJUSTING THE CROP**

● Release the mouse button when you are satisfied with the shape of the rectangle.

● If you want to begin again, click once outside the rectangle so that it disappears.

● You can move the existing rectangle to another position by placing the cursor inside it and holding down the mouse button while you drag the rectangle to a new position.

4 CROPPING THE IMAGE

● When you are satisfied with the area you have selected, double-click inside the rectangle.

● Your picture will be cropped to its new shape.

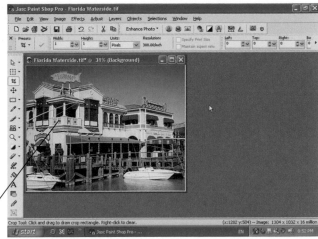

The picture is cropped to size ●

SAVING THE CORRECTED IMAGE

After you have completed the corrective work on your image, it is wise to save the document as a second file, keeping the original untouched. Then, if for any reason you are not happy with the final result when you print the corrected picture, at least you will be able to return to the original and try again. Instead of selecting **Save**, choose **Save As** from the **File** menu. In the **Save As** window, name the document so that it is clearly marked as the corrected image (for example add **Retouched** to the end of the original name), then click **Save**.

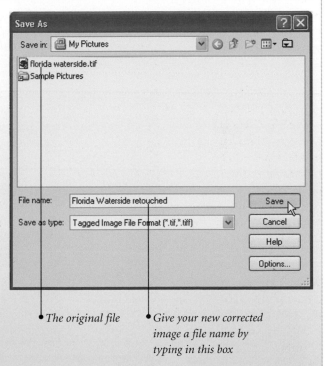

● *The original file* ● *Give your new corrected image a file name by typing in this box*

PRINTING YOUR IMAGE

Your designs are not doing you justice when they are trapped inside a computer screen. Having a color print that you can touch and hold adds real value to your work.

THE PAGE SETUP

The following sequence shows you simply how to print the scanned image that we corrected in the previous chapter. Don't forget, however, that this really is the thin end of the wedge – once you become more ambitious with your scanned images, you will want to start using them in conjunction with desktop publishing software to create your own designs. You may even want to use a graphics program to create illustrations and montages from a series of scanned pictures. Whatever you are printing, the first task is to check the page setup, which dictates the size at which your image will be printed and where it will appear on the paper.

1 OPENING THE PRINT WINDOW

● With your document open, click on **File** and select **Print** from the drop-down menu.

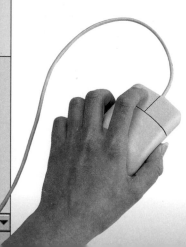

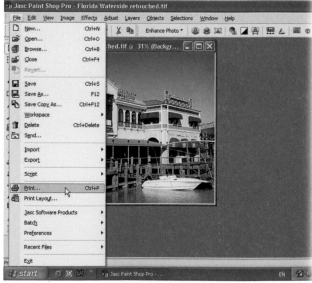

2 CHANGING THE IMAGE SIZE

• The **Print** window will open, showing the size and position of your image as it will appear on the page.

• If you wish to change the size of the printed image, click on the vertical arrows to the right of the **Width**, **Height**, and **Scale** boxes. These three are linked, so a change to any one of them will affect the other two.

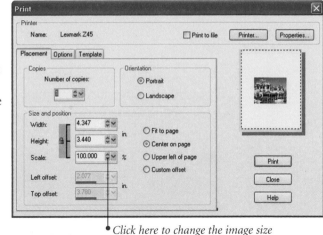

• Click here to change the image size

3 CHANGING THE ORIENTATION

• If you want your document to print so that the image appears on the paper horizontally, click in the **Landscape** radio button so that a bullet appears.

• The preview in the right-hand side of the window will change to show you how your document will appear when it is printed.

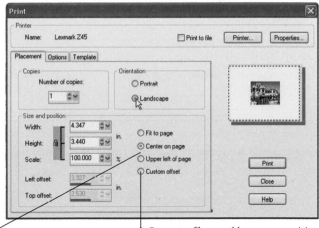

Use these radio buttons to alter the position of the image on the page •

*• **Custom offset** enables you to position the image precisely by defining the **Left offset** and **Top offset***

Printing from other programs

Although the sequence shown demonstrates printing an image from Paint Shop Pro, the process is virtually identical no matter what program you are using. You will find the same settings and options under the **Print** menu (or **Page Setup**) in any software package, even though they may look slightly different.

4 CHOOSING OTHER OPTIONS

● Refer to the annotation below to decide whether you want to activate any other options.

● When you have finished, click on the **OK** button.

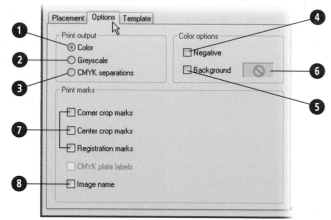

OTHER PAGE OUTPUT OPTIONS

① Prints image in color
② Prints image as grayscale (black and white)
③ Prints four grayscale separations: one page each for cyan, magenta, yellow, and black

④ Prints the image in its reverse colors
⑤ Click here if you want to have a background color to "frame" your image
⑥ Click here to select the background color

⑦ Check the appropriate box if you wish the image to appear with crop or registration marks
⑧ Check this box to print the document name below the image

5 VIEWING THE PRINTER

● To check that the image will be sent to the correct printer, and that the printer is ready, click on the **Printer** button at the top of the **Print** window.

● Click on **OK** if the settings are correct.

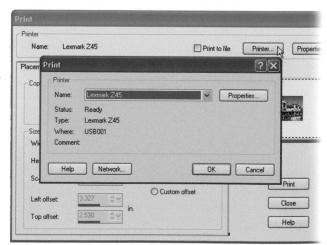

SETTING THE PRINT OPTIONS

The following settings concern the printer itself, and how it outputs your image. The options that you choose here will have a bearing on the final quality of your printed image, so make sure everything is correct before starting the print process.

1 OPENING PROPERTIES
● Click on **Properties** in the top panel of the **Print** window.

2 SELECTING PRINT QUALITY
● The window that opens now will display options for your own particular printer. Your printer may differ from this example, but the same options should be available.
● Select the quality of print that fits the resolution of your image ⌐.

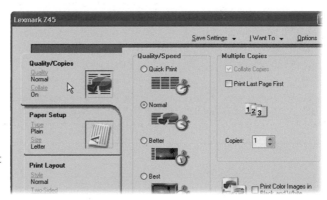

3 SELECTING PAPER TYPE AND SIZE
● Click on the **Paper Setup** tab and select the type of paper that you are using ⌐. Here we are selecting glossy photographic paper.
● Select the paper size that you are using from the list in the right-hand panel.

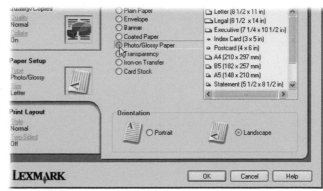

SELECTING PAPER

Selecting the correct paper to use with your inkjet printer is an important issue. Although the printer itself does require compatible paper, the main issue is the quality of the print itself. You will not be able to achieve a photo quality print on conventional paper as it will absorb too much of the ink and the image will have a slightly "soft" appearance. You will need to invest in some photo quality inkjet paper to achieve the best results. As this paper can be quite expensive, it is worth reserving the use of it to your final, edited images only, and use standard matt inkjet paper for everything else. In addition to photo quality paper, the range of materials that you can put through an inkjet printer is ever expanding. You can also purchase glossy film for even higher quality prints, transparency film for use with overhead projectors, and card for greetings.

4 SELECTING THE PRINT LAYOUT

● Click on the **Print Layout** tab to view the various layout options, and make your selection by clicking on the appropriate radio button.

● Here, we are leaving the setting on the default layout for normal single-sided printing.

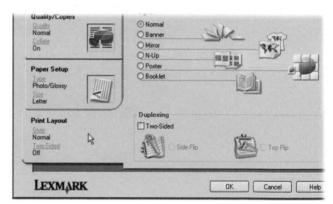

5 COMPLETING YOUR SELECTION

● When you are satisfied with your selected options, click **OK** to return to the Print window.

SHORTCUTS TO PRINTER OPTIONS

● This particular printer offers shortcuts to many of the printer options through

a list of projects from which you can choose.

● Click on **I Want To**, and the quick access drop-down menu appears.

● Make your selection by clicking on the project that meets your needs.

● Here, we are selecting **Print a photograph.**

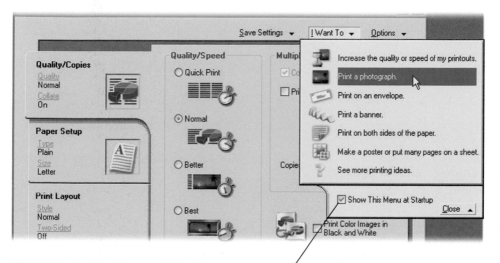

*Click in this checkbox if you would like the **I Want To** menu to appear each time you open the Properties window*

MAKING YOUR SELECTION

● The **Print a Photograph** window opens, allowing you to make a quick selection of print quality and paper size within the same menu, rather than having to open two separate tabs in the printer properties window.

● Click **OK** to return to printer properties, and click **OK** again to return to the Print window.

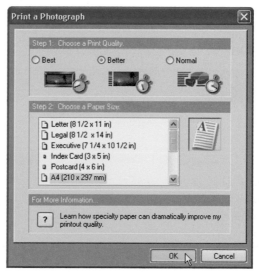

5 PRINTING THE DOCUMENT

● Once all the printing options have been selected, click on the **Print** button to start the printing process.

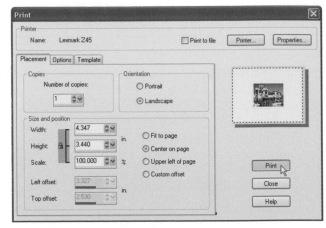

● The Print window disappears and you are returned to the image editing program.

● While the image is being printed, a status screen may appear to tell you how the printing is progressing.

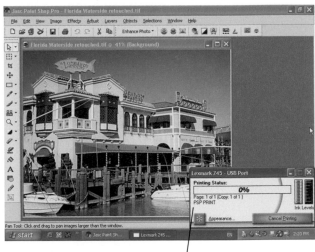

A status bar may indicate the progress of your document as it prints

RESOLUTION AFFECTS PRINT SPEED

You may start to feel frustrated at the length of time it is taking for your document to come out of the printer. However, don't be tempted to pause or cancel the printing process unless you are sure there is a genuine problem. Many inkjet printers take a long time to process and print documents, especially those that are being printed at a high resolution ⬩.

CHECKING THE PRINT STATUS

If your printer software does not provide its own print status window, you can use Windows XP to see how your job is progressing. The Windows XP Printers function allows you to view the progress of all the documents you have sent to the printer, and through it you can pause, restart, or cancel them if you wish.

1 OPEN THE CONTROL PANEL

● While your print job is processing, click on the **Start** menu on the desktop and select **Control Panel** from the pop-up menu.

2 OPEN PRINTERS AND FAXES

● The **Control Panel** window will open.
● Double click on the **Printers and Faxes** icon.

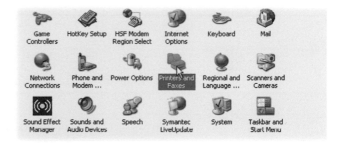

3 OPEN YOUR PRINTER

● In the **Printers and Faxes** window, double click on your printer's icon.

4 PAUSE THE PRINTING

● The status window for your printer will open, displaying a list of the print jobs that are currently being processed.

● For each file being printed, the window shows the status of the job, the size of the file, and the time it was sent to the printer.

● Highlight the document that is currently being printed by clicking on it.

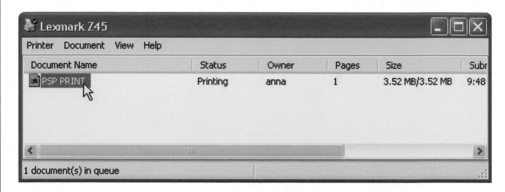

● With the file highlighted, click on the **Document** menu and select **Pause**.

● Your document will temporarily stop being processed. (Note that the options to **Restart** the printing or **Cancel** the printing completely are also available.)

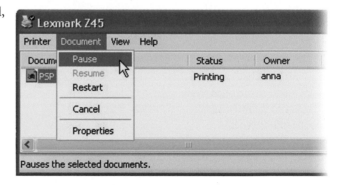

5 RESUME THE PRINTING

● To start your print job processing once more, select **Resume**.

● You can continue viewing the progress of your print job until your document finally leaves the printer, or you can continue working normally.

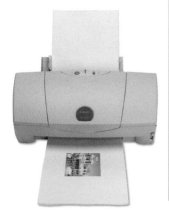

CLEARING PAPER JAMS

Although it does not happen often, occasionally paper will jam inside your printer – either because the paper that you are using is incompatible, or because the paper is not feeding through the printer correctly. Freeing the paper is relatively easy, but don't try to force it, as this could damage the mechanisms inside your printer. Instead, gently pull the paper through the rollers. If the paper really won't give, simply turning the printer off and on again may inspire the printer to spit your page out. Depending on how much of your document has processed, you may have to send your document to print again after you have freed the paper jam. Look in the print status window to see whether the document is still listed and whether or not it is processing.

6 CANCEL THE PRINTING

● If you want to stop your document from being printed altogether, highlight the file in the window and select **Cancel** from the **Document** menu.

I want to cancel all my print jobs

If there are many documents listed in the status window and you want to cancel them all – maybe because the first document printed incorrectly – select **Purge Print Documents** from the **Printer** menu. This will cancel all print jobs and they will disappear from the window.

COMPUTER TROUBLESHOOTING

THE PERSONAL COMPUTER HAS changed our lives in so many ways, allowing us to look after our home finances, produce highly designed documents, and spend hours surfing the internet. However, most users assume that a PC can manage its own affairs despite our bad habits, poor practices, and sometimes thoughtless use of such a highly technical and complex machine. The aim of this section is to help you optimize some performance aspects of your PC and to avoid common problems. You will discover how to maintain your hard drive, keep it clean by defragmenting the files, check for viruses, and delete old files that clutter up and slow down your PC, as well as finding out how to prepare for emergencies that may arise.

ABOUT YOUR PC

In a competition for causing heartache, frustration, and sometimes physical violence, the PC would be in the running for first prize; but it doesn't have to be this way.

LOOKING AFTER YOUR PC

Most of us don't realize (or ignore) how much we abuse the machines on which we depend. However, with some knowledge and a little time, the sometimes tense relationship you have with your computer can be made that much easier.

RECURRING TASKS

Most computer users follow an endless round of activities including installing and uninstalling software, downloading a new version, moving files, making a copy, deleting the old version, and inevitably forgetting where a particular file is saved.

Every computer is subject to these events and, over time, they may result in bad files, duplicate files, unused files, and any amount of unnecessary data clogging up, and slowing down, the performance levels of your machine.

Although the PC is built to cope with an astonishing amount of data, there comes a time when you need to assess exactly what you do and don't need, and carry out a major cleanup of your system. This book introduces a number of simple methods to tidy up your computer.

Although a 100-percent crash-free computer can't be guaranteed, there are steps you can take to reduce the possibility of future problems occurring.

MAKING BACKUPS

Your computer could encounter a problem that causes it to lose all the information on the hard disk, so making regular backups of your work is vital. Later in this book there is a section explaining how to back up all your valuable data.

Your computer has to deal with a colossal amount of data and keep track of its movements.

HELP IS AT HAND

For a PC to operate correctly, there are hundreds of components, as well as the software, that must all work together. Inevitably, performance problems do occur as a result of glitches, and these may either be trivial or, rarely, terminal. The actions you take to resolve a problem when one occurs may have an effect, but sometimes they are inappropriate. For example, restarting your computer can clear a fault, but if your machine is running slowly, restarting your PC is unlikely to solve the problem. Part of the answer lies in knowing what is available

to help you. Among the software on your computer, there are tools for preventive maintenance to help stop faults from developing, and others to rectify problems when they do occur. For example, later in this section we will show you how to clean your PC's hard drives of unwanted files. We will then delve deeper and explain how to use utilities such as Error Checking and Disk Defragmenter to examine, clean up, and repair broken and damaged files on the hard drive. These are simple, but effective, procedures and techniques to keep your PC in good working order.

THE WORKING PC

If you are new to computers, you may be uncertain about the meanings of the terms that are used to describe the different elements that make a PC work. Here we explain the differences between peripherals, software, and hardware.

Peripherals

A peripheral is a piece of equipment that can be connected to your computer and that is used for either inputting (such as a keyboard or scanner) or outputting (such as a printer, monitor, or external modem). Most peripherals require a piece of software to make them run. This is known as a driver and is supplied along with the peripheral. Upgrades to the drivers can sometimes be downloaded from the internet.

Software
Software comes in many shapes and sizes and is usually supplied on a CD-ROM, unless of course you are downloading it from the internet

Monitor

Desktop PC

Hardware
Computer hardware consists of all the physical elements of the system, including the main PC unit, monitor, keyboard, mouse, and any additional peripherals.

CD/DVD drive

Floppy disk drive

Keyboard

Mouse

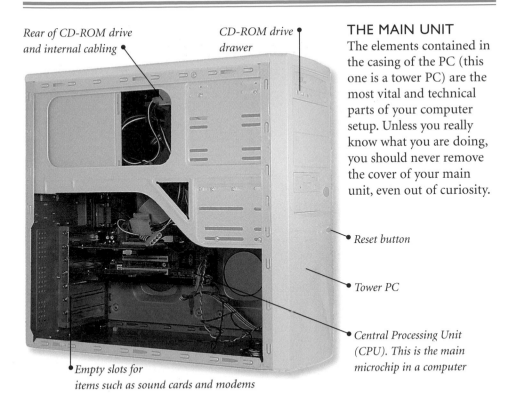

Rear of CD-ROM drive and internal cabling

CD-ROM drive drawer

Empty slots for items such as sound cards and modems

Reset button

Tower PC

Central Processing Unit (CPU). This is the main microchip in a computer

THE MAIN UNIT

The elements contained in the casing of the PC (this one is a tower PC) are the most vital and technical parts of your computer setup. Unless you really know what you are doing, you should never remove the cover of your main unit, even out of curiosity.

HARDWARE

Hardware is made up of the parts of your computer that you can see and touch. The keyboard, mouse, scanner, printer, modem, and monitor are all hardware, as is the PC system box, which may be either a tower unit or a desktop unit. The PC system box houses the microchips, the related circuitry that make the input and output peripherals work, as well as the drives, including the hard disk drive, which store all your software. It is also the component to which all the peripherals are connected. The PC is adaptable and can be easily upgraded.

SOFTWARE

Your computer needs software, or programs, for the hardware to function, and for you to do anything useful with your computer. Software comes in many forms – from simple utilities to immense computer games. Most software is now supplied on CD-ROM.

Computers have more speed and capacity than 10 years ago and software developers make the most of these developments by pushing the hardware faster and harder. Programs have grown so large that many of the major ones are now supplied on multiple CD-ROMs or single DVDs.

BASIC TROUBLESHOOTING

In this chapter, we will deal with fast recovery from problems, isolating and identifying problems, closing a crashed program, and removing unnecessary software and dead shortcuts.

BASIC RECOVERY STEPS

When troubleshooting, keep in mind that computers are completely logical and that there is always a rational reason why a problem has occurred. Correctly identifying the reason and finding a solution will be easier if you work step-by-step. However, try one or more of these basic recovery steps first when you next become aware that your computer is beginning to malfunction.

QUIT AND RESTART
● Quit the program and restart the computer to reload the operating software. Minor problems, especially temporary memory problems, can be solved in this way.

SAVE AS AND REOPEN
● Save your work under a different name and location by using the **Save As** option, quit the program, restart it, and open the new version of your work.

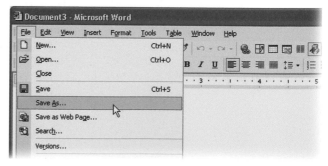

REINSTALLING
● If your software has become corrupted, reinstalling it from the original disks may often resolve the problem.

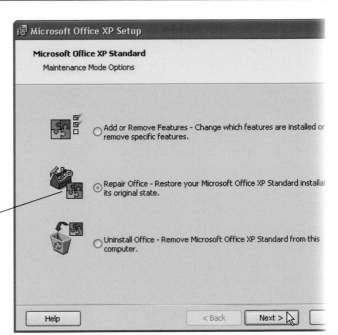

The Microsoft Office install options include a **Repair Office** *function*

DISK REPAIR UTILITY
● Use a disk repair utility, such as Norton Utilities, that scans and repairs your hard drive and carries out other system maintenance.

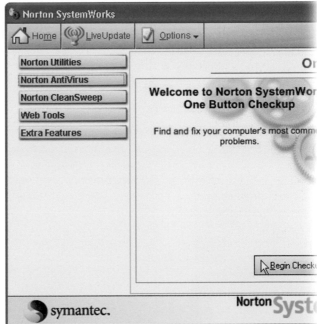

ISOLATING A PROBLEM

The preceding steps should help you to recover from an emergency, but to find out what went wrong, you may need to move on to problem isolation. A distinction to draw is between hardware and software problems. Most systems have only a few major components: monitor, printer, hard drive, sound card, CD-ROM or DVD drive, and the system box, and each can be isolated to identify a problem. In the case of software, every computer is different, but they can share characteristic problems, and the cause can be identified by isolating suspect applications.

HARDWARE ISOLATION

● To take a simple example, if you have no display on the monitor, check the power lights on both the computer and the monitor. If the computer light is on but the monitor light is off, check the monitor for burning smells, have a look at all the cables, particularly the power cords, and listen for a high-pitched whine or squealing sound. All of these (apart from the cables) are symptoms of a failed monitor.

Do not open the monitor

Never take the back off a monitor. Opening the casing of a monitor exposes you to dangerously high voltages from 10,000 to 50,000 volts, even when the monitor has been disconnected. You are endangering your personal safety by attempting to repair a monitor. Limit activities to identifying the symptoms before you seek professional help.

SWAPPING COMPONENTS

If your hardware problem has symptoms that are less obvious, it may be possible to isolate the problem by swapping a peripheral with another model of the same type. If the problem continues with a replacement peripheral, try swapping the cables. If that cures the problem, you have isolated the cause to a fault in the original cable. If not, the problem lies with the system box, which will probably need professional attention.

If you have no display, and yet the computer is switched on and running, the monitor or its power supply has failed.

WINDOWS XP HELP SYSTEM

There are times when even the most proficient PC user will bump into a problem that cannot be easily answered without a little assistance. Micosoft **Help and Support** is an invaluable resource for solving the most basic of "how to" scenarios, to complex networking problems. Chances are that if you have a problem, you will find a solution here. There are also some useful troubleshooting guides and even links to the internet for on-line assistance.

OPEN HELP AND SUPPORT

● To open the main **Help and Support** window, click on the **Start** button and then on **Help and Support**.

At Startup..

When your PC first starts up, it puts itself through a checking process, making sure that everything is working correctly and determining which hardware devices are installed. It also works out whether you are booting the PC from its own hard disk, or a CD-ROM (if you were having problems, you may want to boot from the Windows XP CD-ROM).

● The Microsoft **Help and Support Center** window opens. This introductory page offers you a guide to basic computing with Windows XP, including how to use the internet, printing, scanning, and playing games.

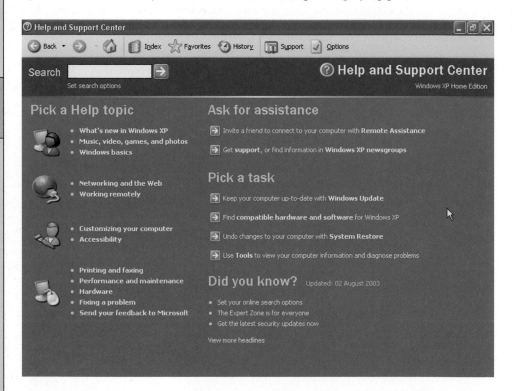

● To get the necessary help, click on the appropriate hyperlinked text.

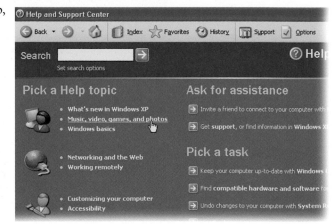

What is a hyperlink?
A hyperlink can be an image, table, or text that links to another item once it is clicked on.

● Near the top of the window, you will find an **Index** that lists the many thousands of items that are contained within the **Help and Support Center**. You can also click on the **Support** button, which has its own links to the internet.

● At the top left of the window, you will find a **Search** panel. Type in a key word to discover more about a particular topic.

● For this example, type in the word **clock** and then click on the green arrow.
● The results of the search are displayed on the right-hand side of the window.

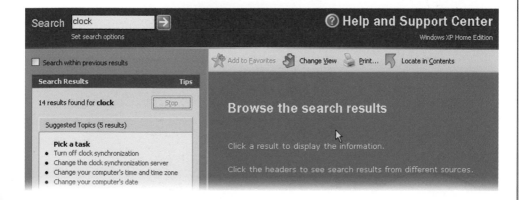

● In this example, we have clicked on the link that says **Changing your computer's time and time zone**. You will see that Windows XP's instructions on how to do this appears in the right-hand side of the window.

● *The topic is displayed on the right-hand side of the window.*

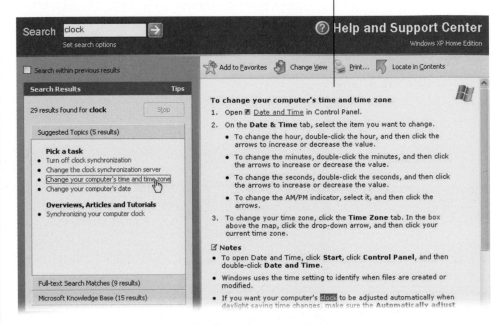

● The search result can be either printed by clicking on the **Print** button, or viewed in its own window by clicking on the **Change View** button.

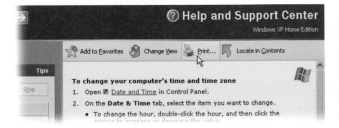

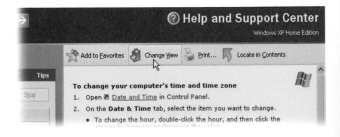

*To change the screen back to how it looked originally, click on the **Change View** button again*

The topic results are now displayed in their own window

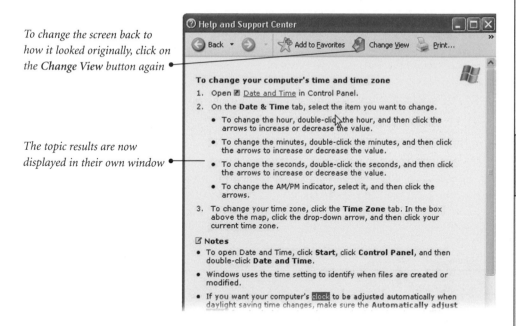

● If you find that you have delved rather deeply into the help system, simply click on the **Home** button.

TROUBLESHOOTING WEBSITES

http://www.troubleshooters.com
This site is a great starting point for any troubleshooting or debugging task.

http://wombat.doc.ic.ac.uk
A free online dictionary of computing.

http://www.everythingcomputers.com/
Has an excellent troubleshooting guide for hardware and software problems.

http://hardwarehell.com/index.shtml
A superb list of help and trouble-shooting websites usefully organized into categories such as modems, scanners, monitors.

http://www.daileyint.com/hmdpc/manual.htm
This site offers detailed solutions for computer hardware problems.

CLOSING A CRASHED PROGRAM

Making a diagnosis of why your computer is not functioning correctly is not always an easy task, and there are numerous reasons why your machine may have failed. Faults sometimes rectify themselves without an obvious reason but, from time to time, your computer will need some help to free itself from a problem.

WHEN YOUR PC FREEZES

One of the most common problems to occur with a PC is when everything "freezes" or "locks up" while you are using an application, and the mouse and keyboard will not respond. This is rarely the fault of the hardware – the problem usually lies with the software in use.

1 FREEZES AND LOCKUPS

● First, give your PC a moment to sort itself out. Never hastily turn the PC off as this can lead to further problems.

2 USING CONTROL, ALT, AND DELETE

● After waiting a while, try to close the locked-up application by using the key combination of: Ctrl + Alt + Del.
● Holding down these keys simultaneously should display the **Windows Task Manager**.

3 WINDOWS TASK MANAGER

● This box shows all the applications that are currently running on your system, and next to the locked-up application there should be a message that reads: **Not Responding**.

● Click on the name of the application in the dialog box, and click on the **End Task** button.

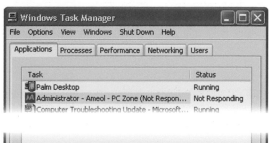
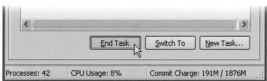

4 END TASK OR SHUTDOWN

● If the software still refuses to close immediately, wait a few moments before pressing Ctrl + Alt + Del again, which should reboot your machine. If the computer still won't respond, then you will have to press the reset button on the front of your PC, if you have one. If you don't have a reset button, then you will need to turn the machine off, wait for 15 seconds, and then turn it on again in the conventional way.

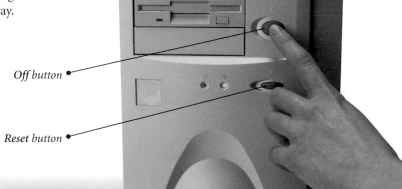

Off button ●

Reset button ●

REMOVING UNNECESSARY FILES

The performance of your PC can be slowed down by the accumulation of unnecessary files. Deleting files one at a time can be a lengthy business. Here, we explain how to locate a folder containing these files and how to delete them.

1 SELECT WINDOWS EXPLORER

● The files that are to be deleted are temporary files stored in a folder called **Temp** within the **Windows** folder. These files are left in the **Temp** folder when your computer crashes, and can safely be deleted.

● To find them, click on the **Start** button, select **All Programs**, followed by **Accessories**, and then select **Windows Explorer**.

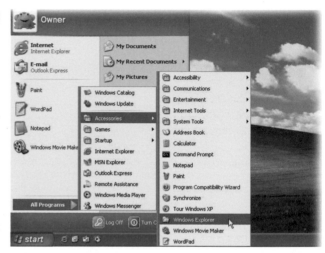

2 FINDING TEMPORARY FILES

● Click on the plus (+) sign next to **My Computer**, then **Local Disk** and finally the **Windows** folder, scroll down to the **Temp** folder and click on it.

● Its contents are displayed in the right-hand panel.

*The **Temp** folder is contained within the **Windows** folder* ●

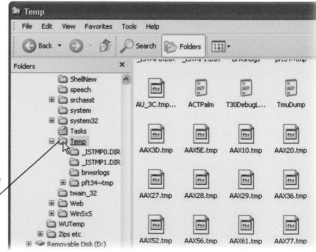

3 SORTING FILES BY TYPE

● Firstly, click on the **View** drop-down-menu and select **Details** from the list.

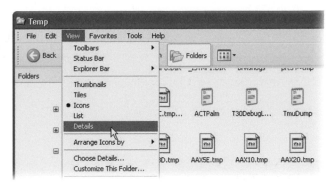

● Next, scroll along the window and click on the **Type** column header to list the files by type, then scroll down to see the start of the **TMP** files.

*The **Type** column header* ●

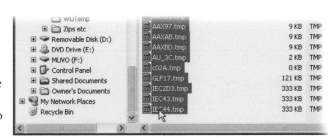

4 SELECTING THE TMP FILES

● Click on the first **TMP** file, scroll down to display the last **TMP** file and, while holding down the Shift key, click on the last **TMP** file to select them all.

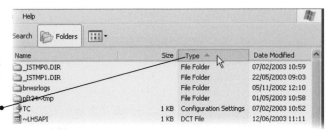

5 SELECTING THE DELETE OPTION

● Click on **File** in the menu bar and select **Delete**.
● An alert box asks you to confirm that the files are to be deleted. Click on **Yes**, and the files are deleted.

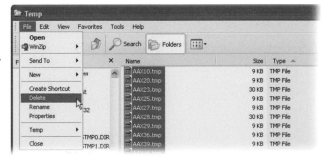

CLEANING UTILITIES

Many problems can be prevented by keeping your hard disk well organized. Windows provides three tools for this task, and commercial cleanup software is also readily available.

USING ERROR-CHECKING

Error-checking can check for damaged files and make sure that your hard disk is storing information correctly. It can also be set up to correct any problems. Error-checking also looks for files and folders with invalid file names, dates, and times, and corrects these problems more thoroughly and quickly than is possible using manual methods.

First aid for files
Error-checking looks for damage and makes repairs.

1 OPENING ERROR-CHECKING

• Open the **My Computer** window by double-clicking on the icon in the **Start** menu or on the desktop.

• When the window opens, right-click on the **Local Disk (C:)** icon (which is usually the one you want to check), and choose **Properties** from the pop-up menu.

2 STARTING ERROR-CHECKING

● When the **Properties** dialog box opens, click on the **Tools** tab at the top of the screen.

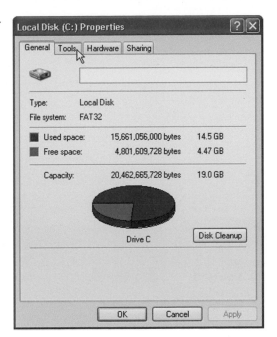

● There are two programs in this section of the dialog box – **Error-checking** and **Defragmentation**. For now, you want to run the first program, so click **Check Now** in the **Error-checking** section of the dialog box.

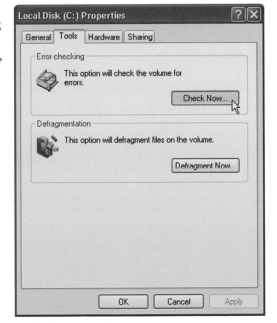

● When the **Check Local Disk (C:)** dialog box opens, leave all the options as they are and click on **Start**.

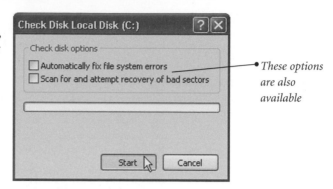

These options are also available

3 RUNNING ERROR-CHECKING

● Windows will then scan your hard disk for errors. As it does so, you will see the green indicator move from left to right along the progress bar.

● When **Error-checking** has finished, it will report back. In this example, no errors have been found. Click on **OK**, and then close the **Local Disk (C:) Properties** dialog box.

ERROR-CHECKING OPTIONS

Running Error-checking in this way simply reports any problems with the hard disk. To fix them as you go, or to perform a more thorough check, click on the **Automatically fix file system errors** checkbox or the **Scan for and attempt recovery of bad sectors** checkbox in the dialog box. These checks cannot be carried out if any other programs are running, so Windows XP will suggest performing the check next time you restart your computer.

Using Disk Cleanup

Windows also contains a piece of software called Disk Cleanup. This program offers options to select files to search for and possibly delete, which creates more free disk space. This is a safe method if you are uncertain about deleting files.

1 OPENING DISK CLEANUP

● Click on the **Start** button, then select **All Programs**, **Accessories**, **System Tools**, and finally **Disk Cleanup**.

2 GAINING FREE SPACE

● The Disk Cleanup program will then estimate how much space it can create on your hard drive by removing unwanted or unnecessary files.

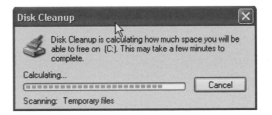

CLEANUP ROUTINES

If you are a fairly frequent user, you could establish a weekly cleaning schedule. Once you have carried out the first thorough clean as described in this section, the process can be quickly carried out.

3 DESCRIPTION DIALOG

● Disk Cleanup now tells you exactly how much space it can free up by deleting unnecessary files, such as temporary internet files, offline web pages, downloaded program files, the Recycle Bin (this means emptying files from the bin, not deleting it!), and other temporary files.

● Select the file types that you want Disk Cleanup to delete by clicking once in each of the check boxes next to them. It is best to accept each of Disk Cleanup's recommended file types.

● Once you have selected the items that you want to clean up, click on **OK**.

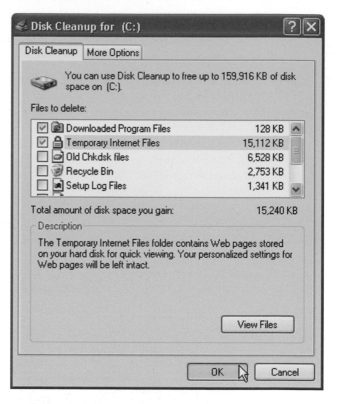

4 BEGINNING THE CLEANUP

● As a final step before starting, a confirmation panel opens. Click on **Yes**.

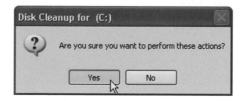

5 FINISHING THE CLEANUP

● After working through the selected options, Disk Cleanup shuts down automatically and you are returned to the Desktop.

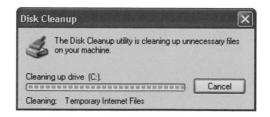

USING DISK DEFRAGMENTER

Through normal use, files on a hard disk are broken up and scattered instead of being placed together. This is known as fragmentation and means that the computer has to work harder to gather all the information it needs to perform the required tasks. Disk Defragmenter reconstructs the fragmented files, meaning that they will load faster as the computer does not have to spend time looking for them. Disk Defragmenter also reorganizes files by putting those that are most frequently used at the start of your hard drive to speed up the working process.

HOW DOES FRAGMENTATION HAPPEN?

Fragmentation is not something that you can physically see or be aware of at the time it occurs. The two panels below illustrate how fragmentation occurs. The process has been simplified to provide a basic representation, although in reality disk fragmentation is very complex and depends on a large number of variables.

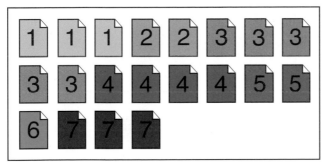

Your hard disk – week one.

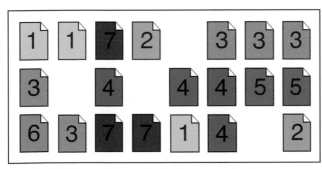

Your hard disk – week three; the files have started to fragment.

THE FRAGMENTATION PROCESS

In week one, the files show no fragmentation. However, by week three, there is evidence of fragmentation. This may be due to old software being uninstalled, work being carried out on existing documents, or the scanning and saving of new images. If a file is opened, added to, and saved, the enlarged file may be split up and placed wherever there is room. After a while, the file structure becomes severely fractured. Defragmenting not only cleans up the drive – it can also increase the performance of your hard disk by up to 10 percent.

1 BEGINNING THE OPERATION

● Click on the **Start** button and select **All Programs**, then **Accessories**, followed by **System Tools**, and finally **Disk Defragmenter**.

2 SELECTING THE DRIVE

● When the **Disk Defragmenter** dialog box opens, it displays the various disk drives currently attached to your computer. Here there are two – drive C and drive D.

● Click on the (**C:**) icon to select your hard disk drive.

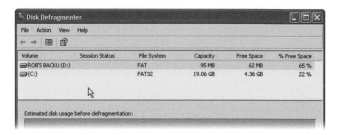

The Screen Saver

It is advisable to turn off your screen saver while running Disk Defragmenter ⬜. Every time the screen saver turns itself on, Disk Defragmenter is forced to start the defragmentation process again.

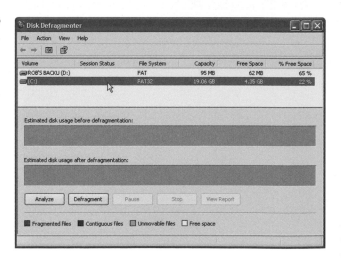

⬜ **Turning Off**
481 **Your Screen Saver**

3 STARTING DEFRAGMENTING

● When you are ready to begin, click the **Defragment** button.

● While Disk Defragmenter is doing its job, Windows provides an animated graphic representation of the process.

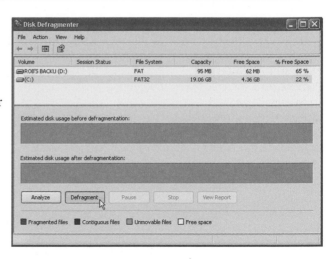

4 THE PROCESS IN ACTION

● **Disk Defragmenter** begins by analyzing your hard disk drive, and it displays its findings in the form of colored lines in the upper window. Red vertical lines indicate fragmented areas of the hard disk that may be slowing down your computer's performance.

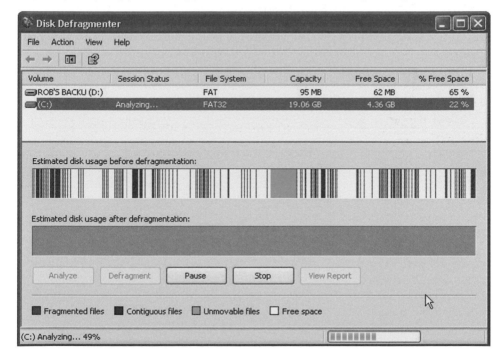

INCREASING DISK DRIVE EFFICIENCY

● As **Disk Defragmenter** carries out its task, it reorganizes the data on your hard disk in order to minimize the amount of fragmentation. This is reflected in the continuous blue bands seen in the lower window on the screen. Your hard disk will perform more efficiently as a result of this reorganization.

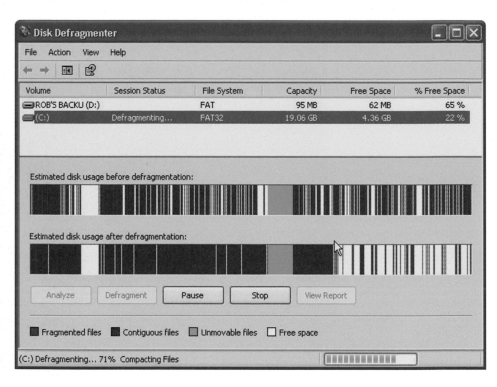

5 PAUSING THE PROCESS

● If you need to monitor the process, but have to leave your computer, you can pause **Disk Defragmenter** at any time by clicking the **Pause** button.

● Click the same button – now the **Resume** button – to continue the process.

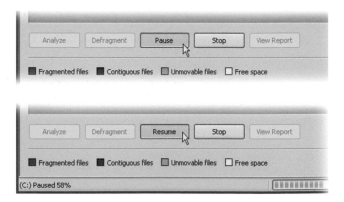

6 SELECTING OTHER SETTINGS

- When Disk Defragmenter has finished analyzing and defragmenting your hard disk, a dialog box will appear offering to display a report of the results. If you would like to see this report, click the View Report button.

- You can look at the report on your computer screen or, if you prefer, print out a hard copy by clicking the **Print** button. When you have finished reviewing the information, click the **Close** button.

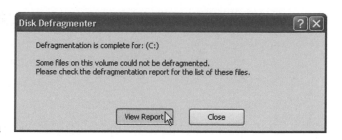

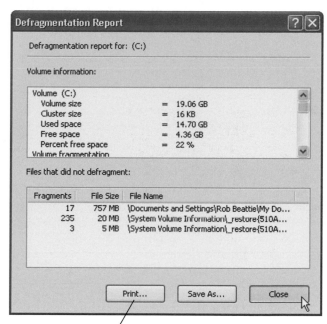

Click on the **Print** button if you wish to keep a hard copy of the Defragmentation Report

---

TURNING OFF YOUR SCREEN SAVER

First, right-click on the Desktop. In the pop-up menu, click on **Properties** at the foot of the menu. The **Display Properties** dialog box opens. Click on the **Screen Saver** tab at the top of the box. In the center of the box is a drop-down menu below the words **Screen Saver**. Click on the down arrow to the right, scroll through the list until (**None**) is highlighted, and click on it. Click on **Apply** and then on **OK**. To reset the screen saver, select one from the **Screen Saver** drop-down menu, click on **Apply** and then on **OK**.

MAKING BACKUPS

Computers fail for many reasons, and when they do
it's important that you have your original program disks to
hand, as well as recent backups of your work.

WHAT DOES BACKING UP MEAN?

Making a backup, in its simplest form, involves copying all the information held on your computer from your hard drive to transportable media, such as a disk or CD, that can be removed from the computer and stored for safe keeping.

BACKUP MEDIA

The best way to recover from a major accident is to have a comprehensive backup on disk. If the computer is stolen or irretrievably damaged, you should be able to rebuild your data from the backups. The main types of media suitable for backing up a home PC are: CD-R (Compact Disc Recordable), Zip disks (in 100MB, 250MB, and 750MB versions) or a portable hard disk (typically with a capacity of 20 or 40 gigabytes). A CD writer is relatively cheap (most new home computers now include one as standard) and blank CDs in bulk cost less than blank Zip disks. Floppy disks are of limited use because of their small capacity – a Zip disk can hold up to 750 times the data of a floppy disk. A CD can hold almost as much, but unless you have a CD re-writer, you can only backup to a CD-R disc once. With a removable drive or Zip disk you can backup as many times as you like on the same disk.

When choosing a backup medium, you should take into account the cost of the drive and the disks, and the storage capacity that each type offers.

BACKING UP TO CD

One of the new features in Windows XP Home Edition is the ability to backup or "burn" your valuable data onto a blank, recordable CD. This is an easy, inexpensive way to keep copies of your important files. In order to use this feature, your computer must have a CD writer, a component now included as standard with most PCs.

1 OPENING THE CD DRIVE

● Before you backup your data to a blank CD, make sure that your recordable CD drive is enabled. Double click on **My Computer** on the desktop.
● Right-click on the icon for your recordable CD drive, and then click on **Properties** in the pop-up menu that appears.

INTERNET BACKUP

If you have a fast, broadband connection to the internet, it may be worth considering backing up your data using that. A number of companies will store your backups on their own, secure computers for a small monthly or annual fee. Go to **www.ibackup.com/index.html** or **www.xdrive.com/** for more information.

DEDICATED BACKUP PROGRAMS

If you choose to buy a removable disk drive, it will probably come with a special program that will give you much more control over the way you backup and restore your data. For example, along with a full backup, you will usually be able to backup files created on or after a specific date, those created by a specific program, or only those files that have changed since you last backed up.

2 ENABLING RECORDING

● When the dialog box opens, click the **Recording** tab at the top.

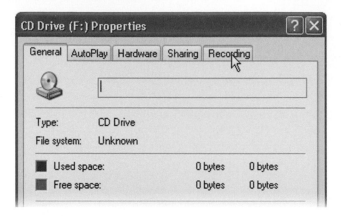

● Put a tick in the **Enable CD recording on this drive** checkbox by left-clicking once in the box. If you would like the finished CD to be ejected once the recording has finished, put a tick in the **Automatically eject the CD after writing** box. Leave the other settings as they are.

● Click on **OK** to close the dialog box.

● Insert a blank recordable CD in the CD drive.

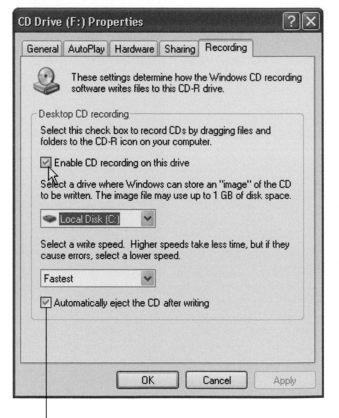

Check this box to have the CD automatically ejected once the files have been copied

3 LOCATING THE FILES

● We intend to backup two Work folders onto a CD. They are stored in the **My Documents** folder, so with the **My Computer** window still open, click on **My Documents** in the list of **Other Places** on the left.

● In the **My Documents** window, select the two **Work** folders by holding down the Ctrl key on your keyboard and then clicking on each folder in turn so they are both highlighted.

● Right-click on one of the highlighted folders and choose **Send To** from the drop-down menu.
● Choose the name of your recordable CD drive from the drop-down list. In this example, the recordable drive is **CD Drive (F:)**.

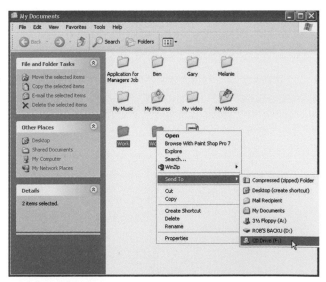

4 PREPARING THE FILES

● Windows XP now copies the files to a special area of your hard disk which has been temporarily set aside for them.

● Once the files have been written to the blank CD, these temporary versions will be deleted. The originals, of course, stay safe on the hard disk, and we can see them in their original locations in the **My Documents** window.

● When all the files have been copied, a message will appear at the bottom of your screen. Follow the instructions and click on the balloon.

● In the **CD Drive** window that opens we can see that the two selected folders are now ready to be written to the recordable CD.

● To begin the process, click on the **Write these files to CD** command in the **CD Writing Tasks** list in the left-hand task pane.

5 WRITING THE FILES

- When the **CD Writing Wizard** window opens, give your backup CD a name. It is a good idea to include the date in the name, for future reference.
- Click the **Next** button.

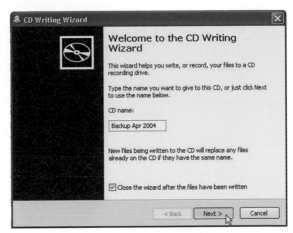

- Windows XP now prepares the files and writes them to your CD.
- When the files have been written, the temporary files are deleted and – if you ticked the checkbox – your finished CD is ejected.
- You can read the data on the CD whenever you like by putting it back into the CD drive. CDs created in this way can be read by all modern home computers.

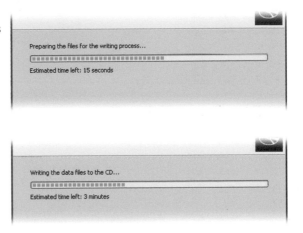

THE REWRITABLE CD ALTERNATIVE

- While recordable CDs can only be used once, re-writable CDs, or CD-RW discs, allow you to record over a previous backup repeatedly. Through the **CD Writing Tasks** menu, Windows XP makes the process very easy.

VIRUSES

We are all susceptible to computer viruses that can come to us as a result of downloading software from the internet, or passing from computer to computer by disk or email.

THE RISKS OF A VIRUS

A computer virus is a program or piece of code that can attach itself to programs on your computer. Some viruses can be considered almost harmless, perhaps throwing up joke messages; but some can delete a few or all of the files on the hard drive, causing a complete system failure known as a crash. A system failure may render your PC completely inoperable – unable even to boot up.

HOW DOES A VIRUS OCCUR?

A computer virus will have been written by someone. Most viruses start as small programs that lie hidden, attached to an application on your computer, until they are activated by running the application. The virus looks for another program to infect. It then changes each program so that it, too, contains a copy of the virus and waits for the next unsuspecting victim. Viruses are created in different ways, that is, they can infect and affect different parts of your computer. For example, a program virus will infect program files. A program file will have a file ending (or extension) such as .COM (command file) or .EXE (executable file). An executable file is the kind of file that you would use to open an application by double-clicking on it. Program viruses are common because they are easier to write.

HOW DOES A VIRUS GET ONTO MY MACHINE?

There are many potential sources that may contain a virus, but by far the most common way of catching one is through down-loading a file from the internet or by opening an infected email.

In the past, viruses could only be conveyed from computer to computer by executable program files, but with the development of "macro" viruses, any document that uses a macro language, such as a document created in Microsoft Word or Excel, can be carrying a virus. Viruses known as "worms" usually arrive attached to email messages.

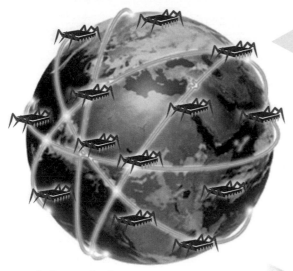

1 The virus is designed and created by a programmer, who will probably start the trail of destruction by means of mass emailing. The emails may have file attachments that contain the virus.

4 Once again, the mail is opened and the virus attaches itself to the new computer. The unsuspecting culprit may email his friends or give copies of the file and the virus now begins to take effect.

3 The file attachment may be passed to a friend via floppy disk or again by email. The virus then spreads.

2 The emails are received and the attachments are opened by the recipients. The virus then contaminates each recipient's computer.

The virus is not selective. Once it has been passed to your system via a floppy disk, downloaded on a piece of software from the internet, or from an email, it will be only a matter of time before it triggers itself and begins to infect your computer.

WHAT DOES A VIRUS CONTAIN?

Replication engine: A successful virus makes copies of itself that move on to other computers.
Protection: A virus protects itself from detection by amending sectors on the hard drive to conceal its presence.
Trigger: The event that activates the virus may be a date and time that is read by the virus from the system clock, or by an action being repeated a certain number of times by the user.
Payload: This is the damage that the virus has been set to cause, which may or may not include loss of data.

VIRUS DEFINITIONS

Boot sector viruses: These are spread when there is an infected floppy disk, bootable or not, in the disk drive when a computer is booted. The virus is copied to the hard drive where it moves the original boot sector to another part of the disk and takes over the computer's operations.

Program viruses: These attach themselves to program files. Running them loads the virus into memory where it replicates.

Macro viruses: These viruses infect files created by applications that use a macro language, such as Microsoft Word. The virus issues commands that are accepted, understood, and executed as valid macros by the application.

Multipartite viruses: These combine the features of boot sector viruses and program viruses. They are able to move in either direction between the boot sector and applications on the hard drive.

SOME KNOWN VIRUSES

SOBIG.F
This is a particularly virulent virus that replicates by sending itself out to all the email addresses it finds in your address book. At the time of writing, it was the fastest spreading virus in history.

KLEZ
Thought by many to be one of the longest surviving viruses, Klez is hard to get rid of because it spreads regardless of the email address book being used, and under some circumstances can disable the very anti-virus software that is supposed to be tracking it down.

JDBG.EXE
A good example of a virus hoax. It arrives as an email message that instructs you to search for a virus called **jdbgmgr.exe.** When you find the virus (it has a teddy bear for an icon) you are instructed to delete it. The email then recommends you forward these same instructions to all the contacts in your address book to inform them about the virus and how to get rid of it. In fact **jdbgmgr.exe** is a legitimate (though little used) Windows program – so little used that if you do delete it by mistake, you probably do not need to re-install it.

SIRCAM
This virus arrived in mailboxes with a friendly message in Spanish or English that led the recipient to believe it was an email from a friend. Sircam was hidden inside an email and, when opened, attached itself to documents at random and sent them out to the email addresses it found in your address book. Worse still, it could delete files on the hard disk or replace them with nonsense.

MELISSA
This common virus modifies Word settings and then infects templates and documents. It also tries to email itself to up to 50 people in your address book. Melissa cleverly hides itself by disabling any menus in Word that might give away its presence.

ANTIVIRUS SOFTWARE

There are a number of antivirus applications available, and some are available free over the internet. However, these tend to detect only the more common viruses. If you require software that is more comprehensive and able to detect the rarer viruses, it is advisable to use an industry-standard virus detector.

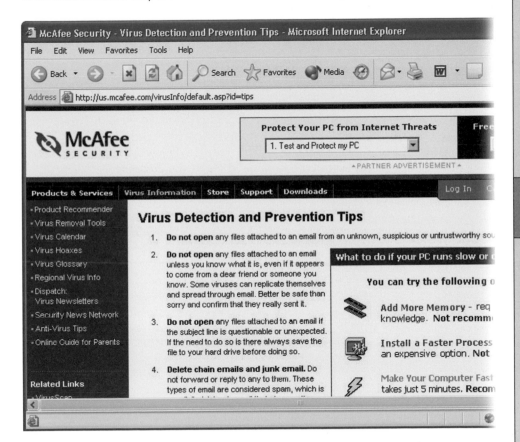

MORE FROM MCAFEE

McAfee's website, **www.mcafee.com**, invites you to download and upgrade antivirus software, much of which is offered on a two-week, free trial period. The site also provides opportunities to report viruses, to browse through their database of 50,000 known viruses, and to view a virus glossary of terms and virus definitions. The virus calendar gives the trigger dates of virus payloads. A database of hoax viruses is also available.

NORTON ANTIVIRUS

Norton AntiVirus – available as part of the Norton SystemWorks suite (shown here) or as an individual program – is one of the most popular and well-known antivirus software packages available. Norton offers excellent protection, a very user-friendly interface, and simple updating available over the internet.

EASILY UPDATABLE

Norton AntiVirus gives protection while you are surfing the internet or retrieving information from floppy disks. It can even be set up to scan incoming emails and their attachments.

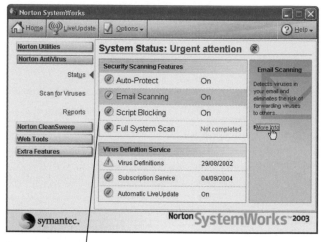

System Status

System Status determines exactly what measures you should take to protect your PC.

● Once you have clicked on the **More Info** link, the **Email Scanning Status** dialog box opens and displays the current settings being used by Norton AntiVirus for scanning incoming and outgoing emails. Close the dialog box to return to the Norton SystemWorks main screen.

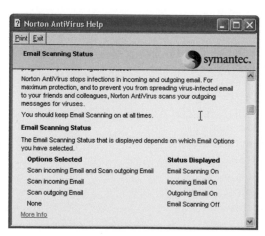

● For further information about any of the items in the list, click on the item to select it. In this instance we have selected **Virus Definitions**.

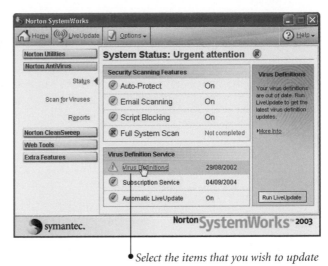

Select the items that you wish to update

● Now click on **More Info**, which appears in the right-hand panel.

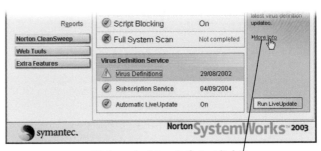

*Click on the **More Info** text link*

● The **Virus Definitions Status** dialog box opens. Although Norton AntiVirus can protect you from many viruses as soon as you install it, you must keep the list of virus definitions up to date by downloading new ones from the website of Symantec, the program's author. If you do not, you risk leaving yourself open to an attack whenever a new virus comes along.

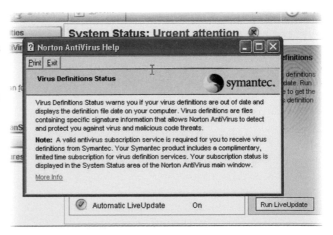

WINDOWS WIZARDS

Windows XP includes a number of clever troubleshooting wizards to help you solve common computer problems. In this chapter, we will examine how to resolve a typical problem.

WORKING WITH WIZARDS

Windows XP's Troubleshooting Wizards are a collection of small programs, each one designed to solve a specific set of problems. For example, if you are experiencing difficulties printing out a photo or if your documents are coming out in the wrong font, you should run the Printing Troubleshooter. Similarly, if you cannot hear sounds from your sound card, or you can hear special effect sounds but not music, you should run the Multimedia Troubleshooter.

WHAT EXACTLY ARE WIZARDS?

The troubleshooters in Windows XP are utility programs that "walk" you through specific problems in a step-by-step, screen-by-screen fashion. When you run one of these wizards, it displays a series of questions on the computer screen to try and discover the nature of your problem. As you respond, the wizard will suggest various possible solutions depending on your answers; if it asks you to change specific Windows settings, it will also tell you exactly how to do so. After each suggestion, you can tell the wizard whether it solved the problem or not. If the proposed solution did not work, the wizard will suggest another one. Wizards are not fool-proof but they do offer helpful, real-life suggestions that even novice computer users will find useful.

⭐ Add to Favorites 　 Change View 　 🖨 Print...

List of troubleshooters

The following troubleshooters are available in Wind troubleshooter by clicking the name in the left colu

Troubleshooter	Identifies and resolves
System setup	Installing and setting up Win
Startup/Shutdown	Starting and shutting down
Display	Video cards and video adap computer screen, outdated drivers, and incorrect settin hardware.
Home networking	Setup, Internet connections printers.
Hardware	Disk drives (including CD-R game controllers, input dev mice, cameras, scanners, a network adapters, and sound cards. Also see t hardware device troublesho
Multimedia and games	Games and other multimed drivers, USB devices, digita sound, joysticks, and relate
Digital Video Discs (DVDs)	DVD drives and decoders.

RUNNING THE DVD TROUBLESHOOTER

Over the next few pages we will show you how to use a typical Windows XP Troubleshooting Wizard. This one is designed to help you resolve problems that you may encounter when watching DVD movies on your computer.

1 LOADING HELP AND SUPPORT
● Click on the **Start** button, and choose **Help and Support** when the pop-up menu appears.

2 FINDING THE DVD WIZARD
● The **Help and Support Center** window opens. Look down the list of help topics on the left-hand side of the window and click on **Fixing a problem**.

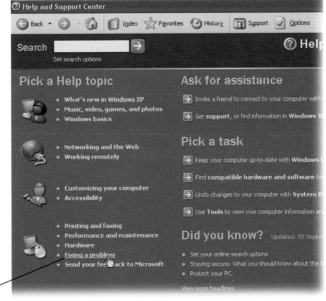

Click here to select
Fixing a problem ●

● When the **Fixing a problem** window opens, click on the first entry in the list on the left – **Troubleshooting problems**.

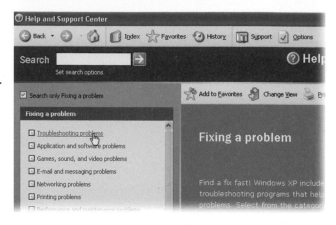

● The text in the right-hand window will change. Look down this list to find **List of troubleshooters**, and click on this entry.

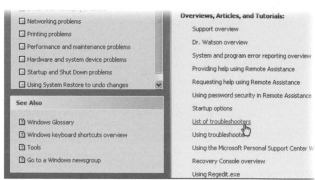

3 STARTING DVD TROUBLESHOOTER

● In the troubleshooters list that appears on the right, find **Digital Video Discs (DVDs)** and left-click on it once.

*Click here to select **Digital Video Discs (DVDs)***

4 ANALYZING THE PROBLEM

● The next screen displays a list of common DVD-related problems. Pick the one that most accurately reflects the problem you are experiencing by clicking on the radio button next to its entry. In this example, we have chosen **When I play a DVD, the video is choppy.**

What problem are you having?

○ I do not hear any sound, or I receive a message about audio.

○ I am having a problem using closed captioning or subtitles.

○ When I try to play DVD, nothing happens.

◉ When I play a DVD, the video is choppy.

○ I receive a message about analog copy-protection.

○ I receive a message about my screen resolution and color quality settings.

○ I receive a decoder error message.

○ I receive a message about digital copy protection.

○ When I play a DVD, the screen is black, or there is some other display problem.

○ I receive a region error message.

○ I receive a video error message.

Next >

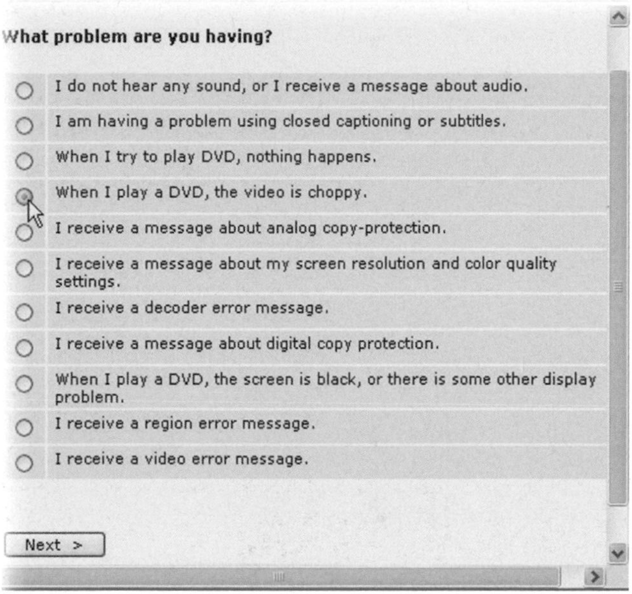

● Click the **Next** button to move onto the next screen.

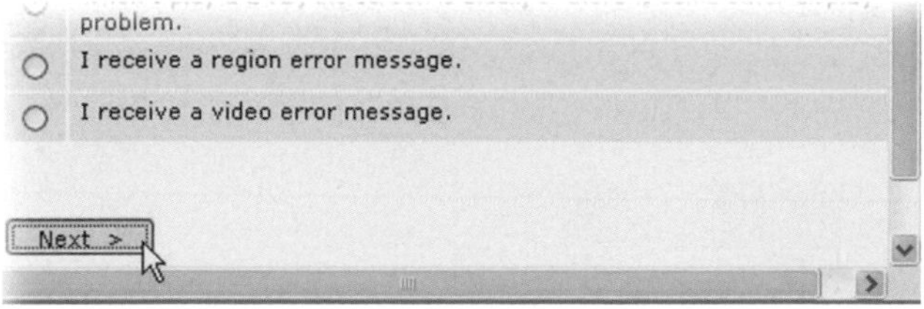

problem.

○ I receive a region error message.

○ I receive a video error message.

Next >

STARTING IN SAFE MODE

If Windows XP doesn't load automatically when you turn your computer on, try the following method. Switch the computer off, turn it back on, and watch the screen carefully. When the words **Starting Windows** appear on the screen, press the **F8** function key on your keyboard. From the menu of startup options that appears, choose **Safe Mode.** This will load a very basic version of Windows XP that you can use to track down the problem. Start by right-clicking on the **My Computer** icon on the desktop, and choose **Properties.** When the dialog box opens, click the **Hardware** tab at the top. Next, click the **Device Manager** button. A list of devices will appear in a new window. Any devices that are causing a problem will be clearly marked 🗎.

501 **When Safe Mode Doesn't Work**

5 SELECTING THE TYPE OF FORMAT

- The DVD troubleshooter makes its first guess and suggests that you may need to adjust your DMA (Direct Memory Access) settings. You may not feel confident doing this on your own, but the wizard will walk you through the process, step by step.
- Notice that **Device Manager** is in blue and is underlined, just like a link on a web page. Underlined text like this is used to indicate a command.
- When you move your cursor over it, **Device Manager** turns red. Left-click once on it.

Add to Favorites   Change View   Print...   Locate in Contents

Is DMA turned on?

The video performance of your DVD player might improve if you turn memory access (DMA).

To turn on DMA

1. Open 🖭 Device Manager.
2. Double-click **IDE ATA/ATAPI controllers**.
3. Right-click **Primary IDE Channel**, and then click **Properties**.
4. On the **Advanced Settings** tab, under **Device 0**, in **Transfer M** click **DMA if available**.
5. Under **Device 1**, in **Transfer Mode**, click **DMA if available**.
6. Click **OK**.
7. Repeat steps 2 through 6, replacing **Primary IDE Channel** with **Secondary IDE Channel** in step 3.

🖾 **Note**

- To open **Device Manager**, click **Start**, click **Control Panel**, click

Is DMA turned on?

The video performance of your DVD player might improve if you turn memory access (DMA).

To turn on DMA

1. Open 🖭 Device Manager.
2. Double-click **IDE ATA/ATAPI controllers**.
3. Right-click **Primary IDE Channel**, and then click **Properties**.

6 CHANGING THE SETTINGS

- The troubleshooter remains on the screen but Windows now opens the **Device Manager** window as well. Use the mouse to position it on the screen so that you can see both this and the instructions in the Troubleshooter Wizard window.
- Follow the instructions and click once on the plus (+) sign next to **IDE ATA/ATAPI controllers**.

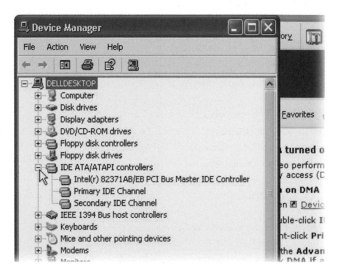

● Now right-click on the **Primary IDE Channel** and choose **Properties** from the drop-down menu.

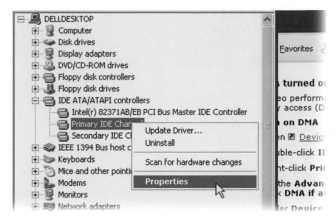

● When the **Primary IDE Channels Properties** dialog box opens, click on the **Advanced Settings** tab at the top.

● Set the **Transfer Mode** of **Device 0** to **DMA if available** by choosing this from the drop-down list that appears when you click on the downward-pointing arrow at the right-hand end of the **Transfer Mode** panel.
● Now do the same for **Device 1**, and click on **OK**.

● Follow the rest of the instructions in the Troubleshooting Wizard window to change the settings for the **Secondary IDE Channel**.

● Try playing a DVD again and see whether the problem has been solved.

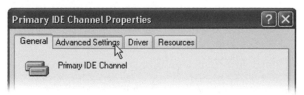

7 TRYING AN ALTERNATIVE

● If the DVD is still running jerkily, click on the radio button next to **No, DMA is on, but I still have a display problem** and then click the **Next** button.

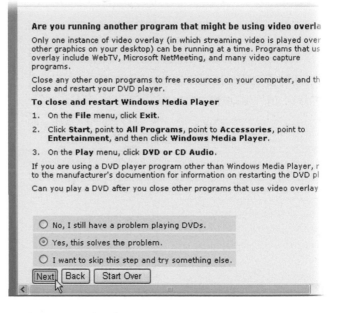

● The DVD troubleshooter now suggests that you may be running another program, such as Microsoft NetMeeting, that may be interfering with the smooth playback of DVD movies.
● It advises you to close any open programs and then close and restart your DVD player program (which is probably Windows Media Player).
● In this example, closing the other programs solves the problem of jerky video.
● Click on **Yes, this solves the problem** and then click the **Next** button.

● The DVD troubleshooter closes and returns you to the **Help and Support Center**, which you can now close, unless you wish to do further troubleshooting.

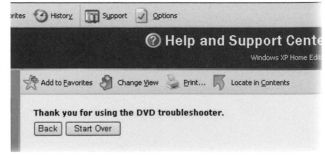

SKIPPING SOME OF THE STEPS

● Sometimes you may feel that the current suggestion is too complicated and that you would rather see if there is a simpler alternative first. To do this, click the radio button next to **I want to skip this step and try something else** and then click **Next**.

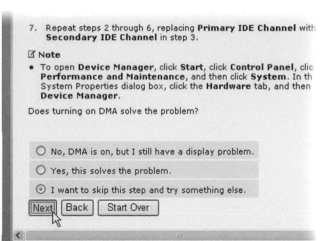

BEGINNING THE PROCESS AGAIN

● You can restart a Troubleshooting Wizard at any time by clicking the **Start Over** button at the bottom of the screen.

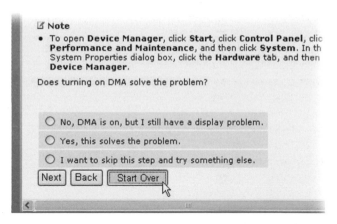

WHEN SAFE MODE DOESN'T WORK

If you cannot start your computer using Safe Mode 🗋, then put your original Windows XP CD in the CD-ROM drive. Switch the computer off, wait a few moments and switch it back on again.

When you see the **Press Any Key to Boot from CD** option appear on the screen, press the Enter ↵ key and choose the command that allows you to repair your Windows installation.

---

497 Starting In Safe Mode

EMERGENCY MEASURES

Sometimes you can pinpoint the moment your PC stopped working properly. Here, we will discuss how Windows XP can "rewind" your settings to a time before the problems started.

USING SYSTEM RESTORE

System Restore first appeared in Windows Me, and it gives you the opportunity to return your PC to a state in which it was working in a satisfactory manner, therefore undoing things that may have caused problems. For instance, you may have installed a new piece of software that has damaged the way your monitor driver operates, corrupting it in some way. System Restore will try to return your computer to a stage before the install.

You can create your own restore points or you can use those already on your PC. The latter are known as System Checkpoints, and they are created when new software is installed.

1 USING SYSTEM CHECKPOINTS

● First, go to the **Start** menu, and then choose **All Programs, Accessories, Systems Tools**, and, finally, **System Restore**.

Restore the restore...
If you perform a restore and are not happy with the results, you can always revert back to the stage from which you performed the restore!

2 CHOOSING A RESTORE POINT

● You have two choices here. The first is to restore your PC to a time that has been determined by your computer, or you can create your own restore point.

● If you have a problem with your PC at the moment, select the **Restore my computer to an earlier time** radio button and then click on **Next** at the bottom of the window.

3 CHOOSING A DATE

● A calendar appears. In this example, no restore points have been created by the user – only System Checkpoints are available. These are shown as slightly bolder numbers in the calendar.

● To restore your PC to one of theses dates, click on the number and then the **Next** button.

● Before you continue, you will be asked to make sure that you do not have any applications open at this time. When you are ready, click on the **Next** button.

● Your computer begins the restore routine, which may take a while. Your computer will then automatically restart.

CREATING YOUR OWN RESTORE POINT

You can create a restore point on your PC at any time. However, the best time is probably when you are happy that everything is operating smoothly, or perhaps before you are about to perform a large install of some new software, something that may damage the smooth running of your computer.

1 FROM THE BEGINNING

● First, go to the **Start** menu, and then choose **All Programs, Accessories, Systems Tools**, and, finally, **System Restore**.

2 CREATING A RESTORE POINT

● In the main window select the **Create a restore point** radio button and then click on **Next**.

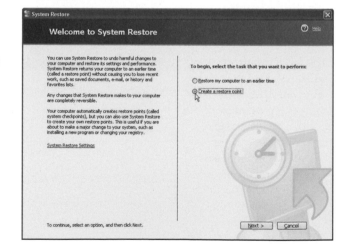

3 NAMING THE RESTORE POINT

● The next window opens and a cursor flashes in a text panel. Give your restore point a name, for example, **My first restore point**.

● If you are happy with the name, click on the **Create** button.

● The **Restore Point Created** window displays the date, time, and name of your restore point.

● Unless you wish to perform another task, click on the **Close** button.

● Now when you use **System Restore**, you can return your computer to the state it was in at this restore point.

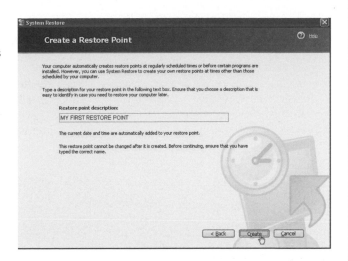

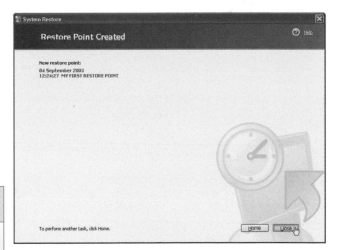

MICROSOFT UPDATE

It is worth using the Microsoft Update feature on your PC, as frequent software updates are available for items such as System Restore. Bugs are fixed and new functionality added to make the software smoother and easier to use.

GLOSSARY

APPLICATION
Another term for a piece of software, usually a program.

ARCHIVE
A file, which is usually compressed, containing back up copies of your work.

ATTACHMENT
Almost any type of file can be sent within an email by "attaching" it to a message that you send.

BACK UP
To create copies of your work on an external device, such as a floppy disk, in case you lose documents or your computer develops a fault.

BOOLEAN MODIFIERS
Words that help you to modify the terms of a key word search.

CCD
Charge Coupled Device. A light-sensitive chip contained within a scanner that converts a scanned image into digital data.

CD-ROM
Compact Disk – Read Only Memory. A disk containing data such as games and programs. Data can only be read from the disk, not written to it.

CMYK
Cyan, Magenta, Yellow, and Black (Key). Printers use inks in these four colors, overlapping them to create full-color images.

COLOR DEPTH
The quality and level of color in a digital image, measured in bits.

COMPRESSION
The act of reducing the size of a file by using software to "compact" it into an archive.

CRASH
The term applied when a computer suddenly stops working during a routine operation.

DEFRAGMENTING
The process of reassembling and arranging badly distributed files on a hard drive.

DESKTOP
The screen that appears once Windows XP has started up, which displays the taskbar and, among others, icons for My Computer, My Documents, and the Recycle Bin.

DIALOG BOX
A rectangle that appears on the screen and prompts you for a reply, usually with buttons, e.g. OK or Cancel.

DOCUMENT
A file containing user data, such as text written in Word.

DOWNLOAD
The process of file-transfer from a remote computer to your own computer.

DPI
Dots Per Inch. The units commonly used to express the resolution of an image.

DRIVER
A piece of software that enables the computer to communicate with attached hardware, such as a scanner or printer.

EMAIL (ELECTRONIC MAIL)
A system for sending messages between computers that are linked over a network.

FILE
A discrete collection of data stored on your computer.

FILE NAME EXTENSION
Three letters added to the end of a file name that indicate what type of file the document is, e.g. .txt (a text file).

FILE PROPERTIES
Information about a file, such as its size and creation date, and attributes that determine what actions can be carried out on the file and how it behaves.

FLOPPY DISK
A removable disk that allows you to store and transport small files between computers.

FOLDER
A folder stores files and other folders, to keep files organized.

FONT
The typeface in which text appears onscreen and when it is printed out.

FORMULA
In Excel, an expression entered into a cell that calculates the value of that cell from a combination of constants, arithmetic operators, and (often) the values of other cells.

FREEWARE
Software that can be freely used and distributed, but the author retains copyright.

FUNCTION
In Excel, a defined operation or set of operations that can be performed on one or more selected cell values, cell addresses, or other data.

GIF (GRAPHICS INTERCHANGE FORMAT)
A widely used file format for web-based images.

GRAYSCALE
An image that is made up entirely of black, white, and tones of gray.

HARD DRIVE
The physical device on your computer where programs and files are stored.

HARDWARE
Hardware is the part of a computer that you can physically see or touch.

HTML (HYPERTEXT MARK-UP LANGUAGE)
The formatting language used to create web pages. HTML specifies how a page should look on screen.

HYPERLINK
A "hot" part of a web page (e.g., text, image, table etc.) that links to another part of the same document or another document on the internet.

HYPERTEXT
Text that contains links to other parts of a document, or to documents held on another computer. Hypertext links on web pages are usually highlighted or underlined.

ICON
A graphic symbol, attached to a file, that indicates its type or the program it was created in.

IMAGE EDITING
The process of altering an image on the computer, either to improve its quality or to apply a special effect.

INKJET PRINTER
A type of color printer that fires small dots of ink from a cartridge onto the paper. The detail that can be achieved is so fine that almost photographic quality can be produced.

INSERTION POINT
A blinking upright line on the screen. As you type, text appears at the insertion point

INSTALLING
The process of "loading" an item of software onto a hard drive. See also uninstalling.

INTERNET
The network of interconnected computers that communicate with one another.

INTERNET SERVICE PROVIDER (ISP)
A business that provides a gateway to the internet.

JPEG
Joint Photographic Experts Group. A compressed file format, ideally used for low resolution images that don't contain a lot of detail, such as web graphics.

LASER PRINTER
A kind of printer that uses heat-sensitive toner to output high quality black and white prints at high speed.

LINEART
An image that is made up of black and white only, with no tones of gray.

MODEM
A device used to connect a computer to the internet via a telephone line.

NETWORK
A collection of computers that are linked together.

NEWSGROUPS
Internet discussion groups on specific topics, where people can post information or contribute to public debates.

NEWSREADER
Software that enables you to access and use newsgroups. Outlook Express has newsreader capabilities.

PARALLEL PORT
A port supplied on most computers, usually used for connecting printers.

PATH
The address of a file on a computer system.

PERIPHERAL
Any hardware device that is connected to your computer.

PIXELS
The individual color or grayscale dots that make up an image on a computer screen.

PLUG-IN
A program that adds features to a web browser so that it can handle files containing, for example, 3D and multimedia elements.

PORT
The socket on the back of a computer, or other piece of hardware, into which you plug the cables in order to connect peripherals.

PROGRAM
A software package that allows you to perform a specific task on your computer (also known as an application).

PROTOCOL
A set of rules that two computers must follow when they communicate.

RADIO BUTTON
Small onscreen button within an application that visibly turns on and off when clicked with a mouse.

RECYCLE BIN
The location on your desktop where deleted files are stored. Files remain here until the Recycle Bin is emptied.

RESOLUTION
The density of the dots that make up an image, measured in pixels or dpi.

RESTORE
To return data from the Recycle Bin to its original location.

RGB
Red, Green, and Blue. An image displayed on a computer screen is created from a combination of these three colors.

RULER
Indicators at the top and left of the screen, with marks in inches or centimeters like a real ruler. Rulers also show the indents and margins of the text.

SCAN
The digital image file that is created by a scanner and saved on your computer.

SCROLL
To scroll is to move up or down the document.

SCROLL BARS
Bars at the foot and the right of the screen that can be used to scroll around the document.

SCSI PORT
Small Computer System Interface. A port that provides fast file transfer, and allows many hardware devices to be connected in a chain.

SELECT
Highlighting files or folders to enable you to perform certain activities on them.

SERVER
Any computer that allows users to connect to it and share its information and resources.

SHAREWARE
Software that is made freely available for use on a try-before-you-buy basis.

SHORTCUT
A link to a document, folder, or program located elsewhere on your computer that, when you double-click on it, takes you directly to the original.

SOFTWARE
A computer needs software to function. Software ranges from simple utilities to immense computer games.

STATUS BAR
The small panel at the foot of an open window that displays information about the items located there.

TASKBAR
The panel at the bottom of the desktop screen that contains the Start button, along with quick-access buttons to open programs and windows.

TIFF
Tagged Image File Format. A file format that retains a high level of information in an image, therefore suited to images that contain a lot of detail.

UNINSTALLING
The process of removing an item of software from the hard drive by deleting all its files.

USB PORT
Universal Serial Bus. A type of port that allows for very simple installation of hardware devices to your computer

USENET
A network of computer systems that carry internet discussion groups called newsgroups.

VIRUS
A program or piece of computer code deliberately created and distributed to destroy or disorganize data on other computer systems.

WEB BROWSER
A program used for viewing and accessing information on the web.

WEBSITE
A collection of web pages that are linked together, and possibly to other websites, by hyperlinks.

WINDOW
A panel displaying the contents of a folder or disk drive.

WIZARDS
Interactive sequences that lead you, step by step, through processes on your computer.

WORLD WIDE WEB (WWW, W3, THE WEB)
The collection of websites on the Internet.

INDEX

ACKNOWLEDGMENTS

Dorling Kindersley would like to thank the following:
Amy Corzine, Sarah Cowley, Julian Dams, Julian Deeming, Sue Grabham,
Clare Lister, and Jane Thomas for their work on the first edition of this book.
Paul Mattock of APM, Brighton, for commissioned photography.
Indexing Specialists, Hove.

Canon Inc.; Hewlett-Packard Company; Iomega Corporation for permission to reproduce
photos of the Iomega Zip 100, 250, and 750MB USB Drives. Copyright© 2003 Iomega
Corporation. All Rights Reserved; Jasc™ Software, Inc. for permission to reproduce screen
shots of Paint Shop™ Pro®; Lexmark International, Inc.; Microsoft Corporation for
permission to reproduce screens from within Microsoft® Windows® XP Home Edition,
Microsoft® Notepad, Microsoft® Paint, Microsoft® Wordpad, Microsoft® Windows®
Explorer, Microsoft® Outlook Express, Microsoft® Internet Explorer, Microsoft® Windows®
Media Player, Microsoft® Word 2002, Microsoft® Excel 2002; Microtek International, Inc. for
permission to reproduce screens from ScanWizard 5 (Copyright © 2002 Microtek
International, Inc. All rights reserved.); Symantec Corporation for permission to reproduce
screens from within Norton SystemWorks 2003; Umax Systems GmbH; Visioneer, Inc.;
WHSmith.co.uk; WinZip Computing, Inc. for permission to reproduce screen shots of
WinZip (Copyright © 1991-2000 by WinZip Computing, Inc. All rights reserved.)

alltheweb.com; altavista.com; askjeeves.com; bigfoot.com; classical-composers.org;
copernic.com; dmoz.org; dogpile.com; download.com; ebay.com; google.com; hotbot.com;
looksmart.com; lycos.com (© 2003 Lycos, Inc.); McAfee.com; metacrawler.com; msn.com
(©2003 Microsoft Corporation); nasa.gov; smartpages.com; tucows.com; turbo10.com;
winfiles.com; yahoo.com; zone.com (©2003 Microsoft Corporation)

HotBot® is a registered trademark and/or service mark of Wired Ventures, Inc.,
a Lycos Company. All rights reserved. Iomega, the stylized "i" logo and product images are
property of Iomega Corporation in the United States and/or other countries. Jasc and Paint
Shop Pro are trademarks of Jasc Software, Inc. and are registered with the U.S. Patent and
Trademark Office and in the European Union. Lycos® is a registered trademark of Carnegie
Mellon University. All rights reserved. McAfee® is a registered trademark of Network
Associates, McAfee.com Inc. and/or its affiliates in the US and/or other countries.
Microsoft® is a registered trademark of Microsoft Corporation in the United States
and/or other countries. Symantec®, the Symantec logo, Norton AntiVirus®, Norton
CleanSweep®, and Norton Utilities® are registered trademarks of Symantec
Corporation. Norton SystemWorks and Speed Disk are trademarks of Symantec
Corporation. WinZip is a registered trademark of WinZip Computing, Inc. Zip is a
registered trademark in the United States and/or other countries.